Marriage and Love
in England

WITHDRAWN

Marriage and Love in England

Modes of Reproduction 1300–1840

Alan Macfarlane

Basil Blackwell

British Library Cataloguing in Publication Data

Macfarlane, Alan
Marriage and love in England :
modes of reproduction 1300–1840.
1. Marriage—England—History
I. Title
306.8'1'0942   HQ613

ISBN 0–631–13992–3
ISBN 0–631–15438–8 Pbk

Library of Congress Cataloging in Publication Data

Macfarlane, Alan.
Marriage and love in England.

Bibliography: p.
Includes index.
1. Marriage—England—History. 2. Family—
England—History. 3. Malthusianism. I. Title.
HQ615.M33 1985 306.8'1'0942 85–13351
ISBN 0–631–13992–3
ISBN 0–631–15438–8 (pbk.)

Typeset by Oxford Publishing Services, Oxford

FSC
www.fsc.org
MIX
Paper from
responsible sources
FSC® C013604

For Jack Goody
in gratitude and admiration

It is a truth universally acknowledged, that a single man in possession of a good fortune must be in want of a wife.

Jane Austen, *Pride and Prejudice*

But all ingenuous men will see the dignity and blessing of marriage is placed rather in the mutual enjoyment of that which the wanting soul needfully seeks, than that which the plenteous body would joyfully give away . . . that which in effect Moses tells us, that love was the son of loneliness, begot in Paradise by the social and helpful aptitude which God implanted between man and woman toward each other.

John Milton, *The Doctrine and Discipline of Divorce*

Therefore shall a man leave his father and his mother, and shall cleave unto his wife: and they shall be one flesh.

Genesis

Contents

Acknowledgements

This book was conceived in 1966 when Isaac Schapera suggested I undertake an M.Phil. thesis on attitudes to incest in pre-industrial England. During the nearly twenty years in which it has grown and taken shape in my mind I have incurred very many debts, only a few of which I can acknowledge.

The inspiration of the work of Keith Thomas, E. A. Wrigley, Peter Laslett, Richard Smith, Roger Schofield, Geoffrey Hawthorn and John Hajnal has been especially important, and I am grateful to all of them for many conversations, suggestions and thoughts. Many of my students, undergraduate and graduate, have given me ideas and tolerantly listened to versions of the book delivered as lectures. Particularly helpful have been Dr Nurit Bird and Julian Jacobs, the latter kindly reading and commenting on the whole text. Dr Alex Monto and Sofka Zinovieff also read the typescript and made a number of helpful suggestions. John Davey's interest and enthusiasm have, as before, been a great encouragement. Many conversations with Raul Iturra have clarified my views on marriage. Sue Phillpott, the copy-editor, and Harriet Barry of Blackwell have helped to see the book through the press. Colleagues in the Department of Social Anthropology and Fellows of King's College have also been supportive, the latter particularly in providing a research fellowship in the early 1970s and support from the Research Centre at King's. The results from the local community studies were achieved through the collaborative work of those who took part in the King's and Social Science Research Council project, 'Reconstructing historical communities with a computer'. To Sarah Harrison, Charles Jardine, Jessica King and Dr Tim King I am enormously grateful, and to Cherry Bryant and Iris Macfarlane who also assisted. Archivists at the Essex, Westmorland and Public Record Offices have always provided a cheerful service. Inge and Astrid Harrison have not only helped in many general ways by giving me insights into family dynamics and being very tolerant of their strange step-father, but have also sorted cards and helped to check references.

The two largest debts I reserve to the end. One is to Jack Goody, to whom this book is dedicated. All those who know Jack will understand why this should be so. He was present at the first stages, as my M.Phil. examiner, he encouraged me in my anthropological interests, and helped to make teaching and administration enjoyable. His theoretical work on marriage systems and his combination of broad comparative and historical interests in the fields of demography, marriage and family life have always been stimulating. Sarah Harrison has once again helped in many ways: she did much of the work on the local records, she helped type and edit much of the book, she checked references. But, much more importantly, she read the book at least four times from start to finish, and firmly pointed out the inadequacies of each version. Of course the book is far from perfect, but it would have been much worse without her constant attention. My thanks, as always, to her and all others, including Cherry Bryant and Tania Li who read the proofs.

Abbreviations, References and Conventions

Spelling and punctuation in quotations have been modernized, except in certain cases where such modernization would alter the meaning, and in poetry or drama.

The footnotes give an abbreviated title and page number. The usual form is author, short title, page number. The full title of the work referred to is given at the end in the bibliography. Some titles are listed under 'A' or 'The', depending on their exact wording.

Inflation makes it impossible to give more than a very rough estimate of the comparative value of money, but £1 was probably worth more than thirty times as much in the seventeenth century as it is now (1985).

When I speak of 'contemporary' or 'contemporaries' in the text, I am referring to those living in the past, during the period under consideration. When I refer to 'this period', I mean the period covered by the book, that is, roughly the fifteenth to early nineteenth centuries.

Note on sample local studies

At various points in the argument it is necessary to use material from local studies. I have drawn particularly heavily from two such studies. One is of the parish of Earls Colne in central Essex over the period 1400–1840. The mid-point population was about eight hundred. A total reconstruction of the records of this parish has been made, using both manual and computerized methods. Another, less complete, reconstruction of a parish at the other end of England, Kirkby Lonsdale in Cumbria, has also been used, and the records for the period 1500–1750 have been analysed. The mid-period population was about two thousand, distributed in nine chapelries, including Kirkby Lonsdale itself and Lupton. The nature of the records which were used is described in Macfarlane, *Guide*. A summary list of some of the more important is given in Macfarlane, *Individualism*, pp. 207–9. Full transcripts of all the Earls Colne documents have been published on microfiche by Chadwyck-Healey Ltd. The manual techniques used in these studies have been described in Macfarlane, *Reconstructing*.

PART I

THE MALTHUSIAN MARRIAGE SYSTEM

1

Charles Darwin and Thomas Malthus

In 1838 Charles Darwin was contemplating marriage. His thoughts on the subject are revealed to us in intimate detail by the chance survival of a scrap of paper. Darwin was now aged twenty-nine, having made his famous voyage round the world after leaving Cambridge. Without a regular job, yet with a small private income, marriage to his cousin Emma Wedgwood was both an attractive and a worrying prospect. In order to help him resolve the question of whether to marry, Darwin decided to set out a balance sheet of the advantages and disadvantages. In pencil on a blue sheet he drew up a cost–benefit analysis.[1] The very setting out of such a sheet is extraordinary. First, at twenty-nine Darwin was quite old by the standards of many societies to be contemplating his first marriage. Secondly, he clearly assumed that the decision was in his own hands. Above all, he saw marriage like some trading venture – as a choice. It was a decision involving costs and benefits which could, as in classic accounting, be balanced against each other. Equally interesting are the arguments Darwin put forward on each side. His sheet was laid out as follows:

This is the question

Marry   Not Marry

Under 'Marry', moving almost immediately from the subject of children to that of a possible wife, and underlining, inserting brackets and crossing out (see the phrase below), he wrote:

> Children – (if it please God) – constant companion, who will feel interested in one (a friend in old age) – object to be beloved and played with – better than a dog anyhow – Home, and someone to take care of house – Classics of Music and female Chit Chat – These things good

[1] Darwin Papers, Cambridge University Library, DAR.210.10.

for ones health – (forced to visit and receive relations – [crossed out])
but terrible loss of time – My God, it is unthinkable to think of
spending one's whole life, like a neuter bee, working, working, and
nothing after all – No, no won't do – Imagine living all one's days
solitarily in smoky dirty London House – Only picture to yourself a
nice soft wife on a sofa with good fire, and books and music perhaps –
compare this vision with dingy reality of Grt Marlb[orough] Str.
Marry.   Marry.   Marry.   Q.E.D.

Thus the arguments for marriage were that there might be
children, about whom nothing more is said, and then, basically, the
advantages of companionship with a wife. Such a wife would be
useful in keeping away loneliness, particularly in old age; she would
be a superior pet, 'better than a dog anyhow'. Furthermore, life would
not have been entirely wasted, for propagation would also produce
something more than a 'neuter bee' would – an apt thought for
Darwin in the year that he discovered the mechanism of the origin of
species through natural selection.

Under 'Not Marry' Darwin started by elaborating further some
arguments which would more logically have come under 'Marry'. Not
to marry would mean 'No children (no second life) no one to care for
one in old age – what is the use of working without sympathy from
near and dear friends – who are near and dear friends to the old
except relatives.' Hence, again, there is stress on old age and
loneliness and on leaving a reminder of one's existence.

He then listed the advantages of not marrying and remaining a
bachelor:

Freedom to go where one liked – choice of Society and little of it.
Conversation of clever men at clubs – Not forced to visit relatives, and
to bend in every trifle – to have the expense and anxiety of children –
perhaps quarrelling – Loss of time – cannot read in the Evenings –
fatness and idleness – anxiety and responsibility – less money for books
etc – if many children forced to gain one's bread (But then it is very
bad for one's health to work too much). Perhaps my wife won't like
London, then the sentence is banishment and degradation with
indolent, idle fool.

Real costs – the costs of children, the costs of a wife – were
therefore set in Darwin's mind against the advantages of companionship and comfort. Such disadvantages would possibly make life less

comfortable and there would certainly be a loss of time and leisure. On the reverse side of the sheet is the following:

It being proved necessary to Marry. When? Soon or Late.
The Governor says soon for otherwise bad if one has children – one's character is more flexible – one's feelings more lively and if one does not marry soon, one misses so much good pure happiness – But then if I married tomorrow: there would be an infinity of troubles and expense in getting and furnishing a house – insisting about no Society – morning calls – awkwardness – loss of time every day (without one's wife was an angel, and made one keep indentures) – Then how should I manage all my business if I were obliged to go every day walking with my wife – Ehem!! I never should know French, or see the continent, or go to America, or go up in a Balloon, or take solitary trip in Wales – poor slave – you will be worse than a negro – And then horrid poverty (without one's wife was better than an angel and had money) – Never mind my boy – Cheer Up – One cannot live this solitary life, with growing old age, friendless and cold, and childless staring one in one's face, already beginning to wrinkle – Never mind, trust to chance – Keep a sharp look out – There is many a happy slave –

Having summed up the costs and benefits, Darwin made his choice. On 29 January 1839, just before his thirtieth birthday, the marriage with Emma was solemnized.

In the same year that he came to balance the advantages and disadvantages of marriage and reproduction, Darwin succeeded in solving the problem of how species evolved through natural selection. The key was provided by an accidental reading of Thomas Malthus' *Essay on Population*, which showed him how high mortality could lead to the survival of only the fittest. Malthus' work may also have been helpful to Darwin when considering his feelings about his individual decision to reproduce. For what Malthus provided was an elegant theoretical model of the marriage system in England in the early nineteenth century, of which Darwin's ruminations are such an enlightening illustration. The *Essay on Population* explains why so many people weighed up the costs and benefits in ways similar to Charles Darwin.

Malthus drew attention to four facts. The first is that mankind is very strongly motivated by a desire for sexual intercourse, or, in his words, 'the passion between the sexes is constant' and very strong. All else being equal, men and women will mate as soon as possible. If mating is only allowed within marriage, 'such is the disposition to marry, particularly in very young people, that, if the difficulties of providing for a family were entirely removed, very few would remain single at twenty-two.'[2] The second fact is that, given low mortality, such early mating will lead to rapid population growth. We know of human groups that have doubled their population every fifteen years. Rapid doublings mean that by geometrical or exponential growth, vast numbers of human beings can be created very quickly. It would have taken 32 doublings of an original couple to raise world population from the original two to our present four thousand million plus. A few more doublings now, and every square inch of the earth would be covered. The third fact is that economic resources cannot keep pace with such growth. This is largely due to the law of diminishing marginal returns, which is implicit in his work. There are periods when rates of three or four per cent per annum economic growth, equivalent to a population doubling in twenty or fifteen years, have been sustained for a few decades. Yet we now know again that these are exceptions to the rule that economic growth tends to be much slower. The final fact is that there is a tendency for any growth in resources to be quickly absorbed by mounting population. A rise in affluence will decrease mortality and also enable people to give freer expression to the 'passion between the sexes'. Population will rise rapidly. It will then meet the inevitable control – namely, the positive checks of 'misery', specifically death by war, famine and disease.

In this theory, as he himself admitted, Malthus was only putting more clearly and with much documentation, the arguments of the political economists of the eighteenth century. In Adam Smith's *Wealth of Nations*, for example, we have a very similar set of assumptions. At the heart of the argument is the statement that 'every species of animal naturally multiplies in proportion to the means of their subsistence, and no species can ever multiply beyond it.' Mankind was included, for 'men, like all other animals, naturally multiply in proportion to the means of their subsistence.' Furthermore, Smith pointed out that an improvement in wealth would lead to a decline in mortality among the common people, hence more children would survive and the population increase. Likewise, increased wealth through increased wages would lead to increased propagation. 'The liberal reward of labour, therefore, as it is the

[2] Malthus, *Population*, ii, 52.

effect of increasing wealth, so it is the cause of increasing population', or, as it is glossed in a marginal note, 'high wages increase population.'[3]

Smith, however, was not appalled by this prospect, for he took the argument one stage further. He argued that it was not food or technology as such which regulate population, but the demand for labour. 'If this demand is continually increasing, the reward of labour must necessarily encourage in such a manner the marriage and multiplication of labourers, as may enable them to supply that continually increasing demand by a continually increasing population.' For 'the demand for men, like that for any other commodity, necessarily regulates the production of men; quickens it when it goes on too slowly, and stops it when it advances too fast.' In other words, the laws of supply and demand could account for population growth and retraction. 'It is this demand which regulates and determines the state of propagation in all the different countries of the world, in North America, in Europe, and in China; which renders it rapidly progressive in the first, slow and gradual in the second and altogether stationary in the last.'[4] Now this rosier picture – although it fails to go into the ways in which population is held stationary, which may include high mortality and misery and hence conform to Malthus' predictions – is not so far from Malthus' own thinking. Similar views to those we shall analyse for Malthus were also advanced by the Scottish political economist Dugald Stewart. He read and approved of the first *Essay on Population* and undertook a very similar analysis to that of Malthus. He placed primary stress on fertility as the major determinant of changes in rates of population growth, and on the effects of ideology and social structure on people's attitudes to marriage and childbearing.[5]

Malthus' arguments were revised in the almost totally new second edition of the *Essay* published in 1803, and there was a substantial alteration. Previously he had elaborated the premises as laws; now he spoke of them as hypothetical tendencies which would naturally work themselves out if all else was equal – or, as we would call it nowadays, a model. The new dimension that altered the whole situation was the 'preventive check', an idea which was in some ways merely an application of Smith's optimism. For Malthus had noticed that while

---

[3] Smith, *Wealth*, i, 89, 163, 90.   [4] Ibid., i, 89; i, 89–90.
[5] Stewart, *Works*, viii, 95–104.

many great civilizations encouraged marriage at as early an age as possible – for example, India or China – this was not the case in Western Europe.[6] During travels in Norway between the first and second editions of the *Essay* he had witnessed various pressures which led to the postponement of marriage, or a moral 'preventive check' (as opposed to contraception and infanticide which he termed 'vice'). In Norway, recruitment to the army so that a man could not marry without producing a certificate of army service, and the informal refusal of certain ministers to perform the marriages of people who were unable to support a family, as well as the absence of employment and housing for the peasantry, all tended to delay marriage.[7] In fact, speaking of Europe as a whole, Malthus wrote that 'it can scarcely be doubted that in modern Europe a much larger proportion of women pass a considerable part of their lives in the exercise of this virtue [i.e., late age at marriage] than in past times and among uncivilized nations.' Thus a delay in marriage, he believed, was 'the most powerful of the checks which in modern Europe keep down the population to the level of the means of subsistence'. In other words, Europe was on the way to escaping from 'misery'.[8]

Malthus did not need to travel to Norway to find an exception to his earlier 'laws' or tendencies. As subsequent historians have pointed out, and as Malthus was fully aware, the most extreme case of the preventive check, through late marriage and non-marriage, was England itself.[9] 'The most cursory view of society in this country must convince us, that throughout all ranks the preventive check to population prevails in a considerable degree.' 'the preventive check to population operates with considerable force throughout all the classes of the community'.[10] Having located the restrained fertility caused by an unusual marriage pattern, Malthus proceeded to provide a fascinating analysis of how, uniquely, the link between growing resources and growing population was transformed.

He looked at each of the four major groupings in English society – the wealthy, the middling, the wage-earners and the servants. The wealthy were reluctant to get married because they would be unable to maintain the standard of living to which they had been accustomed when single. They could not 'afford' to get married. The analysis is so central that we will quote his explanations fully:

[6] Malthus, *Population*, i, 116, 119, 129.   [7] Ibid., i, 155–7.   [8] Ibid., i, 315.
[9] Flinn, *Industrial Revolution*, 66; Chambers, *Population*, 59.
[10] Malthus, *Population*, ii, 236, 238.

a man of liberal education, with an income only just sufficient to enable him to associate in the rank of gentlemen, must feel absolutely certain that, if he marry and have a family, he shall be obliged to give up all his former connections. The woman, whom a man of education would naturally make the object of his choice, is one brought up in the same habits and sentiments with himself, and used to the familiar intercourse of a society totally different from that to which she must be reduced by marriage. Can a man easily consent to place the object of his affection in a situation so discordant, probably, to her habits and inclinations? Two or three steps of descent in society, particularly at this round of the ladder, where education ends and ignorance begins, will not be considered by the generality of people as a chimerical, but a real evil . . . These considerations certainly prevent many in this rank of life from following the bent of their inclinations in an early attachment.[11]

Thus, in Malthus' analysis, there is a combination of economic and social pressure: a mixture of fear of poverty, of loss of social status, of loss of leisure and pleasure, which will hold back the wealthy of both sexes from marriage. Furthermore, 'among the higher classes, who live principally in towns' people 'often want the inclination to marry, from the facility with which they can indulge themselves in an illicit intercourse with the sex. And others are deterred from marrying by the idea of the expenses that they must retrench, and the pleasures of which they must deprive themselves, on the supposition of having a family.'[12] Put very broadly, marriage was viewed as something which bore considerable social and economic costs, which had to be weighed against its advantages.

The pressures on the middling wealthy, the very large group of farmers and tradesmen for which England had always been conspicuous, were a little different, Malthus believed.

The sons of tradesmen and farmers are exhorted not to marry, and generally find it necessary to comply with this advice, till they are settled in some business or farm, which may enable them to support a family. These events may not perhaps occur till they are far advanced in life. The scarcity of farms is a very general complaint; and the competition in every kind of business is so great, that it is not possible that all should be successful. Among the clerks in counting-houses, and the competitors for all kinds of mercantile and professional

---

[11] Ibid., i, 236.   [12] Idem.

employment, it is probable that the preventive check to population prevails more than in any other department of society.[13]

At this level, people were restrained from marriage by the shortage of remunerative employment, of farms or businesses, and of a sufficient salary in merchant and professional employments to permit them to keep a wife and family. On this last group, Malthus' opponent William Godwin was in entire agreement:

> There is a very numerous class in every great town, clerks to merchants and lawyers, journeymen in shops, and others, who either never marry, or refrain from marriage till they have risen through the different gradations of their stations to that degree of comparative opulence, which, they think, authorises them to take upon themselves the burden of a family.[14]

Again, of course, the pressures are not just economic. People could have sacrificed their careers and their station in life in order to marry; but, as with the wealthy, it would have probably meant slipping down several rungs of that steep social ladder upon which everyone was poised.

The next major stratum was wage-labourers. They too were faced with the double hazard of economic cost and social humiliation if they made a mistake and married too young or, in some cases, at all.

> The labourer who earns eighteenpence or two shillings a day, and lives at his ease as a single man, will hesitate a little before he divides that pittance among four or five which seems to be not more than sufficient for one. Harder fare and harder labour he would perhaps be willing to submit to for the sake of living with the woman he loves; but he must feel conscious that, should he have a large family and any ill fortune whatever, no degree of frugality, no possible exertion of his manual strength, would preserve him from the heart-rending sensation of seeing his children starve, or of being obliged to the parish for their support.[15]

Here, plainly, the battle was between a desire to marry, or 'love', and the rational realization of the likely hazards. Again, the rewards

---

[13] Ibid., i, 237.   [14] Quoted in Place, *Population*, 162.
[15] Malthus, *Population*, i, 237.

for labour were so structured that while a single person could manage, the rearing of a family was very difficult.

But what happened, then, to all the young people who, in many societies, would have been married off at, or soon after, puberty? These were the people who would be under the most severe biological pressure to seek a mate and hence to marry. In England many of them were servants; once again, as Malthus points out, they found the economic and social pressures against marriage very strong.

> The servants who live in the families of the rich have restraints yet stronger to break through in venturing upon marriage. They possess the necessaries, and even the comforts of life, almost in as great plenty as their masters. Their work is easy and their food luxurious, compared with the work and food of the class of labourers . . . Thus comfortably situated at present, what are their prospects if they marry? Without knowledge or capital, either for business or farming, and unused and therefore unable to earn a subsistence by daily labour, their only refuge seems to be a miserable alehouse, which certainly offers no very enchanting prospect of a happy evening to their lives. The greater number of them, therefore, deterred by this uninviting view of their future situation, content themselves with remaining single where they are.[16]

Like celibate fellows of Oxford and Cambridge colleges in the past, or monks, they would lose the advantages of security and assured income if they married. If they were apprentices, rather than servants, they would lose their apprenticeships if they broke their contract and married.

What Malthus was in fact describing was a situation where those contemplating marriage had to make a choice. Marriage was not something automatic and universal, arranged by others and occurring like any natural event. It was something to be chosen, a conscious decision which could be made early or put off, and there were costs and benefits in any solution. Godwin agreed with Malthus that people calculated in this way. He thought that early marriages were infrequent in England because

> every one, possessed in the most ordinary degree of the gift of foresight deliberates long before he engages in so momentous a transaction. He

[16] Ibid., 237–8.

asks himself, again and again, how he shall be able to subsist the offspring of his union. I am persuaded, it very rarely happens in England that a marriage takes place, without this question having first undergone a repeated examination.[17]

Malthus was aware of some of the benefits that pulled a person into marriage. Apart from the assuaging of that 'passion between the sexes', the biological urge, there was the desire to live 'with the woman he loves'. Marriage could also bring social advantages, of which, incidentally, he disapproved. He described as 'little better than legal prostitutions' those marriages between fair young women and unattractive older men which had resulted from the 'superior distinctions which married women receive, and the marked inattentions to which single women of advanced age are exposed'. These forced women through 'the fear of being an old maid, and of that silly and unjust ridicule, which folly sometimes attaches to this name' into 'the marriage union with men whom they dislike'.[18] Such costs must be explained to people before it could be fairly said that 'with regard to the great question of marriage, we leave every man to his own free and fair choice.'[19] Yet against these biological, social and occasional economic advantages must be weighed the costs.

The cost at one level was an economic one. In essence, it was more expensive to be married with children than to be single. 'We must on no account do anything which tends directly to encourage marriage, or to remove, in any regular and systematic manner, that inequality of circumstances which ought always to exist between the single man and the man with a family.'[20] Malthus agreed with the judge who claimed 'that the growth and increase of mankind is more stinted from the cautious difficulty people make to enter on marriage, from the prospect of the trouble and expenses in providing for a family, than from anything in the nature of the species.'[21] This economic cost was mixed up with social costs, hence trouble and expenses.

In an assessment of the preventive check, Malthus isolated various considerations which would drive an ordinary man to hold back from marriage:

[A man] cannot look around him and see the distress which frequently presses upon those who have large families; he cannot contemplate his

[17] In Place, *Population*, 162.   [18] Malthus, *Population*, ii, 184.   [19] Ibid., ii, 185.
[20] Ibid., ii, 223.   [21] Ibid., i, 238.

present possessions or earnings, which he now nearly consumes himself, and calculate the amount of each share, when with very little addition they must be divided, perhaps, among seven or eight, without feeling a doubt whether, if he follow the bent of his inclinations, he may be able to support the offspring which he will probably bring into the world.[22]

The cost is also social. In a stratified society such as England, Malthus observes, 'will he not lower his rank in life, and be obliged to give up in great measure his former habits?' Is it not true that the utmost effort he may make will not be able to save his family, if he should have a large one, 'from rags and squalid poverty, and their consequent degradation in the community'? A man will have to work much harder. 'Will he not at any rate subject himself to greater difficulties, and more severe labour, than in his single state?' Furthermore, his children may be downwardly mobile: 'will he not be unable to transmit to his children the same advantages of education and improvement that he had himself possessed?'[23] In effect, a mixture of social and economic arguments was balanced against the psychological and biological pressures towards marriage.

In such a situation, Malthus had no doubt that most people would act in an economically rational way and delay their marriages. Hence, there was no necessity to make laws against early marriage. 'I have distinctly said that, if any person chooses to marry without having a prospect of being able to maintain a family, he ought to have the most perfect liberty so to do . . . I am most decidedly of opinion that any positive law to limit the age of marriage would be both unjust and immoral.'[24] As contraception was both 'vice' and unnecessary, so was such a law both immoral and ultimately unnecessary. But how could Malthus be so sure that people in England would behave in a way which so conspicuously differed from that elsewhere? It appears that he saw the key in the combination of four features, all of which were developed to a very considerable degree in the England of his day.

These four things were a general acquisitive ethic which encouraged people to pursue economic and social gain; a ranked and unequal society which meant that people were constantly striving to move up a ladder and not to sink down; the institution of private property, secured by a just and powerful government, which would enable people to hold on to their gains; and a general standard of

[22] Ibid., i, 12. [23] Ibid., i, 12–13. [24] Ibid., ii, 64.

living well above subsistence so that people would have grown to appreciate the comforts and advantages of civilization. It was this combination which made the situation uniquely propitious for the preventive check to work in England. England, a 'nation of shopkeepers', was famed for its pursuit of gain and wealth through trade and industry. It was noted for having infinite gradations of status and easy mobility between them, whereby wealth could be turned into status. It was the bastion of private property and had long enjoyed powerful government and law in support of such property. It was notably the most affluent country in Europe, and the comforts and luxuries were spread widely through the population in a way unparalleled in the world. Malthus presumed and documented these things as the background to the preventive check.

He saw the acquisitive ethic as the central feature.

The desire of bettering our condition, and the fear of making it worse, like the *vis medicatrix naturae* in physics, is the *vis medicatrix reipublicae* in politics, and is continually counteracting the disorders arising from narrow human institutions . . . it operates as a preventive check to increase.[25]

Despite exhortations on the duties to marry,

each individual has practically found it necessary to consider of the means of supporting a family before he ventures to take so important a step. That great *vis medicatrix reipublicae*, the desire of bettering our condition, and the fear of making it worse, has been constantly in action . . . Owing to this powerful spring of health in every state . . . the prudential check to marriage has increased in Europe.[26]

This force operates most powerfully where it is relatively easy to climb or fall. For labourers there was the easy slide to pauperdom.[27]

It was private property and political security which kept the ladder upright and ensured that an individual's efforts to better his condition would not be wiped away. 'That this natural check to early marriages arising from a view of the difficulty attending the support of a large family operates very widely through all classes . . . cannot admit of the slightest doubt. But the operation of this natural check depends exclusively upon the existence of the laws of property and succession.'

[25] Ibid., ii, 53.   [26] Ibid., ii, 257.   [27] Ibid., i, 12–13.

Abolish inequality, abolish private property, and one would revert to those natural tendencies which could then only be controlled by 'vice' or 'misery'. The 'strong desire of bettering the condition (that master-spring of public prosperity)' led to a 'most laudable spirit of industry and foresight', included in which was the foresight to postpone marriage. 'These dispositions, so contrary to the hopeless indolence remarked in despotic countries, are generated by the constitution of the English government and the excellence of its laws, which secure to every individual the produce of his industry.'[28] Such past security, combined with the desire to better one's condition, had created the final precondition for the preventive check – widespread affluence. 'Above all, throughout a very large class of people, a decided taste for the conveniences and comforts of life ... are observed to prevail.'[29] It was a circular process. A widespread taste for 'decencies and comforts', for good food, good housing, good clothes and leisure would develop; people would become accustomed to that pleasant cushion between mere subsistence and their present lifestyle and wish to increase it. Such a wish would act as a further incentive to civilization and delayed marriage, and would prevent increased wealth being put straight back into reproduction. People would be forced to choose and would grow to prefer their raised standard of living. 'In a civilized country, such as England, where a taste for the decencies and comforts of life prevails among a very large class of people',[30] people would be less prepared to risk all by early marriage. This is what intervened between rising wages and population and broke the vicious spiral. 'It is under these circumstances, particularly when combined with a good government, that the labouring classes of society are most likely to acquire a decided taste for the conveniences and comforts of life.'[31]

Malthus believed that once a circular process had begun, then it would continue and benefit all. He was concerned about the poor, but believed that the solution to their plight was not charitable hand-outs, as in the old Poor Laws. Such indiscriminate charity encouraged early marriages. 'A poor man may marry with little or no prospect of being able to support a family without parish assistance', and this merely led to a situation where the laws 'create the poor which they maintain.'[32] Much better, he argued, to encourage the taste for other things than children and hence improve the bargaining position of the poor. 'This

---

[28] Ibid., ii, 206–7. [29] Ibid., ii, 206. [30] Ibid., ii, 185. [31] Ibid., ii, 135. [32] Ibid., ii, 48.

prudential restraint if it were generally adopted, by narrowing the supply of labour in the market, would, in the natural course of things, soon raise its price.' The delay in marriage would also allow people to save for their marriages, so that when they did marry they had enough to support themselves. Thus 'all abject poverty would be removed from society.'[33] Yet Malthus added one further refinement. He argued that it might well be necessary for economic growth that population did grow, possibly rapidly. This he believed was possible under such a regime.

Elaborating on the framework of Adam Smith, he argued that the forces of supply and demand were bound to operate in the end – and the demand for labour would finally produce labour. The crucial thing, however, was the way in which this occurred and the delay in achieving the increased labour. 'The operation of the preventive check in this way, by constantly keeping the population within the limits of the food, though constantly following its increase, would give a real value to the rise of wages and the sums saved by labourers before marriage.'[34] But how, exactly, did a rise in wealth get delayed in this way; what exactly was the connection between the market and marriage? Here Malthus provided further insights.

His main point was that in a complex market economy such as England, the determining pressure was not simply the level of wages as such, let alone the cost of grain. More important was a heavier demand for labour within the economy. A single man's wages, for example, might be relatively high, but if they were not coupled with a demand for women and children's labour, they might not be conducive to a drop in the age at marriage: 'it will evidently be the average earnings of the families of the labouring classes throughout the year on which the encouragement to marriage, and the power of supporting children, will depend, and not merely the wages of day-labour estimated in food.'[35] It was the total earnings over the whole year that were important. 'An attention to this very essential point will explain the reason why, in many instances, the progress of population does not appear to be regulated by what are usually called the real wages of labour.'[36] A combination of factors prevailed, including the possibility of parish relief, the presence of cheaper foodstuffs, and the availability of piece-work.

Malthus drew on the history of eighteenth-century England to

---

[33] Ibid., ii, 161.   [34] Idem.   [35] Ibid., ii, 139.   [36] Idem.

describe the intervening mechanisms that meant that one had to think of total real income, rather than merely the real wages of labour.

In our own country, for instance, about the middle of the last century, the price of corn was very low; and, for twenty years together, from 1735 to 1755 a day's labour would, on an average, purchase a peck of wheat. During this period, population increased at a moderate rate; but not by any means with the same rapidity as from 1790 to 1811, when the average wages of day-labour would not in general purchase so much as a peck of wheat. In the latter case, however, there was a more rapid accumulation of capital, and a greater demand for labour; and though the continued rise of provisions still kept them rather ahead of wages, yet the fuller employment for everybody that would work, the greater quantity of task-work done, the higher relative value of corn compared with manufactures, the increased use of potatoes, and the greater sums distributed in parish allowances, unquestionably gave to the lower classes of society the power of commanding [i.e., purchasing] a greater quantity of food, and will account for the more rapid increase of population in the latter period, in perfect consistency with the general principle.[37]

Thus, in a society where people were well above subsistence level, it was no longer the supply of food which determined population. In Ireland, where the standard of living was much lower, with the widespread use of potatoes and with low expectations, population would rise rapidly as the food supply increased.[38] But it was the demand for labour combined with people's expectations that would affect the situation in England, and one might even get the curious situation of population rising while the food supply shrank.

When the demand for labour is either stationary, or increasing very slowly, people not seeing any employment open by which they can support a family, or the wages of common labour being inadequate to this purpose, will of course be deterred from marrying. But if a demand for labour continue increasing with some rapidity, although the supply of food be uncertain, the population will evidently go on.[39]

Malthus was very aware that it was aspirations and attitudes that determined the effects of economics. Two principal examples of this were the attitudes to the purposes and functions of marriage, and the

[37] Idem.   [38] Semmel, *Papers of Malthus*, 44.   [39] Malthus, *Population*, ii, 140.

attitude to what was considered an acceptable life. The former was interrelated with the religious and mental systems. The Chinese, Malthus suggested, 'acknowledge two ends in marriage; the first is that of perpetuating the sacrifices in the temple of their fathers; and the second the multiplication of the species . . . In consequence of these maxims, a father feels some sort of dishonour, and is not easy in his mind, if he do not marry off all his children.'[40] In India (quoting from a translation of the ancient Indian *Laws of Manu*), 'marriage is very greatly encouraged, and a male heir is considered as an object of the first importance.' 'By a son a man obtained victory over all people; by a son's son he enjoys immortality; and afterwards by the son of that grandson he reaches the solar abode.'[41] Such views of marriage 'cannot but have a very powerful influence'.

> The man who thinks that, in going out of the world without leaving representatives behind him, he shall have failed in an important duty to society, will be disposed to force rather than to repress his inclinations on this subject; and when his reason represents to him the difficulties attending a family, he will endeavour not to attend to these suggestions, will still determine to venture, and will hope that, in the discharge of what he conceives to be his duty, he shall not be deserted by Providence.[42]

Religion and social pressure combined with the 'passion between the sexes', Malthus believed, could well overwhelm economic prudence.

The force of the economic arguments would again depend very heavily on what was considered an acceptable living standard. If a person was prepared to put up with absolutely basic food and accommodation, and the humiliation of parish relief, then a population could marry early for a long time before it hit the absolute levels of starvation and pestilence. But if a person expected a few of the comforts of life, like some leisure, privacy, warmth, food above and beyond rice, potatoes or black bread, then he or she might be held back from early reproduction. This was a contrast between the English and Irish poor, as Malthus observed it, a difference arising from the fact that the English had grown to think of certain minor comforts as necessities. 'One of the most salutary and least pernicious checks to the frequency of early marriages in this country is the

[40] Ibid., i, 129.   [41] Ibid, i, 116.   [42] Ibid., ii, 184–5.

difficulty of procuring a cottage, and the laudable habits which prompt a labourer rather to defer his marriage some years in the expectation of a vacancy, than to content himself with a wretched mud cabin, like those in Ireland.'[43] Thus we see that a consideration of why the preventive check had become so powerful in England led Malthus deep into a consideration of politics and law, of private property, equality and inequality, of religion and views of the ancestors and after-life, of aspirations and 'habits'.

The applicability of Malthus' analysis to Darwin's case is obvious. What has been less clear until very recently is the great importance of the marriage mechanisms which Malthus outlines. Their significance in explaining the nature of English economic and demographic development has been obscured by a problem which has only recently been overcome. The solution to that problem places Malthusian marriage at the centre of the historical investigation.

[43] Ibid., ii, 250.

2

The Importance of Malthusian Marriage

One of the unanswered questions concerning the recent past is the relationship between economic and demographic growth in eighteenth- and nineteenth-century England. The sudden spurt in population from roughly the middle of the eighteenth century, after a hundred years of minimal growth, is puzzling. The period of slow growth allowed for the accumulation of the infrastructure for industrialization, and the population explosion provided labour for industrial and colonial expansion. What were the reasons for the change in population dynamics?

In the hundred and forty years of continued speculation on this problem, between Darwin's reflections on marriage in 1838 and 1978, there were three major theories put forward to account for the change. The most popular argument, which became enshrined in 'demographic transition theory' and hence vastly influential in population analysis throughout the world, was that the determining variable was mortality. England conformed to the usual pattern observed in many developing countries. There were three stages. Up to the middle of the eighteenth century high fertility was balanced by high mortality. There were then improvements in health and the disappearance of plague. For a while high fertility continued, but the babies and young mothers ceased to die in such numbers and population soared. The balance was achieved over a hundred years later when fertility was brought down through the introduction of birth control. This seemed plausible enough, and since it was clearly what was happening in many other parts of the world, it was widely accepted.

In such a solution, the important topic to study is health and disease. Fertility is a biological constant and unimportant in explaining the change. The argument when applied to earlier periods would be that the reason for continued drops in population after the Black Death was recurring outbreaks of disease. The reason why population was stagnant after the middle of the seventeenth century was the recurrence of further and new diseases. The implications are that this pre-industrial society was at the subsistence level and constantly bumping against Malthus' positive checks. England escaped first from 'the horsemen of the apocalypse' through a number of accidents and discoveries: the curious disappearance of plague, perhaps an improvement in child health through better diet and particularly the increased consumption of milk, the invention of vaccination, and the development of medical care in general.

This view has been the dominant one. The position in 1980 was much the same as it was in 1953 when H. J. Habakkuk wrote, 'Few generalizations are so well established in the books as that which ascribes the increase in the population of England and Wales in the second half of the eighteenth century to a fall in the death rate caused primarily by improvements in medicine, medical skill, and public health.'[1] Thus in 1968 J. Spengler could write that the increase in population growth rates in the eighteenth and nineteenth centuries 'seems to have been attributable mainly, if not entirely, to a decline in mortality.'[2] An example of this approach can be found in the widely read work of Thomas McKeown. An early article in 1955 with R. G. Brown provides the basis for a full-length treatment. McKeown concludes that 'when the modern rise of population is considered as a whole it is clearly a substantial reduction of mortality that has to be explained.'[3] Unable to find an explanation in medical or public health improvements, McKeown suggests that despite massive urbanization and industrialization, the majority of the English population must have experienced a substantial improvement in nutrition sufficient to lead to a dramatic fall in mortality. Although there are no figures to show that this did, indeed, happen, it must have been so.[4]

The other, minority, theory was that the rise was caused by changes in fertility, a view McKeown strongly challenged. Such an interpretation was put forward by T. H. Marshall in 1929, when he argued that 'so far as the Malthusians are concerned, it is evident that . . .

[1] In Glass, *Population*, 269.   [2] 'Historical Population', 434.
[3] McKeown, *Population*, 43.
[4] A plausible case for linking a European decline in mortality to changes in public health is argued by Kunitz, 'Mortality'.

they were absolutely right to regard the birth rate as the key to the situation.' Marshall states that a rise in the economic value of children and a drop in constraints to stop servants and apprentices from marrying may have brought down the age at marriage.[5] This view was supported by Habakkuk in two articles. In 1953, while admitting that detailed parish register evidence still awaited analysis, he argued along the same lines as Marshall: new economic opportunities and resources could have led to a fall in the age at marriage, which in turn could account for the major part of the population increase. Habakkuk quoted K. H. Connell to the effect that 'the question of the age at marriage is at the heart of Irish population history', and added that 'this is probably true of most other pre-industrial societies.'[6] If this were the case it would have enormous implications. If a fall in mortality rates is the main cause of population increase, then 'it is reasonable to consider whether the Industrial Revolution was a response to the challenge of increasing population.' If, on the other hand, the rise of population was 'primarily a consequence of an increased demand for labour, we must look elsewhere for the mainsprings of economic change in this period.'[7] Attacked by McKeown and Brown, Habakkuk was thrown on to the defensive, though maintaining his general position in an article in 1958. 'I am not convinced that we must at this stage reject the possibility that a fall of two or three years in the age at marriage, plus some increase in nuptiality, *could* have caused an acceleration of the rate of growth of the sort we observe in the later eighteenth century.' Yet his lack of confidence is shown in the next sentence: 'The much more doubtful question is whether there were in fact changes in age at marriage of this order of magnitude.'[8]

Thus there was a stalemate, neither side able to show, in the absence of detailed evidence, that their theory was correct. Who was right, the eighteenth-century writers, who tended to ascribe the upsurge of population to changes in fertility, or the majority of later historians who on the whole thought that mortality was the crucial factor?

There were major objections to the eighteenth-century view of the crucial role of fertility. First, such a phenomenon – that is, the very rapid build-up of population being caused by changes in fertility – had nowhere else been observed. Many modern and past societies

---

[5] In Glass, *Population*, 267; 260–1.
[6] Ibid., 275.   [7] Ibid., 271.   [8] Ibid., 153; see also 154.

could be shown to have rapidly increased their population through a planned or accidental drop in death rates, but few if any through a rise in the birth rates, as McKeown pointed out.[9] Secondly, it was also argued by McKeown, from the analogy with Ireland, that 'an advance in mean age of wives at marriage of about 5 years would be needed to reduce the mean number of live births by 1.'[10] Thirdly, a logical objection was voiced by Dr Johnson. When it was mentioned that Russia was likely to become a great empire because of the rapid increase of population, Johnson replied, 'Why, Sir, I see no prospect of their propagating more. They can have no more children than they can get. I know of no way to make them breed more than they do.' When Boswell countered by asking, 'But have not nations been more populous at one period than another?', Johnson answered, 'Yes, Sir; but that has been owing to the people being less thinned at one period than another, whether by emigrations, war, or pestilence, not by their being more or less prolifick. Births at all times bear the same proportion to the same number of people.'[11] This was written in 1769, just as the great burst in population was under way. As Johnson looked around him, he concluded that it was impossible to increase fertility and that Malthus' positive checks, famine, war and pestilence, or emigration, were the forces determining population growth.

Thus, while there were those who saw the phenomenon as a combination of changes in mortality and fertility, the major consensus and the weight of historical and local evidence lay with those who believed that the solution lay in the elimination of Malthus' positive checks. What has happened in the last few years has been a complete overturning of the argument. Before looking at the very considerable implications of this historical reversal, we may look at how it has been established. It has occurred in two stages, the first in two articles in 1965 and 1966. In the first article, John Hajnal outlined the 'European marriage pattern in perspective'.[12] He showed that Western Europe, since at least the sixteenth century, exhibited a curious and possibly unique marriage pattern. The two central features were a very late mean age at first marriage for women, often at 25 years of age or over, and a very large proportion of never-married females, often up to fifteen per cent or more. This 'selective' marriage is just as unusual as late age at marriage. Such a pattern separated off those countries in Europe west of a line drawn

[9] McKeown, *Population*, 42–3. [10] In Glass, *Population*, 297; McKeown, *Population*, 38. [11] Hill, *Life of Johnson*, ii, 101–2. [12] Hajnal in Glass, *Population*.

from Trieste to Leningrad from countries to the east. It was a very different pattern from that found in contemporary Africa, Asia and other parts of the Third World. What, in effect, Hajnal had shown was that fertility was not biologically but socially determined; that there was a gap of ten years or more between sexual maturity and reproduction, and that many never married at all. This important finding was quickly corroborated and examined minutely in an article by E. A. Wrigley.[13] This demonstrated that English women's marriages had indeed been very late; in Colyton, Devon, the mean age at first marriage fluctuated between 26 and 30 in the period 1560–1750. Wrigley's article also showed that, within marriage, marital fertility was relatively low, so low at certain times that he suspected that his Devonshire families were controlling their fertility by the use of some form of birth control.

Unfortunately, it has not yet been possible to show definitely when this pattern of late and selective marriage began. Hajnal thought that it probably did so sometime between 1400 and 1650, but the evidence he put forward, and that of others who are forced to work indirectly from the records of manorial courts, or court rolls, is inconclusive. Poll taxes and other early documents are extremely difficult to interpret, and we cannot be certain about female age at marriage. It remains true that 'there is no convincing evidence to show the age at which medieval women married.'[14]

These two articles removed the logical objection of Dr Johnson, for it was clear that by changing one or more of the three factors (age at marriage, proportion marrying or marital fertility), people could indeed be 'more prolific'. Nor did there have to be such a dramatic shift in age at marriage as McKeown argued: his demographic analogies appear faulty.[15] This explains how we do, in fact, find that a much smaller change in age at marriage in England had a significant effect on fertility. The first objection, however, remains. If it can be shown that it was a rise in fertility that accounted for the population growth, this would indeed make England unusual. It is one matter to show that fertility could have been the important factor; it is another, as Habakkuk pointed out, to prove convincingly that it was.

That we are now in a position to resolve these questions, among the most important and contentious facing historians, is largely due to the work of the Social Science Research Council Cambridge Group for

---

[13] Wrigley, 'Family Limitation'.   [14] Hajnal in Glass, *Population*, 122; Macfarlane, *Individualism*, 158.   [15] Schofield, 'Review', 180.

the History of Population and Social Structure. During the last twenty years they have reconstructed the population history of England through two separate procedures. They have worked out methods of 'back projection' which enable the historian to calculate fertility and mortality rates back to the sixteenth century, from aggregate figures derived from parish registers. This is complemented by the intensive study of parish registers through 'family reconstitution', that is, the linking of baptisms, marriages and burials, so that it is possible to work out ages of mothers at marriage, when giving birth, and at death. During the last four years the results of this work have been published, and it has transformed our understanding of the causes of these puzzling relations. We can now see that the unexpected solution is the right one.

We may briefly summarize the conclusions of the work of Schofield and Wrigley which has finally settled the argument. They have discovered that there was little change in the levels of marital fertility over time. The number of children conceived in each year of marriage hardly varied over the sixteenth to eighteenth centuries, and can consequently be discarded as a major solution to the puzzles we are investigating.[16] Throughout the centuries, when compared to France or Sweden, English marital fertility was surprisingly low, but that is another problem. What did change dramatically were the two features first stressed by Hajnal. The proportions never marrying dropped at the beginning of the eighteenth century. Schofield and Wrigley calculated that in the second half of the seventeenth century as many as 22.9 per cent of the population of both sexes between 40 and 44 years of age were still not married. There was a great change in the second half of the eighteenth century, when the equivalent figure was about 9 per cent not married: a change from about a quarter of the population to one tenth.[17] Thus one important difference in the pattern was the fact that one had moved from a Stuart England where many never reproduced themselves to a Georgian England where most people did so.

Yet the heart of the eighteenth century shift lay elsewhere – namely, in the drop in the age at which people reproduced themselves. In essence, the change hardly looks dramatic. Wrigley tells us that 'during the period in which intrinsic growth rates rose

[16] Wrigley and Schofield, 'Population History', 168.
[17] Ibid., 176, originally put the figure at 5.9%, but Schofield now thinks a 'minimum of 9% is probably nearer the mark' (personal communication); see also the dramatic graph in Outhwaite, *Marriage*, 151.

from zero to 1.67 per cent per annum ... age at first marriage of women fell by about three years.' The drop was from a mean age of 26 to a mean age of 23.[18] Both ages are by many countries' standards very high, and the modification may appear slight. But in the right circumstances, when mortality is relatively low and when it is combined with an increasing proportion marrying, this is enough to have a significant effect on population growth rates. 'Since the middle twenties is in the period of peak fecundity for women, a fall of three years in marriage age is sufficient to make a substantial difference to over-all fertility.'[19] The author estimates that 'the changes which occurred in marriage and marriage-related behaviour in the course of the eighteenth century were sufficient to have raised the annual rate of growth of the population from zero to 1.26 per cent, *even though there was no change in either mortality or age-specific marital fertility*'; hence he is able to argue convincingly that 'about three-quarters of the acceleration in the growth rate which took place over the period is attributable to the increase in fertility brought about by changing marriage behaviour.'[20] The other quarter he ascribes to possible changes in mortality.

One of the associated features of this change, which has led us to talk of 'age of reproduction' rather than age at marriage, is the link with illegitimate and pre-nuptial conceptions. It might have been expected that, as stiff controls which prevented many from marrying and delayed the marriages of others were relaxed, the pent up reproductive energies which had occasionally found outlets in bridal pregnancy and illegitimacy would diminish. The contrary happened. 'Age at marriage fell and with it the proportion of men and women who never married, and yet at the same time illegitimate fertility rose sharply and the proportion of pregnant brides also increased.'[21] This was very different from France, for example, where as marriage age was delayed, 'there was some tendency to more widespread liaisons outside marriage, as if there were a pent-up pressure.'[22] In England

[18] Wrigley, 'Population', 131; Wrigley in Outhwaite, *Marriage*, 148.

[19] Wrigley in Outhwaite, *Marriage*, 148–9.

[20] Ibid., 171. Two articles in the *Journal of Family History* in late 1984/1985 by Roger Schofield and David Weir add to our understanding of the relative contribution of changes in proportion married and age at marriage, showing that celibacy was more important up to the eighteenth century and age at marriage thereafter. I am grateful to Tony Wrigley and Roger Schofield for references to this work.   [21] Wrigley in Outhwaite, *Marriage*, 146.   [22] Ibid., 179–80.

'whatever constrained men and women to marry late also constrained them to avoid extra-marital intercourse, but when earlier marriage was countenanced, inhibitions on intercourse outside marriage were also relaxed.'[23]

We have learnt several important things as a consequence of these discoveries. We know that England, during the sixteenth to nineteenth centuries, exhibited a particular kind of self-correcting, homeostatic regime connecting wealth and population. Instead of population immediately expanding up to the maximum that resources would allow and then being cut back, a comfortable margin was left by the working of the institution of regulated marital fertility. There was a gap which allowed considerable capital accumulation with little population growth, and which also slowed down growth when resources began to be stretched. This was linked to a second feature – what Wrigley calls a 'low-pressure' equilibrium. This had two characteristics. On the one hand, both mortality and fertility were below the maximum for many centuries. This was made possible by controlled fertility. In societies 'where fertility was high, mortality was of necessity also high.' But in England, where fertility was lower, mortality could also stabilize at more modest levels, as Malthus had earlier pointed out.[24] Such a lower-level equilibrium also led to advantageous effects on standards of living. 'A low-pressure equilibrium between population and the resources available to sustain it was consonant with relatively high standards of living. A high-pressure equilibrium was inevitably one entailing for the bulk of the population a life lived close to the margin of existence.'[25] In this respect England was different from other traditional societies and other countries in western Europe at the time.[26] In a lengthy comparison with France, Wrigley shows that the fertility and nuptiality patterns of the two countries were very different in the eighteenth century: 'the contrast between the history of marriage in England and France in this period is remarkable.' It was thus not mortality 'which appears to have distinguished England from other countries so much as her fertility history'.[27]

Above all we know that the crucial variable was marriage and associated sexual behaviour. 'Thus marriage now emerges holding

---

[23] Ibid., 146.   [24] Wrigley, 'Population History', 209; Malthus, *Population*, i, 240.
[25] Wrigley, 'Population History', 209.   [26] Wrigley and Schofield, 'Population History', 184.   [27] Wrigley in Outhwaite, *Marriage*, 174–6.

the centre of the stage', for the 'changes in nuptiality in England in the early modern period were on a large enough scale in themselves to move population growth rates between the minimum and maximum to be found in pre-industrial societies.'[28] Marriage and the family system become of central importance in helping us to understand the unique and early development of England. As Wrigley points out, the work of Hajnal and Laslett had suggested in the 1960s 'the possibility that the pre-industrial west European family pattern – late marriage for women, a large proportion of women of child-bearing age remaining unmarried, a separate household at marriage, small households comprising only a single conjugal family – was unique among all traditional societies'. This meant that the study of the family became of central importance.

> Was it a key to the understanding of the transformations of the eighteenth and nineteenth centuries? If it was not the industrial revolution that had produced the modern conjugal family system, might it not have been the existence of an unusual complex of marriage and co-residential patterns that helped to produce the radical economic changes of the industrial revolution period?

The connection is not merely temporal. It is possible to see how the homeostatic, low-level-equilibrium structure of England could actually encourage, or at least not extinguish, economic growth.

> A pre-industrial society in which overall fertility is comparatively low because women marry late is one in which a comparatively favourable balance between population and productive capacity is attainable. Once attained, it is easier to sustain where age at marriage is sensitive to economic and social circumstances and not largely determined by a biological event such as menarche. Higher real incomes imply a different structure of demand and a greater chance of provoking the type of changes that precede and accompany an industrial revolution.[29]

A set of long-standing puzzles has been solved and the solution has important implications. Yet, as Wrigley points out, in solving these a fresh set of problems has been raised. We now know that what needs to be explained is the pattern of marital and sexual relations which allowed population to behave in this way. We know that 'English

[28] Wrigley, 'Population', 133.   [29] Wrigley, 'Reflections', 76–7.

society was so constituted that at times of low over-all fertility every aspect of the reproductive career of women up to the point of marriage was conducted conservatively.'[30] But how, exactly, was it so constituted, and why? Until we have an answer to this, we will not be able to answer the many new questions now thrown up: 'Why should nuptiality have increased so remarkably in eighteenth-century England? Why should illegitimacy and prenuptial pregnancy have such a distinctive relationship with nuptiality? And why should what is observable in England have contrasted so markedly with the parallel phenomena in France in the same period?'[31]

Thus what now faces us as a central problem is the nature of the English pattern of marital and sexual relationships, and above all how the decision to reproduce was reached, either through marriage or outside marriage. Before embarking on analysis of this we may accept three further pointers from the work of Wrigley and Schofield. First, it is obvious that there is a relationship between decisions to reproduce and real income. It is argued that 'there was a tight relationship between the secular behaviour of prices and the rate of population growth from the sixteenth century until about 1800.'[32] Furthermore, 'there is evidence that the secular changes in nuptiality which took place . . . were closely associated with the secular trends in real wages, with the former taking place some 20–30 years later than the latter.'[33] But, as Wrigley states, even if a relationship is demonstrated, this does not explain 'how economic changes became transmuted through social norms in a manner which resulted in an "appropriate" change in individual decisions about marriage and reproduction both within and outside marriage'.[34] A particular problem is the lag of twenty years or so.

A second important suggestion is that we are dealing with a long-enduring pattern and that we need to look for a solution in the effects of enduring rules rather than changes in the rules themselves. At first, when the dramatic change of the mid-eighteenth century was pinpointed to changes in fertility, it seemed attractive to believe that this reflected some massive transformation in social structure or in the nature of marriage. One appealing argument was that as the labouring groups, those dependent entirely on wages, increased as a proportion of the population, so a hitherto minority pattern of early

---

[30] Wrigley in Outhwaite, *Marriage*, 184.   [31] Ibid., 183.   [32] Wrigley, 'Population', 136.   [33] Wrigley in Outhwaite, *Marriage*, 183.   [34] Idem.

marriage became dominant. Thus changes in fertility reflected the growth of proletarianization.[35] Wrigley, however, points out that 'the downturn in nuptiality in the early nineteenth century', which seems to have once again reflected a downturn in real wages, 'is fatal to this viewpoint since proletarianization went forward steadily.'[36] Nor is there evidence of a major shift in the nature of marriage itself or of its relations to economics. Thus 'there appears to have been a substantial uniformity of reaction to changing real income trends between the sixteenth and nineteenth centuries.'[37] When trying to explain the shift in the middle of the eighteenth century Wrigley comments that 'it is highly probable that this did not reflect any major alteration in the way in which young people made their decisions to marry, to delay marriage or to remain single, but that instead the inducements to marry grew steadily greater and the disincentives less with rising real incomes over a period which lasted more than a century.'[38] In other words, it is possible that between the sixteenth and nineteenth centuries, and possibly earlier, we are looking at a framework of decision-making, a set of rules and customs, which remain broadly the same. What changes is the outcome produced by these rules in differing economic circumstances. Prima facie, this makes sense; it does not need a radical change in the structure and nature of marriage to change a mean age at first marriage for women from 26 to 23.

The final suggestion links the former two and provides a possible explanation for the difference between the English pattern on the one hand, and the French and Swedish on the other. In the continental variety, 'it is tempting to see in the nuptiality history . . . a "peasant" variant', while in England one has a 'wage' variant. 'In the former the number of viable holdings might be supposed to be growing less rapidly than the population, which might make matches harder to make, while in the latter a system of "ecological niches" had given way to one in which current and prospective earnings had replaced access to land as a criterion for eligibility to marry.' This, Wrigley states, is merely 'speculation', an 'hypothesis to be tested'.[39]

Solutions to the problem of how the Malthusian regime worked and when it became established have not only an historical but also a present-day significance. Rapid population growth is one of the

---

[35] Levine, *Family Formation.*   [36] Wrigley, 'Population', 144.   [37] Idem.
[38] Ibid., 148.   [39] Wrigley in Outhwaite, *Marriage*, 183.

gravest threats to world resources and peace. In the period between about 1950 and 1975 the population trends in the Third World led to extremely gloomy forecasts. Many governmental and other attempts to bring down fertility to match the lowered levels of mortality through family planning campaigns were failing, and a large literature arose to show why such schemes would be unlikely to succeed.[40] Then an extraordinary thing happened. In a growing number of countries, fertility rates started to drop. Rather like the strange fertility transition which occurred throughout most of Europe in the period 1870–1915, this change occurred across ethnic, religious, political and other boundaries. It was noticed particularly in islands (Mauritius, Taiwan, Japan, Sri Lanka) and in 'Confucian' cultures – Singapore, Taiwan, parts of Thailand, for example, and later, dramatically, in China.[41] But it also started to occur in large land-locked states, in Catholic as well as Protestant countries (for example, certain countries in South America). The one major exception, where fertility rates rose rather than declined, was sub-Saharan Africa. Like the fertility transition within Europe, the reasons remain a mystery. There is no obvious association with sociological or economic variables. In both cases it looks as if some kind of 'fashion' has changed. But it became apparent that in fact the fertility changes were due to *two* major changes – a Malthusian revolution to late age at marriage, and a neo-Malthusian one to contraception.

Using a simple model developed by the demographer Matras, we can point to four major types of fertility regime:[42]

		Fertility	
		Uncontrolled	Controlled
	Early	A	B
Marriage	Late	C	D

In Western Europe today we employ D, though sometimes reverting to B. It was expected by many that when the hoped-for demographic transition occurred in the Third World it would involve a direct move from A to D. This has indeed sometimes happened – as with the massive campaigns in China where there has been some

---

[40] Davis, 'Population Policy'. [41] Maudlin, 'Family Planning'; Tabah, 'Population'.
[42] Cited by Spuhler in Zubrow, *Demographic Anthropology*, 211.

success in moving a quarter of the world's population in a few years from A to D, by way of late marriage and one-child families achieved through contraception and abortion. But equally common is the move from A to C, which may have a similar effect, but probably arises from different causes.

A brief summary of what is happening is provided by Ansley Coale. He points out that there is a 'Malthusian element in current population trends that is usually overlooked. The preventive check of 'moral restraint' that Malthus proposed is contributing very significantly to the reduction in human fertility occurring in the past 10 or 15 years in the third world.'[43] He notes a significant rise in the age at marriage leading to a drop in fertility in Morocco, Tunisia, Kuwait, the Central Asian Republics of the Soviet Union, Sri Lanka, Singapore, Malaysia, Hong Kong, Taiwan, Korea and China. He cites, as an example, Korea. There, over the period 1930–75, the overall fertility declined by approximately a half, the birth rate dropping from 43 to 23 per thousand. This was due more to the rise in the age at marriage than to birth control; the proportion married among women of childbearing age declined by 33 per cent, and marital fertility decreased by 23 per cent. The decline in the proportion married among women aged 15 to 50 was 'wholly the result of a very large increase (from 16 to nearly 24 years) in age at first marriage.'[44] Coale notes that in Taiwan the mean age at first marriage rose from 18 in 1905 to 23 in 1970, in Sri Lanka from 18 in 1901 to 25 in 1975. The difficult case is China, for which little information was then available. Coale's hunch, based on fragmentary reports that there had been a substantial rise in the age at marriage there, now appears confirmed, and consequently the 'rising age at marriage has been as important as birth control in reducing Chinese fertility.'[45] If this is true, then Coale concludes that the Malthusian preventive check (later marriage) 'has been as effective in contributing to the recent reduction in the birth rate in the third world as the much more publicized spread of "family planning".'[46] Yet this has gone so totally unnoticed that there has been little speculation on the reasons for the change.

From the work of Malthus and certain recent demographic and economic historians we can draw certain conclusions. The relation-

---

[43] Coale, Malthus, 10.   [44] Ibid., 11.   [45] See recent issues of *Population and Development Review*.   [46] Coale, 'Malthus', 12.

ship between economic growth, and population trends is central to an understanding of European economic growth and particularly the remarkable upsurge of wealth and productivity in England in the eighteenth and nineteenth centuries. An important distinguishing feature of Europe, the pivot on which the system turned, was the flexible marital regime, which allowed population to adjust to economy. Malthus had shown that population will tend to grow rapidly even before there is any economic growth; it will destroy any chance of a rise in the standard of living, since it will increase as soon as mortality loosens its grip. Such population expansion will also make economic growth more difficult through the law of diminishing marginal returns on further labour input. What was needed was a breathing space. 'The constant effort towards population, which is found to act even in the most vicious societies, increases the number of people before the means of subsistence are increased.'

This produces a negative spiral. Food becomes scarcer, the poor 'consequently must live much worse, and many of them be reduced to severe distress'. Then wages fall, with a superabundance of labour. This leads to a fall in population, through 'the discouragements to marriage and the difficulty of rearing a family'.[47] What was needed was a situation where, instead of population growing rapidly and being held in check by 'misery' or 'vice', a set of tastes and institutions could be created which would induce people to pursue other than biological goals. A game needed to be devised in which there would be prizes of different sizes, assured by the firm system of government – prizes that people really wanted. This game is known to us as capitalism. Whatever its costs, Malthus believed that its benefits recommend it to us.

What, in effect, Malthus and his followers have done is to isolate a problem. In the 'natural' situation, fertility is uncontrolled and is held back by two major mechanisms. Either there is high perennial mortality, particularly of infants, which contains population. Or, more usually, there is a wave-like movement with population climbing moderately rapidly and then being savagely cut back by a 'crisis', usually the pestilence and famine associated with war. This latter 'crisis' pattern has been observed from India, China and much of Europe until the middle of the eighteenth century.[48] In such situations it is the control of perennial and crisis mortality, often by

[47] Malthus, *Population*, i, 15.   [48] Macfarlane, *Resources*, 304ff.

such indirect measures as the institution of peaceful government or good communications, which causes population to explode. Any improvement, in food, technology or other factors, would quickly, as Malthus argues, be absorbed. These are what Wrigley would call 'high-pressure' regimes. They make it extremely difficult to accumulate in the long term and they tend to force down the living conditions of the masses. By an accident whose nature and causes we do not yet understand, England seems to have escaped from this 'natural' situation by at least the sixteenth century. It had escaped into a 'low-pressure' regime, much more like that of present-day 'post demographic transition' societies. That is to say, both fertility and mortality were well below their theoretical maximum and were more or less balanced. Such a homeostatic situation has been observed in some simple hunting-gathering societies and among certain species of animals, and became widespread in Europe in the nineteenth century. There are now signs that it is developing in parts of the Third World, particularly in South-East Asia. Yet it is so generally unusual that it is very tempting to link it to other well known unusual features of the society – a precocious growth of industry, urbanization and democracy.

3

The Malthusian Marriage System and its Origins

A number of the central features of the marital and family structure which Malthus believed to be present can be abstracted from his analysis. Most important are certain characteristics which he takes for granted, hardly bothering to mention them with any emphasis, or simply ignoring them. One of these was a set of assumptions about the nature and purposes of marriage, which were self-evident and 'natural' to an English clergyman living at the turn of the eighteenth century but are unusual in comparative perspective.

Malthus assumed monogamy, though most societies at his time practised polygamy; a fairly egalitarian relationship between husband and wife, while most societies assumed male dominance; unbreakable marriage, though many permitted easy divorce; permissive remarriage, though the majority either forbade remarriage or made it mandatory; independent residence after marriage, though the majority of societies have been virilocal or uxorilocal;[1] a fairly equal contribution to the conjugal fund, though the usual situation was for wealth to flow preponderantly from either bride's or groom's group. These structural features, which would have seemed so extraordinary to those living in China, India, Africa, Eastern Europe and South America at the same time as Malthus, are the assumed foundations of his scheme. They were the basis for beliefs about the nature of marriage choice which were equally unusual at that time.

Malthus' 'preventive check' was based on the assumption that it was the individual man and woman who would decide whom to marry. But the vast majority of people believed that, on the contrary, marriage was not a matter to be left to the couple themselves, but was to be arranged by the parents and wider kin. Malthus' analysis was

---

[1] 'Virilocal', residence at husband's place; 'uxorilocal', at the wife's.

also founded on the presumption that there were few positive rules restricting the choice of spouse, and in particular, that the individual could marry whomever he or she could 'catch'. The very elaborate rules which in the greater part of the world dictated that an individual should marry within a certain group or category defined by kinship, geography, caste, class, religion or occupation, are not apparent in his analysis. All this betrays an even deeper assumption – that there was choice in the matter of marriage. Malthus believed that to marry or not to marry at all was a matter for decision by the individual concerned. The almost universal view at his time was that marriage is an automatic, 'natural' event, like birth or death, but such a way of looking at things was not contemplated in his scheme. Both as to when one married and whether one married at all, it was confidently assumed that the matter was open to choice. Marriage was like choosing a career; but there was also an element of 'calling' or vocation, and not all were called.

A further cultural assumption which would have startled other parts of the world was the view that marriage, and particularly the rearing of children, would be economically and socially 'costly'. The whole Malthusian analysis was based on the weighing up of the advantages and disadvantages of marriage, regarded from the individual standpoint. Malthus argued that the state should not tamper with the balance by increasing the Poor Law provisions, thereby favouring those who took the risk and married young. Such people should be forced to bear the full cost themselves. Behind this argument is the assumption that the participants were faced with real costs. Most human societies contemporary with Malthus would not have seen any opposition between individual desire (biological and psychological forces) and individual wealth (economic and social pressures). Usually, the two have run alongside each other rather than conflicted. Unusually, it is precisely marriage, and above all the children and their labour which marriage produces, that bring wealth of all kinds. To talk of the cost of marriage, to see children as an expense and marriage as likely to threaten individual prosperity, has been until recently an almost incomprehensible view. Wives and children are wealth and happiness.

Although the assumptions revealed in Malthus' scheme and Darwin's personal reflections were unusual at the time in a world context, they are now so familiar to us that we tend to take them for granted. They show a set of cultural and social features which have frequently been dissected in the contemporary world when theorists discuss the differences between the 'traditional', 'familist' system and the 'modern', 'individualistic' one – Malthus and Darwin fitting well into the latter. To elaborate more fully the nature of the marriage system of which Malthus wrote, we may examine a few more examples from the vast literature in this field.

Just after the Second World War an American social demographer, Kingsley Davis, wrote a textbook in which he outlined the major features of what he called the 'Great Transition' to the 'modern family system', the movement from 'familistic' to 'individualistic' societies. In the 'familistic' society – for instance, Hindu India, where the immediate family is controlled by the extended family – there is likely to be plural mating (either polygyny or concubinage), an authoritarian power of husband over wife, young age at marriage, marital choice determined by parents, and an absence of romantic love. Economic exchanges at marriage are complex, 'embracing not only a wide range of goods and services but also a wide circle of relatives', and the newly married couple will tend to live with the parents. There will probably be a high fertility rate to compensate for high mortality. Inheritance will either be automatic or strictly along kinship lines. The familistic system has historically 'prevailed to a much greater extent than the other' (individualistic) system. Yet it is now being destroyed by the 'small family system' which is 'now being diffused, along with other features of industrialism, to the rest of the world'. The individualistic system is the mirror image of the structure described above. For instance, 'mass romanticism – the deification of romantic courtship – has reached its pinnacle'; couples wish to set up a separate home; the 'sole effective kinship group is now the immediate family, and even this unit has lost its size and function.'[2]

This contrast has been elaborated in the work of W. J. Goode, who outlines the major features of the 'modern' conjugal family system.[3] The most important characteristic is the 'relative exclusion of a wide range of marital and blood relatives' from the affairs of the young couple. From this flow a number of other features. The young will establish 'neolocal' or separate residence after marriage and will be relatively independent. The courtship system will be based on the mutual attraction between the future husband and wife, rather than the interests of the wider kin. The age at marriage will rise, for 'the

---

[2] Davis, *Human Society*, 417–18; 424; 422.   [3] Goode, *World Revolution*, 8–9.

youngsters must now be old enough to take care of themselves; i.e. they must be as old as the economic system forces them to be in order to be independent at marriage.' The couple decide the number of children they want, rather than their choice being dictated by the needs of a wider group. The husband–wife relationship becomes the most important of all ties, and 'the emotions within this unit are likely to be intense, and the relationship between husband and wife may be intrinsically unstable.' Remarriage is likely to be widespread 'because there is no larger kin unit to absorb the children and no unit to prevent the spouses from re-entering the free marriage market.' Goode then proceeds to analyse how far this system has already penetrated in the Middle East, Africa, India, China and Japan. He argues that there is a rapid spread, based as much on a cultural or ideological pressure as on any link with Western economic or technological systems. 'The ideology of the conjugal family is a radical one, destructive of the older traditions in almost every society.'[4]

A complementary depiction of this marital and family system, specifically linking it to the Malthusian and demographic arguments, is provided by John Caldwell. Caldwell's major thesis is that there is a great difference between the two main types of social–demographic regime. In many traditional societies there is no economic or social advantage from restricting fertility or avoiding marriage because, on balance, children are an economic and social advantage. The net flow of assets is upwards, from children to parents. Children contribute more to their parents than they consume. This results not from the nature of the means of production – for instance, the type of agriculture or industry – but from the set of cultural expectations about relations within and outside the nuclear family. Thus one finds that even in an urban–industrial setting such as the city of Ibadan in West Africa, children are a net advantage to their parents.[5] Caldwell argues that 'as long as children ungrudgingly share their earnings with their parents it will pay to have a large family and to educate them.'[6] Here we have a society where there appears to be little 'cost' in marrying and having children; both activities expand a person and add to his material and social wealth.

What transforms the situation, according to Caldwell, is the importation of the 'Western' family system, or what we have termed

---

[4] Ibid., 19.   [5] Caldwell, 'Fertility', 243.   [6] Caldwell, 'Rationality', 16.

the 'Malthusian' marriage system. This alters the situation, so that wealth flows preponderantly down rather than up. Hence children begin to become a cost to their parents. 'What causes this emotional nucleation of the family whereby parents spend increasingly on their children, while demanding – and receiving – very little in return?' asks Caldwell. His answer is that it is 'undoubtedly the import of a different culture; it is westernization.' This process of 'westerniz-ation' is 'the central feature of our times'.[7] It is the culmination of a long history, mounting in the nineteenth century through the pressure of missionaries, traders and Western imperial governments, and today pushed by the mass media and mass education. Yet we may wonder what the specific content of this 'westernization' is, that leads to 'family nucleation and the reversal of intergenerational wealth flow', which Caldwell believes will 'almost inevitably . . . guarantee slower global population growth'.

The central features are precisely those which were illustrated by Malthus and Darwin. They are the 'predominance of the nuclear family, with its central conjugal tie and its ideology of concentrating concern and expenditure on one's own children'.[8] The theme is an application of Davis' and Goode's ideas to demography; it is the rise of the dominant husband–wife relationship, the decrease of obliga-tions to wider kin, and the concentration on children. The whole package is succinctly presented in Caldwell's explanation of our own assumptions and how they hinder a Western observer from understanding Third World societies. In the West there is a 'strong nuclear family' with few obligations outside immediate relatives; a deep bond between spouses; an increased expenditure on children 'accompanied by a decline in moralizing about what is good for them'; 'property bought on an open market largely regulated by the State', with little community or family ownership. Caldwell does not discuss at this point the other parts of the system that we have noted, particularly individual 'love marriage', but his scheme fits well with the earlier analyses. And Darwin's self-examination and Malthus' general scheme fit excellently with his analysis. Caldwell helps to show why it is that marriage and childbearing become, instead of automatic and self-fulfilling, a matter of choice and of the weighing of advantages. He is correct in seeing this as a vast transformation without which contraception and a deferred marriage system are

[7] Caldwell, 'Restatement', 352, 356.   [8] Ibid., 356.

unlikely to occur. He is also right in arguing that the origins of the change lie in the 'perhaps unique familial and social structure' that had somehow emerged in the West at least by the time of Darwin and Malthus.[9]

Caldwell's major field research has been undertaken in West Africa. It is supported by the analysis of anthropologists who have worked in the same area – for example, Meyer Fortes. Fortes notes the peculiarity of the Western family system assumed by Malthus and Darwin, that is, 'the monogamous, independently co-resident, conjugal or nuclear family'.[10] In contrast to this family structure, with its emphasis on marriage and husband–wife relations, is the system in West Africa where 'the critical factor is *parenthood.*' There, marriage is 'valued primarily as the indispensable condition for the achievement of parenthood', rather than as an end in itself. This is because the 'achievement of parenthood is regarded as a *sine qua non* for the attainment of the full development as a complete person to which all aspire.' While, in the West, people 'have children incidentally to conjugal or other sexual relationships', and with the Welfare State 'there is no need for parents to have children with a view to augmenting family income or insuring against penury or loneliness or in old age', in West Africa 'the supreme purpose of marriage', Fortes tells us, is procreation. To attain any kind of political status, as well as personal wealth, one must have children.[11] Because of the 'enormous investment individually and collectively, emotionally and morally' in offspring in West Africa, it is, Fortes argues, 'inevitable that members of a filial generation will strive to achieve marriage and parenthood as early as they are permitted to.' In such a situation, 'no one is a complete person until he or she marries and achieves personhood', and 'there is a deeply ingrained ideal that normal men and women should continue to beget and bear children throughout their fecund years.' Thus a 'woman becomes a woman when she becomes able to bear children and continued childbearing is irrefutable evidence of continued femininity', just as masculinity is equated with virility and the fathering of children.[12]

This description of West Africa is indeed a long way from the world of Malthus and Darwin, for here a fulfilled life, marriage and childbearing are all deeply associated. The kind of oppositions and

---

[9] Caldwell, 'Fertility', 246–7.   [10] Fortes in Hawthorn, *Population*, 124.
[11] Ibid., 125, 127, 128, 132.   [12] Ibid., 137, 141.

choices which were taken as axiomatic in the Western discussions in the early nineteenth century and by family planners today, would and do strike people in these cultures as most extraordinary. We could summarize the contrast between the two polar extremes of these ideal types in a different way, as follows.[13]

In familistic societies, those that analysts often term 'tribal' and 'peasant' or having a 'domestic mode of production', the central feature is that production and consumption are inextricably bound to the unit of reproduction, or family; units of social and economic reproduction are identical. The farm and family are bound together as the place where both wealth and children are produced. As T. Shanin puts it, 'the family farm is the basic unit of peasant ownership, production, consumption and social life. The individual, the family and the farm, appear as an indivisible whole.'[14] Or as A. V. Chayanov summarized the position, 'The first fundamental characteristic of the farm economy of the peasant is that it is a family economy. Its whole organization is determined by the size and composition of the peasant family and by the coordination of its consumptive demands with the number of its working hands'.[15]

In many societies, historically, the basic or smallest unit of production and consumption is not the individual, but the members of a family, which may merely consist of parents and children, or a larger group. All those born into this minimal group have an equal share and rights in the resources; labour is pooled in the group; the 'estate' is passed on undiminished from generation to generation. In this situation each new child is an asset, giving of his or her labour and drawing off the communal resource. Each member contributes to the welfare of parents and wider kin (especially as the parents pass their prime), increasing the prestige and political power as well as the economic well-being of the group. The unit of production and the unit of reproduction coincide. To increase production, one increases reproduction; likewise, as Malthus would have argued, if productivity increases, so will reproductivity. Where the basic unit of production and consumption is the domestic group, whether co-residential or operationally united in work and consumption, there fertility will be highly valued – as in much of traditional China, India, Africa and Eastern Europe. Each small group will try to maximize its size.

[13] What follows is based on Macfarlane, 'Reproduction'.
[14] Shanin, *Peasants*, 241. [15] Wolf, *Peasants*, 14.

Economics, social structure, politics, ideology and demography have become intertwined; to control fertility is to alter part of a delicate structure which also threatens many other good things in life. Deeper than this, it is not even a matter of choice; one is not weighing advantages, for there is no contradiction between the different interests of parents and of kin, between psychological and economic needs.

The opposite situation is the one described by Davis, Goode and Caldwell as the 'Western', capitalist, nuclear family and individualist systems. Here the central feature is that the lowest unit of production and consumption is not the family but the individual. And the individual only expands his or her self in one way – through marriage, to one person. In such societies the husband–wife bond is stressed, there is no communal, family ownership of property or permanent joint consumption unit. Production is not based on the family but on non-familial links. The permanent basic unit is either the lone individual or the married pair. By focusing on the individual rather than the family, many demographic features are changed. Instead of a population expanding in quantity as Malthus has predicted, an increase of productivity is used in the first place to increase the quality of life for the individual, rather than the wider kin group. Hence a rise in productivity will not immediately be channelled into reproductivity: there may well be that delay, that deferral of gratification, which Malthus pleaded for.

In this individualistic variant, parents do not see production and reproduction as inextricably connected; sex and childbearing are separable activities. Women's main role is no longer as a productive and reproductive machine; extra children do not necessarily increase the prestige and well-being of a wider group, or even of their own parents. In fact, children, and certainly a large number of them, become a threat to the happiness of their parents, to their mother's health and to their father's peace and pocket. Many children are seen as a drain on the individual, who is not recompensed by labour invested in a common resource which will provide a store for the future. In such a situation, marriage and child bearing incur a cost, celibacy has its attractions and family limitation is likely to be encouraged. Marriage age is likely to be high, and people will pause and reflect both before marrying and later, on procreation.

Thus in a familial mode of production, fertility increases the well-being of the smallest units of society, even though it may be disadvantageous to the society as a whole. While there is no tension between social, economic and productive ends for the individual, there may be a new tension between the needs of the family and of the nation. Such a congruence between a family system and reproduction is nicely illustrated by two examples. A Spanish farmer told the poet Laurie Lee, 'Buy land and breed sons and you can't go wrong. Come war and thieves and ruined harvests – they don't signify at all . . . If a man's got strong blood like me, and scatters his seed wide enough, that man must flourish.'[16] Or as a Punjabi water carrier explained to the anthropologist M. Mamdani, mistaking him for the family planner who visited him years before,

> You were trying to convince me in 1960 that I shouldn't have any more sons. Now, you see, I have six sons and two daughters and I sit at home in leisure. They are grown up and they bring me money. One even works outside the village as a labourer. You told me I was a poor man and couldn't support a large family. Now you see, because of my large family, I am a rich man.[17]

Here, to invest in reproduction is to increase production and consumption, but it would not have been so if the children had refused to hand over a substantial part of their wages to a family fund. If they had kept their own money, set up separate homes, paid their taxes to the government who might have provided some security for the old, the situation would have been quite different. In that case, an individual would have had to choose between children and leisure goods, between a child and a mortgage, between a child and geographical and social mobility, perhaps between a child and a career. Acquisitive or possessive invidualism alters all the equations. It leads to a world where the assumptions of Malthus and Darwin make some kind of sense.

That world of expectation and family obligations predominated in the first half of the nineteenth century in England, and is now spreading by way of Europe and America over much of the world. This leads us to ask where it came from, how it originated. Ultimately we wish to know how it worked and what caused it. In order to understand this we first of all need to know how long it has operated as a system. If it had started in the eighteenth century, then certain explanations can be advanced; if earlier, then others. Since the

[16] Lee, *Rose*, 24.   [17] Mamdani, *Myth*, 109.

pattern of marriage is both at the heart of the problem and also clearly of so much contemporary importance, it is not surprising that there has been growing speculation as to its origins. As we shall see, there is a good deal of confusion about the historical facts, even in relation to England.

The current state of uncertainty in the matter, with almost radically opposed views on most of the central issues concerning timing, is well surveyed by Michael Anderson in his summary of the historiography of the present situation.[18] It is therefore unnecessary to go into detail here. A number of writers have argued that the curious family system which underlies our modern world and that of Malthus and Darwin is a recent phenomenon. Thus the anthropologist A. R. Radcliffe-Brown wrote that 'we must remember that the modern English idea of marriage is recent and decidedly unusual, the product of a particular social development.'[19] It was the product of the industrial and urban revolutions, and hence basically a phenomenon created in the eighteenth and nineteenth centuries.[20] Others see the changes starting in the sixteenth century, after the Protestant Reformation, but only reaching their modern, nuclear family form with 'love marriage', in the later seventeenth or eighteenth centuries.[21] Some discern a deeper continuity, stretching back into the later Middle Ages, for they can discover no major revolution in structure or sentiment in the sixteenth to eighteenth centuries.[22]

Interestingly, it is the demographic sociologists and historians who have seen the deepest roots and greatest continuity. Thus Kingsley Davis wrote that 'Western European society tended to set the nuclear family apart a long time ago – a fact which is borne out by Western legal history, kinship terminology and courtship customs ... a product of cultural peculiarities extending back at least into mediaeval times.'[23] Richard Smith, speaking of the Malthusian demographic system, writes that 'the regime was most likely in existence when

[18] Anderson, *Western Family*; for a further recent survey of approaches to the English family see Houlbrooke, *English Family*, ch.1. A particularly strong difference exists between my views and those of Stone, *Family*. My detailed criticisms of Stone's position are given in Macfarlane, 'Review'.

[19] Radcliffe-Brown, *African Kinship*, 43.

[20] Notestein, 'Population Change', 16; Lowie, *Social Organization*, 220.

[21] Stone, *Family*; Goode, *World Revolution*; Shorter, *Modern Family*.

[22] Mount, *Subversive Family*; Pollock, *Forgotten Children*; Houlbrooke, *English Family*.   [23] Davis, 'High Fertility', 35.

More wrote his *Utopia* as well as when Marx wrote *Das Kapital*.'[24] Caldwell argues that 'For reasons that lie deep in its history, the family was increasingly nucleated in Western Europe centuries ago; indeed some social groups may have crossed the divide reversing the intergenerational wealth flow as early as the seventeenth century', and elsewhere he takes it back even further. The individualistic family system, he argues, could occur even 'before the creation of the modern economy. This seems to be what happened in Western Europe. The feudal system, built on the inherited ruins of the urbanized civilizations of the ancient world, went far towards making a nuclear family economically viable.'[25] A few have even argued that the basic premises of the system go back to the thirteenth century or before. These include Goody, Fortes and myself.[26] The causes are disputed, but the roots are thought to be very early. As Fortes argues, the preoccupation with marriage and other features of the modern pattern is claimed by some to be 'based on the religious ideology and the sexual morality and procreative ideal of Christianity, but I myself believe that it goes back even further in the history of Europe, probably to the Germanic tribes described by Tacitus.'[27]

Our present situation can be summarized briefly. We can see that the emergence of the Malthusian regime is of fundamental importance both in explaining the social and economic history of Western Europe and particularly England, and in analysing current developments in much of the world. Yet we are still very unsure about how that system worked as a set of interlocked institutions, and of when it emerged. In order to deal with these questions we shall be faced with great problems of variation and of evidence. Just to list a few of the difficulties gives an idea of the very high level of generalization and abstraction in which we shall be engaging.

We will be examining the central nature of marriage over the period roughly from Chaucer to Malthus, that is, from the late fourteenth century to the early nineteenth, a period of more than four hundred years. This is slightly shorter than the five-hundred-year period which F. W. Maitland dealt with in one lecture on the forms of action at common law. Like Maitland, we can say that this is 'enormously long', but like him we can also argue that we 'do not

---

[24] Smith, 'Fertility', 615.   [25] Caldwell, 'Restatement', 356, 346.   [26] Macfarlane, *Individualism*; Goody, *Family and Marriage*; Fortes in Hawthorn, *Population*.
[27] Hawthorn, *Population*, 124.

know that for our present purpose it could be well broken into sub-periods.'[28] Obviously, as we shall see, there were major changes over the period, and only a few of these can be highlighted. The difficulties of dealing with such a long span are compounded by the changing nature of the evidence. Many new sources become available, particularly from the middle of the sixteenth century onwards, so that questions we are unable to answer for the later Middle Ages suddenly become partly answerable. One of the aims of the following analysis is to see how far the world of Malthus was a creation of his time, and how far it was already in essence present a century or more before the Reformation. In attempting to do so there will be a tendency, in describing a timeless model, to stress continuity. Obviously the physical, social, political, religious and economic world changed in numerous ways over this period, yet only by taking a long period can these questions be illuminated.

A second problem concerns differences in attitudes and structures between the various levels in society. Over the whole of this period England was a highly stratified society with vast differences of wealth and life style between the levels. Observations about one level cannot be extrapolated to others. In particular, anyone who has considered the evidence will be aware that the demography and familial structure of a small elite were in many respects different from those of the majority of the population, as T. H. Hollingsworth and Lawrence Stone have shown.[29] In essence, it would seem that as very large fortunes became involved, some of the characteristics of the domestic mode of production and reproduction emerged: marriages were more like alliances, arranged between kin groups, male dominance asserted itself, heirs were more important. This wealthy group has already received extensive attention, and the fact that many of the more obvious records were generated at the top makes its particular features especially prominent. In order to redress the balance, and because from the demographic and social point of view the rest of the population and its behaviour are equally important, we will concentrate here on the rest of the social strata. This encompasses basically the four groups which Malthus outlined, that is, from the minor gentry downwards.

The relative size of the two segments of the population in the seventeenth century can be seen from Gregory King's scheme of the

[28] Maitland, *Forms of Action*, 43.
[29] Hollingsworth in Glass, *Population*; Stone, *Family*.

English population in 1688.[30] King gives the whole population as roughly 5.5 million. Of these, some 19,720 or about 0.36 per cent were among the temporal and spiritual lords and baronets. If we add for good measure knights and a thousand of the 'Persons in greater Offices and Places', as well as the top lawyers and clergy and many of the wealthier gentry, we are still only dealing with less than 1 per cent of the population. Our concern in the following pages will be mainly with the other 99 per cent below that rank. In trying to present a clear picture of the heterogeneous groups below the aristocracy we will necessarily iron out differences between the poor, the middling and the rich, between professions and occupations. Like the ironing out of the subtler changes over time, this is the price one pays for attempting a general synthesis. Differences in education will likewise be minimized.

A third homogenization is a geographical and social one. Although it would seem that England by the start of this period had a remarkably uniform culture, there still remained important regional differences, particularly between the highland north and west with its pastoral economy and the lowland south and east with its arable agriculture. Although we have selected for intensive study and example communities located in each of these areas, this does not overcome the problems of variation. Furthermore, there are the differences between urban and rural populations. Can the inhabitants of London, Bristol or Norwich be lumped in with those of small villages in Essex or Westmorland? We have had to do so, and the extremely high urban–rural mobility which ironed out many of the strong oppositions found in many countries between country dwellers (*paysans*) and town dwellers (*bourgeois*) may partially justify this. Yet there is the same danger of compression into a single stereotype. Likewise, there were clearly very considerable differences between religious sub-groups – Quakers, Catholics, Anglicans – and between political groups – Cavaliers and Puritans, or Whigs and Tories. None of these are dealt with in any depth.

A further problem concerns the degree to which England was merely a part of a much wider 'West European' pattern, or somehow peculiar. Throughout the following chapters I will be concentrating on the English evidence. This reflects my own interests and a belief that, as with the language, legal system and political structure, there was something distinctive about England within Europe. Yet, just as

[30] Laslett, *Lost World*, 36–8.

the language is one example of a wider European, or even Indo-European, language family, so it is reasonable to believe that many of the family features we are examining are not unique. While concentrating on England, I do not necessarily imply that the peculiarities noted inevitably separated it off from Europe, and particularly from north-western Europe. As an anthropological historian, the comparisons I am making are usually not with other parts of Western Europe, but with non-European, peasant or tribal societies. Thus the book is primarily about England, but also has implications for the contrasts both within Western Europe and between it (including offshoots in America, Australia and elsewhere) and other non-European civilizations. The characteristics of English society, particularly the unspoken assumptions and rules, become easier to consider when we set them within this broader comparative framework.

A final over-simplification of a very important kind should be noted. Much of the discussion will be concerned with those areas of reproduction and sexuality which affect women even more than men. There are clearly ways in which men and women feel and behave differently. Yet nearly all of our sources of a personal kind were written by men, and the author of this work is a man. It should thus be noted that there will be a male bias in the discussion from both these causes, which not even the reading of Aphra Behn, Jane Austen and Dorothy Osborne, or the advice of female friends, can rectify.

If one had taken each geographical area separately, multiplied this by social class, added in the time dimension broken into reasonable slices of about a hundred years, and looked at this from both male and female points of view – in other words, applied the sort of microscope that enables an anthropologist to study one community of a few thousand people for one year of its history – this book would have turned into thousands. As it is, what I have attempted to do is distil from a variety of sources some of the quintessential structures and sentiments. Readers interested in particular periods, places or persons can judge for themselves how far the general description fits what they know.

PART II

THE VALUE OF CHILDREN

4

The Benefits and Costs of Children

We have seen that the central characteristic of marriage in most societies has been that it is entered into in order to have children. Children are seen as wealth and as an expansion of individual and family power and position. That this was not so in Malthus' scheme is clear. In order to understand the roots of his views we may start by turning back two centuries in England. If we situate ourselves in the sixteenth or seventeenth century and in the large middling rank of yeomen and tradesmen, how would the question of procreation have struck us? The first outstanding assumption is that people believed, once married, that children were inevitable. There is little evidence of either desire for, or knowledge of, contraceptive practices. Such as they were, contraceptives were mainly for use in illicit relationships. It was assumed that children were the normal fruit of a marriage. Thus it was also assumed, with Malthus, that the passion between the sexes was constant and that such constant biological drives would lead to pregnancies and childbirth.

Children born in wedlock were welcome. Children were a psychological gratification to their parents, fulfilling their needs in various ways: the biological craving of women to reproduce, the desire of all humans to see mirrors of themselves, the desire for companions, the desire for objects to love and care for. As the midwife Mrs Sharp put it, 'to conceive with child is the earnest desire if not of all yet of most women.' Culpeper wrote, 'all Men and Women desire Children.'[1] This desire is shown clearly enough in the reactions to the birth of children in contemporary diaries.[2] To take one example,

[1] Sharp, *Midwives*, 93; Culpeper, *Midwives*, 68.
[2] Blencowe, 'Burrell', 131; Rye, *Isham Journal*, 41; Jackson, *Thornton Autobiography*, 98; Winchester, *Tudor Portrait*, 105.

Ralph Josselin, a seventeenth-century clergyman, described how he himself was born 'to the great joy of father and mother being much desired as being their third child and as it pleased God their only son'. He was delighted to find that his wife was pregnant, blessing the name of the Lord when 'some hopes of my wives breeding' proved to be true 'to our great joy and comfort.' He described as his daughter and son were on the point of dying how he would surrender them to God, for 'thou art better to me than sons and daughters, though I value them above gold and jewels.'[3] That people for various reasons were eager to have children is clear from the fictional *Ten Pleasures of Marriage* attributed to Aphra Behn. The newly married wife who fails to conceive 'begins to mump and maunder at her husband; vaunting much of her own fitness and not a little suspecting her husbands; and oftentimes calling him a Fumbler, a dry-boots, and a good man Do-little etc.' When finally the child is conceived and born, 'who can imagine or comprehend the jollity of this new Father'.[4]

The joy at the birth of children was clearly related to a widespread and deep affection felt towards them. This has recently been amply documented from English diaries over the sixteenth to nineteenth centuries, and so we need not labour the point.[5] Joy at birth led to delight in their youth, with affection and deep concern.[6] Contemporaries took this deep feeling for granted. If the mother finds it too painful to breast-feed the child, 'it goes to the very heart of both father and mother to put the child out to nurse.' The dangers were those of favouritism and too much affection leading to children being over-indulged. Culpeper warned that many people spoiled their children 'because they cocker [pamper, fondle, indulge] them in their youth.' They indulge them because of the natural propensity to feel tenderly towards them.[7] As John Locke wrote, parents looked after their children because God had 'placed in them suitable inclinations of tenderness and concern', he had 'woven into the principles of human nature such a tenderness for their offspring that there is little fear that parents should use their power with too much rigour; the excess is seldom on the severe side, the strong bias of nature drawing

---

[3] Macfarlane, *Josselin Diary*, 1616; July 1641; 26 May 1650.

[4] Behn, *Pleasures*, 51, 84.   [5] Pollock, *Forgotten Children*.

[6] For example Greven, *Protestant Temperament*, 156, 183, 266ff; cf. also Illick in De Mause, *Childhood*, 312–13.

[7] Behn, *Pleasures*, 93; Bacon, *Essayes*, 20; Fuller, *Holy State*, 11; Culpeper, *Midwives*, 215.

the other way.'[8] There arc no grounds for thinking that there was any basic shift in this deep affection for children during our period. Documenting this feeling from start to end of the seventeenth century, Keith Wrightson concludes that 'there seems no reason to believe that parental attitudes towards or aspirations for their children underwent any fundamental change in the course of the seventeenth century.'[9] It is now clear that the period could be extended: throughout the four centuries we are considering, we find that a basic premise is a deep affection and love for young children, though this could also be combined with intolerance and severity at times.[10]

It would appear that both sons and daughters were welcomed, with only a slight preference for sons. The absence of a very strong male bias is noteworthy. Anthropologists have pointed out that a very strong preference for sons is a characteristic of many settled peasant societies; they are the ones who will stay and look after the parents – daughters require dowries and go elsewhere. 'The villagers say that daughters make a man poor'; the care of a daughter is 'watering a neighbour's tree'; girls are valueless and boys everything.[11] The contrast between such male preferences in densely populated, settled agricultural societies in Eurasia and a lack of sex preferences in sub-Saharan Africa has been explored by Jack Goody.[12] We might have expected such a marked preference in England in these centuries.

There are indeed indications of some preference for sons. Particularly for those with large estates, it was preferable to have a male heir: daughters, the Duchess of Newcastle wrote, 'are but branches which by marriage are broken off from the root from whence they sprang, and ingrafted into the stock of the other family, so that daughters are to be accounted but as movable goods or furnitures that wear out.' Clarissa Harlowe's brother hated the thought of giving dowries away: 'Daughters are chickens, bought up for the table of other men,' he was fond of saying. Hence, when a daughter was born to the Lisle family in the early sixteenth century, a commiserating letter was written which mixed congratulations with the hope that 'by God's grace at the next shot she shall hit the

[8] Locke, *Government*, 32, 34.   [9] Wrightson, *English Society*, 118.
[10] Pollock, *Forgotten Children, passim.*
[11] Bailey, *Caste*, 71; Dube, *Indian*, 148; Stirling, *Turkish*, 116.
[12] Goody, 'Strategies of Heirship' in Goody, *Production*.

mark.'[13] But even at this level of society there was a desire to mix the genders. Thus Lucy Hutchinson recalled how 'after my mother had had three sons she was very desirous of a daughter.' Sir Ralph Verney, we are told, 'was devoted to girls: his love for his own little daughter had been so great he had often thought right to "dissemble" lest his boys should regard her as his favourite, he ceased not to mourn her loss.'[14]

For the majority of the population there is very little evidence of a strong preference for sons. Though there may, as today, have been a slight bias, it is likely that Aphra Behn caught the general spirit of the times when she made those attending the 'gossips' feast wish that a couple should the following year 'have a daughter to your son, or a son to your daughter'.[15] Although people were clearly interested in the sex of the next child – and hence astrologers were visited by clients who wanted to find this out, and popular almanacs contained methods for determining sex – there are few indications that in the middling ranks the absence of sons was the disaster it is held to be in many Third World countries today.[16] Even when compared to other parts of Europe in the past, it may be that our current lack of concern to have male children is a very ancient feature.[17]

Children were welcomed and loved for a number of reasons, including the pleasure they gave to their parents. One of the aspects of this pleasure was the delight in children as entertainment, and as objects for affection and discipline. As Culpeper wrote, one of the three main 'reasons' why all desired children was that they were 'pretty things to play withall, every like desiring to play with his like'. Among the reasons given for marriage in a letter written to provide a model for letter-writers was 'the joy of procreation', one of the two explanations for this 'joy' being the fact that 'infancy cackling with a pleasant lisping sound, shall become an incredible delight to the parents hearing.' As Lady Mary Wortley Montagu, in the early eighteenth century, explained to her daughter, she could not take much credit for her love towards her child in infancy, for 'there was so great a mixture of instinct' that love was natural. But afterwards

[13] Cavendish, *Letters*, 184; quoted in Watt, *Rise of Novel*, 253; St Clare Byrne, *Lisle*, 201.

[14] Hutchinson, *Memoirs*, i, 24; Verney, *Memoirs*, iii, 60.

[15] Behn, *Pleasures*, 114.

[16] Thomas, *Religion*, 317; e.g. *The Husbandman's Practice*, 170.

[17] Marwick in De Mause, *Childhood*, 283; Origo, *Merchant*, 45(Italy); Huarte, *Men's Wits*, 286(Spain); Campbell, *Patronage*, 56(Greece).

she felt that she had shown real love when compared with 'other mothers, who generally look on their children as devoted to their pleasures, and bound by duty to have no sentiments but what they please to give them; playthings at first, and afterwards the objects on which they may exercise their spleen, tyranny, or ill humour'.[18] She regarded her daughter as her 'real friend', a 'companionship value' of children which some demographers regard as one of the hallmarks of a modern demographic regime.[19]

The likening of children to other playthings is evident in many ways. Pictures often grouped children with pets, and ballads extolled the pleasures they gave.[20] After listing the other advantages of marriage, a poet described the advantage of having a child:[21]

> With such a pretty child as this:
>   joy there to me doth rise,
> Had I no wife all this I misse,
>   then 'tis not otherwise.
> The babe doth grow, and quickly speaks,
>   this doth increase my joy,
> To hear it tattle, laugh and squeake,
>   I smile and hug the boy:
> I with it play with great delight
>   and hush it it when it cries . . .

Children, supposedly like parrots, 'soon learn foreign languages'.[22] The essence of the attitude revealed in this poem lay in three things: children gave pleasure by their smallness, their dependence and their ability to learn – like domestic pets. They were ultimately non-utilitarian goods – again like pets. They were around the house – not ultimately kept for their economic or other usefulness but for the emotional and aesthetic pleasure they gave. Finally, like pets, they would leave their 'owners': pets died, children left home and withdrew emotionally. It all happened very quickly: 'a child's a plaything for an hour', for 'the Truth is, they are really no more ours than the curls of our hair, or parings of our nails.'[23]

---

[18] Culpeper, *Midwives*, 68; Day, *Secretorie*, 140; Wharncliffe, *Letters of Montagu*, ii, 414.

[19] Tabah, 'Population', 362.

[20] King-Hall, *Nursery*, illustrations between pp. 32 and 33.

[21] Rollins, *Pepysian Garland*, 359–60.   [22] Moryson, *Itinerary*, iii, 352.

[23] Mary Lamb in Cohen, *Penguin Dictionary*, 229; Osborne, *Advice*, 71.

This attitude, which nowadays makes it possible for economists to treat children as 'consumer durables' offering security, amusement and other functions on a par with a house or car, is decidedly odd.[24] It does not mean that children were not desired or deeply loved. But it was a love for something that was essentially a luxury, and a transitory one at that. They might be 'jewels', but man can ultimately live without jewels. It is an attitude which does directly parallel the need for pets, except that this pet has the fascination of being biologically linked to its owner and capable of speaking the same language.[25] A revulsion at this hedonistic and, it would seem, self-centred attitude was shown by Montaigne when he argued that the 'natural propensity', the second deepest instinct after survival, that is, 'the affection which the begetter has for his offspring', combined with reason, should mean that as we come to know children more and more our love should grow. But 'very often it is the other way, and we are generally more excited by the kickings, the silly, playful childish movements of our infants, than we are later by their grown-up actions; just as if we loved them for our pastime, as if they were apes and not human beings.'[26] This delicate delight in infants and small children is early shown in the thirteenth-century dictionary *De Proprietatibus*.[27]

Children were thus welcome as 'pretty things to play withall' and as mirrors of their parents. They were also welcome as a way of partially overcoming mortality. As Darwin reflected, what was the point of working and working 'like a neuter bee' and leaving 'nothing after all'? Or as Bacon noted, children may 'increase the cares of life, but they mitigate the remembrance of death.'[28] Thus we find in books of advice and morality the assumption that people wanted their 'name' and line to continue. Children were 'living monuments and lively representations' of their parents; one of the aims of marriage was 'by children and succession, to have his family and name extended'; having children was 'the hope of posterity', and there were those who cried, 'Give me Children, or else my Name dies.' We find diarists showing a concern that their 'seed' should continue.[29] Again Josselin is a good illustration. 'Lord mar not my inheritance,' he wrote when

---

[24] E.g. Leibenstein, 'Interpretation'.

[25] For pets, see Thomas, *Natural World*, pt iii.   [26] *The Essays of Montaigne*, i, 374–5.   [27] Anglicus, *Properties*, 298–303.   [28] Bacon, *Essayes*, 20.

[29] Gouge, *Domesticall*, 210; Becon, *Workes*, dcxlix; Whateley, *Bride-Bush*, 17; Osborne, *Advice*, 70.

death threatened his children, and he prayed, 'oh be my God and of my spouse, and our seeds after us.' He clearly saw his family as a tree or vine, with his wife and him as the trunk and his 'Children like plants and branches'.[30]

Yet though the desire to leave heirs is present, it seems less pronounced than in the accounts we earlier saw of African and Indian societies. Many treatises and diaries either omit any mention of the desire for heirs, or touch lightly on it. The lack of emphasis appears when we compare the situation with that in the many societies where the line must be perpetuated for economic, social and ritual reasons. In such cases, heirs are adopted if they are not produced naturally. The middling and lower ranks of society in England give little evidence over the centuries of an overwhelming desire or need to perpetuate the family line.[31]

The only other reason that Culpeper could suggest, why 'all men and women desire children', was for religious motives. They are blessings from God, and so godly persons desired them. That children were blessings was a widespread conviction, and that people should be anxious to have them for that reason was a view put forward by those advocating population increase.[32] Sir William Petty stated that it was 'the first command of God to increase and multiply'.[33] Procreation, according to the marriage service, was the first reason why marriage was instituted. Yet, if we examine the religious motive to have children we find that it is singularly weak. As Culpeper admitted, for every person who was moved by religion, there were a hundred swayed by lust or psychological motives.[34] There is very little evidence that propagation was seen by many people as a way of pleasing God. Later, having numerous children was seen as a Popish vice; the clergy, it was said, 'begin to look plump, and get children without mercy: as if they had nothing else to follow but the Catholic cause of generation.'[35] But it would be over-simplifying to put this disinterest down to Protestantism, for it went much deeper.

The religions of India and China, Malthus had suggested, with

---

[30] Macfarlane, *Josselin Diary*, 20 July 1673, 1 September 1644; Macfarlane, *Ralph Josselin*, 83.

[31] See on adoption and heirship in Goody, *Production*.

[32] Coverdale, *Matrimony*, 72; Perkins, *Oeconomie*, 115.

[33] Landsdowne, *Petty Papers*, ii, 49; cf. also Becon, *Workes*, ccccclxxxiii.

[34] Culpeper, *Midwives*, 68.   [35] Aylmer, *Diary of Lawrence*, 47.

their insistence that a man leave sons to venerate him at his funeral and to ensure this well-being in the after-life, produced strong pressures to high fertility. The linking of procreative success and spiritual success in Hindu and Confucian religions has long been obvious.[36] Likewise, Muslims emphasize the need for sons, and in the ancestor cults of tribal religions we often find similar stress.[37] Among the Semites, Edward Westermarck tells us, 'he who abstains from marrying is guilty of bloodshed, diminishes the image of God, and causes the divine presence to withdraw from Israel.'[38] Christianity, for whatever reasons, like Buddhism, has never directly linked ritual status with fertility.[39] Though Roman Catholicism sometimes stresses the need for uncontrolled fertility, Christianity is on the whole neutral as to child bearing. A man's salvation in the afterworld and his relations to God are not affected either way by his procreative ability. Celibacy is the highest calling and marriage a poor second. Children are the product of sinful lust, one of the 'curses' on Adam and Eve; our Saviour himself led a life of bachelordom and most of the great saints were celibates. Childbearing is consequently played down.

The extreme form of this absence of stress on fertility is in ascetic Protestantism, but it is only the extreme. Malthus, as a clergyman, rejoiced in the fact that his religion fitted so well with the marriage system he was advocating. 'In the religion of Mahomet ... the procreation of children to glorify the Creator was laid down as one of the principal duties of man; and he who had the most numerous offspring was considered as having best answered the end of his creation.' On the other hand, 'it is a pleasing confirmation of the truth and divinity of the Christian religion ... that it places our duties respecting marriage and the procreation of children in a different light.'[40] Certainly, the historical evidence supports Malthus' assessment in England. There is very little evidence, either before or after the Reformation, that people linked religion with procreation. Children were 'blessings', but there is a singular lack of insistence on the need for children for religious or ritual purposes. God could be glorified in many ways: a numerous progeny was not one of the most important.

[36] Goode, *World Revolution*, 208; Goode, *Family*, 112; Westermarck, *Marriage*, i, 379.

[37] E.g. Freeman in Goody, *Developmental Cycle*, 29; Marshall *Natality*, 128.

[38] Westermarck, *Marriage*, i, 377.   [39] Ekvall in Spooner, *Population*, 280.

[40] Malthus, *Population*, ii, 165.

One advantage of having a large family, and particularly sons, is political. In situations where public order is fragile, then the more weapon-bearing kin a man has, the better. This is the case in tribal societies where each child expands the lineage, and in many peasantries where close kin are the only ones you can trust to guard the family land and the family honour against rapacious landlords and fellow villagers. Those who breed most successfully increase their advantages. We are told, for instance, that in parts of Africa 'to become powerful it is important, almost indispensable, to have many children.'[41]

Against this background there is in England a conspicuous absence of political motive. I do not recall any statements to the effect that children were needed as protection, as a potential army. This corroborates what we know from other sources, that over this period England was, on the whole, an orderly and highly governed society. The policing functions that the family usually performs had long ago been taken over by the state through a complex system of government and justice, and little room was left for vendetta, mafia, patronage and 'amoral familism'.[42] Hence, as we have seen, children could be regarded as pets; as pretty and enjoyable, but not ultimately as guard dogs. Sons, we have seen, do not seem to have been particularly desired for their fighting prowess, or daughters for the alliances they would bring. Political life was structured on other principles than the family, and hence political influence either at village or national level was not related to the number of children one had. This is so much a part of our present experience that it is difficult to realize the cultural achievement that had led to a world where it was not politically necessary or even desirable to have the maximum number of children. There is no real sign of any major shift in this motivation over the period we are considering.

Another notable silence concerns the advantage of children as a way of increasing prestige and social esteem. In many societies each extra child adds to its parents' social prestige: infertility is a terrible curse, and a large and growing family a blessing. The virility of the man is shown through his many children and he gains esteem through each successive birth.[43] But in England it is difficult to find evidence,

---

[41] Forde, *African Worlds*, 177. [42] See Macfarlane, *Justice*, final chapter.
[43] E.g. Fortes in Hawthorn, *Population*, 141; Osborn, *Population*, 100.

for example, of people commenting admiringly on prolific fathers.[44] Indeed, as we shall see, people began to be worried and anxious after a number of children had been born.

Children are often even more important for women than for men. It is not the wedding ceremony itself, but the bearing of children, that cements a marriage and alters a woman's status to that of adulthood.[45] It is the fertility of the womb that a lineage has paid for with the brideprice, and thus women are reproductive assets whose value, and hence esteem, increase with each child.[46] Women are ascribed status according to the number of children they have borne: the more, the higher.[47] In Turkey, we are told, wife and children are linguistically inseparable and it is absolutely essential for a woman to have a son – an attitude with a long history.[48] In the early eighteenth century Lady Wortley Montagu wrote home from Turkey that 'without any exaggeration, all the women of my acquaintance have twelve or thirteen children: and the old ones boast of having had five-and-twenty or thirty apiece, and are respected according to the number they have produced.'[49] For a woman, her children are her main support; they are her allies in the new family she finds herself in, and through the years, particularly in widowhood, they will be her main comfort. Each birth is further insurance. Each child brings praise from husband and kin and a growing respect in the eyes of other women.

In so far as it is possible to judge these matters from literary and autobiographical evidence, there is only a minimal reflection of such pressures in England through the centuries. Although Jorden in the seventeenth century might write that 'being the mother of children is the highest honour, and most exalted state of satisfaction, that the fair sex can attain to in married life', and we have seen that newly married couples wished to emulate their friends and have children, it is difficult to detect much emphasis linking female status to high reproductivity.[50] Portraits do not concentrate on pregnant figures, poetry does not extol the fecund womb or mother of many children, even the cult of the Mother of God (who was, of course, a *virgin*

---

[44] Stubbes, *Anatomie*, fol.54v., refers to admiration for those who beget bastards, but this alludes to virility rather than legitimate childbearing.

[45] Evans-Pritchard, *Nuer Kinship*, 67, 72; Salisbury, *Stone*, 37.

[46] Lorimer, *Human Fertility*, 370.   [47] Mitchell, 'Fertility', 298.

[48] Stirling, *Turkish*, 154, 114.

[49] Wharncliffe, *Letters of Montagu*, ii, 41.

[50] *A Rational Account*, 55; Behn, *Pleasures*, 50ff.

mother) was very weakly developed in England. Motherhood was no doubt often a source of satisfaction, and people delighted when the first few children came. But it was not the central, only, and defining role of women. They were certainly not, as reported for a part of France, '*une machine à enfantement*'.[51] That necessary prerequisite for modern contraception – the basing of women's adult status on something other than childbearing – seems long ago to have been established.[52] Women's satisfactions and securities came from many sources, of which children were only one.

Thus children were desired – in moderation – as an added pleasure of life. That they were not essential is shown in the attitude towards barrenness or infertility. Where children are the major aim of marriage, a failure to produce any, or enough of the right sex, is a disaster. Only the birth of children cements the marriage and hence marriages automatically dissolve if they are childless. There is 'an abhorrence of childlessness', one cannot risk having no children. Childlessness is for many women 'the greatest personal tragedy and humiliation'.[53] Such an attitude Lady Montagu found to her amazement in Turkey. She wrote home, 'you won't know what to make of this speech; but, in this country, it is more despicable to be married and not fruitful, than it is with us to be fruitful before marriage.'[54] In reverse, the Turkish ladies would have found Pepys' attitude – a growing gladness that his wife was childless – very difficult to comprehend.[55] Nor could they have understood how Oliver Heywood could knowingly have married a wife of whom 'many said, and we feared that she would never be able to bear children, because of the littleness and weakness of her body.'[56] Clearly people in England, as today, were often upset by barrenness, and doctors, astrologers and leechbooks were consulted as to how to overcome such a defect.[57] But barrenness was not considered as a ground for divorce, there is little evidence of abuse or anger at childless women, and the inability to produce children seems to have been regarded as a misfortune rather than the terrible tragedy and humiliation we find it to be in many societies.[58] In a discussion of barrenness in 1682 an

[51] Shorter, *Modern Family*, 77.　[52] Goode, *Family*, 111.
[53] Mead, *Cultural Patterns*, 104; Campbell, *Patronage*, 58; Caldwell, 'Fertility', 203; Lorimer, *Human Fertility*, 265.　[54] Wharncliffe, *Letters of Montagu*, ii, 54.
[55] Latham, *Pepys*, i, xxxv.　[56] Turner, *Heywood*, i, 63.
[57] Culpeper, *Midwives*, 91; *Culpeper's Herbal*, 16.
[58] Arensberg, *Irish Countryman*, 90; Schapera, *Married Life*, 106; Mead, *New Guinea*, 240.

author explained Rachel's overwhelming longing for a child, and then commented, 'but you shall find but few women of this mind now a days.'[59] The failure to produce male heirs did not lead to the widespread adoption of heirs, a device used in India and China to overcome gaps in certain families.[60]

In England the absence of contraception, either preventive or *post hoc* in the form of instituted infanticide and abortion, suggests that most people found that the 'blessings from God' came in about the right numbers – or at least not intolerably many. Today it has been estimated for the West that, given our present age at marriage, natural birth intervals and the likelihood of infant and child mortality, a couple who do not practise contraception would be likely to produce up to 12 children who would be alive to succeed their parents.[61] The desired number is between two and three. Contraception is clearly essential to bridge the huge gap. If we take into account the same parameters for the seventeenth century, the late age at marriage and moderately high mortality would have meant that many parents would have had only four or five children, of whom only two or three would be alive at their death.

When for various reasons people began to have well above these numbers, it is clear that instead of welcoming each extra child many became apprehensive. When in 1667 (after her eighth child) Alice Thornton found herself pregnant again, she wrote, 'if it had been good in the eyes of my God, I should much rather ... not to have been in this condition.'[62] Frances Clarke wrote to her father Sir John Oglander in 1651 that she had just borne her tenth child, 'and I pray God, if it be His blessed will, it may be my last'; and William Blundell wrote to one of his children that his wife had been well delivered of her tenth child, commenting, 'you may well think this is not the way to grow rich.'[63] The wife of the Lord Chancellor, wondering whether to remarry if her husband died, thought 'she would willingly do it' on the condition 'that she might have no more children.' When Thomas Wright's first wife died, having given birth seven times, 'some people advised me to marry an old woman that would have no more children.'[64] Contemporaries were aware that some people 'feareth he

---

[59] From *The British Midwife Enlarged* (1682). I owe this reference to Dr Audrey Eccles.

[60] Goody, *Production*, ch.6.　　[61] Tabarah, 'Demographic Development'.

[62] Quoted in Notestein, *English Folk*, 198.　　[63] Ashley, *Stuarts*, 17–18.

[64] Notestein, *Four Worthies*, 95; Wright, *Autobiography*, 144.

shall have too many children', and even when they were most required, in the heirship to the great properties of the nobility, there seems to have been caution.[65] Thus Henry Percy in his *Advice to His Son* wrote that to possess many children was 'an unhappiness, and that he is happy by misfortune that hath none at all, and less happy by consequent that hath but a few ... the plentiful blessing of children leads on with it an increasing charge.'[66]

The increasing cost took two main forms: the economic cost to the parents, and particularly the father, and the physical cost to the mother, whose body and health were stretched every two years or so in producing another child. Each time, death was close and pain extreme. The Duchess of Newcastle saw no reason why a woman should desire children in their own right, for 'she hazards her life by bringing them into the world and hath the greatest share of trouble in bringing them up.'[67] It is not surprising that some women uttered protests. An underground theme through the centuries is the suffering of women, from a medieval writer who argued, 'if only God had given some share to man; if only God had given him the child-bearing', through to the nineteenth century Oxfordshire villager who held that 'the wife ought to have the first child and the husband the second, then there wouldn't ever be any more.'[68] As Jane Sharp noted in the later seventeenth century, 'some there are who hold conception to be a curse, because *God* laid it upon *Eve* for taking of the forbidden fruit, *I will greatly multiply thy conception*.'[69]

That children were to be welcomed as God's gift was a constant theme of contemporary preachers and moralists: 'Your children (most assuredly) is the very blessing of god, for the which you ought to give him most hearty thanks, and be contented, and with such as he doth send you, be they many or few, sons or daughters. For if they be many, he will provide for them if they be faithfull.'[70] The doubts of increasing cost, however, were not so easily to be quelled. As we have already partly seen, in many societies the idea of the cost of children does not arise: children are wealth and each child is a profitable investment. There is no contradiction between biology and economics. There is now a considerable demographic and anthropological literature to show that in many parts of the world people believe that

---

[65] Coverdale, *Matrimony*, fol.26v.   [66] Percy, *Advice*, 55–6.
[67] Cavendish, *Letters*, i, 184.
[68] Power, 'Women', 409; Thompson, *Lark Rise*, 128.   [69] Sharp, *Midwives*, 93.
[70] Furnivall, *Tell-Trothes*, 187.

having children adds to one's wealth. This belief is correct. In parts of India, 'the optimal course of action is for them to have large numbers of children.'[71] Likewise in Bangladesh, 'high fertility and large numbers of surviving children are economically "rational" propositions.'[72] In Taiwan there were traditionally powerful economic incentives to have as many sons as possible.[73] Thus both males and females often replied in interviews that 'they see their reproduction as potentially increasing their economic position.'[74]

We do not have to travel as far as Asia or Africa for such a view. In comparing England and Ireland in the later eighteenth century, Arthur Young noted that in the latter, their children were not 'burthensome'. 'In all the enquiries I made into the state of the poor, I found their happiness and ease generally relative to the number of their children, and nothing considered such a misfortune as having none.'[75] This was the case among the very poor as well as the more affluent. Hence, as Mamdani argues, in certain parts of India 'people are not poor because they have large families ... they have large families because they are poor.'[76] Although high fertility is not necessarily beneficial to parents in all agricultural societies, often the poor 'find themselves in a vicious circle of low income and low education, where large numbers of children represent the only hope of making a break-through.'[77] A change from this situation where people cannot afford not to have children, to one where they cannot afford to have many of them, is one of the most significant underpinnings of the Malthusian revolution. The motivation for childbearing, we are told, 'was largely economic in the past, as it remains in the developing countries', but in the West it 'is today esentially affective.'[78] Westermarck observed that 'the desire for offspring has become less intense in western societies. A large family instead of being a help in the struggle for existence, is often considered an insufferable burden.'[79] When did this change occur in England?

At the level of perception and attitude, there are signs back at the

[71] Monica das Gupta in Epstein, *Fertility*, 115; see also Beals, *Gopalpur*, 13; Marshall, *Natality*, 185.

[72] Cain, 'Children', 224.

[73] Arthur Wolf in Zubrow, *Demographic Anthropology*, 229.

[74] James Ryder in Kaplan, *Fertility*, 98.   [75] Hutton, *Young's Tour*, ii, 120.

[76] Mamdani, *Myth*, 14; e.g. Cain, 'Extended Kin', 5.

[77] George Mkangi in Epstein, *Fertility*, 176.   [78] Tabah, 'Population', 362.

[79] Westermarck, *Marriage*, iii, 105.

beginning of the sixteenth century that children were widely regarded as a 'cost', that is, that there was a net loss on them. Hence there was a contradiction between emotion, biology and inclination on the one hand, and prudence, economy and social status on the other. This is clearly the case in the later nineteenth century, at both village and middle-class levels. Flora Thompson records of Oxfordshire villages that there were diverse opinions about the cost of children. As a child of twelve remarked, 'What's the use of having a lot of brats you can't afford to feed?' and a woman said that she 'didn't never hold wi' havin' a lot o' poor brats and nothin' to put into their bellies. Took us all our time to bring up our two'; she could not have made her meagre savings if she had had a 'great tribe o' children.'[80] Here the absence of children was a cause of prosperity.[81]

These Malthusian views were behind the rapid adoption of birth control in the middle classes in the later nineteenth century.[82] Even the pro-natalist Cobbett implicitly recognized the conflict: 'How is it when the sixty-fourth year has come? And how should I have been without this wife and these children? I might have amassed a tolerable heap of money; but what would that have done for me?'[83] These views go back through Darwin and Malthus to a much earlier period.

Eighteenth-century observers were aware of the conflict between children and wealth. As Lord Kames remarked, 'idleness begets profligacy, and the profligate avoid loading themselves with wives and children.'[84] In England avarice and children were in opposition. Moralists expostulated that 'when a Man does not marry for fear of the charge of children, it is pity his father had ever any', and pointed out that 'the greatest enemy to marriage is the covetous man: he loves to get everything but children.'[85] To counter this, it was argued that it was a service to the country to have children. Thus Goldsmith 'was ever of the opinion that the honest man who married and brought up a large family, did more service than he who continued single, and only talked of population', but not all could afford them.[86] As Corbyn Morris put it in 1751, writing of London, 'the unmarried Ladies and Gentlemen in this City, of moderate Fortunes, which are the great Bulk, are unable to support the Expence of a Family with any Magnificence ... they, therefore, acquiesce in Celibacy; Each Sex

[80] Thompson, *Lark Rise*, 324, 70.   [81] Davies, *English Village*, 286.
[82] See Banks and Banks, *Family Planning*.
[83] Cobbett, *Advice*, 204.   [84] Kames, *Sketches*, iii, 54.
[85] *Characters*, 193; ibid., 196.   [86] Vicar of Wakefield in Cohen, *Penguin Dictionary*.

compensating itself, as it can, by other Diversions.' 'As marriage produces children, so children produce care and disputes.'[87]

The same was true at the lower levels of society. We are told that one of the regular categories of parish pensioners was 'parents overburdened with children.'[88] Tom Paine proposed family allowances which would mean that 'widows will have a maintenance for their children ... and children will no longer be considered as increasing the distresses of their parents.'[89] The 'no longer' is significant: clearly an increase of children was held to lead to destitution. The practical choices are indicated by Thomas Wright in the eighteenth century. After the death of his first wife who had left him seven children, he had been advised to marry an old widow, so as to have no more. He ignored his friends' advice, though even with his first wife, 'as my family now increased apace, and my income began to pinch us', he had been forced to sell his land. Having remarried a young and pretty girl, he found 'I have got a house full of fine children, and straitened circumstances', though he loyally wrote that he would 'a thousand times rather choose this situation, than be bound for life to a person I could not love, though in the midst of affluence and worldly prosperity'. That people were faced with the choice of either affluence or children is the crucial fact.[90]

It is clear that there was the same choice in earlier centuries. Francis Bacon drew attention to 'some foolish rich covetous men that take a pride in having no children, because they may be thought so much the richer.'[91] Thus Henry Percy advised his son that having many children led to great expenses, 'and either must you give yourself a continual slave to the want of your own pleasures; or grieve, that beggary must be left them for their last portions.' William Gouge noted as one of the motives that impeded sexual intercourse the 'fear of having too many children'.[92] Ballads suggested that it was better to marry an old widow than a young maid, precisely to avoid this danger.[93] As one contemporary proverb put it, 'an old child sucks hard', or as another stated, 'the chidren in their youth oft make their parents smart, being come to riper years, they vex their very heart.'[94]

[87] Quoted by Hajnal in Glass, *Population*, 113; Wharncliffe, *Letters of Montagu*, i, 230.

[88] George, *London Life*, 213.   [89] Quoted in Thompson, *Working Class*, 102.

[90] Wright, *Autobiography*, 116, 145.   [91] Bacon, *Essayes*, 22.

[92] Percy, *Advice*, 56.   [93] Rollins, *Pepysian Garland*, 265.

[94] Bruce, *Diary of Manningham*, 12 ; Behn, *Pleasures*, 243.

Thus a fictional character in a sixteenth-century text lamented, 'I remember me of Children, six sons and three daughters, of whom I am the unhappy Father . . . The common upon which industry should depasture is overlayd; Numerousness spoils all, and poverty sells all at an under value.'[95] The poet Quarles wrote of the poorer sort:[96]

> Seest thou the fruitful Womb? how every year
> It moves the Cradle; to thy slender chear
> Invites another guest, and makes thee Father
> To a new son, who now, perchance, had'st
>   rather
> Bring up the old, esteeming propagation
> A thankless work of supererogation
> Perchance thou grumblest, counting it a curse
> Unto thy faint estate, which is not able
> To increase the bounty of thy slender Table;
> Poor miserable man what e'er thou be.

The very poor were often driven to desperate measures, for instance to infanticide, which was blamed by Mrs Cellier on the 'want of fit ways to conceal their shame, and provide for their children.'[97] From nobility such as the Earl of Wiltshire who blamed his relative poverty partly on his wife's over-fertile womb, through the middling like the newly marrying clergy who found themselves impoverished by their wives and children, to the very poor who had their children taken from them and put on parish assistance, all found that, as Adam Martindale wrote of his brother, those with fertile wives had 'a great charge of children'.[98] Engels in the nineteenth century took the mid-European, and almost universal, view that children were valuables, returning more than was invested in them. As we have seen, Malthus, with his English attitude, saw them as basically a cost.[99] It would appear that the Malthusian tradition was deep-seated, going back until at least the start of the sixteenth century.

Of course there are numerous instances in many other societies of children being seen as costly, particularly daughters. But what seems

[95] Furnivall, *Tell-Trothes*, 142.

[96] Quarles, *Divine Poems*, 236–7. I owe this reference to Christopher Hill.

[97] Cellier, 'Royal Hospital', 191.

[98] Stone, *Crisis*, 81; Hoskins, *Leicestershire*, 18–19; Parkinson, *Life of Martindale*, 32.

[99] Meek, *Marx and Engels*, 61.

to have been unusual is the very widespread and deep-rooted view that all children were a 'burden', a 'care', a 'cost', something which you might or might not be able to afford, a luxury of a kind, something for which one saved up, like a house or furniture. The next task is to account for this belief. Was it 'false consciousness'? Was it that, as in almost all other agrarian societies, children were really of net value for their parents, each one expanding the family estate, but that for some reason people were unaware of this? In order to see whether this was the case we need to examine more closely the costs and benefits of children in a comparative perspective. How is it that they are 'valuable' in many pre-industrial societies, and how far did such value exist in the English past?

There has been much discussion about the costs and benefits of children. This brings out a number of points. For a start, there is the absolute cost, that is to say, how much a child consumes in the way of food, space, energy, money. Although somewhat to over-simplify, it might be argued that the amount that has to be invested will vary over the life cycle: as more has to be spent – for example, on education, food and clothing – so the cost will increase and people will find they cannot afford children.[100] But this absolute cost is influenced by a number of factors which make it, in itself, fairly useless as an indication.

First, there is the question of whether children can be maintained out of surpluses from the farm, or whether it is necessary to earn extra money to purchase the necessities for them. The degree of intrusion of money is crucial here, and the difference between an early monetized economy such as England and subsistence peasantries is excellently documented by Arthur Young in contrasting England and Ireland in the eighteenth century. 'The Irish poor in the Catholic parts of the country are subsisted entirely upon land; whereas the poor in England have so little to do with it, that they subsist almost entirely from shops, by a purchase of necessaries.'[101] Consequently each added child in England was a money expense: only by increasing his wages could a person hope to be able to support children. The fact that, as we know, the majority of the population were earning wages or equivalent cash incomes from at least the fourteenth century is enormously significant in affecting the cost of children.[102]

[100] Mitchell, 'Fertility', 298ff; Lorimer, *Human Fertility*, 389; Notestein, 'Population Change', 16.

[101] Hutton, *Young's Tour*, ii, 120.   [102] Macfarlane, *Individualism*, 148–9.

A second factor affecting the cost is the loss through mortality. The characteristically high infant and child mortality rates of many societies mean that for every surviving child a good deal has been invested in children that die. Malthus pointed out that 'in a public view, every child that dies under ten years of age is a loss to the nation of all that had been expended in its subsistence till that period'; of course, the loss fell particularly on those who had raised it.[103] In Brittany in the eighteenth century 'roughly half of the children do not reach their tenth year.'[104] In Colyton, Devon, probably between two thirds and three quarters of those live-born reached their fifteenth birthday. Though the English mortality is lower, these are high death rates by modern standards. Figures which suggest losses of one fifth of national income on children who die before a productive age in developing countries today are not fully applicable, but still of interest.[105] Thus for each living child there was the added cost of dead siblings.

A third factor in the calculation is the sex of the child. As Cain has pointed out,[106] in many societies the rearing of daughters is seen as pointless expense. When the daughter also needs a dowry, cost is added to cost. Here, as we have seen, there was some feeling in the English past that girls were marginally more of a cost. It is likely that their slightly lower value was compensated for by fewer costs – particularly in education and apprenticeship. Certainly in the middling groups the education and setting up of a son was usually more expensive than that of a daughter.

A fourth factor is the question of who bears the costs and who reaps the advantages. Demographers have frequently pointed out that there is a fundamental distinction between societies where almost all the costs fall on the nuclear family – basically mother and father – and those where they are distributed more widely – both upwards, to grandparents, and to wider kin, particularly parents' siblings. In those familistic societies where costs are spread, each added child calls on a wider pool of support in terms of labour and other resources, and hence a large production unit is not likely to find each additional child a 'burden'.[107] Thus Kingsley Davis argues that the modern Western nuclear family system which 'held married couples responsible for

---

[103] Malthus, *Population*, ii, 252.   [104] 'Historical Population', 599; ibid., 571.

[105] *The Determinants of Population*, 280.   [106] Cain, 'Extended Kin', 7.

[107] Halpern, *Serbian Village*, 140; also Caldwell, 'Fertility', 221; Clark, *Population Growth*, 186–7.

their children' is one of the major factors which made children a cost and hence delayed marriage.[108] Although there are occasionally instances of help to cousins, siblings or grandchildren in the historical sources, on the whole it would appear that it was assumed from as soon as our records start that 'married couples were responsible for their children.' In other words, the early establishment of the nuclear family pattern in England, probably before the fourteenth century, is a powerful pressure towards considering children 'costly'.[109] Basically, the situation prevented the spreading of costs through kinship, for brothers, cousins and others contributed little to the parental fund. The adult pair, given other factors such as the returns for labour, could not afford more than a smallish dependent group. This is noted by observers through the centuries. For instance, John Locke reported that 'we humbly conceive that a man and his wife, in health, may be able to maintain themselves and two children.' He recommended that all children over the age of three should be taken over and funded by the state.[110] In the early twentieth century it was still the case that 'only in households where adults outnumber the children can these be brought up under conditions which give scope to full development of their faculties.'[111]

A further factor concerns the alternatives to investment in children, that is, the opportunity cost of children. It has often been pointed out that in many societies the alternatives to investing in children are either non-existent or unattractive. There are no banks, no stocks and shares, no pension schemes, and no other forms of long-term storage for temporary profits. In such situations 'it is not surprising that men's efforts should be directed towards building up and maintaining through the generations links of marriage and kinship.'[112] Sometimes one can hoard gold, cloth and other 'valuables' – but these treasures are highly susceptible, as the Bible warned, to moth and rust, and to thieves, including landlords, who break in and steal. Although children may for a while be a burden, as is all saving, they are at least one way of accumulating resources against times when they will be needed.

From this point of view, the singular feature of English society from as early as the fourteenth century or before is the highly developed, and fairly secure, alternatives to investment in children. A developed

---

[108] Davis, 'Theory', 357.   [109] Macfarlane, *Individualism*, 136–8.
[110] Quoted in George, *London Life*, 380.   [111] Davies, *English Village*, 149.
[112] Krige in Forde, *African Worlds*, 75; Myrdal, *Asian Drama*, iii, 1540ff.

market in land and other property and a widespread system of lending and mortgaging meant that those who wished to invest and save in ways other than in children could easily do so. Although banking, pension schemes and insurance companies, as such, did not develop into formal institutions until the seventeenth and eighteenth centuries, it is evident that many of their functions were performed indirectly by bills, bonds and investment in property for many centuries before. It would seem that, as today, a person had a real alternative: he or she could invest in children, or he could invest in property of other kinds. The alternative property might well bring a better yield, as it is likely to do today.

One feature of this situation was not merely the availability of alternatives, but the risk involved. Here we see the importance of the point made by Malthus that not only was it necessary for there to be private property in which people could invest, but also this property, the web of investments, must be secured by a powerful government. The well known orderliness of English society from the thirteenth century onwards, in which there were few rampaging armies, little excessive taxation, scarcely a class of arbitrary landlords, and no successful revolutions which overthrew property laws, provided a cosy context in which people could spread their risks. The central concern of English law and government to preserve private property, the basis of English political philosophy for Locke and others, contributed to a world where people could grow rich with few or no children.

We are dealing here with an equation, or balance, between costs and advantages. The crucial question is the relationship of the two. We are told, in an intensive study of this topic, that 'very few parents in present-day society ever receive back a fraction of the money that they spend in bringing up their children.' A recent estimate is that, taking into account the opportunity cost of lost earnings by the mother, a first child will cost a middle-class family in England up to £80,000. In America, 'the actual per-child cost has risen to over $16,000 by 1944, and in 1959 is probably above $25,000', a figure which would have to be quadrupled by 1985.[113] The parents are very unlikely to recoup much if any of this in a monetary form.

The precise value of children has now been the subject of several studies. Although some, for example E. Mueller, have argued that 'children have negative economic value in peasant agriculture',

[113] Wynn, *Family Policy*, 274; Hunt, *Love*, 302.

despite the beliefs of the natives to the contrary, it seems that often they are valuable.[114] This is shown by Mamdani's study in the Punjab, at least for sons, and has been shown in Bangladesh.[115] In Nepal and Java, even with dense population, Nag and associates have argued that 'children probably have a net positive economic value to their parents in these villages, aside from the old-age security they provide them'; in Java 'each individual household, by increasing its size . . . obtains *not less, but more*, of a share of these opportunities.'[116] A characteristic of this situation is that it takes time for the children to become an advantage. Thus, in Bangladesh 'male children appear to become net producers at least by age 12, compensate for their cumulative consumption by age 15, and compensate for their own and one sister's cumulative consumption by age 22.'[117] So it may be generally true that in the early part of the reproductive phase parents have to work very hard and the children are, like forced saving of all kinds, a burden. As L. K. Berkner writes of the seventeenth-century Austrian peasantry, 'during the first half of a peasant family's life cycle the economic well-being of the family declines as each new child adds to consumption.'[118] But after that the older siblings become net producers, and the parents regard their children, like a maturing orchard, as a protection in their declining years . Thus it is during the 'latter phase of their development' that economic success comes to peasants with large families.[119]

The essence of the equation, Caldwell argues, is the direction of the net flow of assets. 'The key issue . . . the fundamental issue in demographic transition, is the direction and magnitude of inter-generational wealth flows, or the net balance of the two flows.' The great divide is between those societies, the majority, where most 'wealth' flows from children to parents and where high fertility is 'rational', and those where most flows from parents to children, where low fertility is economically rational.[120] Basically, in the domestic mode of production, where resources are pooled between the generations and parents and children form one economic and social unit of consumption and production, each parental generation benefits from children.

If the point at which children become net producers is roughly as in

[114] Quoted in Caldwell, 'Fertility', 193.   [115] Mamdani, *Myth*, 77–8.
[116] Nag, 'Children', 301, 298 (italics in original).
[117] Cain, 'Children', 224.   [118] Berkner, 'Stem Family', 414.
[119] Nag, 'Children', 300.   [120] Caldwell, 'Restatement', 344.

Bangladesh, it is very easy to see how two parents could benefit from children. In an 'open frontier', the returns might be much greater. On the basis of figures from North America, Adam Smith in the eighteenth century remarked that 'labour is there so well rewarded that a numerous family of children, instead of being a burthen is a source of opulence and prosperity to the parents. The labour of each child, before it can leave their house, is computed to be worth a hundred pounds clear gain to them', and this was possible even with the children leaving home and setting up independently at a young age.[121]

The great transformation, Caldwell argues, comes when children become a net loss, and this is caused by changes in relationships in the set of obligations within the nuclear family. It is not necessarily the result of a change from agriculture to industrial occupations, from rural to urban dwelling. 'High fertility remains rational in nonagricultural urban conditions as long as the flow of wealth is predominantly from the younger to the older generation', as Caldwell documents for groups in Ibadan in Nigeria where 'the return from investment in children is greater for urban than rural residents and is the greatest of all among the city white-collar and professional class.'[122] This is a restatement of Adam Smith's insight. Having contrasted the profits to be made from children in North America with the 'burthen' they were in Europe, Smith pointed out that 'the value of children is the greatest of all encouragements to marriage.' Hence in North America 'a young widow with four or five children, who, among the middling or inferior ranks of people in Europe, would have so little chance for a second husband, is there frequently courted as a sort of fortune.'[123] But whereas Smith lays the stress on the returns on labour, in other words, its relative scarcity and productivity *per se*, Caldwell adds in the relations of production, that is to say, the degree to which parents can appropriately call on the fruits of their children's mature years. Here, paraphrasing the argument, the dramatic change is from societies where parents and children share production and consumption and hence children automatically feed back their costs plus a bit more to their kin, to capitalist societies with individual profits. In the latter, children soon learn that they will one day run an economic enterprise independently from their parents, where what they return is negotiable and not automatic.

---

[121] Smith, *Wealth*, i, 79. [122] Caldwell, 'Restatement', 348.
[123] Smith, *Wealth*, i, 79.

The great question for Caldwell thus becomes 'what causes this emotional nucleation of the family whereby parents spend increasingly on their children, while demanding – and receiving – very little in return?'[124] And he argues that until family morality 'decays', and children stop automatically feeling that they are 'the debtors of their parents for life, warmth and love, [and] hence ought, and wish to channel wealth upwards, the children will probably be a net profit.'[125] There is nothing intrinsically determining about the means of production: children are useful in agricultural tasks, but they can also be essential in industrial jobs, as the history of child labour in nineteenth-century Europe or twentieth century South East Asia shows. It is important that their labour is needed, as Adam Smith pointed out. But even more important is whether parents or children reap the major rewards from the children's labour. As we have seen, the two extreme forms are the domestic and capitalist modes of production. In between these extremes are situations where, even though children ultimately reap individual rewards, their labour is sufficiently valuable and their emancipation sufficiently delayed that they are of net value; or other situations where there is so little employment for children that the family benefits little from them. The shortage of demand for children's labour is shown by calculations which suggest that the 'break-even' age of children is 16 for Nepal, 21 for Java, 25 for the Philippines and 28 for Sri Lanka, because of underemployment.[126] The high demand for children's labour was demonstrated on the frontier of North America, and perhaps partly explains the rising fertility in the eighteenth century when a growing demand for children's labour was apparent in the early industrial revolution.

All this cost–benefit analysis may seem curiously artificial, not to say unrealistic, and it is certainly ethnocentric. Anthropologists and demographers have pointed out that the model is 'over-rational' and may bear little resemblance to how people today in developing societies think.[127] This is true. But the interesting thing is that this very way of thinking is part of the revolutionary change which we are trying to account for. As long as the psychological/biological/social and other patent advantages of children are fully in accord with the economic situation, such thinking is irrelevant. But part of the

---

[124] Caldwell, 'Restatement', 352.
[125] Caldwell, 'Education', 247.   [126] Cain, 'Extended Kin', 7.
[127] Cassen, *India*, 21; Das Gupta in Epstein, *Fertility*, 98, 233.

transformation brought by capitalism is to make children seem a problem, a burden, a cost. As children pick up the message, they reciprocally turn their old people into burdens, problems and costs.

Given the fact that costs are incurred roughly up to puberty, and profits made after that, the crucial factor to determine is the historical point at which control over the children's earnings was lost to parents or other kin. When did children stop 'costing' and start 'producing', and for how long? It seems likely that children often started to work relatively young in England in past centuries. There are many agricultural and domestic tasks – carrying, herding, collecting, watching – which are labour intensive and which children can do nearly as well as adults. Particularly around the house, and in periods of peak labour demand such as harvesting and weeding, their labour is especially valuable. A census of the poor mentions as the youngest persons 'idle' people aged 6, 8, 9, 10 and 12 years; small children helped carry peat, and often they were apprenticed out at 6 or 7.[128] They could earn wages early on which, between the ages of 6 and 14, could be a 'great help to their poor fathers and mothers.'[129] Yet it may be that the opportunities for work around the home and farm, or of obtaining paid work, were more limited than in many societies. A moderate demand for human labour may have meant that children helped, but did not slave. As John Locke complained, 'the children of labouring people are an ordinary burden to the parish, and are usually maintained in idleness, so that their labour also is generally lost to the public, till they are twelve or fourteen years old.'[130] In a very detailed eighteenth-century listing of inhabitants, only about a quarter of the girls aged 5 to 9 and none of the boys were listed as having occupations.[131] Just as the English in general were regarded as leading a leisurely life, filled with holidays and amusements, so their children often did not seem to be needed as drudges. They could even let their offspring attend schools whose terms continued over the harvests, whereas in Scotland and Ireland the school terms had to be fitted in with seasonal demands for help with harvesting.[132]

Here we may detect a major shift in the eighteenth century, particularly among the poor. It is likely that the demand for child

---

[128] Pound, *Census, passim*; Ford, *Warton*, 84; George, *London Life*, 182, 377, 424.
[129] Lodge, *Account Book*, xxxiii; George, *London Life*, 182.
[130] George, *London Life*, 380.   [131] Schofield, 'Mobility', 264.
[132] E.g. for Scotland, see Graham, *Scotland*, 437.

labour increased markedly, and consequently, as Adam Smith had argued, their value increased and so population rose to produce more hands. The growing industrial upsurge created a sort of internal frontier, somewhat like the external frontier in America. In the early eighteenth century, Defoe noticed the change with delight in the cradle of industrialism, the area around Halifax. Here he found in the growing cloth industry that 'the women and children . . . are always busy carding, spinning, &c. so that no hands being unemployed, all can gain their bread, even from the youngest to the ancient; hardly any thing above four years old, but its hands are sufficient to it self.'[133] Here was an altered situation. No longer were the children of the poor idle to 14, but self-sufficient from 4. And even if we accept the view of Alice Clark for the seventeenth century that 'above 7 years of age, children began to contribute towards their own support but they are not completely self-supporting before the age of 13 or 14',[134] if Defoe is to be believed, the age of self-sufficiency had been lowered by nearly ten years. By the age of 10 they might have produced a surplus and by 14 have accumulated a good deal. The crucial fact was that during this period children were likely to be contributing to the domestic economy without the pressure to start to save for their own home and marriage.

The demand for children's, and women's, labour, as Malthus noted, is vital in estimating the effects of changes in wages on the fertility pattern, for it is the total earning power of the family, not just the wages of the husband, that is important. The demand for child labour grew apace. It is graphically described at the end of the eighteenth century by Sir Frederick Eden.[135] It had reached such a peak that children were practically kidnapped from their homes and then set to work through day and night: Eden pointed to the 'manufacture, which, in order to be carried on successfully, requires that cottages and workhouses should be ransacked for poor children; that they should be employed by turns during the greater part of the night.' We have many descriptions of the very young age and long hours of work in the nineteenth century, which not only horrified some contemporaries, but would have amazed Englishmen two centuries earlier.[136] As Habakkuk noted, reflecting Malthus, it was 'an increase in the economic value of children in industrial

[133] Defoe, *Tour*, 493. [134] Clark, *Women*, 72.

[135] Quoted in Stewart, *Works*, viii, 184.

[136] E.g. Thompson, *Working Class*, 367–8; Anderson, *Family Structure*, 75.

employment', as well as changes in poor payments, that reduced that set of 'costs' which had deterred people from marrying young.[137] Children may not have been a profit to their parents, but they were no longer such a conspicuous loss. As Arthur Young observed, 'Employment is the soul of population' – 'Away! my boys – get children, they are worth more than ever they were'.[138] This remark can be misleading. It is difficult to show that people came to consider children so 'valuable' that they altered their marriage strategy in order to produce more. Yet the opportunities for child labour took away some of those preventive pressures to earlier marriage of which Malthus had written. Thus J. Rickman commented on the 1821 census that rapid population growth was related to the fact that 'in many manufactures, children are able to maintain themselves at an early age, and so entail little expense on their parents, to the obvious encouragement of marriage.'[139]

The most important fact, however, is how long children see their primary responsibility to be to channel wealth upwards. In almost all societies, it is at least until marriage; where this is the case, the parents often put some pressure on their children to delay marriage. Thus we find a reluctance to allow marriages in some Mediterranean societies.[140] In very many countries the obligation continues automatically for life, since parents and children run a joint, undivided economy. So in Nigeria 'most parents receive continuing assistance from adult, married children irrespective of their state of health or feebleness.' On average, over 10 per cent of the parents' income tends to come from absent children. As long as children 'ungrudgingly share their earnings with their parents, it will pay to have a large family and to educate them.'[141] It is not just that, as in peasant Poland,[142] children cannot dispose of any of their earnings during adolescence, and that therefore the rough period up to twenty or so 'repays' the cost of childhood. In many instances, for the rest of life there is a flow upwards.

In order to examine the returns on children we need to know what the relative obligations and power of children and parents were. To

---

[137] Habakkuk in Glass, *Population*, 280.
[138] Quoted in Chambers, 'Vale of Trent', 56.
[139] Quoted by T.H.Marshall in Glass, *Population*, 267.
[140] Pitt-Rivers, *Countrymen*, 122.
[141] Caldwell, 'Fertility', 231; Caldwell, 'Rationality', 23, 16.
[142] Thomas, *Polish Peasant*, 93–4.

what extent did children still living at home automatically contribute to a 'family budget' and continue to do so after they were living away from home? When did children leave home? What were the responsibilities of married children to their parents? These are some of the questions we shall now seek to answer.

5

Setting up a Separate Economic and Social Unit

At first sight, the fact that children married very late or not at all in sixteenth- and seventeenth-century England would seem likely to favour parents. The unmarried could devote all their surplus to parents; the mean age at first marriage for both men and women of twenty-five or older could have meant that at least ten years of earnings went back into the family fund. But what is important is not just the gap between puberty and marriage, or whether a person is married or not, but rather what is regarded as the normal pattern of wealth flow between members of the family. In particular, as Moni Nag points out, the value of children is related to the parents' 'ability to retain control of their children's labour by postponing their dispersal from the household'.[1] It is not so much, in fact, the actual dispersal from the household that is important, but that emotional and also economic nucleation whereby at a certain point parents and children come to an agreement that the earnings should primarily go to the child. It is quite possible for a child to stay as a kind of boarder in the parental home and only contribute his or her keep, or, conversely, for the children to leave home, earn money in cities or even abroad, and yet conceive of themselves as contributing all earnings to a family fund, from which they can then draw.

The view of two recent social historians is that children may have contributed relatively little to the parental generation. Richard Smith notes of 'pre-industrial England' that 'children were not necessarily an important source either of labour or of security in old age.' Keith Wrightson suggests for the seventeenth century that 'certainly parents did not seem to have regarded their children as a source of labour to any significant extent', and the 'evidence of wills makes it clear

[1] Nag, 'Children', 302.

enough that though parents invariably helped children into adult life, they rarely expected economic aid in their turn.'[2] If this was true, how can it have occurred within a system of late marriage?

One part of the explanation lies in the unusual legal status of children in England and particularly their rights to control their own assets, whether inherited or accumulated. In classical Roman law which in revised form dominated the Continent throughout our period, the property of children was automatically absorbed into that of parents for a number of years. The paterfamilias was in a very powerful position.

> His children had no rights against him, and, though there was a shadowy *condominium*, in historical times they could own no property, whatever their age: everything was his. A son was, in this matter, like a slave: all that he acquired vested in the father, except in the Empire his earnings etc., or military service and in the later Empire his earnings in some other public services.[3]

In contrast, a very early feature of the English situation was that parents do not seem to have had an automatic right in their children's property. This is clearly the case nowadays.

> A parent, it seems, has no rights as such in the property of a child of any age; thus in the absence of any agreement he has no claim on a child's wages, and even an arrangement by which the child promises to pay his father or mother a weekly sum is not enforceable . . . Similarly, property bought by a child out of his income will remain exclusively his own.

The only exception is 'the domestic services of their children under the age of 18 actually living with them as part of their family'.[4] 'The child's property is his own: anything given to him by the parents or from outside vests in him, though his powers of administration are very limited in infancy. A parent is not liable upon any of those contracts which an infant can validly make for himself.'[5]

This was equally true in the nineteenth century. 'As to the property of his child, a father has no right to it; if he enter into possession of land, he will be regarded as the child's bailiff, and have to account for

[2] Smith, 'Fertility', 618; Wrightson, *English Society*, 112, 114.

[3] Buckland, *Roman Law*, 40.   [4] Bromley, *Family Law*, 458, 304.

[5] Buckland, *Roman Law*, 39.

the rents and profits he has received.' It thus 'seems doubtful whether he can take the child's earnings gained by service to a stranger.'[6] Like many features of English law, this appears to be very ancient. It is described in similar terms by Maitland.

Contrasting the general position in thirteenth century England with that under Roman law, Maitland wrote:

> the law of the thirteenth century knew, as the law of the nineteenth knows, infancy or non-age as a condition which has many legal consequences . . . but the legal capacity of the infant is hardly, if at all, affected by the life or death of his father, and the man or woman who is of full age is in no sort subject to paternal power . . . Our law knows no such thing as 'emancipation', it merely knows an attainment of full age.

Thus 'an infant may well have proprietary rights even though his father is still alive.'[7] He or she may inherit land and will come into court to defend his or her right in this as an independent person. 'An infant can sue; he sues in his own proper person, for he can not appoint an attorney.' It is entirely consistent with this that children should have power over their own earnings: above what was due as payment for board and keep, such fruits of their labour did not automatically belong to the paterfamilias. The contrast between the Roman law and English common law rights of children was noted by Sir Thomas Smyth in the sixteenth century. 'Our children be not in *potestate parentum*, as the children of the Romans were . . . That which is theirs they may give or sell, and purchase to themselves, either lands and other movables the father having nothing to do therewith.'[8]

The separate property rights of children are well indicated by their rights to bequeath their estates. If they could accumulate goods which were really their own by their labour, one index of this would be the right to leave such goods to whom they chose, irrespective of their parents' wishes, and this was indeed the case. The leading expert on last testaments and wills summarized the position at the end of the sixteenth century as follows: 'howbeit a boy after the age of fourteen years, and a girl after the age of twelve years, may make a testament and dispose of their goods and chattels; and that not only without the authority or consent of their curator or guardian, but also without the authority and consent of the father, if he or she have any goods of his

---

[6] Geary, *Marriage*, 433–4; Blackstone, *Commentaries*, i, pt 2, 452–3.
[7] Pollock and Maitland, ii, 438, 439, 440.   [8] Smyth, *De Republica*, 106.

or her own.'[9] Swinburne contrasts this with the situation under 'civil' or Roman law, where property was in the hands of the parents. In equity, there were similar rights. 'An infant female may make a will, and dispose of her personal estate at twelve, an infant male at seventeen, or at fifteen if proved to be of discretion.'[10]

All this would have been pointless if children had no property rights. It is thus no coincidence that under sections headed 'Parent and Child' in books on modern English family law there is discussion of 'Parental Obligation' but not of 'Children's Obligation'.[11] It came to be taken as axiomatic that obligations, like emotion, flowed down. Children need not maintain their grandparents, for 'natural affection descends more strongly than it ascends.'[12] Even with parents, children by the Poor Law Act of 1601 were only obliged to give support to 'poor, old, blind, lame and impotent people' who were 'not able to work'. If the parent did not fall into any of these categories, no assistance was required. Furthermore, any assistance that was required was not founded on affection, but duty. A child is 'equally compellable if of sufficient ability, to maintain and provide for a wicked and unnatural progenitor, as for one who has shewn the greatest tenderness and parental piety'.[13] Children thus became the first in line to pay tax or maintenance towards their destitute parents. If the children had travelled far off, it would be impractical to levy this. Significantly, while a Justice of the Peace could issue warrants to seize the rents and grounds of parents and husbands who had run off and left their children or spouse to parish relief, no similar warrants are mentioned for children who had abandoned their parents.[14]

Linked to this, and providing another part of the explanation for the generally small contribution by children to parental income, is the peculiar English tradition of sending young children away from home in order to earn their separate keep. There were institutions which from an unusually early age in children's lives broke up the joint domestic unit of consumption and production and separated the parental and the children's generation. The peculiarity and antiquity of the various mechanisms for doing this are well illustrated in the famous observations of an Italian visitor to England in the late fifteenth century. He described how the English,

---

[9] Swinburne, *Wills*, 67.   [10] *A general abridgement*, 283.
[11] Bromley, *Family Law*; Hall, *Family Law*.   [12] Burn, *Justice*, pt 3, 657.
[13] Blackstone, *Commentaries*, i, pt 2, 454.   [14] Burn, *Justice*, pt 3, 659–60.

having kept them [children] at home till they arrive at the age of 7 or 9 years at the utmost, . . . put them out, both males and females, to hard service in the houses of other people, binding them generally for another 7 or 9 years. And these are called apprentices . . . and few are born who are exempted from this fate, for every one, however rich he may be, sends away his children into the houses of others, whilst he, in return, receives those of strangers into his own.

The effect was that parents could 'enjoy all their comforts themselves' while their children started at the bottom. Nor did the children ever return, 'for the girls are settled by their patrons, and the boys make the best marriages they can.'[15] There is now ample evidence of this pattern working throughout the whole period from the fifteenth to nineteenth centuries.

Particularly well documented is the institution of sending children away as servants. It was often specifically non-adult labour that was sought, and usually it was one's own children who provided it. They might not be fully employed, but at crucial points in the agricultural cycle the children in a family were irreplaceable, that is, unless there was a well developed labour market of young people of all ages and skills who could be hired as needed. This was exactly what servants provided. The hiring of labour when required – that is, servants as an alternative to large families – has been recognized by a number of demographers and economists as of central importance in determining the attitude to having large families.[16] Whereas in many societies it was essential to produce, or even over-produce, children in order to provide the right labour force in terms of age and sex, and to adopt children if nature did not give the right number, in England it was possible to use the much more flexible mechanism of hiring children for a year at a time as servants, or taking an apprentice for a longer period. Wrigley points out that the institution of service could act as a form of *ex post facto* family planning. Surpluses of children could be sent off, or labour shortages made up by hiring children. As Ann Kussmaul puts it, farm service was 'wonderfully adaptable, filling both the roles of family-balancer to small farmers, and labour force to larger farmers'. Servants dealt with those problems of fluctuating over- and under-supply of labour which face peasant societies and which Chayanov shows are solved by other means elsewhere.[17] Thus

[15] Sneyd, *Relation*, 24–5.
[16] Boserup, *Population*, 182; Cain, 'Extended Kin', 7; Cassen, *India*, 70.
[17] Kussmaul, *Servants*, 26, 27, 23ff.

servanthood undermined one of the major pressures towards high fertility.

Service also broke the economic and social link between the generations. A child who was just reaching economic self-sufficiency would be sent away from home to earn his keep in another family. To the new family he would give his labour, and from them he would receive his rewards. Henceforward he would be cut off from his parents' domestic economy. At first he or she would earn little more than keep and some clothing. Gradually, as wages increased, it would seem that the larger part would be kept by the individual, preferably being saved as a contribution to the later costs of setting up a home or business. Although there are hints that servants sometimes sent part of their wages home to their parents in the second half of the nineteenth century and the early twentieth century, there is singularly little evidence of such remittances in the earlier centuries.[18] And I have come across no evidence in the numerous sources that money was sent home in significant amounts; for instance, none of Josselin's daughters who became servants seem to have done so, or to have been expected so to do. Wrightson, who has also examined parallel sources, can find 'no firm evidence' that 'some children . . . remitted part of their wages to their parents', and Richard Smith, likewise, can find little or no evidence.[19] Most significantly, Ann Kussmaul, who has worked extensively on farm servanthood over the sixteenth to nineteenth centuries, has found only one reference to such a practice: even that is merely 'an indirect suggestion'.[20] Here there is probably a very marked difference with patterns on the Continent and among Irish and perhaps Scottish immigrants, where servants sent home a large part of their earnings.[21] As Kussmaul writes, 'farm service gave the children of the poor a chance to save the wages they received in order to stock small farms or common land, or simply to furnish the cottage they would inhabit when they married.'[22] Likewise, children of farmers and husbandmen saw it as a chance to save for themselves, rather than to supplement a domestic economy they had never broken away from.

Apprenticeship was an equally ancient and unusual institution, unknown in most civilizations. The idea was that the apprenticed

---

[18] Thompson, *Lark Rise*, 158.

[19] Wrightson, *English Society*, 113; Smith, 'Nuclear Family', 12.

[20] Kussmaul, *Servants*, 76.

[21] See Scott and Tilly in Rosenberg, *Family*, 166.   [22] Kussmaul, *Servants*, 76.

child would gradually master an art or skill which he or she would then use to support himself or herself. Widespread apprenticeship appears to be a post-Roman, north-European phenomenon. Adam Smith noted that

> apprenticeships were altogether unknown to the ancients. The reciprocal duties of master and apprentice make a considerable article in every modern code. The Roman law is perfectly silent with regard to them. I know no Greek or Latin word (I might venture, I believe, to assert that there is none) which expresses the idea we now annex to the word Apprentice, a servant bound to work at a particular trade for the benefit of a master, during a term of years, upon condition that the master shall teach him that trade.[23]

The absence of an economic payment upwards in apprenticeship was even more explicit. It cost money to apprentice a child, whether to a craft or trade or to a profession by way of school, university or Inns of Court. Often, as we shall see, it was very costly indeed. There were few if any payments to the apprentice during this period. Smith pointed out that the abolition of apprenticeship would mean that masters 'would lose all the wages of the apprentice, which he now saves, for seven years together'.[24]

Apprenticeship, along with 'schooling', was an investment in children by parents, from which parents could expect little or no return during the period of apprenticeship itself. Between them, servanthood and apprenticeship covered a very large proportion of the population and kept them occupied outside their own domestic economies, either living away from home or, at the least, not contributing to their parents' domestic enterprise. These institutions, which filled that long period between economic self-sufficiency and marriage, are thus of central importance in understanding the Malthusian marriage regime.

It has been increasingly observed in contemporary societies that as formal education becomes more institutionalized it has an enormous effect on intra-family economics and sentiments. It breaks the link between children's earnings and their parents' domestic economy. It increases the cost of each child, who has to be supported for longer, with payments to the 'educators' and with no returns on his or her

---

[23] Smith, *Wealth*, i, 137.   [24] Ibid., i, 138.

labour.[25] In the words of Caldwell, 'schools destroy the corporate identity of the family.'[26] They do this in a number of ways. As well as increasing the cost of the child, education reduces his or her potential for work for the family's benefit; it creates dependency of a sort, society regarding the child as a future rather than a present producer; it encourages the spread of new 'Western' values and ideas such as that a person should have complete control over his own earnings, or that the husband–wife, rather than the parent–child relationship, is the most important in life.[27]

We can extend this analysis to all those institutions of child training of the past. Although schools were widespread in England from the sixteenth century, they constituted merely the stratum above the other forms of 'apprenticeship' of which we have spoken. Servanthood was widespread in England from the thirteenth to the nineteenth centuries.[28] Service in husbandry, one branch of servanthood, was practised 'without intermission from the sixteenth to the nineteenth century . . . very few changes in the form of the institution can be discerned in these centuries.'[29] About 60 per cent of the population aged 15 to 24 in the period 1574–1821 were servants; thus approximately a third to a half of hired labour in early modern agriculture was provided by servants in husbandry.[30] Of some two thousand people who wished to settle in a parish, from the seventeenth to nineteenth centuries, 81 per cent of the examinants had been servants. As Kussmaul concludes, 'service in husbandry was the usual occupation of early modern rural youths. They left their parents as children, and departed from service as adults.'[31] Laslett estimates that between a quarter and a third of families in Stuart England had servants of one kind or another,[32] including house servants. If we then add the numerous apprentices in villages and towns, both those apprenticed to learn a craft and those apprenticed to a 'master' to learn a profession such as law or medicine, we can envisage a society where the vast majority of children were already leaving home at an early age, or working for people other than their parents.

---

[25] Nag, 'Children', 303; *The Determinants of Population*, i, 81; Dore, 'Fertility', 76.
[26] Caldwell, 'Education', 243.   [27] Ibid., *passim*.
[28] Laslett, *Family Life*, 47; Anglicus, *Properties*, i, 305; Macfarlane, *Individualism*, 147–9.   [29] Kussmaul, *Servants*, 119.   [30] Ibid., 3, 5.   [31] Ibid., 19, 70.
[32] Laslett, *Lost World*, 13.

Although servants would tend to leave home, and apprentices and scholars often did so, many stayed for some years with their parents. It was once argued, as the Italian visitor to England suggested, that almost all children would have left home by their early teens during these centuries.[33] It was thought that Flora Thompson's description of an Oxfordshire village in the nineteenth century, where 'there was no girl over twelve or thirteen living permanantly at home', might be an accurate portrayal of earlier centuries.[34] With the more detailed analysis of listings it became clear that this picture was too extreme. Schofield analysed an eighteenth-century listing for Cardington and found that many children were still at home over the age of 15. An analysis of four listings for 1697, 1782, 1801 and 1841 also found many children staying at home in their late teens and early twenties.[35] There was clearly variation, both geographically and temporally. Yet the mean age at entering service was 13 to 14,[36] and there is very extensive literary and other evidence of children of all groups being sent off young. Two of Josselin's own children went off at 10, two at 13, one at 14, and two at 15.[37] Apprenticeship could start at any age from three onwards, with many becoming bound apprentice at seven or eight.[38]

While servants were often sent off to live with others, and apprentices might or might not still live at home for the first few years, others lived at home but began to attend school. Brinsley in the seventeenth century commented that 'for the time of their entrance with us, in our country schools, it is commonly about 7 or 8 years old: six is very soon.' Revealingly, he continued, 'if any begin so early, they are rather sent to the school to keep them from troubling the house at home, and from danger, and shrewd turns, than for any great hope and desire their friends have that they should learn anything in effect.'[39] Far from being a labour asset, they were a nuisance and the school acted as does a modern crèche. The same was probably true of apprenticeship. Adam Smith pointed out that 'long apprenticeships are altogether unnecessary for most trades . . . a few days might be sufficient.' In fact, masters gained from their apprentices' labour.[40]

---

[33] See Macfarlane, *Ralph Josselin*, App. B.   [34] Thompson, *Lark Rise*, 148.

[35] Schofield, 'Mobility'; Wall, 'Leaving Home', *passim*.

[36] Kussmaul, *Servants*, 70.   [37] Macfarlane, *Ralph Josselin*, 93.

[38] George, *London Life*, 239, 377, 424: it should be noted that guild and parish apprenticeships were significantly different in their conditions and costs.

[39] Quoted in Furnivall, *Meals and Manners*, lxii.   [40] Smith, *Wealth*, i, 138.

The tradition whereby schools act as absorbers of redundant labour over a period of up to fifteen years was established early and widely. Thus Smith also noted of public schools and universities that 'no better method, it seems, could be fallen upon of spending, with any advantage, the long interval between infancy and that period of life at which men begin to apply in good earnest to the real business of the world.'[41] It has been estimated that in 1660 there was an endowed grammar school for every 6000 of the estimated population in the ten counties round London, and one school for every 4,400 if we count the non-endowed schools. This was a higher level than for most of the nineteenth century. Before the Education Act of 1870 there was only one school for every 23,750 persons.[42]

The final point about all these forms of contractual relationship, whether of education, of servanthood or of apprenticeship, was that they were generally incompatible with marriage. Children at school or university could not marry; apprentices were bound by their indentures not to marry; house servants could not often marry and keep their job, and even servants in husbandry were, on the whole, put under heavy pressure not to marry. As David Hume wrote, 'at present all masters discourage marrying of their male servants and admit not by any means the marriage of the female.'[43] Arthur Young noted the difference between England and Ireland. In the latter, marriage was common in classes 'which with us do not marry at all; such as servants; the generality of footmen and maids, in gentlemen's families, are married, a circumstance we very rarely see in England.'[44] Here we find a mechanism for delaying marriage. Yet, instead of parents profiting from the new-found energies of those between 14 and 24, it was the masters of these servants and apprentices who did so. A certain amount also went to the servant in wages, and to the apprentice in a future right to a skill which would provide him with a living. Formal education was also a promise of future rewards, which would be provided in the form of a profession.

The cost of rearing children up to marriage was thus not generally recompensed by a proportional return to the domestic fund. Parents invested in their children's long-term future. How much, in fact, did they invest? Elsewhere I have undertaken a detailed analysis of the

[41] Smith, *Wealth*, book v, ch.1, pt 3, 295.

[42] Jordan cited by M.Curtis in Nicoll, *Shakespeare*, 58.

[43] Hume, *Essays*, 1907 edn, i, 387.

[44] Hutton, *Young's Tour*, ii, 120.

costs of each of the children in the family of Ralph Josselin.[45] Basing the analysis on contemporary estimates that it cost at least from £5 to £10 per year to keep a child, I concluded that during the period 1641–83, the education, rearing and dowering of his children cost about £2,000, or one third of his total income. It was considerably more than he spent on any other item, including himself and his wife, or his purchase of land and buildings. Another contemporary estimate for the very poorest orphans in a foundling hospital in the late seventeenth century was that a person who asked to redeem an orphan could do so for £25 for one under five years, £40 for 5–7 years, £50 for 7–10, and each year after that an extra £10 had to be paid.[46] The middling Adam Martindale, who had looked after his grandson for five years (from age 1 to 5), said he 'would not take any man's £30 to do for his child what we have already done for it, and are further to do ... £80 or £90'.[47] James Jackson, a Cumberland yeoman, provides similar figures, boarding out children at between 1s 4d and 1s 6d per week. He then paid for a son's apprenticeship £10 plus four crowns. When the son set up in trade, he gave him another £150.[48] The payments continued late into the child's life. We shall later consider the dowry and portions paid at marriage, but there were also other expenses. Thus Martindale gave his son furniture when he became a schoolmaster, having paid for him through university. Even after marriage, the Revd Moore spent £68 11s 9d in settling his daughter.[49]

These sums, of course, are trifling when compared with those for the gentry and above. As Alice Thornton ruefully put it, 'the education, maintenance, and learning of my dear son Thornton, will amount to so prodigious a sum as perhaps may not be credited.'[50] The proverb that old children sucked hard is fully borne out. One Verney daughter boarded out at 18 cost her parents £18 per annum in diet and £12 per annum in clothes, and another daughter £25 for food and £12 for clothes.[51] Even at that age, where in many societies a daughter would be a net producer – both in labour and in children – many English parents found their children a financial commitment. It

[45] Macfarlane, *Ralph Josselin*, 46–54.   [46] Cellier, 'Royal Hospital', 196.

[47] Parkinson, *Life of Martindale*, 221.

[48] Grainger, 'Jackson's Diary', 117–23.

[49] Parkinson, *Life of Martindale*, 219; Blencowe, 'Giles Moore', 117.

[50] Jackson, *Thornton Autobiography*, 143.

[51] Verney, *Memoirs*, i, 434.

was not surprising that the vicar of Warton in 1695 should lament, 'I am much in debt and my charge is great, nine poor children in number to maintain, every one daily chargeable unto me and not one of them prefer'd. One of them indeed is more chargeable than the rest because we are forced to board him out being eight years of age.'[52]

John Locke believed that all this investment gave the parents certain permanent rights in the children, and engendered certain obligations on the part of the children: 'the honour due from a child places in the parents a perpetual right to respect, reverence, support, and compliance too, more or less, as the father's care, cost, and kindness in his education has been more or less.'[53] We have seen that the bread cast upon the waters did not tend to bring in considerable returns to the parents before their children married.

The next phase to consider is the period after the children married. Assuming the parents married at 25 and the children also, a parent would be approaching his or her mid- to late fifties when the children started to marry. Such children would now either have made savings from their wages as servants, or the deferred savings of a craft through apprenticeship or university. For the first time he or she would be economically self-sufficient. To what extent was this earning potential shared with the ageing parents? This depends very much on the cultural rules concerning residence and economic co-operation after marriage.

Rules that determine where the bride and groom settle are among the most important aspects of a marriage pattern. They are very closely linked to the main puzzles we are attempting to solve for, if Malthus is right, 'one of the most salutary and least pernicious checks on the frequency of early marriage in this country is the difficulty of procuring a cottage.'[54] But, as Malthus realized, the matter is not merely a physical one concerning actual structures; a comparison with the hastily constructed shacks of the Irish, or the shared households of many societies, shows that cultural expectations of what is considered a reasonable dwelling for a married couple are central. In order to understand the peculiarities of the English system, we need to examine it briefly in a comparative context.

It has been argued by a number of anthropologists and sociologists

---

[52] Report of the Lancashire Record Office, 1970, p.30; for other costs see Clark, *Women*, 70ff. [53] Locke, *Government*, 34. [54] Malthus, *Population*, ii, 250.

that marriage residence is an important determining cause of different kinship systems. In anthropological terminology, 'if custom requires the groom to leave his parental home and live with his bride, either in the house of her parents or in a dwelling nearby, the rule of residence is called matrilocal. If the bride regularly removes . . . patrilocal . . . When a newly wedded couple . . . establishes a domicile independent of the location of the parental home of either partner . . . neolocal.'[55] Surveying a sample of 171 human societies, G. P. Murdock found that 101 had patrilocal systems, 24 had matrilocal systems, 13 had neolocal systems, and the rest had various mixed systems. Thus, a neolocal system such as that practised widely in Europe and the West at present is, in statistical terms, not typical. Murdock argued that 'the shift to neolocal residence results in the emergence of the isolated nuclear family.' Kingsley Davis also stresses neolocal residence as a vital feature of the nuclear family system.[56] This raises the important question of when such an unusual system started. Before investigating this further, we need to stress two distinctions.

The first is between living in the same settlement as a parent and living in the same household. As Murdock implies, the distinction may not matter very greatly; even though brothers live under different roofs from their parents and each other, they may operate a joint economic and social unit. The physical structure is largely immaterial.[57] The second distinction is the one we have encountered frequently, between explicitly recognized rules, formal or informal, and statistical tendencies. Murdock points out that in most societies it is custom that determines residence. In other words, there are strong cultural constraints; people know that at marriage they will move in a certain way – perhaps always to live with their husband's people. We need to examine the records to see if there were such rules in England. We also need to see if there were any less obvious statistical tendencies. Although there may not be any rules, it may be frequently the case that sons settle near their parents, thus setting up a sort of patrilocal system within an apparent system of neolocality.

We may look first at the 'custom' of the society as expressed in formal statements about what was right and proper. A search of

---

[55] Murdock, *Social Structure*, 16–19.
[56] Ibid., 208; see also ibid., 201, 203–4, 221; Davis, *Fertility*, 21.
[57] Goody in Laslett, *Household*, 103–24.

proverbs, travellers' observations, autobiographical and other materials, has given no indication whatsoever that it was considered
proper and necessary for the young couple to move at marriage to the
village of either husband's or wife's kin. Although the wedding itself
often took place in the bride's home, subsequent residence was not, it
would seem, a matter about which there were positive rules. For
example, the rule that prevails in most human societies, namely, that a
woman will leave her village of birth to join her husband's kin, is
absent. In terms of positive rules, the situation seems to have been left
open. This is termed 'neolocal residence'. Though there are no
formal rules discoverable, we might expect there to be informal
pressures leading to statistical differences.

We may make a preliminary examination of these problems
through the analysis of local records. One way of looking at actual
patterns of residence is to find a parish with a listing of inhabitants
and to see how many parents had married children of each sex living
in the parish with them. In Kirkby Lonsdale in 1695, of 103 married
couples only nine had married children living in the same parish.
Several of these had more than one married child, so we find that
there were ten married sons and five married daughters living in their
parents' parish. Thus there was a tendency towards sons remaining,
but given the fact that these parents at the time of the listing would
have had over a hundred married children between them, the
outstanding point is how few had settled in their parents' parish.

Without a listing, one has to approach the problem in a different
way. In Earls Colne between 1580 and 1750, some 947 couples are
recorded as being married. In these marriages, only 183 of the males
had been baptized in the parish, So three quarters were outsiders. In
the case of women, a higher proportion seem to have remained
between baptism and marriage: a little less than one third of those
who married in Earls Colne had been baptized there. But in order to
determine patrilocality, matrilocality and neolocality in a society of
high mobility we need to know at least two other things.

One is the proportion who remained for a substantial period after
marriage – for it might be the custom for a woman to come back for
the marriage and then disappear, or to move away after the marriage
for other reasons. In the case of the males, almost all of those who had
been baptized and married in Earls Colne remained there for a
number of years: only 6 out of 183 men disappear from the parish
records after marriage. In the case of women, the proportion is larger:

39 of the 306 women baptized and married in the parish disappear after the wedding. The second fact we need to know is how many were marrying into a parish where their father or mother was still alive. Given the mortality rates and the late age at marriage, it soon appears that the majority of those who married within their natal parish had already lost both their parents. Of the 183 men we have been considering, only sixty, or one third, had both parents alive or a parent and step-parent alive at the time of their marriage. In the case of the women, there was a slightly higher proportion (124 of the 306 cases). If we now take into account all these factors – the total number of marriages recorded, the number of men and women who seem to have moved away straight after marriage, and the survival of parents – we can calculate the approximate frequency with which those who married in Earls Colne would be doing so in a parish where a parent was alive, and would then settle there. In the case of men, about one in nineteen did so, in the case of women, about one in eleven. There was some sort of bias towards women remaining in their birthplace until marriage; but more importantly, it is clear that neolocality was far more important than either matrilocality or patrilocality.

The scattering of children over the countryside at marriage is clearly linked to two other important features of the pattern. One is the age at marriage. Murdock made the assumption, as do most anthropologists, that at the time of marriage the respective partners will be living at home, and hence marriage forces a move from one kinship group to another: thus he wrote that 'custom requires the groom to leave his parental home', or vice versa.[58] This is a reasonable assumption to make in the vast majority of familistic societies in which people remain with their parents until, and often after, their marriage. An Indian girl married off at twelve in the early twentieth century would almost certainly be living at home. Nowadays, of course, we are used to a situation where many people have left home for a few years before marrying. Which pattern do we find in England over these centuries?

It would seem that with a mean average marriage age of 25 for women and roughly the same for men, the chances that both parties were still resident in their parental homes would be slight. Thus in Earls Colne, between 1585 and 1650, of the 884 recorded persons marrying there we know that 221 were born there. This will, if

[58] Murdock, *Social Structure*, 16.

anything, inflate the number, since people who were living away may well have returned to their natal parish just for the wedding. Within this quarter, a maximum of only a quarter involved both partners from the parish. The pattern is likely to be that they had been away not only from their own home but even from their village, for three or four years, working as servants or apprentices, or in other jobs. With the young persons established in a setting other than the parental one, it would have been an entirely different matter suddenly to re-absorb them into the parental house or village. If a person has grown apart, assumed responsibilities, made a living, made decisions, it is very much more difficult for him or her to return home and become a child again. In such a situation, neolocal residence is natural.

The second feature of the pattern flows directly out of this: it concerns the yearning for independence and the nature of the authority structure in the family, which led to a set of strong cultural rules against parents living with their married children. To live within a parental household, sharing socially and economically, seems to have been something which very early on many of the English disliked. Although we do find such arrangements among the very rich and powerful, with their large estates and large houses, for the rest of the population there is strong evidence of two kinds that co-residence, or even sharing within the same village, was largely avoided.

The first kind of evidence is provided by contemporary statements. That such a 'parent and married child avoidance' was widespread amongst the English in the eighteenth century was noted by Arthur Young, who wrote, 'if they marry therefore, where are they to live? No cottage is empty – they must live with their fathers and mothers or lodge: the poor abhor both as much as their betters and certainly in many cases run into licentious amours mainly for want of a cottage or a certificate.'[59] Neither the reasons for the difficulties, nor the evidence of the dislike of sharing with parents, were a new phenomenon. They were shown in the writings of William Whateley. In *A Care-Cloth or a Treatise of the Cumbers and Troubles of Marriage* published in 1624, he advised his audience that

> when thou art married, if it may be, live of thy self with thy wife, in a
> family of thine own, and not with another, in one family, as it were,

[59] Tate, *Parish Chest*, 214, quoting Arthur Young.

betwixt you both ... The mixing of govenours in an household, or subordinating or uniting of two Masters, or two Dames under one roof, doth fall out most times, to be a matter of much unquietness to all parties: Youth and age are so far distant in their conditions, and how to make the young folks so wholly resign themselves unto the elders as not to be discontented with their proceedings; or to make the elder so much to deny themselves, as to condescend unto the wills of the younger ... in the common sort of people is altogether impossible. Whereof, as the young bees do seek unto themselves another hive, so let the young couple another house.[60]

That it was thought 'altogether impossible' for parents and children to live together in one household would have struck most people elsewhere in the world as surprising. Generally speaking, a young couple is absorbed into the household of either bride or groom. Although, of course, there are often growing frictions between daughter-in-law and mother- in-law, and between brothers' wives, at least such a joint arrangement is attempted and often lasts for a number of years, until the estate is divided and the parents 'retire'.

The popular dislike of parents' sharing with their married children and the difficulties it created are particularly well expressed in a letter from the sectarian Ludowicke Muggleton to one of his troubled followers in the mid-seventeenth century. A widow had encouraged her married daughter and son-in-law to come and live with her, and then the daughter had died. The widow was a school teacher, and she had shared the running of the school with her daughter and son-in-law. The son-in-law was talking of a second marriage to a maid servant, and Muggleton was asked for his advice. He first outlined the serious nature of the problem, 'for I perceive you are so involved and entangled in your estate, and in your way of livelihood, by reason of your daughter's living with you, after she was married, that it will be hard to separate and divide, what is your own, and what is your son-in-law's own.'

This was the basic problem. With individual property rights, how could a system of joint householding work? If it broke down, as it would often do, it was extremely difficult to re-allocate the property. Muggleton noted that 'these are commonly the fruit that parents do reap, when children do live with them when they are married.' As a result, 'I being sensible, and having had great experience of the

---

[60] Whateley, *Care–Cloth*, sigs A6–A6v.

inconveniences of this, by several, it was always my advice to any friend, not to do any such thing.' The reason why 'one house cannot hold two families, being both of one profession' did not merely lie in the economic entanglements, or the conflict between the principles of individual and communal production and consumption. There was also the conflict of authority, the political dimension. It was a basic principle that an adult was free and not subservient, but how could this be reconciled, except in marriage itself, with living together as adults? 'Here,' Muggleton continued, 'lieth the knot hard to be untied, how you two shall live together, and manage the employment together, as your own daughter and you did . . . Now where two are equal in power, or two mistresses, there will be some differences; but where one doth rule, and the other a servant, there is good government.' There cannot be two masters: thus a wife ultimately deferred to her husband, a child to its parents, or a servant to its master. If the widow was prepared to defer and become subservient, it would work, but Muggleton could not 'wish you, in your old age, to become servant to any'. He saw directly to the heart of the two problems which made co-residence of parents and married children so difficult. Private property and adult freedom clashed with joint living.[61]

We may now turn to actual residence patterns. That the upper gentry and above frequently lived in households where there were two married couples of the same family is clear from diaries and autobiographies.[62] But the diaries and autobiographies kept by those from below that level do not show such a pattern. As far as I am aware, none of the well known autobiographies and diaries of the period – Pepys, Josselin, Heywood, Martindale, Eyre – show any trace of the pattern of co-residence after their marriages. Neither did the diarists themselves live with their parents after marriage, nor did their children reside with them when married. This could be dismissed as in some way unrepresentative if it were not fully corroborated by listings of inhabitants.

Ever since such listings started to be analysed, from the middle of the 1960s, one of the most intriguing findings has been the absence of extended or joint households. Summarizing extensive analysis in this area, Peter Laslett concluded:

[61] Reeve and Muggleton, 322, 325, 324.
[62] Jackson, *Thornton Autobiography*; 'Diary of Mrs Venables', 11–12.

in all the communities for which evidence has so far been recovered the presence of children living at home after marriage was even rarer than the presence of parents living with married children. There were three such families at Chilvers Coton out of the 176, there were none amongst the 86 families living at Ealing in 1599, none at Clayworth in either 1676 or 1688 . . . What was true in these villages is now known to have been true for dozens of others.[63]

In Kirkby Lonsdale township, for example, in the 107 households in the 1695 listing of inhabitants, only one definitely included parents and married children.

The English findings are so unusual, particularly when compared with much higher rates of co-residence in many communities on the Continent, that the first reaction of historians was to attempt to undermine them. The most notable attempt to do so was by Berkner, on the basis of evidence from Austria.[64] His main argument was that while at any point in time only a few families would have co-resident married couples – it being a short-lived stage in the life cycle – it might still be the normal thing for most people to go through. By analogy, only a few people are married each year, but most go through a wedding. Obviously there is something in this. Yet if we apply the argument, for example, to the Westmorland evidence, however much we attempt to inflate the figures we are left with the conviction that the great majority of the population would never live with their married parents after marriage.

A second type of qualification is that offered by Margaret Spufford, who argued that wills suggest that quite frequently it was envisaged that a widow or widower would remain in the house with his or her married children. Of course, this is a separate question. It might well be that in order to deal with old people, after the parental generation's marriage was broken, a parent would share a house with a married child, having lived in a separate house for many years. Structurally, this has a completely different effect from settling down together immediately after marriage. Yet even this type of arrangement is less common than we might suspect. The detailed analysis of listings shows that over half of those living as 'solitaries' in the seventeenth

[63] Laslett, *Lost World*, 95.
[64] Berkner, 'Stem Family', *passim*.

century were widows or widowers.[65] It is as if Whateley's warnings concerning the difficulty of mixing two governors in a household continued through life. Far more frequently than a bereaved parent turning to his or her married children, the widow or widower remarried. It would seem that once the psychological, economic and social split had occurred, it was hard to reintegrate children and parents again into one unit. Like young bees, they had set up a new hive; the joining together of a new and old hive within one structure was very difficult.

It could be argued that what is important is not the actual physical residence, but the nature of the economic and social co-operation between members of the family. It is quite possible to run a joint unit of production and consumption with brothers living in separate houses from each other and their parents, and even with one brother living in a nearby town. Orders may still be given by the father, and the married sons and their wives may pool their labour and share the rewards. In such a situation the marriage of each child has a very considerable impact on the domestic economy of the other children and the parents. The important feature is the operation and relationships between siblings and parents. The crucial question then becomes: is there evidence for the centuries up to the eighteenth that parents and married children continued to operate as a joint economic and social unit after marriage, to own property in common, to share labour, to share out the rewards of their work? These are big questions, and very difficult to answer. Hence, perhaps, the almost total absence of historical analysis of how domestic budgeting worked among the populace in general. Here we can only offer a few preliminary impressions.

One critical feature is the co-ownership of property after marriage, which I indirectly addressed in an earlier work.[66] After surveying a number of different kinds of source – legal textbooks, autobiographical materials, the actual operation of property laws at the village level – I concluded that there was a highly developed concept of private and individual property in England from at least the thirteenth century. Although there have been a number of criticisms, no one has challenged this central finding. It does seem clear that parents had the right to alienate and sell their property – it was theirs, and not part

[65] Spufford, *Contrasting Communities*, 114; Laslett, *Lost World*, 289, note 107.
[66] Macfarlane, *Individualism, passim*.

of a shared pool. Likewise, children were not at the mercy of their parents' demands. If a married child died, there is absolutely no evidence that parents in any sense inherited from them, unless a child had specifically made a will in their favour. Indeed, it was a long established principle, stressed by Maitland, that property in English law always descended and never ascended.[67] Even the elderly did not have rights in their children's property. The rights to certain property, known as 'widowright' and 'free-bench', were not rights in children's property, but parts of the parental estate that had been reserved.

In all the litigation over property, in the numerous settlements and transfers, in the autobiographical materials which have survived for these centuries, there is scarcely any trace of a concept of a joint estate between parents and children which continues after the marriage of the children – in contrast to many other societies. The children might expect to receive something from their parents at retirement or death, just as parents might expect their children to shelter, clothe and feed them in old age. But this was based on voluntary acts, not on any legal joint ownership. The domestic economy of the vicar of Earls Colne, which we can reconstruct in detail through his diary, shows how the system worked. Most of the children did inherit, receiving sums of money or land. But at least one son, John, was threatened time and again with total disinheritance.[68] There is no hint in the many passages on his relations with his children that Josselin envisaged his and their budgets and property as somehow linked. He never added up their various properties and accounted for them alongside his own. He never made calculations on their labour reserves and on how they might be deployed in his activities. It is absolutely clear that, after their marriage, he conceived of his own and their economic and social worlds as separate. They might meet for Christmas or christenings, but they were not acting together as a joint business. A similar very strong impression emerges if we look at the account books and papers of others in the sixteenth and seventeenth centuries.

Of course, it could be argued that people literate enough to leave us accounts and diaries were exceptional, and to a degree this is true. To penetrate a little lower we need to examine the numerous court cases about property. In neither Earls Colne, Kirkby Lonsdale nor any other village study have I come across any convincing evidence from

---

[67] Pollock and Maitland, ii, 286.   [68] Macfarlane, *Ralph Josselin*, 120–3.

the sixteenth century that parents and married children co-owned houses, fields or any other assets. The one exception would be where there was a family firm. But such firms – 'Smith and Son' – were exactly the kind of phenomenon that indicates how remote England was, in general, from communality of property. In many societies, every argicultural or artisan enterprise is a family firm, in which all members of the family, and the spouses they bring in, are partners. In England such a situation had to be artificially created by explicitly setting up such firms and companies.

Three types of evidence from the fifteenth to the eighteenth centuries might be used in examining questions concerning the pooling of labour in joint production. First, there are legal disputes in the various courts of the realm. There can be little doubt that if there had been a widespread pooling of labour after marriage, this would have come out in the numerous types of economic suit in Exchequer, Chancery, manorial courts and elsewhere. Parents would have complained about children not doing enough, a brother would have argued that he and his wife and children had put in more than another brother and hence should receive a greater inheritance, wives might have complained that an undue proportion of their husbands' labour was going into educating younger siblings and so on. The numerous records of disputes that we have surveyed, particularly the records of the many property disputes in Chancery, indicate a complete absence of such allusions to pooled production. The absence is reflected in the system of common law and equity itself. There were no discussions in the great manuals of law by Bracton, Fortescue, Coke or Blackstone of the complex issues that are raised when joint production occurs within the family. There were no manorial customs to deal with such questions, as there were in areas like widows' rights. The church courts, whose interests encompassed inheritance, had nothing to say on the matter. Swinburne in his treatise on wills and last testaments does not suggest that children should have more or less because they contributed a greater or lesser amount by their labour.[69]

It might be suggested that the silence was caused by the fact that in practice everyone assumed that parents and married children would work together, the cultural rules were so strong that no one needed to mention the subject, and there was no friction. Although far-fetched,

---

[69] Swinburne, *Wills, passim.*

this is just possible. Yet if we look at a second source that mainly includes autobiographies and diaries, once again there is little evidence of such joint production. Pepys, Josselin, Heywood, Eyre, Martindale and the rest envisaged a separate life for parents and children, with no pooled labour force. The Muggleton example of the school-mistress widow is a partial exception. One of the most interesting side effects of a situation of pooled production is that in cultures where it is widely established, for example India or parts of Ireland, even when a child marries a long way from home and sets up a separate household he or she may continue for years to send large sums of money back, to share a bank account, and so on. Likewise, parents will send money, food, younger siblings or whatever is appropriate when the children need support. Such a system maintained over long distances will most easily be detected by the historian through letters written by members of a family to each other. An examination of some such series of letters – Paston, Cely, Verney – provides no evidence of such a situation. The final type of autobiographical material relevant to this issue, account books of the period – Lodge, Fell, Fleming, Harlakenden and others – tell the same story.[70] A third kind of evidence lies in detailed local records. Through an analysis of wills, which would give various hints of such a situation – for example, bequests to a married child stating that he or she had contributed particularly to the parents, inventories of possessions indicating that certain things had been accumulated through the efforts of a certain child, lists of debts and assets at death which would include the intertwined economics of the children – we might expect some evidence. Again there is silence. Or we might expect to find evidence in manorial records, accounts of the manorial officers, surveys of rights, transfers of property. But in none of these do we come across evidence that parents and married children normally worked as a unit.

I have stressed the point because it is so important in understanding the nature of marriage. If marriage expands the labour force, widens the social and economic grouping and powerfully affects parents and siblings, it will be regarded and planned in certain ways. If, on the other hand, a couple set up a separate social and economic unit at, or even before, marriage, they can be allowed far greater

---

[70] Lodge, *Account Book*; Penney, *Sarah Fell*; the account book of Daniel Fleming is in the WRO, that of Richard Harlakenden in the ERO.

freedom. In this case marriage affects the individual, but does not alter the production group.

The analysis can also be extended to the consumption aspect. Where property is held jointly by parents and children, where the 'name is on the land' and all pool their labour, then the family acts as a unified consumption group. The fruits of all their labour and capital will be divided equally. If one child sinks, they all sink; if one child is successful, they all profit. The same range of historical sources as those just mentioned shows that this was not the case in England in the centuries leading up to the industrial revolution. There is very little evidence indeed that married children, unmarried children and their parents regarded themselves as a linked unit of consumption. Of course, as we see in Josselin's case and as is still true today, wealthy parents might send choice presents from their garden or estate to their children. One might even find a brother sending presents to a sister. But the important fact is that these were presents, voluntary gifts not requiring a return and not automatically expected as part of a communal consumption pattern.

6

Children as Insurance

It is generally agreed that one of the chief advantages of investing in children is that they are secure: 'children represent, as it were, a sort of investment or insurance policy.'[1] Children's value often 'lies not so much in their bringing prosperity to their parents, as in protecting them against disaster', a risk-avoidance strategy that makes absolute sense in the precarious economic and political world which most peasants inhabit.[2] 'The emphasis in tropical Africa . . . tends to be far more on security and on being guaranteed survival through times of duress than it is on maximizing the profit in good times.'[3] There are two elements in this situation. The risks are very high: people live at subsistence level and just a small change in the weather can lead to famine. There is huge political insecurity, disease is prevalent and mortality very high. Children are the only real protection. To help in sickness, in harvest shortage, in old age, is not only a duty for children but a privilege; it is also to contribute to bailing out a ship in which the child also sails.

What transforms this state of affairs is the lowering of the risks and the abandonment of the ship by the children. As far as the former is concerned, it is now apparent that England had moved away from the political and economic cliff-hanging situation by at least the fourteenth century. Compared to England today, of course, the state of housing, public health and old age provision may not have been elevated,[4] but compared to the position in many present-day pre-industrial societies, the English population as a whole was well above the level of meagre subsistence. It was relatively affluent in

[1] Murdock, *Social Structure*, 9.
[2] Cassen, *India*, 73; Caldwell, 'Restatement', 339.
[3] Caldwell, 'Fertility', 213; see also Cain, 'Extended Kin', 9.
[4] See Thomas, *Religion*, ch.1 on the risks.

clothing, in diet, in housing; but this is not the place to document something that many economic and other historians have been long aware of.[5] It will have to suffice to quote some delightful comments written in the early nineteenth century by Cobbett:

> No man shall make me believe, that our ancestors were a rude and beggarly race, when I read in an Act of Parliament passed in the reign of Edward the Fourth [1461–83], regulating the dresses of the different ranks of the people, and forbidding the LABOURERS to wear coats of cloth that cost *more than two shillings a yard* (equal to *forty shillings* of our present money), and forbidding their wives and daughters to wear sashes, or girdles, *trimmed with gold or silver*. No man shall make me believe that this was a rude and beggarly race, compared with those who now shirk and shiver about in canvas frocks and rotten cottons. Nor shall any man persuade me that that was a rude and beggarly state of things, in which [reign of Edward III] an Act was passed regulating the wages of labour, and ordering that a woman, for *weeding in the corn* should receive a penny a day, while a *quart of red wine* was sold for a *penny*, and a pair of men's shoes for *two-pence*.[6]

All the evidence suggests a prosperous society, particularly in that very large middling rank for which England was famed. In the seventeenth century, Thomas Fuller described the yeoman thus: 'he wears russet clothes, but makes golden payment, having tin on his buttons, and silver in his pocket . . . In his house he is bountiful both to strangers, and poor people . . . at our yeomen's table you shall have as many joints as dishes . . . solid substantial food.'[7] Alongside this relative economic affluence went political security. England was seldom marched over by warring armies, nor subject to a particularly extortionate state. Taxation was light, and the lords kept in check. Yet the state was powerful enough to reduce physical insecurity by providing the 'insurance' of a well organized and effective system of self-policing, courts and law.[8] Relative to other peasantries in both Europe and the rest of the world, it would seem that the English peoples were indeed fortunate through many centuries. The need for risk insurance was thus not quite as urgent.

Nevertheless, the world was still very uncertain. Poverty, sickness,

[5] E.g. Macfarlane, *Individualism*, ch.7; Laslett, *Lost World*, ch.5.
[6] Cobbett, *Advice*, 218.
[7] Fuller, *Holy State*, 106.
[8] For importance, see Cain, 'Extended Kin', 10.

accident, and particularly old age, were never banished, any more than they are today. What mechanisms existed to deal with such risks? In most societies it is the family and, particularly as they grow older, the children, who provide the necessary help. Observers today stress that it is the shift in the burden of responsibility from kin to some wider, non-kinship, group that helps to make possible a new attitude towards children. Ron Lesthaeghe, for instance, links drops in fertility in the Third World to the increasing role played by the state and the wider community, a 'greater reliance on neighbours, or organizations like guilds and corporations', which takes away from the family the responsibility for assistance.[9] McNicoll points out that the rapid decrease in fertility in China is related to the growing reliance on non-kinship structures: 'the new structures have succeeded in shifting importance away from lineages and official kin ties and toward team and brigade boundaries.' Thus the contrast between Bali, where community structure has been strengthened and kinship weakened, and Bangladesh, where 'locally defined villages, and administrative villages, all have little role in the society', arises from a falling fertility in one community and continuing high fertility in the other.[10] The anthropologist Fortes has made the same point in contrasting West Africa, where traditionally the kinship group provided the organizational principle, and European society, where a person is a citizen by birth, with rights to support as well as obligations to contribute. Thus the movement from 'family morality' to a 'community-wide morality', particularly in regard to responsibilities in poverty, old age and sickness, is fundamental.[11]

The central question here for England is the date at which the major support in times of risk – particularly after accident, in illness or old age – shifted from the children to other, wider units. Before the Reformation there were basically four main ways of dealing with the poor, including the elderly. There was the manorial organization. The duty of relieving the poor was 'legally incumbent upon the manor', and we are told that 'instances of the observance by manorial lords of ancient custom that each lord should maintain the poor of his own manor occur as late as the middle of the seventeenth century.'[12] A study of the Poor Law of three Cambridgeshire manors concluded

[9] Lesthaeghe, 'Social Control', 531–2.   [10] McNicoll, 'Institutional Determinants', 447, 448, 450.

[11] In Hawthorn, *Population*, 128–9; Caldwell, 'Education', 236.

[12] Tate, *Parish Chest*, 188 and note.

that 'it is difficult to overrate the importance of the customary land law as a method of poor relief.'[13] Secondly, in the towns the guilds took on many similar functions and provided support for their members.

Thirdly, the Church was heavily involved in poor relief, both through the monastic organization, one of whose main functions was to help the poor, and through the parish organization. According to the Webbs, 'throughout all Christendom the responsibility for the relief of destitution was, in the Middle Ages, assumed and accepted, individually and collectively, by the Church.'[14] Richard Burn summarized the situation thus: 'anciently, the maintenance of the poor was chiefly an ecclesiastical concern. A fourth part of the tithes in every parish was set apart for that purpose. The minister, under the bishop, had the principle direction in the disposal thereof, assisted by the churchwardens and other principal inhabitants.'[15] Later many of these tithes became appropriated by monasteries, who added their donations to the fund. Thus an automatic way of raising relief for the needy had been established in the early Middle Ages. In 1391, for example, 'the second Statute of Mortmain ordered that upon the appropriation of a benefice a proportion of its fruits should be reserved for distribution among the poor of the parish.'[16] The Church administered many charities for the poor; churchwardens continued to be responsible for acting as poor relief officers in the centuries after the Reformation.[17] Finally, private charity by the rich, either directly or funnelled through these institutions, was encouraged. The Webbs provide a classic account of how these institutions worked.[18]

Thus, when in the sixteenth century the state started to take over responsibility for the poor, it did so as a successor not to the family but to other institutions: manorial and guild structures were withering, and the Church and monasteries had lost much of their land. Simultaneously the rapidly rising population of the sixteenth century saw a great increase in the numbers of the poor. In this situation we see the emergence of a state system of provision, the famous Tudor Poor Law, which continued in operation until 1834.

[13] Page, 'Poor Law', 133.   [14] Webb, *English Poor Law*, i, 1.
[15] Burn, *Justice*, iii, 306.   [16] Tate, *Parish Chest*, 189.
[17] Hale, *Precedents*, 221; and generally Webb, *English Poor Law*, i, 9–10; Campbell, *English Yeoman*, 329; Tate, *Parish Chest*, 85.
[18] Webb, *English Poor Law*, i, 16–22.

This built on a tradition which, while universal in Christendom, also had a unique feature, noted by the Webbs. 'Peculiar to Britain' was the fact that from the Middle Ages to 1834, the 'unit of obligation' was also a unit of local government and ecclesiastical organization – the parish. The parish took on the responsibility of administration.[19] Earlier provisions were codified in 1601. The central provision was that the churchwardens and a number of substantial citizens should act each year as overseers of the poor. They would have the duty of maintaining the poor and setting them to work; the funds would come from a 'poor rate', deriving from a taxation of all the inhabitants who could pay, plus money from tithes.

In 1662 the Act of Settlement attempted to strengthen the hands of those who wished to prevent the wandering poor becoming a burden on their poor rate. It was the duty of a parish to support for life the poor born within it or residing there for more than a year and a day. Thus the poor were often sent back to be sustained by a particular parish, not asked where their children were living. On other occasions a written agreement from the natal or settled parish to pay if destitute was enough, and the poor stayed where they were. This Act of Settlement was very close indeed to vagrancy statutes of 1388.[20] In essence, from the fourteenth to the nineteenth centuries, the parish, guild, manor, Church and state between them accepted ultimate responsibility for the poor. In particular emergencies – for instance, when plague or fire hit a certain town – then a 'brief' or circular letter would be sent all over the country to raise special sums.[21] The nation, rather than the wider kin, was appealed to.

The problems of poverty and of old age are closely connected. It is particularly in dealing with the economic and social problems of old age that children are valued. In India, for instance, under the mortality conditions of 1961, 'by the time a woman reaches fifty to fifty-five . . . it is likely that she will be a widow and be dependent on her sons for economic support.'[22] It is consequently not difficult to see why children are desired as a support.[23] 'In all peasant societies based on a household economy,' we are told, 'elderly parents depend largely on their offspring for care and sustenance.' Thus we find, for instance, in a Javanese community, that 'in only 13 of 121 cases do the elderly people have living children in the village.'[24] Even in Japan,

[19] Ibid., i, 5–6. [20] Tate, *Parish Chest*, 189.
[21] Ibid., 119–24. [22] Poffenberger, 'Fertility', 142.
[23] Marshall, *Natality*, 188. [24] Nag, 'Children', 298, 299.

'the successful rearing of a large family may continue to be considered the surest way of ensuring economic security in old age.'[25] Particularly important is the degree to which children consider such aid as their responsibility and parents believe it to be their right. Physical closeness is also important. Though money and provisions can be sent home, 'the giving of care and help is possible for the most part when the children and parents live in the same households or neighbourhood.'[26]

The two great changes that are occurring in many parts of the world today are in these two areas. Higher geographical mobility separates kin, and a new morality justifies children in putting their own economic welfare before that of their parents. In the situation of the joint estate, the flow of wealth continues upwards to death and it is the prime duty of children to maintain their aged parents, but the nuclear family system based on the conjugal bond changes the equation.[27] The injunction to 'leave father and mother' and cleave to a married partner is taken as a charter to put the new family first. Many people from the Third World have commented that the most striking characteristic of the Western family system is the heartless attitude towards old people. To take only two examples: 'again and again West Africans deplore in conversation and in the press the failure of *Western* families to take in uncomplainingly their aged parents', or as an old Californian Indian put it, 'we are getting like the white people and it is bad for the old people. We had no old people's home like you. The old people were important. They were wise. Your old people must be fools.'[28]

Throughout the period from Chaucer to Malthus there was a central ambiguity, a certain anxiety and uneasiness, a lack of a clear and obvious set of duties and responsibilities in relation to the old. Two contrary messages were being transmitted: that the primary responsibility of individuals was towards themselves, their wives and children, but that at the same time they somehow also had a responsibility towards their parents. This latter duty was ultimately optional: just as parents had the right to disinherit their children, so, reciprocally, children had the right to 'disinherit' their parents. What is so surprising to those societies into which this view is penetrating is

[25] Dore, 'Fertility', 77.

[26] Nag, 'Children', 299.

[27] Dube, *Indian*, 152; Campbell, *Patronage*, 166; Goode, *World Revolution*, 354.

[28] Caldwell, 'Rationality', 25; quoted in Hoebel, *Primitive*, 356.

the element of *reluctance*, of bargaining and negotiation between the generations, reflecting a conflict of interests. Where parents and children have never broken apart, it is not a matter of choice or conflict. To support a parent is to support oneself, to expand one's own being; it is entirely natural and automatic. The idea that by paying taxes and insurance parents should have saved enough outside the family to support themselves through life and not have to rely on children seems strange.

The ambivalence is well shown in the sixteenth and seventeenth centuries. On the one hand there was a wealth of (mainly religious) exhortation urging people to treat their parents well. This theme appears from the medieval moralists onwards and its very presence is revealing. Under 'Of the Duty of Children towards their Parents', Thomas Becon in the early sixteenth century wrote of the following family duty:

> if their parents be aged and fallen into poverty, so that they are not able to live of themselves, nor to get their living by their own industry and labour, then ought the children, if they will truly honour their parents, to labour for them, to see unto their necessity, to provide necessaries for them ... forasmuch as their parents cared and provided for them, when they were not able to care and provide for themselves.[29]

A favourite image was the stork, which was believed to care for its parents.[30] In the seventeenth century Fuller described the good child:

> he is a stork to his parent, and feeds him in his old age. Not only if his father hath been a pelican [i.e., self-sacrificing to children], but though he hath been an ostrich unto him, and neglected him in his youth. He confines him not a long way off to a short pension, forfeited if he comes in his presence, but shows piety at home ... and learns to requite his parent.[31]

Thus a child should reverence his parent, 'though old, poor and forward', for 'as his parent bare with him when a child, he bears with his parent if twice a child.' As Blackstone wrote, 'they who protected the weakness of our infancy are entitled to our protection in the infirmity of their age.'[32]

---

[29] Becon, *Works*, 358.   [30] E.g. Perkins, *Oeconomie*, 148.
[31] Fuller, *Holy State*, 14.   [32] Blackstone, *Commentaries*, i, 453.

Yet it was also conceded that this duty met with a strong counter-tendency. Both the exhortation of 'undutiful children' and the fear of them are well illustrated in the very widely read manual, *The Whole Duty of Man*, which was first published in 1658 and ran into many editions through the late seventeenth and eighteenth centuries. Children should love their parents – a love based on gratitude for the love bestowed. Yet what if all these kindnesses and parental attempts 'should not succeed to their wishes, as very often they will not'? Even if there is no love, 'the obligation is the same on the child.' 'How therefore can we account for the wickedness of those children, who dare curse their parents either openly or in their heart?' The author cannot explain this, but warns such people that God will bring them an untimely death.[33] One of the duties arising from this love is to 'minister to all their wants under the infirmities of body, the decay of understanding, and the poverty of their condition'. Thus the author of Ecclesiastes, too, exhorted children to help their parents. This should be remembered by those children 'who deny relief to their distressed parents, and will not part with their own excesses and superfluities . . . to relieve the necessities of those to whom they owe their very being; or, which is worse, in the midst of their pride, scorn to own their parents in their poverty'.[34]

The ambivalence towards parents is widely apparent. There was the satirist who described how 'the young gallant bribes him with a guinea to know when his miserable father will have the civility to go to heaven.'[35] Parents were frequently warned to be careful not to hand over too much to their children and become dependent on their charity. Whateley related how 'many a child puts his mother to after-throes more terrible, than those with which she brought him into the world at first. Many a father is in travail of his old child, that knew not the labour of his first bringing forth.' Sometimes parents give almost all their estate to their child, then he 'begrudgeth his parents food and attire'. Ralph Houlbrooke summarizes the work of Daniel Rogers who warned, in the middle of the seventeenth century, that 'no prison . . . could be more irksome than a son's or a daughter's house.' Rogers wrote that 'love must descend, not ascend: its not natural (saith Paul) for children to provide to parents, but for parents to provide for them, therefore invert not providence . . . be sure to hold stroke sufficient in your hand, for the securing of love and duty

---

[33] *The Whole Duty*, 200.   [34] Ibid., 204.   [35] Thomas, *Religion*, 316.

from your children.'[36] This fear, majestically realized as the central theme of *King Lear*, can be discerned from the thirteenth century at least.[37] It was an ever-present anxiety for parents. For instance, a man who wished to leave land to his three daughters in his sixteenth-century will was frightened to do so in case, if his son and daughter-in-law heard of it, he might be maltreated in his last illness.[38] Lord Kames wrote of London in the eighteenth century that 'it is common to see men in good business neglecting their aged and diseased parents.' They did so, Kames concluded, because the parish was bound to find them bread and the children could hence avoid their responsibilities.[39]

The same point was made by Blackstone.

> The abuse of the poor laws, and of charitable institutions in general, have tended much to the dissolution of family obligations. The patriarchal roof is unknown in England. Children able to maintain their parents seldom redden to see them become suppliants for parish, and other mendicant relief. Perhaps the laws which render the maintenance of an indigent parent imperative upon his more able offspring, are too seldom enforced.[40]

A memorable instance occurs in the life of Daniel Defoe. In order to avoid the attempts of his enemies to destroy his estate, he legally conveyed his property to his son Daniel during the remainder of his life, for the benefit of his wife and his two unmarried daughters. The son proceeded to convert the property to his own use. Defoe's last letter described what happened. Speaking of his son he wrote in 1730:

> I depended upon him, I trusted him, I gave up my two dear unprovided children into his hands; but he has no compassion, and suffers them and their poor dying mother to beg their bread at his door, and to crave, as if it were an alms, what he is bound under hand and seal, besides the most sacred promises, to supply them with: himself, at the same time, living in a profusion of plenty.[41]

---

[36] Whateley, *Care-Cloth*, 51–2; Houlbrooke, *English Family*, 190, citing Daniel Rogers, *Matrimoniall Honour* (1642), 92–3.
[37] Homans, *Villagers*, 155.   [38] Margaret Spufford in LPS, 7(1971), 30.
[39] Kames, *Sketches*, iii, 59.   [40] Blackstone, *Commentaries*, i, pt 2, 453, note 19.
[41] Wright, *Life of Defoe*, 380.

It was from such a background, and in directly similar circumstances, that seventy years earlier Muggleton advised a widow to
maintain her independence. Being persecuted for her religion with
the threat of huge fines, she was considering handing over her goods
to a friend to keep for the use of her children. Muggleton pointed out
that

> if you should make over your estate to any friend whatsoever, your
> condition will be seven times worse than to stand to the persecution of
> the nation, let their persecution extend ever so far. Therefore let me
> advise you, that is now a freed woman, a widow, that hath full power as
> any lord in the land, over your husband's estate, for the good of your
> children; . . . so you are the lady of all, and hath the possession of all, as
> your husband had; and for you to make over your estate to another
> man, you will become a mere servant, and your children mere servants
> to another man.[42]

He therefore advised her to keep her property.

This is not to argue that all, or even most, children mistreated their
parents. Evidence from contemporary diaries and other sources
shows this was not so. The late-seventeenth-century *Antiquities of
Myddle* provides several cases of fathers returning to children to be
maintained in their old age.[43] Ralph Thoresby recalls how his
father-in-law decided to 'live upon his children', and hence moved
from his daughter to his two sons in turn.[44] But even here we note the
ambivalence. Thoresby was worried about the expenses, for he could

> by no means quit my father-in-law, who gave over house-keeping, and
> came with wife, daughter, and servant, to live upon his children, and,
> though he sometimes went to brother W's and R's, yet I think he was
> half, if not two-thirds, of his time at my house; and, being of a
> generous spirit, was too liberal of my liquor to visitants, that I saw it
> absolutely necessary to give over wine.[45]

It was often with high hopes that the arrangements were made.
Thus the autobiographer William Stout noted in 1702 that a man
'sent to London for his daughters Bethia and Elizabeth', obviously
unmarried and living there with their grandmother, 'in hopes and

---

[42] Reeve and Muggleton, 563–4.   [43] Gough, *Myddle*, 126.
[44] Hunter, *Thoresby Diary*, i, 185.   [45] Idem.

expectation that they might be assistant to him and their mother in his trade and otherways in their old age. Accordingly they came, and it was hoped and expected by all their friends that it was well projected.'[46] Others were less fortunate. Elias Pledger of Little Baddow records that after the death of his wife in 1708 his son went off to be an apprentice, leaving him alone. He thought that he would 'leave off housekeeping and to live retired in lodgings'.[47]

Even when the father returned to a child's home this could be thought of as almost a lodging house. Thus an old seventeenth-century Cambridgeshire man described in a deposition how 'his wife being dead, and his children grown up, he now liveth as a sojourner with one of his sons.' Margaret Spufford, who cites the case, points out that 'sojourner' has the meaning of rootless, fatherless, wandering. She continues, 'once a man retired and had given up all his land, he was a sojourner, although he might live in the house that had once been his own. There he had, by right, no abiding place.'[48] No wonder that parents were warned to beware of Lear's fate and not to hand over all their property to their children. It was not merely that the children were undutiful, but – more fundamentally – that their duty was not, ultimately, to their parents. They were to forsake mother and father and cleave to their wives. If they had children their responsibility was more to their children than to their parents. This view is held by Muggleton in a letter to one of his followers. Exhorting the parents to forgive their daughter for having married against their wishes, he informed them that 'the law of God and the law of nature doth bind parents to have a care of their children, and to forgive them their offences, and not to cast them off and disown them in a passion; but children are not bound to have a care of parents.'[49]

Many of the problems and ambivalences are well illustrated in the detailed diary of Ralph Josselin. Josselin clearly felt that he would like to support his own father, even though he had not been able to hand over a patrimony to Josselin.

> In reference to my father I bless god to give me a spirit careful to please him so that I had his blessing being a joy and not a grief of heart unto him. [He was] grieved that he should leave me no estate and I told him if he had enough for himself I hoped god would so bless me as that

---

[46] Marshall, *Stout Autobiography*, 140–1.   [47] 'Diary of Pledger', fol.84v.
[48] Goody, *Family and Inheritance*, 174.   [49] Reeve and Muggleton, 348.

I should if need were be helpful to him; tis a continual comfort to me to think of my tender love to him.

He also housed his father-in-law, who 'delighted to be with us until his death'. As for his own children, there is little evidence that he received much material support from them, though he clearly hoped for it. On hearing that his wife was pregnant again, he prayed for a safe delivery: 'give it life and grace to serve thee and comfort our grey hairs.' His general views, which directly reflect the views of other religious moralists, were given in a sermon of which we have notes:

> If any widow have children or nephews, let them learn first to shew piety at home, and to requite their parents: for that is good and acceptable before god; this is pleasing to god ... Now to requite is when that we do, carries a proportion to what we have received. Now what have we received from our parents? We received from them our life under god, and our bringing up, and education, with a great deal of care and labour, and with all love and tenderness. Now to return that love and tenderness to your parents with all willingness, this is to requite them; and this is well pleasing to god. Oh then children, requite your parents for the cost they have laid out about you, follow their counsels, and cheer up their spirits in their grey hairs.[50]

In fact Josselin received very little back, beyond some affection. He lived to the age of sixty-eight, but right up to his last illness he retained control of his wealth and his estate, never fully retiring or handing over to his children. Retirement, such as it was, was a gradual process, as he distributed parts of his property to each of his daughters as they married. He was never left dependent on the support of his children or others, and in his will he left his wife sufficient land and movable property to protect her. He also left 'her dwelling in three or four rooms of the mansion house wherein I now dwell together with free ingress, egress and regress out of the same into the yard ... with all the wood, logs, broom, coal, or whatsoever in the yard is laid in for firing during her natural life'.[51] He spent one third of his total income on his children and handed a great deal of property to them, yet there is no evidence that his children gave him anything, beyond small gifts. They did not work for him, and there is no evidence that they sent back any wages to him. They did not come

---

[50] Macfarlane, *Josselin Diary*, March 1632, 1641, 16 November 1650; extracts in Macfarlane, *Ralph Josselin*, 223.   [51] Macfarlane, *Ralph Josselin*, 211.

back to look after him, though his daughter Mary did help nurse him occasionally.

The degree to which children maintain their parents in their old age and retirement, and the ways in which they do so, are well shown in what historians describe as 'maintenance' or 'retirement' contracts. David Gaunt, who has surveyed these documents, has found widespread in Scandinavia and parts of Europe a class of material bearing on retirement. The earlier automatic sharing of the late Middle Ages was giving way to a more formal specification of obligations so that, between the sixteenth and nineteenth centuries, parents would decide to hand over control of their farm to their children in return for a specified amount of food, clothing, firewood, living space and so on. All this was drawn up in a written agreement between the parties. Gaunt rightly sees this as an important stage in the evolution from peasant, subsistence economy to fully market-integrated, monetized, capitalist farming.[52]

If we compare these retirement or maintenance contracts with the surviving English evidence, the surprising conclusion is that they were very rare indeed in England. We do occasionally find a retirement agreement, but this does not seem to have been a widely favoured way of dealing with old age. Analysis of medieval and early modern manor court rolls, wills, law cases and other materials suggests that while parents did retire, and widows and widowers did maintain an interest in their properties, the retirement contract between two ageing parents and their children is very uncommon.

The reason for the general absence of retirement contracts in England throughout the centuries from the thirteenth to the eighteenth lies in the nature of English family property rights. Where there is 'family property', as in the areas surveyed by Gaunt, an heir will automatically inherit. The contract merely specifies on paper what, exactly, is to be the relationship between the generations. It does not create a new right for the child. In the English situation, where for many centuries there had been no family property, no indestructible right of inheritance, no 'family farm', parents never need to hand over control of their land to their children, and are certainly advised not to do so during their lifetime. If parents wish for an income in their old age, they are presented with many alternatives to the practice of obtaining payment in kind from their children. They

---

[52] Gaunt, 'Retired Farmers', *passim*.

can mortgage their estate, sub-let it, sell off parts. But none of these is possible where children have inalienable rights. Even if it were possible to partly alienate the family holding, the absence of a wide-scale money economy would make it very difficult for parents to convert their capital assets into cash income. Nor would there be the market available in which the food, clothing and services needed in old age could be bought for money. Thus the absence of retirement contracts is an indication of individual property rights and a developed market economy. In north and central Europe, such contracts were eliminated in the later nineteenth century; in England there is no convincing evidence of their having existed, as far back as the thirteenth century. This absence broke the links between parents and children, with money intervening once again. Nowadays a pension scheme makes children an option rather than a necessity, but the pension is just the latest in a line of devices to provide for old age.

In general, then, children were only one of the mechanisms by which people in England dealt with risk. Indeed, children were less secure than other treasures. This view of the value of children fits into other recent work on the elderly. Laslett has surveyed the subject and noted that, while in Scotland a wide group of relatives were legally responsible for the old, in England this was not the case.[53] He has shown that there were large numbers of 'solitaries', that is, single old men or women living alone. We have already seen how, in general, the old and their children lived apart, and how the nature of the property and power system of England could lead to this state of affairs. It is very difficult for two independent adults, whether father and son, mother and son, or any combination of parents and children, to live together. It is not surprising that Wrightson should conclude that 'children, then, were not regarded as either a potential labour force or as a form of insurance against old age.'[54] The obligations to support wider kin – siblings, uncles, nephews and nieces – were minimal. The reputation the English have long had for not caring for their old is thus in one sense justified; loneliness is a price that is paid for economic and political individualism.

It is now possible to see why it was that the central aim of marriage was not the procreation of as many children as possible. Consequently, we may wonder why people decided to marry at all. To the large topic of the reasons for marriage, and its control, we may now turn.

[53] Laslett, *Family Life*, 174ff.
[54] Wrightson, *English Society*, 114, cf. also Smith, 'Fertility', 618.

PART III

THE PURPOSES OF MARRIAGE

7

Who Controls the Marriage Decision?

That from very early on marriage in England does not seem to have been primarily aimed at maximizing procreation is intimately linked to a number of other equally unusual features. These are clustered round the reasons people have given for wanting to marry or to stay single, and the degree to which the choice has lain in the hands of the individual or of a wider group. This is of crucial importance in understanding the roots of the Malthusian regime. As we have seen, Malthus took it for granted that the choice of marriage partner and of whether and whom to marry would be in the hands of the individuals marrying. This is consistent with deferred and selective marriage, and the weighing of costs and benefits of the kind he advocated. Yet it is culturally an extremely unusual approach.

The idea that marriage is based on the personal feelings or inclination of those marrying may strike us as self-evident. Yet the majority of societies would take the view that marriage is far too important a matter to be left to the individuals concerned and that 'feeling', 'emotion', 'love', between the prospective partners are largely irrelevant. This is not to say that 'love' or deep affection between members of the opposite sex are unknown. There is plenty of evidence for these emotions in simple societies, and to a certain extent in tribal societies 'love matches' are recognized as a basis for marriage.[1] It is therefore wise to follow Goode's advice to eschew an absolute dichotomy between societies which base their marriages on personal attraction and those which arrange them.[2] Nevertheless, particularly in peasant societies, marriage is largely based on

[1] Westermarck, *Marriage*, ii, ch. 21; Evans-Pritchard, *Nuer Kinship*, 53, 55; Kardiner, *Psychological Frontiers*, 141; Malinowski, *Sexual Life*, 57, 71 and suggested long ago by Kames, *Sketches*, i, 360.
[2] Goode, 'Love', 41.

arrangement by kin or other wider interests, and the personal feelings of an often very young couple are not of concern. In order to show how unusual the individualistic 'love-based' marriage system was that Malthus took for granted, we may cite a number of comparative sociologists and anthropologists.

Nineteenth-century anthropologists noticed the contrast with their own society. Lewis H. Morgan wrote of 'savage' societies that 'men did not seek wives as they are sought in civilized society, from affection, for the passion of love . . . was unknown among them.'[3] The findings were confirmed by the generation of British and American anthropologists of the first half of the twentieth century. Ralph Linton summarized the position: 'all societies recognize that there are occasional violent attachments between persons of opposite sex, but our present American culture is practically the only one which has attempted to capitalize these and make them the basis for marriage.'[4] E. A. Hoebel echoed this view: 'few people are so given to romantic love as are Americans. In our individualistic sentimentalism we exalt the ideal of marriage based on love – that mysterious psychophysiological reaction.' Robert Redfield concludes that 'not many societies have been able to afford some approximation of romantic love as realized in marriage; peasant societies are certainly not among them.'[5]

The anthropologist Robert Lowie succinctly summed up the evidence. In most human societies

> practical points of view are foremost in inaugurating and maintaining the conjugal state. They eclipse romance not only among aborigines, but virtually everywhere except in small circles of Western society. Romance need not be absent, but it is held inessential for that serious part of life which is marriage. For the Japan of the 1890s, Lafcadio Hearn, himself the husband of a Japanese woman, has made the matter very clear. His Nipponese pupils in a course on English literature were quite bewildered by the Anglo-Saxon novelists' emphasis on love between the sexes as a prelude to wedlock.

Elsewhere Lowie went even further. He wrote concerning the basis of marriage that 'individual attraction, we repeat, is not the basic factor; our own immediate ancestors and virtually every other society

[3] Morgan, *Ancient Society*, 463, cf. p.484.   [4] Quoted in Hunt, *Love*, 308.
[5] Hoebel, *Primitive World*, 214; Redfield, *Human Nature*, 317.

in human history would have rejected contemporary Western conceptions as absurd and vicious in principle.'[6] Furthermore, he wrote ironically, 'but of love among savages? . . . Passion, of course, is taken for granted; affection, which many travellers vouch for, might be conceded; but love? Well, the romantic sentiment occurs in simpler conditions, as with us – in fiction.'[7]

A recent survey of friendship and love by a British anthropologist confirms the cultural specificity of the link between individual choice, based on emotion, and marriage. Although finding slight evidence of the 'romantic love complex' in non-Western societies, Robert Brain concludes that 'the combination of spiritual love, frustrated sex, and marriage is a uniquely Western contribution.'[8] This leads him to pose the question: 'what are the social and cultural factors that have led us – unique among the societies of the world – to marry for love?'[9] The uniqueness and importance of the phenomenon has been apparent to others, too. The literary critic C. S. Lewis, referring to the poetry of the later sixteenth century with its idealized love, described it as 'a highly specialized historical phenomenon – the peculiar flower of a peculiar civilization, important whether for good or ill and well worth our understanding'. Two centuries earlier Adam Smith observed that 'love, which was formerly a ridiculous passion, became more grave and respectable. As a proof of this it is worth our observation that no ancient tragedy turned on love, whereas it is now more respectable and influences all the public entertainments.'[10]

These generalizations were based on contrasts between living in a society which took love between courting couples to be the ultimate basis of marriage, and accounts of societies where marriages were arranged by parents and wider kin. Whether in Hindu India, in New Guinea, amongst Brazilian tribes, in parts of Africa or in parts of continental Europe until recently, it was usually found that marriages were arranged *for* individuals.[11] Although she herself was put under great pressure by her parents in the question of marriage, Lady Wortley Montagu was aware of a huge contrast in the early eighteenth century between the relative importance in England of the future couple's feelings and the situation in the arranged marriage society of

[6] Lowie, *Social Organization*, 220, 95.   [7] Quoted in Goode, 'Love', 40.
[8] Brain, *Friends and Lovers*, 222ff.   [9] Ibid., 245.
[10] Lewis, *Allegory*, 360; Smith quoted in Radcliffe-Brown, *African Kinship*, 45.
[11] Von Furer-Haimendorf, *Merit, 153; Mead, New Guinea*, 133; Chagnon, *Fierce People*, 69; Little, 'Modern Marriage', 422; Friedl, *Vasilika*, 56–7.

Turkey, which she visited with her husband. While even in France it was 'a species of indelicacy' for a 'young lady to interfere, or claim a right of choice' in marriage, the situation was far more extreme among the Armenians in Turkey. There they are 'always promised very young; but the espoused never see one another till three days after their marriage.'[12] As another eighteenth-century writer noted, in England the 'strange passion' of love was 'so common, in a greater or less degree, among the youth of both sexes', whereas, it was reported, 'in Africa . . . the passion is unknown.'[13]

The Malthusian marriage system depends on there being freedom of choice by the individuals concerned. The flexibility resulting from a balancing of costs and advantages, which allows marriage age to rise and decline in relation to economic demand, is lost if parents and wider kin are under tremendous pressure from 'custom' to marry off their children, particularly their daughters, at a very early age. Relatively late age at marriage and considerably large numbers never marrying, the two central demographic features of the regime, are intimately linked to personal choice by the marriage partners.[14] In turn, the lateness of the marriage affects the degree of control of parents. It is one thing to marry off a teenage daughter, but quite another with a girl of twenty-six who has perhaps been away from home for ten years.

The shift along the continuum from arranged marriage to individual choice has implications for demographic features because it alters the balance within the family. The romantic–love ideology justifies children in breaking away from family control. They marry for 'love' and can now put their conjugal relationship first, above their ties to parents and siblings. Thus in Africa, the introduction of love marriages gives ideological support for the shift from familism to individualism, enabling children to move upward socially with their wives and children, and away from the parental generation.[15] This change is a part of that switch from the upward to the downward flow of wealth which we have discussed at length. It is one of the features which isolates the husband–wife, rather than the parent–child, relationship as the most important psychological and social bond. The concept that marriages should be based on individual love is projected

---

[12] Wharncliffe, *Letters of Montagu*, i, 19; ibid., ii, 77.
[13] Wright, *Autobiography*, 59.   [14] Cf. Glass, *Population*, 132.
[15] Little, 'Modern Marriage', 416, 415.

in education and in the media all over the Third World nowadays, and is very rapidly subverting the arranged marriage systems it encounters.[16] The consequences are mixed – loneliness, frustration, freedom, satisfaction – but the power of the ideology is unquestioned.[17] The invention of the tradition of courtly love, somehow intertwined with love marriage, 'effected a change which has left no corner of our ethics, our imagination, or our daily life untouched and they erected impassable barriers between us and the classical past or the Oriental present.'[18]

It is not clear when the transformation to individual choice occurred in England. A few points are certain. First, there appears to be no relationship between depth of emotion between husband and wife and mortality: although it might be thought that people could only 'afford' to become deeply involved and 'fall in love' when high mortality rates dropped, by any reckoning, love marriage had emerged at least a century before the dramatic fall in mortality of the later nineteenth century. Secondly, while it is undoubtedly true that romantic love as an ideology can be spread by writing and word of mouth, this cannot be the root of the institution. It was a commonplace in the eighteenth century to blame novels for the 'new fangled' views justifying individual love – as implied by Adam Smith. As *The Court Letter Writer*, a set of model letters, suggested in a letter to a person supposedly in love, 'I really fear thy brain is disordered with novels and romances', or as the Duchess of Newcastle a century earlier had written, 'the truth is, the chief study of our Sex is Romances, wherein reading, they fall in love with the feign'd Heroes and Carpet-Knights.'[19] There is no doubt that, just as today television and romantic novels reinforce and spread assumptions concerning the need for love and the inescapable nature of it, so in the past poetry, plays, songs, paintings, chapbooks and ballads did the same. But there have been many highly literary civilizations that have contained all these art forms without producing romantic love. The Japanese pupils who were amazed when Lafcadio Hearn tried to explain English novels to them came from a culture with a highly developed literary tradition.[20]

---

[16] Caldwell, 'Education', 240. [17] Brain, *Friends and Lovers*, 245–8.

[18] Lewis, *Allegory*, 4.

[19] *The Court Letter Writer*, 175; Cavendish, *Letters*, 39–40.

[20] For a recent comment on the Anglo-Saxon and Japanese attitudes, see Takizawa, 'Germanic Love'.

In order to further investigate the mechanisms of marriage choice, which have such a central part to play in the Malthusian scheme, we will need to turn to the historical evidence for England. We may start by looking at the degree to which parental consent was needed for marriage. The initiative in locating a likely marriage partner could be taken by a number of people: by the couple themselves, by parents, by relatives, by friends. It was the young couple themselves who often made the first choice, based on mutual attraction. Thus Wrightson suggests that for the seventeenth century it 'seems reasonable to conclude that among the greater part of the common people marriage partners were freely chosen, subject to the advice of friends and a sense of obligation to consult or subsequently inform parents if they were alive and within reach.' In his analysis of the numerous marital problems that were brought to the astrologer Napier in the seventeenth-century, Michael MacDonald concludes that 'in most cases the children appear to have assumed the initiative in courting.'[21] People might deplore the tendency of the young to 'wholly follow their own will and let out the reins unto their own unbridled and unsettled lusts, making matches according to their own fickle fantasies, and choosing unto themselves, yoke fellows after the outward deceivable directions of the eye', but they were fully aware how common it was.[22] Dr Johnson described the normal procedure leading to marriage thus: 'such is the common process of marriage. A youth or maiden meeting by chance, or brought together by artifice, exchange dances, reciprocate civilities, go home, and dream of one another ... find themselves uneasy when they are apart, and therefore conclude that they shall be happy together.'[23] When the initiative came from the couple, the counterbalancing forces would come from several levels – from parents, from friends, from neighbours and others.

Those with the strongest vested interest in the couple's intended marriage and the most powerful sanctions were parents. Here we come to one of the central features of the English marriage system, which sets it apart for centuries from most other societies – namely, the lack of the need for parental consent. Part of this difference was noted by Montesquieu in the eighteenth century. He pointed out that

---

[21] Wrightson, *English Society*, 78; MacDonald, *Mystical Bedlam*, 94.

[22] Campbell, *English Yeoman*, 283–4; cf. also Ingram in Outhwaite, *Marriage*, 49.

[23] Johnson, *Works*, iii, 381–2.

English daughters 'frequently' married 'according to their own fancy' without consulting their parents, because they were allowed to do so by law, whereas in France there was a law which 'ordains that they shall wait for the consent of their fathers.'[24] It was noted a century later by Engels that 'in Germany, in countries with French law etc. – the children are bound to secure the consent of their parents for marrying. In countries with English law, the consent of the parents is by no means a legal qualification of marriage.'[25]

The difference goes back many centuries.[26] G. E. Howard described the position, according to the law of the Church, by the end of the twelfth century – a position which remained unchanged in essence in England until the middle of the eighteenth century.

> There was no absolute requirement of parental consent or of a certain age. All persons on reaching the years of puberty were declared capable of wedlock solely on their own authority. No religious ceremony, no record, or witness was essential. The private, even secret, agreement of the betrothed, however expressed, was declared sufficient for a valid contract. All these things might be enjoined under the sanction of severe discipline for their neglect; but the marriage, if formed without them, was not the less binding . . . Even the Council of Trent, while making the validity of the marriage depend upon its conclusion in the presence of a priest and two or three witnesses, declined to go further and give an equal sanction to banns, registration, or the benediction, though these were enjoined in its decree. After the council as well as before children barely arrived at the age of puberty might contract a valid marriage without the consent, or even against the will, of their parents.[27]

Thus a marriage formed by partners aged seven years or over 'without consent of parent or guardian, and even in opposition to it was held to be legal'.[28] This revolutionary doctrine – that marriage is a contract which ultimately involves only the couple themselves – is now fully established from the decretals of the twelfth century onwards. They acknowledge no rights of either lordship or family in setting up a valid marriage.[29] This principle, the basis of modern

---

[24] Montesquieu, *Spirit*, ii, 6. [25] Engels, *Origin of the Family*, 88.
[26] Homans, *Villagers*, 160, who argues to the contrary.
[27] Howard, *Matrimonial Institutions*, i, 339. [28] Ibid., 357.
[29] Sheehan, 'Choice', 8.

romantic love marriage, was established in canon law by at least the twelfth century, and no doubt it was founded on older principles of free contract in the earlier Germanic customs out of which canon law is known to have grown.

In much of Europe the force of this doctrine was muffled by the growing reascendance of Roman law. This gave great power to the father, and hence made the canon law of little effect. In the eighteenth century, for example, Richard Burn pointed out that by 'civil' (that is, Roman) law, men under the age of 25 and women under 20 could not marry without parental consent.[30] Westermarck noted that as late as 1907 under the French Civil Code, a son under 25 and a daughter under 21 could not marry without parental consent. He concluded a wide survey of 'consent as a condition of marriage' in Europe by stating that 'generally speaking, in France as other Latin countries the Roman notions of paternal rights and filial duties have to some exent survived among the people throughout the Middle Ages and long after.'[31] In only one part of Europe – England – did Roman law never reassert itself. There the common law, equally based on old Germanic custom, instead of stifling the canon law, lent it support in emphasizing that marriage was solely a contract between the two parties. To be valid, like all contracts, it needed their consent; but it was not, ultimately, a contract that required any other parties' agreement.

The medieval English position is summarized by Maitland:

> after some hesitation the church ruled that, however young the bridegroom and bride might be, the consent of their parents or guardians was not necessary to make the marriage valid ... Our English temporal law, though it regarded 'wardship and marriage' as a valuable piece of property, seems to have acquiesced in this doctrine.[32]

As regards 'wardship and marriage', Maitland wrote elsewhere that

> the law does not go so far as actively to constrain the ward to marry the mate provided by the guardian, nor does it declare null a marriage solemnized without the lord's consent ... The maxim was admitted, strange as this may seem to us, that 'marriages should be free', and the church would neither have solemnized nor annulled a sacrament at the bidding of the lay tribunals.[33]

---

[30] Burn, *Ecclesiastical Law*, ii, 403.   [31] Westermarck, *Marriage*, ii, 341.
[32] Pollock and Maitland, ii, 389.   [33] Ibid., i, 319.

Thus from the twelfth to eighteenth centuries marriage for men from 14, for girls from 12, was valid against all pressures from the outside world. Ironically, it was Hardwick's Marriage Act of 1753(26 Geo.II.cap.33) which inched English law for the first time towards the continental laws. It was at the very time when many commentators believe the major transformation from parentally arranged to individual marriage took place, that under English law the marriage of those under 21, not being widows or widowers, was made illegal without the consent of parents or guardians. Thus it was that Coleridge could write in the early nineteenth century that 'up to twenty-one, I hold a father to have power over his children as to marriage; after that age, authority and influence only',[34] a remark that would have been inaccurate between the thirteenth and mid-eighteenth centuries.

While the law was hardened in England, it was not changed in America or Scotland, where parental consent continued to be unnecessary.[35] Even in England the change was relatively short-lasting. The Hardwick Marriage Act was repealed by Statute III, G.IV.cap.75 (1823), and Blackstone remarks that 'by the present marriage act, viz. stat.4.G.IV. c.76,16, such consent is directed to be obtained; but, although wanting, the marriage is not therefore void or voidable.'[36] It was not until 1929 that the 'Age of Marriage Act' made all marriages under the age of 16 void.[37]

An example of the recognition of children's ultimate freedom to do what they wished if they were prepared to face the consequences is given in the advice which Muggleton gave to parents who had cursed a daughter who had married (her third marriage) against their wishes. He pointed out that 'she hath committed no evil to her parents in this thing, because she was a free woman, and hath had two husbands before, and hath not been under her parents tutoring, but hath been free of herself, to give her person to whom she will, and her estate; nor no others can hinder her, it is all in her own power.' Muggleton then proceeded to point out that the laws of God and those of England 'doth justify her in it altogether'. Thus parents' only course 'with children that are free of themselves' is to forgive them, and not cast them out.[38]

If the consent of parents was not legally necessary in England,

---

[34] Quoted in *Table Talk*, 155.   [35] Westermarck, *Marriage*, ii, 343.

[36] Blackstone, *Commentaries*, i, pt 2, 452, note 15; cf. also Westermarck, *Marriage*, ii, 343.   [37] Bromley, *Family Law*, 24.   [38] Reeve and Muggleton, 345, 348.

neither was any other permission necessary for the marriage to be valid. Elsewhere, the state is often concerned with marriage, and the couple may need express permission to marry: such state intervention has been noted in central and Eastern Europe and in Scandinavia in the past.[39] On the whole, in England, marriage was a private contract, of no concern to the state.

Equally surprising, it does not seem to have been of concern to lords of manors. We have seen that even in the matter of wardship and marriage there was freedom. Again, in many parts of Europe in the past, the landlords have held their tenants' marriages in their hands, particularly in areas of serfdom.[40] On the island of Barra in Scotland, the chieftain of the clan arranged the marriages of his tenants.[41] In England, the situation seems to have been different. Of course, up to the fourteenth century unfree tenants on manors often had to pay a 'fine' in order to have the the lord's leave to marry, or for permission to marry off their children.[42] This was exactly similar to the wardship and marriage system whereby a ward could 'buy' the right to his own marriage from the man who held it. But in both cases, ultimately, we are talking about monetary rights. It seems clear that if ever an unfree tenant married without the lord's consent, the marriage would be valid, even if the tenant was fined or thrown off the manor. Economic sanctions could be imposed, but the marriage once contracted could not be broken. Coulton states that 'by a decree of Pope Hadrian IV (1150) the serf's marriage was made legally binding under all conditions, the ancient disabilities surviving only in the fine which was paid generally in all cases, and always when he married off the manor.' In other words, here was a licence, but it was not necessary. As Sheehan points out, in English thirteenth-century church legislation concerning marriage, 'the role of family and lord was virtually ignored.'[43]

We thus have a situation where marriages needed no consent or witnesses in order to be valid. Parents, employer, lord, friends, could all advise, could put enormous physical, moral and economic pressure on the individuals, but ultimately the simple words of the pair – if the man was over the age of 14 and the woman 12 – would constitute an

---

[39] Mitterauer, *European Family*, 122–3; Malthus, *Population*, i, 155.
[40] E.g. Mitterauer, *European Family*, 122–3.   [41] Martin, *Western Islands*, 161.
[42] Turner, *Brighouse*, 55, 57, 58, 59.
[43] Coulton, *Medieval Village*, 469; Sheehan, 'Choice', 17.

unbreakable marriage from the twelfth to the twentieth century in England (with a lapse between 1754 and 1823). It is difficult to envisage a more subversively individualistic and contractual foundation for a marriage system.[44]

As well as this principle there was an equally important and complementary one – namely, that a marriage, like any other contract, was not valid *without* the free consent of the partners to the contract themselves. All that was needed for a valid marriage was a 'full, free and mutual consent'[45] but without such consent there was no marriage. In other words, while children did not need parental consent, parents had to have that of children. Such was the law in the eighteenth century, and it was widely recognized.

The New Whole Duty of Man was unequivocal about children's rights and duties. When a parent 'will enjoin a child, upon mere motives of advantage, to marry, where there is no foundation of love, nor prospect of content; it is hardly to be thought, that such instances are to be complied with.' Thus, if 'parents offer to their children what they cannot possibly like, and what all considerate people cannot but disapprove, there is no doubt to be made, but that, in such a case, children may refuse; and if their refusal be made with decency and humility, that it will not fall under the head of sinful disobedience.'[46] Such refusal made the marriage impossible. Dr Johnson admitted that certain parents seemed to think they had a right to dictate their daughters' marriages, but he firmly rejected the idea. 'There wanders about the world a wild notion which extends over marriage more than over any other transaction. If Miss . . . followed a trade, would it be said that she was bound in conscience to give or refuse credit at her father's choice?'[47] Boswell noted that 'at Streatham, on Monday, March 29 (1779), at breakfast, he maintained, that a father had no right to control the inclinations of his daughter in marriage'; in fact, what right there is is only conditional and not absolute. 'The parent's moral right can arise only from his kindness, and his civil right only from his money.'[48]

If we go back two centuries to the early sixteenth century, we find the same legal and moral position. Thus Thomas Becon thought that

[44] Bromley, *Family Law*, 24–5. [45] *A Treatise of Feme Coverts*, 25.
[46] *The New Whole Duty*, 202–3.
[47] Hill, *Life of Johnson*, iii, 377, note 3 quoting *Piozzi Letters*.
[48] Ibid., iii, 377.

it was necessary for children to give consent. It is for this reason that at the start of the marriage ceremony each person is asked solemnly, 'Wilt thou have this woman [man] to be thy wedded wife [husband]?' If either of the partners says no, then the marriage service cannot proceed. Mutual consent is central: people cannot be married in their absence or without making such a statement. Marriage by proxy was only allowed if one of the partners was abroad: thus a person resident in England 'may validly contract a marriage by proxy in a country the law of which permits such marriages'.[49] After the declaration of consent, it is time for each in turn to plight their troth, each taking his or her individual decision to enter holy matrimony. Such formal instituted acceptance was paralleled in more informal customs. In Yorkshire in the mid-seventeenth century we are told that when the bride was dressed and ready to go to church, the bridegroom arrived and said publicly, 'Mistress, I hope you are willing', or else kissed her in front of assembled neighbours and family.[50] These public occasions could also be used by either partner to halt the proceedings, a fact illustrated by a contemporary seventeenth-century joke: 'Two being a marrying, the priest said to the man – dost thou take this woman to thy wedded wife? Yes, then he said to her wilt thou have this man to thy wedded husband? No. What do you here then? Because (quoth she) I have told my friends so often enough; and now come to tell you.'[51]

The medieval position has already been partly described by Howard. Michael Sheehan has pointed out that the consent of the partners was necessary from the twelfth century onwards.[52] Likewise, Christopher Brooke has shown that while it is generally believed that freedom of marriage is a relatively recent invention, the right of children to make the choice is upheld by the Council of Westminster in 1175, which repeated an earlier form stating that 'where there is no consent, there is no marriage.' Indeed, Brooke argues, 'the idea of consent and the kernel of choice it contains, was spread about in the twelfth century in a way, and to a degree, that was extremely unusual in the early Middle Ages.'[53] Sheehan sees this as a new and revolutionary theory of marriage. In the works of the twelfth century,

---

[49] Becon, *Works*, 372; Bromley, *Family Law*, 19.

[50] Best, *Rural Economy*, 117.   [51] Fleming, 'Notebook', fol.12v.

[52] Sheehan, 'Choice', 7, 32.

[53] Brooke, 'Marriage', 15; Outhwaite, *Marriage*, 28; Brooke, 'Marriage', 19.

he states, 'a theory of marital consent was elaborated, the practical implications of which were to have immense social consequences.' This was the spread of a 'revolutionary theory of marriage', carried by instruments which gave expression to 'the new theory'.[54]

While agreeing with Sheehan as to the importance and explosive consequences of such a view, we should note that he offers no explanation of how it was suddenly 'invented'. In view of this, it seems plausible to suggest that what was now elaborated was not new at all, but rather the strengthening and dissemination of an older view that we find, for example, several centuries earlier in the Anglo-Saxon law codes. This was noticed long ago by Westermarck, who provides the clue to the origins of this 'revolutionary' view.

> Canon Law adopted the principle that no marriage can be concluded without the consent of the persons who marry ... An edict of Clothaire I in 560 prohibited the forcing of women to marry against their will. According to the Laws of Cnut, no woman or girl could be compelled to marry a man whom she disliked. In an Anglo-Saxon betrothal formula from the tenth century the girl's consent is unconditionally required. And various early Teutonic law-books in continental countries likewise prohibited the forcing of a woman into marriage against her will.[55]

Westermarck cites his authorities, and his view is confirmed by more recent work on Anglo-Saxon England. For example, Dorothy Whitelock notes that before the end of the Anglo-Saxon period, 'the law states categorically: "No woman or maiden shall ever be forced to marry one whom she dislikes, nor be sold for money."'[56] There may or may not have been a temporary change for a short period after the Norman Conquest, but by the later twelfth century the necessity of consent was reinstated. It has remained present ever since in England, a deep and ultimately unbridgeable obstacle to arranged marriage.

While the broad legal rules of the game thus favoured the children, nonetheless huge pressures were exerted on them by those who took an interest in their lives. To this *de facto* situation we now need to turn in order to survey the long battle between personal inclination on the part of children, and the interests of their parents and friends.

---

[54] Sheehan, 'Choice', 7, 32.   [55] Westermarck, *Marriage*, ii, 338–9.
[56] Whitelock, *English Society*, 151.

The relative rights and power of children have been a matter of constant discussion over the centuries. It was a widespread view that although the consent of parents was not strictly necessary for marriage, it was the duty of a child to attempt to obtain it, if at all possible. If parents did not have a moral right to advise their children, they often had the economic and social power to influence their children's decisions. Such power varied enormously according to the age, gender and birth position of the children. Older children tended to be more difficult to control than young ones, boys less controllable than girls, first-born children more dependent on their parents. The nature and size of the resources controlled by parents also influenced the situation. Large landholders obviously had far more power than the parents of children who had gone into a craft apprenticeship or wage labour. For most of the period the ideal for the middling ranks seems to have been for parents to advise the children and to suggest a range of possible partners, delimiting a field of eligibles and making sure that passion did not lead children to 'throw themselves away', 'ruin themselves', or in any way cross those invisible status lines which were so important. Just as today parents may attempt to introduce their children to suitable partners, and dissuade them from unsuitable ones, so it was in the past.

The delicate compromise was beautifully illustrated in a metaphor by Fuller in the middle of the seventeenth century. The 'good child' in marriage 'first and last consults with his father: when propounded, when concluded. He best bowls at the mark of his own contentment, who besides the aim of his own eye, is directed by his father, who is to give him the ground.'[57] The sort of advice about the ground that parents could offer is illustrated in the prudent suggestions of Dudley Ryder's father to his love-struck son in 1714.

> My father was then very sensible of my passion and told me the inconvenience of marrying so soon out of business, and besides said her fortune could not be anything considerable, a £1,000 or £1,500 would be the most could be expected. Besides her family was nothing, could bring me no acquaintance nor friends that could serve me in my business. That her father was nothing but a common ordinary tailor at first, but by great industry arrived at something considerable. He might be worth 5 or £6,000 but hardly more. As for Mrs Marshall, she was agreeable but nothing extraordinary.

[57] Fuller, *Holy State*, 14.

Having pointed out the costs and disadvantages, Ryder's father continued, 'if I was so deeply engaged in love as to interrupt me in my study or that I could not be easy without her, he could freely consent to my marrying of her, and would go himself to Mr Marshall and make up the match.' This approach had a salutary effect on Ryder, who suddenly discovered that he was 'in hopes to be able to overcome my passion', which he duly did.[58]

Just as children were warned not to upset the delicate balance by marrying without consulting their parents, there was an equally old and vocal tradition of criticizing those parents who took too much power into their own hands. The warnings were widespread in eighteenth-century aphorisms: 'that man that is against his sons and daughters to marry, has sons and daughters that wish their father's death.' 'The reason why your Great Folks seldom like the Persons they marry is because they seldom marry the Persons they like.' Their motives were 'the raising of an Estate, instead of Children, or the clearing off some heavy Mortgage; that's all'. Such marriages were 'often made up without Courtship, or even seeing the party'. Yet 'every parent that disposes of a daughter in Wedlock' was counselled to 'fairly ask himself this Question: whether he is not more careful to lay the foundation of her happiness when she becomes a widow, than while she continues a wife.' The barbarous practices of the wealthy were disparagingly contrasted with the majority of the population: 'it is your common people make the happiest marriages: for they marry purely for love and for nothing else.'[59] As Dr Buchan explained in his textbook on medicine, 'love is perhaps the strongest of all the passions', yet 'there is no passion with which people are so ready to tamper as love, although none is more dangerous.' Parents should therefore be very careful. 'The first thing which parents ought to consult in disposing their children in marriage, is certainly their inclinations. Were due regard always paid to these, there would be fewer unhappy couples, and parents would not have so often cause to repent the severity of their conduct, after a ruined constitution, a lost character, or a distracted mind, has shewn them their mistake.'[60] It might be thought, if we were to restrict ourselves to the eighteenth century, that this was the upsurge of criticism that would lead to a

---

[58] Matthews, *Ryder Diary*, 326–7.
[59] *Characters*, 169, 191, 191, 191, 194, 191.
[60] Buchan, *Domestic Medicine*, 119–20.

new individualistic, affective marriage regime. Yet we can pursue these criticisms further back in time.

We might think it was the Jacobeans who originated the criticism. Certainly there were many who deplored forced marriage and warned of its consequences. Fuller told the 'good parent' that when dealing with a child he 'moves him to marriage rather by argument drawn from his good, than his own authority. It is a style too Princely for a parent herein, to will and command, but sure he may will and desire. Affections like the conscience are rather to be led than drawn; and 'tis to be feared, they that marry where they do not love, will love where they do not marry.'[61] Milton wrote angrily, 'as for the custom that some parents and guardians have of forcing marriages, it will be better to say nothing of such a savage inhumanity.'[62] Half a century earlier Angel Day printed a model letter dissuading a man from marrying off his daughter to a rich old miser, pairing the 'matchless favour of so young and dainty a piece, to the filthy tawny deformed and unseemly hue, of so wretched and ill favoured a creature' – an activity 'so repugnant to reason, or any manner of considerate and sage advisement.'[63] George Whetstone wrote:

> I cry out upon forcement in Marriage, as the extremest bondage that is ... the father thinks he hath a happy purchase, if he get a rich young ward to match with his daughter: but God he knows, and the unfortunate couple often feel that he buyeth sorrow to his child, slander to himself and perchance the ruin of an ancient gentleman's house by the riot of the son in law not loving his wife.[64]

Philip Stubbes, with characteristic exaggeration, attacked the practice whereby 'little infants, in swaddling clouts, are often married by their ambitious parents and friends, when they know neither good nor evil, and this is the *origins* of much wickedness.'[65]

The *Tell-Trothes New-Yeares Gift* of 1593 put in a particularly passionate plea for consideration by parents. The author set out to analyse why so many marriages were filled with jealousy and strife. The first cause was forced marriages. Such marriages were constrained, 'when as parents do by compulsion couple two bodies, neither respecting the joining of their hearts, nor having any care of

---

[61] Fuller, *Holy State*, 12. [62] Milton, *Works*, iii, 210.
[63] Day, *Secretorie*, 144, 143. [64] Campbell, *English Yeoman*, 284.
[65] Stubbes, *Anatomie*, fol.55.

the continuance of their welfare, but more regarding the linking of wealth and money together, than of love with honesty.' 'What is the cause of so many household breaches, divorcements, and continual discontentments,' the author continued, but 'unnatural disagreements by unmutual contracts?' The birds and beasts are free to choose their mates, and 'only man is injurious unto himself, by unnatural usage of his dearest blood.' For parents 'do not match them with the mates their children's eyes have chosen, but with the men their own greedy desire have found out: little fore-thinking of their childrens after-grieving and their own repenting'. The solution propounded is the same balance of interests: 'it is most requisite that the children should have their free liberty in liking, as the fathers have had theirs in choosing. For as those matches are best, where there is a mutual agreement between parents and their children, so do those for the most part love best, that have the privilege of choosing for themselves.'[66]

Forty years earlier the same advice was offered by Becon. In the instructional catechism given by a father to his son the father asks, 'ought not the consent of the children also to be considered in this behalf no less than the authority of the parents?', to which the son replies, 'God forbid else!' The son proceeds to explain how Rebecca was asked whether she wished to marry Isaac. 'Here see we, that though the authority of the parents be great over their children, yet in the matter of marriage the consent of the children may not be neglected.' Parents must not abuse their authority and must act with the 'good-will and consent of the children, to whom the matter chiefly pertain'. The father then explains that 'some parents greatly abuse their authority, while they sell their children to other for to be married for worldly gain and lucre, even as the grazier selleth his oxen to the butcher to be slain.' The son replies in horror, 'these be wicked parents, and marriages thus made for the most part have never good success, as experience daily teacheth.'[67]

It seems likely that this theme was already old when Becon took it up. In a survey of literary advice on marriage, Kathleen Davies has shown that there was very little new in the post-Reformation or Puritan advice on marriage in England. The two novelties she locates regarded the rating of celibacy and the possibility of divorce with remarriage. Regarding consent, in the stress on choice by partners

---

[66] Furnivall, *Tell-Trothes*, 5, 6, 7. [67] Becon, *Works*, 372.

qualified by parental advice there is no marked change caused by the Reformation.[68] The theme is taken up by Langland in the later fourteenth century: marriages should be based on a combination of father's will, friends' counsel and the individual's assent.[69] It would be possible to go back further. In his *Handlyng Synne* Robert Mannyng translated an English work written in the reign of Edward I, in which child marriages were condemned as an 'outrage' from which would come 'great folly'. When children wedded in this way grew up and the wealth that prompted the wedding was spent, all was 'sorrow and care', for 'love' and goods were all gone.[70] The jaunty attitude of the children was nicely expressed in a late-thirteenth-century poem.[71]

> You seem indeed to be a scholar,
> You speak so soft and still;
> For love of me you never shall
> Endure such pain and ill.
> Father, mother and all my kin
> Shall never thwart my will;
> So you be mine, an I'll be yours,
> And all your joy fulfil.

The insistent criticism from the earliest sources up to the end of the nineteenth century arose out of the potential conflict of interests of the generations. Ultimately it was the children who would have to live together, but parents often felt they knew best and that children should be directed on how to make the most of opportunities that the parents themselves had partly created. The tensions were especially prevalent in the best recorded and most wealthy families, from whom stem almost all our personal records. In the balance of tension between individual emotion (psychology) and long-term interests (economics), the balance favoured the children of the middling to poor most, and the parents of the rich. It is obvious that 'noble or upper strata will maintain stricter control over love and courtship behaviour than lower strata',[72] but from top to bottom there was a perennial conflict between interest and emotion over these five centuries.

Much of the greatest literature – poetry, novels and plays – was

---

[68] See K.Davies in Outhwaite, *Marriage*.   [69] Homans, *Villagers*, 160.
[70] Homans, *Villagers*, 163.   [71] *Medieval English Verse*, 212.
[72] As Goode, 'Love', 46.

generated by this very tension. Though often accord would be reached, there was also bound to be endless failure in bargaining. As the eighteenth-century doctor, Buchan, pointed out, 'an advantageous match is the constant aim of parents; while their children often suffer a real martyrdom betwixt their inclinations and duty.'[73] Whichever group took the initiative, there was a danger that the other would disagree. 'When a couple have agreed to go together, the parents are generally against it. When the parents make up the match, they are married most commonly against both their consent.'[74] Naturally, the records tend to be filled with cases where there was tension, and thus exaggerate the difficulties. It is worth looking briefly at a few examples to show the system we have been describing bearing on particular people's lives.

At the level of the gentry, one of the earlier accounts is in the Paston letters of the fifteenth century. These letters are often taken as evidence of simple arranged marriage. Yet it is worth noting that in one case a son married without his mother's knowledge, apologizing after the marriage for not having introduced his bride to her before. In another instance a woman resolutely refused a suitor offered to her. In a third, a girl became secretly engaged, for love, to her father's bailiff. The parents tried every pressure to break up what they considered an unsuitable love match, beating the girl and finally expelling her from the house. Yet the couple prevailed, were supported by the bishop, and the marriage was effected. The bailiff continued to be employed.[75]

Letters and autobiographies begin to be common in the seventeenth century, and here we find a wide range of responses from children. Alice Thornton married in accordance with her mother's request, though it was 'contrary to my own inclination', while Sir Simonds D'Ewes recorded that 'I was motioned by my father to a match that liked me not, which I with thanks for his love refusing, like a most loving father he pressed me no further.'[76] Lucy Hutchinson, writing about her mother, described how she was much perplexed because 'her mother and friends had a great desire she should marry, and were displeased that she refused many offers which they thought advantageous enough; she was obedient, loath to displease them, but

---

[73] Buchan, *Domestic Medicine*, 120.   [74] *Characters*, 170.

[75] Bennett, *Pastons*, 36; Gairdner, *Paston Letters*, iii, 120; ibid., ii, 351, 363.

[76] Jackson, *Thornton Autobiography*, 62; Bourcier, *D'Ewes Diary*, 171.

more herself, in marrying such as she could find no inclination to.' Lucy's father had been in an equally difficult predicament. He had fallen in love with Lucy's mother and decided to tell his father. But his father 'had concluded another treaty, before he knew his son's inclinations were this way fixed, with a party in many things much more advantageable for his family, and more worthy of his liking.' However, his father 'was no less honourably indulgent to his son's affection, than the son was strict in the observance of his duty', and Lucy's parents were duly married.[77]

Thomas Isham's journal records several cases of elopement and marriage without permission, including the fourteen-year-old son of the Earl of Winchelsea who was said to have married without his father's consent.[78] Sir John Bramston noted the marriage of his brother's son with his daughter, a marriage of 'cousins german' of which Sir John strongly disapproved. 'Her marrying without my consent, nay, expressly against my command, was the only fault I can charge her with towards me; a great sin it was, as she herself called it, and expressed great sorrow for, and often asked pardon of God for, of me also, which I fully forgave her, but not easily forgave him, but I have fully done it, and I hope God hath also fully wiped it so out that he will not lay it to their charge.' In fact, though against his wishes, he had given her eleven hundred pounds for her portion, with which the husband had bought the lease of a parsonage.[79]

Negotiations are evident in many eighteenth-century sources, with no apparent softening on the parents' side, particularly in relation to daughters. There were some who were prepared to take a negative veto from their daughters seriously. Thus Blundell was aware that his daughter Mally might be difficult: 'I do not find my daughter any more inclinable to marry than she was . . . I thought it would be rude to let any one come to court her, and then for her to declare she would not marry . . . But if Mr Strickland or any other deserving gentleman think it worth while to try if he can gain her affection I am not against his coming.' His own position was plain: 'I long since told her I would not compel her to marry, much less to marry one she could not love and so to make her miserable as long as she lives, so leave her entirely to please herself.' But she must marry within a certain field: 'all I require is that he be a Gentleman of a competent

[77] Hutchinson, *Memoirs*, i, 93, 97.   [78] Rye, *Isham Journal*, 49, 75, 103.
[79] Bramston, *Autobiography*, 28, 348.

Estate, one of a good character, and a Catholic.'[80] This is a far cry from the more extreme form of parental pressure represented in Richardson's *Clarissa Harlowe*, where Clarissa is finally driven to elopement and shame as the only protection against family pressures to marry an unattractive suitor.

Clarissa's situation had certain curious resemblances to the pressures put on Mary Wortley, later Lady Wortley Montagu. She herself wrote, 'to say truth, the first volume [of *Clarissa Harlowe*] softened me by a near resemblance of my maiden days', yet she found 'on the whole 'tis most miserable stuff', and Clarissa she thought 'so faulty in her behaviour as to deserve little compassion'. Anne Wortley was very pessimistic about her chances of being allowed a say in her marriage. 'People in my way are sold like slaves; and I cannot tell what price my master will put on me.'[81] In a letter to her future husband she summarized the dilemma which faced the daughters of wealthy parents from the Pastons onwards.

I have no reason to believe that I am going to be otherwise confined than by my duty; but I, that know my own mind, know that is enough to make me miserable. I see all the misfortune of marrying where it is impossible to love ... I wanted courage to resist the will of my relations; but, as every day added to my fears, those, at last, grew strong enough to make me venture the disobliging them. A harsh word always damps my spirits to a degree of silencing all I have to say.

She therefore decided to plead by letter with her father, 'the disposer of me', and said that 'in attonement for not marrying whom he would' she would be prepared to promise 'never to marry at all'.[82]

Such letters were already provided in volumes of 'model letters'. For example, the 1773 *Court Letter Writer* included a specimen letter 'From a Young Lady to her Father, earnestly conjuring him not to insist upon her marriage with a gentleman in years, who paid his addresses to her', which delightfully sets out the conflict of duty and inclination.[83] Anne Wortley was sent for by her father, and 'he told me he was very much surprised that I did not depend on his judgement for my future happiness; that he knew nothing I had to

---

[80] Blundell, *Diary*, 222–3; cf. also 231.
[81] Wharncliffe, *Letters of Montagu*, iii, 23; ibid., i, 174–5.
[82] Ibid., i, 189.   [83] *The Court Letter Writer*, 144–5.

complain of, &c.' He said that if she refused this suitor he would never provide a settlement for any other marriage she might wish for, either during his life or after his death. Thus she could choose whether to marry well, with a settlement, or be largely disinherited and marry where she liked. Anne was pleased, though her relatives were shocked and afraid she would 'ruin' herself. She replied that she 'did not love' her father's choice. 'They made answer, they found no necessity for loving; if I lived well with him, that was all that was required of me.' She then told her father, who said he would 'confine me, where I repent at leisure.' As for the prospective man she ultimately married, her father warned her that 'he would never have agreed to your proposals, having no inclination to see his grandchildren beggars.'[84]

In the face of this blank show of economic force, with the old conflict of love and interest, we may wonder how Anne Wortley solved the equation. A few days later we have a moving letter from her to her lover: 'I tremble for what we are doing. – Are you sure you shall love me for ever? Shall we ever repent? I fear and I hope. I foresee all that will happen on this occasion. I shall incense my family in the highest degree. The generality of the world will blame my conduct ... yet, 'tis possible, you may recompense every thing to me.' The following night she explained where and when they were to meet. 'Reflect now for the last time in what manner you must take me. I shall come to you with only a night-gown and petticoat, and that is all you will get by me.'[85] The two eloped and were married, and gradually Lady Montagu re-established some of her links with friends and relations. The fear of fathers continued up into the nineteenth century: thus Elizabeth Barrett's letters show her awe of her father, which drove her and Robert Browning into a secret wedding and elopement in 1846, when she was forty.[86]

The daughters of the upper gentry and aristocracy, as we have seen, are at the extreme end of the continuum of arrangement – a situation they faced for at least five centuries. When we move down the scale to the bulk of the population, children seem to have been far freer. Even at the level of the upper-middling – the clergy, merchants, professional men and others who wrote diaries and autobiographies – there is ample evidence of independence.

[84] Wharncliffe, *Letters of Montagu*, i, 189–91.   [85] Ibid., i, 196.
[86] Stack, *Love-Letters*.

In the eighteenth century Thomas Wright described how he decided to marry 'in spite of the old folk's opposition'. The trouble was that his bride was only fifteen. The couple therefore eloped to Scotland. On his return, much to his irritation, he was forced humbly to ask his in-laws' forgiveness, which was given.[87] James Fretwell in 1722 described how his cousin related that 'her daughter Mary (who was her only child) was married, . . . without her parents' knowledge, much less with their consent; but, since it could not be undone, they took him to them, and instructed him in her father's business, who was a tanner . . . I suppose she was not quite 17 years of age when she was married.'[88] Here we see that it tended to be daughters, and very young ones at that, who were still partly under the control of their parents. The situation in the seventeenth century is well illustrated in two sources.

The first is the 'Life' of Adam Martindale, a northern Puritan schoolmaster. His sister insisted on going to London against parents' and friends' advice, and despite the fact that 'if she had a mind to be married, my father was then in a good ordinary capacity to prefer her.' There she met a gentleman who, 'being fallen in love with her', married her, and the couple kept an inn, with initial help from her parents. Martindale's brother was equally fancy-free. Being the eldest brother, the parents hoped he would marry someone equally wealthy. A suitable match came along, 'but when things were nearly accomplishing, he on a sudden slights her, and sets his affection upon a young wild airy girl, between fifteen and sixteen years of age; an huge lover and frequenter of wakes, greens, and merry-nights, where music and dancing abounded.' Moreover 'as for her portion, it was only forty pounds. This was a great surprise upon us, and we were all full bent against it.' Martindale himself was only ten at the time but remembered that he had been 'apprehensive of the difference of these two matches'. Yet 'say and do what we could, he was uncounsellable, have her he would, and at last with much ado, he procured my father's unwilling consent, and married her about Shrovetide, 1632, as I take it.' As Martindale ruefully admitted, the lightsome girl turned into a civil, religious and 'exceeding good wife', while the other girl went to the bad.

Another of Martindale's brothers, 'growing wild, and unmanageable, did to all our griefs marry a papist, and went with her into

---

[87] Wright, *Autobiography*, 72, 90–1. [88] Fretwell, *Family History*, 201.

Ireland'. In the marriage of Martindale's daughter Elizabeth, then aged eighteen, again plans went wrong. She was out at service and 'fell in love with a fellow-servant that was an unsuitable match for her'. When Martindale heard of this he took her away and provided her with 'a far more lovely match, for person, parts, goodness, and estate, and one that dearly loved her, but could not prevail'. At the age of 25 she died, unmarried. Martindale's oldest son, Thomas, also a schoolmaster, lost several good matches through careless behaviour. Finally he heard of a lady in London that was reputed to have £600 for her portion, whom he married but 'never had so much with her, that I have heard of'. This 'foolish marriage' left him with a wife devoid of a portion, and, having married, he lost his schoolmaster-ship. Failing to get a job he returned to the north, where he did not at first dare approach his father 'whom he had so offended by despising my counsel and otherwise'. But a neighbour acted as mediator and Martindale received them back and gave them support and help.[89]

Martindale's life reveals a world where parents tried to advise and direct children, using duty, morality and economic pressures. Ultimately the choice was the child's. In the south of England at the same time and level, the clergyman Ralph Josselin's diary reveals the same attempt at balance. We have seen that the second son and heir, John, married without even informing his father. Josselin's treatment of his daughters is equally interesting. In his sermons he upheld the theoretical right of parents to control their children's marriages, giving his daughter Elizabeth a long talk when she seemed reluctant to marry the man he approved of. He made unsuccessful motions in a match for his son Thomas, yet in practice it is clear that his four married daughters chose their own husbands. Aged respectively 25, 24, 19 and 16 at marriage, they had all left home for some time before they married – Jane, the eldest, for over fourteen years, Mary for fifteen, Elizabeth for two, and Rebecca for six years. It is noticeable that the pressure was much the greatest on Elizabeth, who had only been away from home for two years and was just under 17 when she married.

With a twenty-five-year-old daughter who had been earning her own living for fourteen years and living far from her parents, it was more difficult to exercise control. Jane found her husband in her own village, although a relative newcomer there. The young man came to

[89] Parkinson, *Life of Martindale*, 6, 16, 21–2, 208, 212–13.

Josselin and asked for his consent, which he freely gave, the suitor being 'a sober, hopeful man, his estate about £500'. Two wooers of the other girls came to stay at Christmas, to be seen and presumably approved by the parents. The one obvious tension came with suitors for Mary. When she was 18 a Mr Shirley, son of a local clergyman, courted her and she seems to have been interested, but nothing came of it. Then at 23 she terminated another courtship with a neighbouring clergyman. Her arguments against the match were 'his age being 14 years older, she might be left a widow with children. She checked at his estate being not suitable to her portion . . . he seemed to her not loving.' Here we see that children also combined in themselves the balancing of passions and interests – love and estate, as well as age. Josselin admitted it was 'no small grief to me' but 'I could not desire it, when she said it would make both their lives miserable.' He also admitted that 'Mr Rhea's estate was not as I thought.'[90]

Detailed diaries and autobiographies below the gentry level are very rare before the seventeenth century. It is therefore impossible to pursue the same theme back in time. Nor is it possible to probe with this source down to the level of artisans or husbandmen, let alone the poor. We will have to approach these levels indirectly. What seems clear here too is that parents should be consulted – even if they were, as often, far away. Thus a model letter of 1653 was 'From a young woman in service, to her mother in the country, to ask her advise, whether she should marry her master's apprentice.'[91] As for the suitors suggested by parents, there were numerous model letters describing how to dissuade them, from the gravely dismissive 'From a young lady, to a gentleman, whom she could not love, but whose addresses her parents had compelled her to receive', to the outright abusive 'A guardian virgin, being designed by him that hath her in his tuition for some rich fool, whose mind and body she equally hates, thus staves him off by letter.' The latter ends thus: 'I shall esteem more highly of a wise man in his shirt, than of a fool in his richest trappings; and for my own part I cannot love you, you know my resolution. Farewell.'[92]

There is also, of course, an enormous amount of discussion of these themes in the drama of the Elizabethan, Jacobean and

---

[90] Macfarlane, *Ralph Josselin*, 96; Macfarlane, *Josselin Diary*, 2 June 1681.
[91] *The Court Letter Writer*, 128.   [92] Ibid., 142; S.S., *Secretaries Studie*, 23.

Restoration periods, all going over the same arguments, from Wilkins' *Miseries of Enforced Marriage* back to the early-sixteenth-century *Ralph Roister Doister*. Likewise in poetry and balladry these topics were explored. To cite only one instance, a conversational ballad of about 1620 set out the stages whereby the young couple courted and agreed with each other, then persuaded the boy's mother to side with them, who in turn helped to persuade the father.[93] In general, the nature of the evidence seems to confirm a peculiarity noted by Taine in nineteenth-century England. 'When a young man has made up his mind he begins by declaring himself to the girl, only asking for her parents' permission thereafter. This is the opposite of the French custom.'[94]

Ecclesiastical court records provide further material for the study of the relations between parents and children. They show that children were concerned to obtain parental consent and well aware that aggrieved parents could apply pressure and break up a courtship. Thus one suitor said to his prospective wife in the later sixteenth century, 'Ellen I pray you be careful what you do, and think that it is no jesting or trifling match [to plight troth and then break it] for fear of your parents you be forced to deny that which you have promised, as I ensure you I fear they will do what they can to keep us asunder if their good wills be not first requested.' In Essex, a man deposed that he

> [being] free from all contracts of matrimony did divers and sundry times talk of marriage with the articulate Anne Savedge to be had between them. And did bear her goodwill in the way of marriage and she the same Anne Savedge for her part likewise did bear him the like goodwill. But she would not grant to make him any contract of marriage without the consent of her father and promised either the other marriage upon the consent of their parents . . . and he declared the matter to his father William Reynolds what good will was passed between him this respondent and the same Anne Savedge and desired his good will and consent, and also that his said father would require the goodwill of the said Mr Savedge.[95]

In about 1570 in northern England, a man asked a woman to 'bestow one of her daughters' on him, he 'having good farmhold to

---

[93] Rollins, *Pepysian Garland*, 133–8.   [94] Taine, *Notes on England*, 78.
[95] LRO, Consistory Court Depositions, 1578, fol.56; ERO, D/AED/1, fol.9.

bring her unto'. This looks like the prelude to an arranged marriage, but any such impression is dispelled by the mother's reply: 'her daughter was in talk with one aged man of Mcdomsley, whom she liked not so well as the said Thomas; and therefore, if they break off, she could be content that the said Thomas should be a suitor to the said Agnes.'[96] Another discussion between mother and prospective son-in-law also indicates the way in which the initiative was taken by the couple. The young man declared to his sweetheart's mother 'that he had obtained the good will of her daughter, Margaret Raime; and in talking of marriage, requested her that she this deponent would grant her good will, likewise, and to give her consent.' The mother replied: 'I perceive you are both agreed, and that it was their own match, she was contented, and prayed to God that they might do well.'[97]

If possible, a trial of strength should be avoided. Yet the Church was ultimately on the side of the couple. Betrothal even without parents' consent or presence was absolutely binding. We do not find people successfully pleading parental opposition as grounds for breaking marriage contracts. Indeed, in general, ecclesiastical depositions showed a great deal of freedom for the partners, whether in the sixteenth century or the fourteenth; a study of the Ely register for 1374–82 reveals, we are told, 'little evidence of family control over choice of spouse'.[98]

We have concentrated on the most important relations of parents and children, but there were also others whose 'goodwill', though not legally necessary, was highly desirable. These fell into two categories – relatives and non-relatives. Unfortunately, the boundary between the two is blurred because the word 'friends' was used for relatives as well as non-relatives until the eighteenth century. The 'friends' might include the employers of the couple, their guarantors, their guardians or more distant relatives. As we shall see, such 'friends' were important in helping to finance the wedding, and thus they had a stake in the proceedings and in the success of the marriage. There are numerous examples in the ecclesiastical records of the need to obtain the 'goodwill', if not formal consent, of such friends. Thus in 1592 in Essex, William Peacock stated that he 'has Alice Stane goodwill in the

---

[96] Raine, 'Depositions', 236.   [97] Hale, *Precedents*, 170.
[98] Ingram in Outhwaite, *Marriage*, 48, referring to Sheehan, 'Stability'; Houlbrooke, *English Family*, more generally.

way of marriage: and intends to marry with her so soon as he can obtain his friends and her friends goodwill.' This was put forward to explain his sexual incontinency with her. In the same year William Moyse explained his incontinency with another woman by saying, 'he is most hartily sorry, that he is lawfully contractd and that for his part is very willing to marry her as soon as he can obtain her friends good will.'[99] The friends were especially important at the gentry level. Lucy Hutchinson in the mid-seventeenth century described how 'the friends on both sides met to conclude the marriage.' Yet it is equally clear that, as with parents, the veto by friends was not binding. Pepys thought it worth noting that 'Sir R. Ford's daughter is married to a fellow without friend's consent.'[100] At a lower level, Adam Martindale's son married against both his father's and his friends' wishes.[101]

The popular attitude – that it was advisable, if not absolutely necessary, to obtain friends' 'goodwill' – is well illustrated in an ecclesiastical court case from Leicestershire in 1590.[102] It was alleged that a certain Hugh Harold took Rosa Clarke by the hand and said to her:

> 'Rosa so it is that we have been in love together a long time and have stayed, thinking to have our friends goodwills. But we see that we cannot procure it, therefore let me know what you say to it' unto whom the said Rosa did presently answer 'you are the man that I do make choice of and therefore I do not care for their goodwills or consent, I shall have never a groat the more than this is my own therefore I will look to myself', with which words the said Hugh replied and said 'let us then conclude that when our friends or others will go about to break it they may not.'

They then proceeded to plight their troth. Yet, like the parents, friends could exert such pressure that the couple were forced apart:

> Many matches have been broken,
>   though both parties were content,
> When the maids good-will is gotten,
>   then her friends will not consent.[103]

[99] ERO, D/AEA/16.fol.70v; ERO, D/AEA/16.fol.31, quoted in the Browne Transcripts, D/AZ/1/5, 585.

[100] Hutchinson, *Memoirs*, i, 96; Latham, *Pepys, iii, 264*.

[101] Parkinson, *Life of Martindale*, 212; cf. also, Macfarlane, *Josselin Diary*, 28 December 1646.

[102] Moore, 'Marriage Contracts', 296.   [103] Rollins, *Pepysian Garland*, 232.

Sometimes the opposition of friends was a useful protection for a somewhat unwilling partner who hesitated to marry, who 'under the shadow of obedience covers the craft of cosonage'. The carefree popular attitude was represented by the view that, 'she that will entertain lovers, and repay their courting with kindness, will care as little for her friends counsel, happening on a mate she can fancy, as the horse will for hay, that hath his manger full of provender.'[104] This view is reflected in a pre-contract case in Essex in 1636 where the girl, being pressed to 'yield him her love' replied that 'she would be willing if he would procure his friends good will, and he said that he had his father's good will, but for the rest of his friends he cared not.'[105]

Basically, as with parents, the *de jure* position was that the couple could marry, whatever their friends advised. On the other hand, in the important matter of laying a sound economic foundation to the marriage, it was clearly wise to obtain the goodwill and support of those who might help with connections, advice and gifts. Especially important, as we have seen, was the approval of one's employer. The late age at marriage is clearly linked to the fact that employers and other friends would not be prepared to give their support and consent until the couple were felt to be economically self-sufficient, to have mastered some trade or craft or obtained some form of living.

---

[104] Furnivall, *Tell-Trothes*, 55.
[105] ERO, D/ABD/8, fol. 143.

8

The Purposes of Marriage

One of the keys to the Malthusian marriage pattern lies in the reason for marriage. In the majority of societies marriage is ultimately about reproduction, the begetting of heirs. It is also of political, religious and social importance. The Malthusian vision is only comprehensible where procreation is no longer the chief aim of marriage and where the central concerns are the economic and psychological aims of the couple. We thus need to investigate how marriage was regarded, what people saw its chief aims to be, and how individuals decided whether and whom to marry.

It is again necessary to stress that we are forced to gloss over considerable variations in order to present a succinct interpretation. One obvious difference was between the attitudes of men and women. Most of the accounts are written by men, and we therefore have a distorted picture of motivation. The two major distortions are probably in relation to procreation and status. For a woman, a biological urge to have children may have been a considerable motive. When she chose a husband, a prime concern was that he should be a good father to her children, both in the sense of procreating the kind of children she would like to produce and of being good at bringing them up. It seems likely that a number of women actually married so that they could have children, though I have not been able to discover any direct statement by the few women writers. Working against the urge to procreate was the rational knowledge of the pains and dangers of childbearing. As Peg the maid put it in Aphra Behn's *Ten Pleasures of Marriage*, having witnessed her mistress give birth, 'does this come of marrying? I'll never venture it as long as I live. I do believe that it is very pleasurable to lie with a Gentleman, but the Child-bearing hath no delight at all in it.'[1] Given the high maternal mortality and the

[1] Behn, *Pleasures*, 82.

sadness of losing children, it was a dangerous path to embark on. Thus childbearing was a mixed experience for women.

Likewise, the effects of marriage in relation to women's status were greater both for good and for ill. The advantage might be great in terms of protection and security. As Aphra Behn again sardonically put it, 'he will (if all falls out well) be your comforter, your company-keeper, your care-taker, your Gentleman-Usher; nay all what your heart wish for, or the heavens grant unto you.'[2] On the other hand, there was the dependence and the loss of liberty. Often it is marriage that gives a woman adulthood, but in England it was not so clear-cut. She was already a free and independent adult, irrespective of marriage. Marriage might give her a certain new status, placing her higher up the table than her 'spinster' sisters and enabling her to wear certain clothes,[3] but in relation to one man she had become, as it were, a subject. Cobbett nicely reminded his readers of 'what a young woman gives up on her wedding day'.

> [She] makes a surrender, an absolute surrender, of her liberty, for the joint lives of the parties: she gives the husband the absolute right of causing her to live in what place, and in what manner and what society, he pleases; she gives him the power to take from her, and to use, for his own purposes, all her goods, unless reserved by some legal instrument; and, above all, she surrenders to him her *person*.[4]

Given the mixed blessings of marriage, it is not surprising that there should have been a cynical tradition which suggested that marriage for women was chiefly an advantage because it might lead to a rich widowhood. From the Wife of Bath with her five marriages in Chaucer's *Prologue*, to Gay's *Beggar's Opera*, the theme of 'the merry widow' is present. In the latter, Peachum asks his daughter Polly whether she did not have 'the common views of a Gentlewoman' in her marriage to the highwayman, Macheath. When Polly asks innocently what these are, she is told, 'of a jointure, and of being a widow'. Polly remonstrates that she does not want to part with the man she loves, to which her father replies, 'Parting with him! Why, that is the whole scheme and intention of the marriage articles. The comfortable estate of widowhood, is the only hope that keeps up a wife's spirits.'[5]

[2] Ibid., 17.

[3] Gouge, *Domesticall*, 211; Van Meteren in Wilson, *Shakespeare's England*, 27; Parkinson, *Life of Martindale*, 7; Whateley, *Care-Cloth*, 61.

[4] Cobbett, *Advice*, 167–8.   [5] Gay, *Beggar's Opera*, 64.

Yet, despite the dangers and disabilities of marriage for women, the advantages seem to have been sufficient to lure many of them into the state – a triumph of hope over experience. Indeed, it was a widespread view at times that the demand for husbands exceeded the supply. The Duchess of Newcastle noted in her seventeenth-century letters that there was more demand for husbands than there are 'husbands to be sold ... husbands are so scarce, especially good ones',[6] and a Pepysian ballad of the same period rhymed:

> A young man need never take thought how to wive,
> For widows and maidens for husbands do strive,
> Here's scant men enough for them all left alive,
> They flock to the Church, like Bees to the hive.[7]

There were several suggestions in the later seventeenth and early eighteenth centuries that laws should be brought in to force bachelors over twenty-five to marry, in order to remedy the situation. An Act of 1695 (6 & 7 W. & M. cap. 6) made a start by taxing all men above the age of twenty-five so long as they remained bachelors. Widowers without children who did not remarry were taxed larger amounts, continuing an earlier tradition of taxes on celibacy.[8] This is not to suggest that women desired marriage more than did men. Dr Johnson may well have been right: 'Marriage, Sir, is much more necessary to a man than to a woman; for he is much less able to supply himself with domestic comforts.' But for various demographic and cultural reasons there were large numbers of bachelors in the late seventeenth century.[9]

As well as the difference in outlook between men and women, there were clearly huge differences depending on the social and economic level of the families. The marriage of the eldest son of a duke was clearly motivated by a number of considerations which were irrelevant in the marriage of a carpenter's eldest son. Bearing this and other differences in mind, what then were the aims of marriage?

A constant stream of moralistic literature from the fifteenth century to the nineteenth suggests that there were three main reasons for which marriage was instituted. These were summarized in the

---

[6] Cavendish, *Letters*, 100.　　[7] Rollins, *Pepysian Garland*, 235.

[8] Jeaffreson, *Bridals*, ii, ch.6.

[9] Hill, *Life of Johnson*, ii, 471. On the bachelor phenomenon, see Watt, *Rise of Novel*, 165.

marriage service, where the purposes were explained to each couple. 'One was the procreation of children, to be brought up in the fear and nurture of the Lord, and praise of God. Secondly, it was ordained for a remedy against sin, and to avoid fornication ... Thirdly, for the mutual society, help, and comfort, that the one ought to have for the other.'[10] Commentators often varied the order. Stubbes placed the avoidance of whoredom first, mutual comfort second and propagation third, adding a fourth cause – marriage as a symbol of spiritual wedlock, Christ's wedlock with his Church. Boswell interpreted God as having ordained wedlock 'for the mutual comfort of the sexes and the procreation and right educating of children'.[11] An analysis of the order of priorities has shown that there is no obvious change at the Reformation from earlier times, and that an almost equal proportion before and after the Reformation put 'mutual comfort' first.[12]

We have already discussed the 'propagation' motive at some length. Though it was clearly present in England, it does not seem to have had that dominating and overriding importance that we frequently find elsewhere. The 'avoidance of fornication' argument is a curious one. Few other societies lay such a stress on marriage as being largely justified as a 'remedy against sin', a safe outlet for the inherently evil tendency of lust. Sir Thomas More explicitly assumed that the major reason why people married was that it was the only way to obtain sex, that society and the Church had managed to harness biological drives.[13] This 'remedy against sin' view was not something inherently Catholic that died away after the Reformation. Some of the most influential and radical Nonconformists took exactly the same view, for instance Richard Baxter in the later seventeenth century.[14] People might scoff, joking that with the proliferation of alternative facilities marriage was really a pretty inefficient and costly way to obtain sex: 'it fareth with married men for the most part, as with those that at great charges wall in ground and plant, who cheaper might have eaten melons elsewhere than in their own gardens cucumber.'[15] But this was More's very point. As long as illicit sex could be controlled, marriage would be necessary. Yet the equation is clearly too simple. We have seen that illicit sex increased in the later eighteenth century, at the very same time that marriage occurred at a younger age and

[10] *The Prayer-Books*, 410.
[11] Stubbes, *Anatomie*, fol.51v; Pottle, *Boswell's Journal*, 304.
[12] Davies in Outhwaite, *Marriage*, 62–3.   [13] *More, Utopia*, 103.
[14] Schucking, *Puritan Family*, 24.   [15] Fleming, 'Notebook', 29v.

became more universal. Today there is little compulsion to marry in order to obtain sexual satisfaction, yet many continue to do so. There must be other powerful pressures, other than procreation and sex.

We have seen that Malthus recognized that a number of the major motives for marriage in other civilizations did not apply to early-nineteenth-century England. It is worth considering how far back these absences are apparent. There is little talk of the political advantages of marriage, that is to say, the advantages of creating alliances with other kin groups, which is such an important element in many societies. Occasionally there is a reference to the importance of marriage as a way of creating 'nie kindred', so that a person 'may increase our kinsfolk, our friends and our allies'.[16] But apart from the top 1 per cent of the population, this motive does not seem to have been of great importance.

Encompassed in the 'procreative' motive was the suggestion that marriage had its value in bringing children into the world who might be godly Christians. Likewise, we have seen that marriage was sometimes urged as a metaphor, a symbol, of God's relationship with man, of Christ and the Church.[17]

But, strangely enough, there is little general emphasis on religion. Usually marriage was a surprisingly neutral matter as far as religion and ritual were concerned, a fact brought into prominence by comparison with other world religions. As Lady Montagu found out when she was in Turkey, Islam laid an enormous emphasis on the necessity of marriage. She noted as a 'very extraordinary' point of doctrine that 'any woman that dies unmarried is looked upon to die in a state of reprobation. To confirm this belief, they reason, that the end of the creation of woman is to increase and multiply; and that she is only properly employed in the works of her calling when she is bringing forth children, or taking care of them, which are all the virtues that God expects from her.' As a result, 'many of them are very superstitious, and will not remain widows ten days, for fear of dying in the reprobate state of an useless creature.' Lady Montagu summed up the gulf between this and Christianity, both pre-and post-Reformation: 'This is a piece of theology very different from that which teaches nothing to be more acceptable to God than a vow of perpetual virginity.'[18]

[16] Becon, *Workes*, dcxlix; Camden, *Elizabethan Woman*, 80.

[17] Perkins, *Oeconomie*, 107.

[18] Wharncliffe, *Letters of Montagu*, ii, 25, 26; cf. for another reference, Westermarck, *Marriage in Morocco*, 359.

In Roman Catholic doctrine there were some awkward contradictions. On the one hand, marriage was for long a purely private, non-religious matter. Howard states that 'primitive and medieval marriage whose development has thus been traced to the thirteenth century . . . was . . . a lay marriage. There is no trace of any such thing as public licence or registration; no authoritative intervention of priest or other public functionary. It is purely a private business transaction.' Slowly between the thirteenth and fifteenth centuries the Church asserted its authority in matrimonial matters. It maintained the uncomfortable position that marriage was only a second best, inferior to continence, yet also a sacrament. 'In the eyes of the medieval church marriage was a sacrament; still it was but a remedy for fornication.'[19]

The ambiguities continued after the Reformation in England. Marriage was downgraded, it was no longer a sacrament. Luther declared it to be a 'temporal, worldly thing' which 'does not concern the church'; it is 'of itself a thing indifferent', nothing but a civil contract.[20] It appears to be no longer of any interest from a religious point of view: it is just a contract between two consenting individuals. Yet, as Howard points out, though this was the technical position, marriage still continued to be something more than a civil affair.[21] People were encouraged to marry with the blessing of the Church. Furthermore, the demotion from sacrament was balanced by frequent attempts by reformers to dignify marriage. They attacked as one of the least pleasant aspects of medieval Catholicism its prurient views of marriage as a second-best remedy for lust. While universal marriage was not enjoined, Christians were exhorted to see it as equally praiseworthy with celibacy. Thus *The Second Prayer Book of King Edward the Sixth* opened its form of solemnization by stressing the worthiness of marriage. It was an 'honourable estate, instituted of god in Paradise, in the time of man's innocency, signifying unto us the mystical union that is betwixt Christ and his Church: which holy estate Christ adorned and beautified with his presence, and first miracle that he wrought, in Cana of Galilee, and is commended of Saint Paul to be honourable of all men'. These were forceful arguments to show that marriage was not a product of the Fall and of sin; it was created in 'man's innocency', it was honourable, as Christ

---

[19] Howard, *Matrimonial Institutions*, i, 285; i, 325.

[20] Ibid., i, 388; Perkins, *Oeconomie*, 10; Selden, 'Table Talk', in Cohen, *Penguin Dictionary*. [21] Howard, *Matrimonial Institutions*, i, 393.

and Paul had shown, and it was a sign, if not a sacrament. Yet the dislike continued. What is certain is that the full force of belief and ritual did not pressurize people into marriage. An unwilling daughter, for instance, could not be bludgeoned into submission by religious arguments.

Many people who marry in most societies end up as affectionate friends. But one of the major lessons to be learnt from the anthropological discussions of marriage is that the Western concept of 'companionate' marriage is unusual. Elsewhere marriage is not entered into for the sake of companionship; it is not the marriage of true minds, it is not the joining of two halves, it is not the completion of a search for someone before whom one can reveal one's inner soul, a companion in life, a mirror. Usually the worlds of men and women are separate, and this is the case after marriage as it was before. A wife will remain much closer to her female kin and neighbours than to her husband; a man will spend his time and share his interests with other men. The couple will often eat apart, walk apart, and even, for most of the time, sleep apart. They may even dislike each other intensely and yet both honestly proclaim that it is a satisfactory marriage because the economic, political and reproductive ends have been satisfied. The blending of two personalities, two psychologies, is not involved. Often the couple did not know each other the day before they were married and see relatively little of each other for years afterwards, perhaps even being embarrassed to be left alone together. This does not mean that the relationships in such societies are shallow and that affection is absent, but merely that love and affection run towards kin by blood. Yet the Malthusian marriage system is based on the premise of a deep bond between husband and wife. How early was conjugal closeness important as one of the central features of marriage, and how widespread was it?

The 'companionship' motives illustrated by Darwin were widespread in nineteenth-century England. Later in the century, the Frenchman Taine observed that 'every Englishman has, in the matter of marriage, a romantic spot in his heart. He imagines a 'home' with the woman of his choice, the pair of them alone with their children. That is his own little universe, closed to the world.'[22] The primary desire to overcome isolation, loneliness, to find a 'soul-mate', is beautifully expressed in the autobiography of Mark Rutherford in the late nineteenth century.

[22] Taine, *Notes on England*, 78.

I found companions for whom I cared, and who professed to care for me; but I was thirsting for deeper draughts of love than any which they had to offer . . . I longed to prove my devotion as well as to receive that of another. How this ideal haunted me! It made me restless and anxious at the sight of every new face, wondering whether at last I had found that for which I searched as if for the kingdom of heaven. It is superfluous to say that a friend of the kind I wanted never appeared.

Rutherford later said of a possible wife: 'marrying her, I should be relieved from the insufferable solitude which was depressing me to death, and should have a home.'[23]

This companionly ideal of marriage, marriage for friendship, is the living embodiment of the Christian ideal of marriage which sees as its third *raison d'être* that 'mutual society, help, and comfort, that the one ought to have of the other.' Another nineteenth-century expression of the ideal can be found in the work of the erstwhile ploughman's son, William Cobbett. Of a celibate existence he writes,

what a life to lead! No one to talk to without going from home, or without getting some one to come to you; no friend to sit and talk to: pleasant evenings to pass! Nobody to share with you your sorrows or your pleasures: no soul having a common interest with you: all around you taking care of themselves, and no care of you: no one to cheer you in moments of depression: to say all in a word, no one to *love* you, and no prospect of ever seeing any such one to the end of your days. For, as to parents and brethren, if you have them, they have other and very different ties.[24]

The nature of this companionly view of marriage, and the fact that such a view was not merely a middle-class phenomenon, is well illustrated by the self-educated baker's son, Francis Place, at the end of the eighteenth century. When his wife was buried he recorded his unmitigated grief: 'I had lost, and for ever my *friend* my long cherished *companion* in all my various changes of life, she who had my entire confidence, she who gave me hers, and had loved me most sincerely during thirty seven years.' Writing to his absent son John he explained,

---

[23] Shapcott, *Rutherford Autobiography*, 24, 58.
[24] Cobbett, *Advice*, 200.

> I loved her as well at the close of thirty six years after our marriage as I
> did on the day we were married . . . My greatest pleasure was to have
> her as my *companion*, my delight was to see her and hear her voice . . .
> The only relaxation I really either coveted or courted was her society
> . . . A man may be the friend of another man, a *woman* alone can be his
> *companion* . . . I had no one to converse with no one to talk over as I had
> been accustomed to do the occurrences of the day, no one to whom I
> could unreservedly communicate my thoughts, no one to sympathize
> with me in any thing I was doing'[25]

Even the French, within the European marriage pattern, found the
system odd. Taine noted of England, 'it is accepted here that one
ought to marry for love, there must be a decided inclination', and
almost a century earlier in 1784 La Rochefoucauld had described
how in England 'husband and wife are always together, they belong to
the same society. It is extremely rare to see one of them without the
other . . . they do all their visiting together. It would be more
ridiculous in England to do otherwise than it would be in Paris to go
around always with one's wife. They give the impression of the most
perfect harmony.'[26] Cobbett noticed that 'in general, English wives
are more warm in their conjugal attachment than those in France.'[27]

If we move back to the eighteenth century we find the ideal of the
companionate marriage already flourishing. Dudley Ryder sounds
just like Darwin:

> I wish I could reason myself into an easy state of mind under the
> thoughts of never being married, but I find a strong inclination towards
> it, not from any principle of lust or desire to enjoy a woman in bed but
> from a natural tendency, a preposession in favour of the married state.
> It is charming and moving, it ravishes me to think of a pretty creature
> concerned in me, being my most intimate friend, constant companion
> and always ready to soothe me, take care of me and caress me.[28]

That women were prepared to give such devotion is shown by a
passage in a letter written only two years later by Anne Wortley to her
suitor, who had been teasing her that she might encourage other
gallants: 'whoever I marry, when I am married . . . I abandon all

---

[25] Thale, *Place Autobiography*, 254, 255–7.
[26] Taine, *Notes on England*, 73; quoted in Flandrin, *Families*, 168.
[27] Cobbett, *Advice*, 23.   [28] Matthews, *Ryder Diary*, 309–10.

conversation but yours; I will part with anything for you, but you.' As Locke put it, marriage 'draws with it mutual support and assistance, and a communion of interests too'. There were many instances of this close companionship and love, like the couple described by Richard Gough in *Myddle*, where 'there was a sympathy in nature between them, and therefore they lived a loving and comfortable life together.'[29]

Moving back to the middle of the seventeenth century, model letter writers assumed that the central advantage of marriage was the mutual society and companionship, the identity of interests in an otherwise competitive and individualistic world – in other words, true friendship. A 'worthy wife is a second self', a 'virtuous woman is still her husband's truest friend.'[30] The multiple roles of wives are summed up in Lord Bacon's aphorism: 'Wives are young men's mistresses; companions for middle age; and old men's nurses.'[31] The homily 'On Matrimony' put as the first reason for marriage: 'to the intent that man and woman should live lawfully in a perpetual friendship.'[32]

Perhaps the most elevated expression of the idea of companionate marriage is in the writings of John Milton. Marriage, Milton argued, was primarily created by God to control the separateness, the loneliness of an individual. It was instituted 'in words expressly implying the apt and cheerful conversation of man with woman, to comfort and refresh him against the evil of solitary life'. Thus sex is 'an effect of conjugal love', rather than the central purpose of marriage. The loneliness which is to be overcome is not merely physical loneliness, expressed in the 'want of copulation', for God sought to provide 'for the worthiest part of man, which is his mind'. God said, 'it is not good that man should be alone. I will make him an help meet for him'; thus it was God's intention that 'a meet and happy conversation is the chiefest and the noblest end of marriage.' 'Conversation', of course, did not mean merely verbal communication, but a total communication – physical, emotional, mental – between people. Thus Milton lays prime emphasis on 'this pure and more inbred desire of joining to itself in conjugal fellowship a fit

---

[29] Wharncliffe, *Letters of Montagu*, i, 187; Locke, *Government*, 40; Gough, *Myddle*, 147.

[30] I.W., *Speedie Poste*, sig.C3v; *The Court Letter Writer*, 157.

[31] Bacon, *Essayes*, 23.   [32] *Sermons or Homilies*, 'On Matrimony', 1.

conversing soul (which desire is properly called Love)'. The very foundation of matrimony is God's realization that 'it is not good for man to be alone', hence the creation of Eve; 'that which in effect Moses tells us, that Love was the son of loneliness.' Hence, when Milton elaborates the necessary elements of marriage, he lays great stress on mutual comfort: 'there must be first a mutual help to piety; next, to civil fellowship of love and amity; then, to generation; so to household affairs; lastly, the remedy of incontinence.' The magic of creating woman and man was that they were similar yet sufficiently dissimilar – complementary, each remedying the other's defects. Thus the human soul needs relaxation, which cannot be achieved so well 'as where the different sex in most resembling unlikeness, and most unlike resemblance, cannot but please best.'[33] It was on the basis of these high ideals that Milton advocated divorce on the grounds of incompatibility: if love and companionship were dead, then marriage should not be artificially prolonged. A similar view to Milton's is laid out in a series of epigrams describing the 'Good wife', in a work published in 1626.

[She is] a world of happiness . . . a comfort as exceeds content, and proves so precious as cannot be paralleled, yea more inestimable than she may be valued. She's any good man's better second self, the very mirror of true constant modesty, the careful housewife of frugality, and dearest object of man's heart's felicity . . . She's a blessing given from God to man, a sweet companion in his affliction, the joint co-partner upon all occasions.[34]

Half a century earlier we find in the sonnets and plays of Shakespeare the same concept of marriage as a total relationship of minds, spirit and body, expressed in language that has never been surpassed. At a humbler level, we find women described thus:

why are women accounted weak, but because their nature is pure? Or, wherefore are they necessary, but that man cannot live without their company? When we are succourless, they comfort us; being melancholy, they cheer us; and they are the means to redeem us from the gates of hell. Being mad, their musical tongues chase away the evil spirits; being bewitched, their love charms the tormenting devils; and being swallowed up by the gulf licentiousness, the heavens have created them the help to redeem us from that hellish furnace.[35]

[33] Milton, *Works*, iii, 181, 342, 332, 187, 192, 192, 333, 331.
[34] Reprinted in Earle, *Microcosmography*, 248.   [35] Furnivall, *Tell-Trothes*, 103.

In a more caustic and abrupt way, Stubbes castigated those who took no heed of the dangers of marriage before a sufficient living had been gained. They were motivated by a purely egocentric desire and affection: 'no, no, it maketh no matter for these things, so he have his pretty Pussy to huggle withall.'[36]

These themes we shall pursue further when we consider the central necessity for love as a basis of marriage. We may conclude this brief survey by looking back at one of the very earliest accounts we have of the marital relationship. In about 1230 the English Franciscan, Bartholomaeus Anglicus, compiled an encyclopaedia. Written in Latin, it was the most popular work of its kind, and the first encyclopaedia to be translated into English. Its description of a man stated that

> in the contract of wedding he plighteth his troth to lead his life with his wife without departing, and to pay her his debt, and to keep her and love her afore all other. A man hath so great love to his wife that for her sake he adventureth himself to all perils; and setteth her afore his mother's love; for he dwelleth with his wife, and forsaketh father and mother.

The spouse tries to win her love with gifts and deeds before the marriage; 'he speaketh to her pleasantly, and beholdeth her cheer in the face with pleasing and glad cheer.' He then weds her and brings her home where

> [he] maketh her fellow at bed and at board. And then he maketh her lady of his money, and of his house, and meinie [estate]. And then he is no less diligent and careful for her than he is for himself: and specially lovingly he adviseth her if she do amiss, and taketh good heed to keep her well, and taketh heed of her bearing and going, of her speaking and looking, of her passing and ayencoming, out and home.

Consequently, 'no man hath more wealth, than he that hath a good woman to his wife, and no man hath more woe, than he that hath an evil wife.'[37] Nor was this merely theory. As the leading student of medieval women, Eileen Power, concluded after reading many accounts of marital relationships – the medieval world is 'full of married friends'.[38]

[36] Stubbes, *Anatomie*, fol.55v.   [37] Steele, *Medieval Lore*, 55–7.
[38] Power, 'Women', 416.

Ultimately the Church upheld the view that marriage was of prime concern to the married couple themselves, to be based on a close social, sexual and economic relationship. The couple would become one heart, one mind, one blood. There were, however, two difficulties in pursuing marriage on this basis. One arose from the fact that one had to live as well as to love; in other words, complex considerations about economics and social status also needed to be weighed in the balance. These might well clash with personal inclination. Indeed the clash of economics and psychology, which we have already seen exhibited in the conflicts between parents and children, also occurred within the children themselves. A second difficulty, closely linked to this, was how to make sure that one chose the right mate. It is obvious that if marriage was the most important of all relationships, and unbreakable, then it was imperative to choose aright. The two problems are to a certain extent separate, but also intertwined. However much one might be attracted physically and psychologically, a great economic disparity could ruin a marriage.

The general view seems to have been that the individual and his advisers should try to achieve an optimum mix of characteristics. Although written for the sons of the richer members of society, the advice of Lord Burleigh, in the later sixteenth century, gives a very good index of the major desiderata and how they were to be balanced. First, a prospective bride should be of good character: 'inquire diligently of her disposition, and how her parents have been inclined in their youth.' Secondly, she must have sufficient wealth. 'Let her not be poor, how generous [i.e., well connected by blood] soever: for a man can buy nothing in the market with gentility.' But beauty should not be sacrificed for wealth: 'nor choose a base and uncomely creature, although for wealth; for it will cause contempt in others, and loathing in thee.' Nor should she be 'a dwarf or a fool', for 'by the one thou shalt beget a race of pigmies: the other will be thy daily disgrace, and it will irk thee to hear her talk – and thou shalt find to thy great grief, that there is nothing more fulsome than a she-fool.'[39]

In his advice to his son, Henry Percy, the Earl of Northumberland's principles concerning choosing a wife were 'first, that my wife should neither be ugly in body nor mind; secondly, that she should bring with her meat in her mouth to maintain her expense; lastly, that her friends should be of that eminency that they might probably appear to be steps for you to better your fortune.'[40] The last piece of

[39] Percy, *Advice*, 38.   [40] Ibid., 94.

advice was particularly appropriate for an Earl of Northumberland, for kin connections were of especial importance to the nobility.

On the whole, it was wise to aim for someone about equal in every respect to oneself. Aphra Behn at the end of the seventeenth century advised:

> search not after great riches, but for one of your own degree; for the rich are insulting, self-conceited, and proud. Admire no outward beauty; because they are proud of their beauty, and imagine themselves to be Goddesses . . . Shun those who are much lesser than your self: For when a mean one finds her self promoted by a great match, she is much prouder and self- conceited than one of a good extraction . . . Follow the advice of understanding friends. For to be wise, and in love, was not given to the Gods themselves.[41]

One should seek 'an equal yoke fellow' who would be 'of due proportion in state, birth, age, education, and the like, not much under, not much over'. Thus Thomas Wright in the eighteenth century was satisfied that he was equal to his bride 'in family, fortune, education, or moral character'.[42] 'The happy marriage is, where two persons meet, and voluntarily make choice of each other, without principally regarding or neglecting the circumstances of fortune or beauty.'[43] There should be a balance, in other words, between psychology and economics.

The perfect wife was thus 'fair, rich, young, wise, airy, and hath the very majestical countenance'.[44] A seventeenth-century poem enumerated the characteristics of the ideal partner, a balanced compromise:

> 1. A maid, yet willing to become a mother.
> 2. Young, yet full ripe. A fair one, and yet black.
> 3. The white side turned to me, black unto other.
> 4. Silent, yet one that no good tongue did lack.
> 5. Rich, only to contentment, not to excess.
> 6. Wise, not to teach, but her own wants to know.
> 7. Holy, striving with lover her faith to express.
> 8. Well born, yet not so high to set me low.[45]

---

[41] Behn, *Pleasures*, 224–5.
[42] Whateley, *Care-Cloth*, 72–3; Wright, *Autobiography*, 73.
[43] *The Court Letter Writer*, 155. [44] Behn, *Pleasures*, 135.
[45] Grosart, *Farmer MS*, pt 2, 152.

People were warned to avoid too much stress on beauty on the one hand and too much greed on the other. 'When you marry a woman purely for beauty's sake; tell me how long her beauty will last, and I'll tell you how long you will love her.' To choose someone merely on the basis of a beautiful face is foolish; such a face is 'commonly a lure to call eagles to the carcase'.[46] Fuller wrote; 'they tell of a floating island in Scotland: but sure no one will cast anchor there, lest the land swim away with his ship. So are they served (and justly enough) who only fasten their love on fading beauty, and both fail together.' He warned, 'neither choose all nor not at all for beauty.'[47] On the other hand, it was equally dangerous to marry people merely for their wealth.

In the late sixteenth century people were condemned for an over-covetous attitude. In marriage, 'he that bids most shall speed soonest; and so he hath money, we care not a fart for his honesty.' One writer thought that 'it hath not been so' in the past, and 'I hope it will not be long so', for this is a 'pitiful partnership, where there is no greater love.'[48] Such a complaint echoes that two centuries earlier in *Piers Plowman*, where 'meed' or corruption is reprimanded because she 'is married much more for her goods than for virtue or fairness or freedom by birth'.[49] Often in these criticisms we find the assumption that at an earlier period the balance had been better. Thus a ballad of about 1625 rhymed:

> Young maidens are bashful, but widows are bold,
> They tempt poor young men with their silver and gold,
> For love nowadays for money is sold,
> If she be worth a treasure no matter how old.[50]

Looking back from the middle of the seventeenth century to about 1580, a man recalled how his grandfather, Sir William Oglander, 'as soon as he was out of his wardship married Mistress Dillington, and had not with her above £50, for in those times men married more for love than money.'[51]

As well as beauty, blood and wealth, people were constantly reminded of character and virtue. Women should be chosen with greater regard 'to be had of virtue and honesty than of beauty or

[46] *Characters*, 180; Percy, *Advice*, 111.   [47] Fuller, *Holy State*, 208.
[48] Furnivall, *Tell-Trothes*, 61–2.   [49] *Piers Plowman*, 29.
[50] Rollins, *Pepysian Garland*, 236.   [51] Long, *Oglander Memoirs*, 169.

portion'. As Becon wrote in the middle of the sixteenth century, rather than respecting 'riches, beauty, favour, nobility, friendship etc.' as was the manner of the world, people should consider 'the godly qualities of the mind, the honesty of her parentage, her virtuous bringing up, her housewifeliness, and ready disposition to do good'.[52]

There were a number of scales upon which a prospective spouse was measured. Naturally, a very high score on one might offset other disadvantages. Indeed, one of the most interesting features of the market system seems to have been the ease of this trade-off, particularly as between wealth and blood. Generally it is extremely difficult to make such exchanges: a rich bourgeois may find the noble estate barred to him, just as a rich lower caste boy may find it impossible to marry a poor Brahmin girl. But as many commented for centuries, the older families were prepared to marry off their children to rich tradesmen's children. We have seen this bluntly put by Lord Burleigh: 'a man can buy nothing in the market with gentility.' In Vienna, Lady Montagu found 'the pedigree is much more considered by them, than either the complexion or features of their mistresses.'[53]

Another primary characteristic is the importance attached to the character of the wife. This is obviously consistent with the view of marriage as a central, companionly relationship, in which the couple become very close indeed. It was essential to make sure that one's partner had all the requisite traits. One of the most complete catalogues of these, with detailed guidance on how to assess each one, was given by Cobbett in *Advice to a Lover*. He listed the desiderata as '1. Chastity. 2. Sobriety. 3. Industry. 4. Frugality. 5. Cleanliness. 6. Knowledge of domestic affairs. 7. Good temper. 8. Beauty.'[54] Nothing was mentioned of childbearing or mothering potential, wealth, or blood. The tone of Cobbett's advice is very similar to that of Becon some three centuries earlier. Wives should be 'honest, godly, and virtuous maids', they should not be wasteful or gamblers, but 'such as will lay their hands to work, help to get the penny, save such things as the man bringeth in, dress meat and drink, spin and card'. Husbands should be chosen who are godly, 'come of an honest stock, have been well brought up, have honest occupations to get their livings, are desirous to live with truth and honesty'.[55]

---

[52] Comenius, *Orbis*, 241; Becon, *Works*, 347.
[53] Stone, *Open Elite*; Wharncliffe, *Letters of Montagu*, i, 300.
[54] Cobbett, *Advice to a Lover*, 10.   [55] Becon, *Works*, 356.

It seems clear that the majority of the population were constantly attempting to maximize as many of these criteria as possible. But the weighting given to each would vary. Thus Pepys' cousin was pushed by the loss of his sister, who had been his housekeeper, into looking for what was more or less a wife–housekeeper. He asked Pepys 'to look him out a widow between thirty and forty years old, without children and with a fortune . . . A woman sober and no high flyer as he calls it'.[56] This kind of wife would have an advantage over a female servant, but it would not have suited every man. As Cobbett later pointed out, a wife was better than such a servant for 'it is the want of a common interest with you, and this you can obtain in no one but a wife.'[57] A wife might be an economic necessity, particularly for a small farmer or tradesman. Cobbett was adamant that 'a bare glance at the thing shows, that a farmer, above all men living, can never carry on his affairs with profit without a wife.'[58] Thus children might not, as we have seen, be necessary, but a wife was an advantage. Thomas Wright in the eighteenth century, having lost his first wife and then been deceived by servants, decided that 'I must have a wife, or be ruined.' Another man proposing to a girl explained, 'I am a sole man, I pay for my diet and lodging at Mrs Widdowson £10 by the year, which I am put to for want of a wife.'[59]

From very early on, those who recounted what sort of person they had married usually provide some sort of implied response to the check-list of desiderata we have outlined. Thus a suitor was told in the fifteenth century that the 'day that she is married, my father will give her 1 mark. But and we accord, I shall give you a greater treasure, that is, a witty gentlewoman, and if I say it, both good and virtuous.' In a description of a likely wedding partner, a widow of forty, the lady was recommended as follows: 'first she is goodly and beautiful, womanly and wise, as ever I knew any, none other dispraised: of a good stock and worshipful', and then her wealth was described.[60] Among the various attractions of one young girl, also in the fifteenth century, was that as well as rich parents, 'she is young, little, and very well favoured and witty, and the country speaks much good by her.'

It was the combination of wealth and appealing temperament that

[56] Latham, *Pepys*, iv, 159.   [57] Cobbett, *Advice*, 199–200.
[58] Campbell, *English Yeoman*, 255; Cobbett, *Advice*, 199.
[59] Wright, *Autobiography*, 144; LPS., 2(Spring 1969), 57.
[60] Gairdner, *Paston Letters*, iii, 168; Stapleton, *Plumpton Letters*, 123.

was sought. Thus a man rejected a very rich widow, because she was 'reputed a very ill-conditioned woman, which kills my heart to stir any further in it'. Others were more fortunate: moving to the later seventeenth century, we encounter a man who 'had a great fortune' with his wife, 'but that which is worth all, she is a loving wife, a discrete woman, and an excellent housewife.'[61] Thomas Turner in the eighteenth century described the balance he had struck in his second marriage. At this shopkeeper level there is no mention of blood or outstanding wealth, but his prospective bride was industrious, sober, prudent, cleanly, well made. Thus she measured up well against most of the criteria to be listed a century later by Cobbett. She was, however, plain, her education was somewhat inadequate and she was rather quiet; 'I have it's true, not married a learned lady, nor is she a gay one', but he trusted that she was 'good-natured' and would do her utmost to make him happy.[62]

The balancing of practical necessities with the personal inclinations of the individuals was one of the major preoccupations through these centuries. And it posed a problem for people in the past, it has also made it difficult for historians brought up in the later nineteenth and twentieth centuries to understand the Malthusian marriage system. They read the complaints about people being sold off like cattle, they hear the talk of marriage as a market, they read the letters and settlement contracts which seem so concerned with details of money, and they are often repelled. That there were so many financial details to be settled seems to make a mockery of love, or even affection. Thus editors of historical documents were puzzled when alongside the advantageous, highly organized financial dealings they found also affection and even love.[63] If we remember that marriage was both a psychological and an economic enterprise, then it is not so difficult to see the strain between the two, and the resolutions of the two threads. Such a tension and resolution is well illustrated by Aphra Behn. She shows two lovers 'kissing and slobbering' in one room, while next door 'the friends' of the two parties are trying to settle the financial details. Often there is disagreement: 'many times the portion of one is too great, and what's given with the other is too little.' Yet the young couple are determined, 'for there's fire in the flax, and go how it will, it must be quenched.' The lover is 'so struck to the heart with such

---

[61] Hanham, *Cely Letters*, 152; Rye, *Gawdy*, 157; Gough, *Myddle*, 130.
[62] Turner, *Diary*, 75–6.   [63] Kingsford, *Stonor Letters*, i, xxviii, xliii.

firy flames of love' that he's resolved never to leave his lady, and an agreement is finally patched up.[64] Here is the epitome of the clash between desire and reason, impulse and calculation, passions and interests – which is one of the central features of those delicate balances that make up the Malthusian marriage pattern.

The analogy between marriage and buying in the market was a common one. Thus we come across a pamphlet, one of many, entitled 'A Market for young Men; or, a Publick sale in sundry places in and about London, where young beautiful virgins and grazed widows are to be sold for clipped money, at reasonable rates.' Likewise, there was a market for men: 'there are more customers that go to hymen's markets, which are churches, plays, balls, masks, marriages etc. than there are husbands to be sold.'[65]

It was, however, a market with a difference. First, the information available about the goods was often very inadequate. As a seventeenth-century model letter writer put it, 'if you buy a horse, you may look in his mouth for his years, you may try his pace how you like him.'[66] This sounds like a conscious echo of Sir Thomas More's remarks in *Utopia*, when recommending the inspection of potential brides without their clothes on. The inhabitants of Utopia pointed out that

> when you're buying a horse, and there's nothing at stake but a small sum of money, you take every possible precaution. The animal's practically naked already, but you firmly refuse to buy until you've whipped off the saddle and all the rest of the harness, to make sure there aren't any sores underneath. But when you're choosing a wife . . . you're unbelievably careless, you don't even bother to take it out of its wrappings. You judge the whole woman from a few square inches of face, which is all you can see of her, and then proceed to marry her – at the risk of finding her most disagreeable, when you see what she's really like.[67]

Secondly, unlike a market, the goods could neither be returned as faulty nor disposed of by any means such as re-sale or destruction. 'A

[64] Behn, *Pleasures*, 14–15.

[65] The Pepys Ballads, vol.iv, 236, in Magdalene College, Cambridge; Cavendish, *Letters*, 100; for other texts attacking the commercial marriage market in the sixteenth to eighteenth centuries, see Thomas, 'Women', 338.

[66] I.W., *Speedie Post*, sig.D; see also *Characters*, 190.

[67] More, *Utopia*, 103; Pollard, *Chaucer Works*, 158, uses the same analogy: all were based on Horace.

wife once had you must keep her', she's 'got to last you a lifetime'. The choice is 'like a stratagem of war, wherein a man can err but once.'[68]

This combination of poor information with non-returnability made marriage into more of a lottery than a market, people concluded. The unpredictable nature of the system was recognized in various ways. Dr Johnson concluded that random marriage allocation would probably lead to as much happiness as the personal choice system. 'I believe marriages would in general be as happy, and often more so, if they were all made by the Lord Chancellor, upon a due consideration of characters and circumstances, without the parties having any choice in the matter.'[69] There are references during the seventeenth century to people drawing lots for their 'valentines', putting in names and then picking at random. Furthermore, although the choice seemed to have been determined from outside, by forces larger than the individual – by the stars, God, destiny – it was no secret that the god of love, Cupid, was almost blind. Sometimes he was represented as totally blind, but Milton argued that 'though not wholly blind, as poets wrong him, yet having but one eye, as being born an archer aiming, and that eye not the quickest in this dark regime here below', his arrows often went astray.[70] Thus marriage was a gamble and one where the odds of the draw were often considered poor. A popular seventeenth-century manual offering advice on practical affairs gave a method for calculating whether a wife be honest or dishonest; the chances were fifty-fifty. A preacher argued in 1603 that 'women are like a cowl [tub] full of snakes amongst which there is one eel, and a thousand to one if a man happen upon the eel; and if he get it with his hand, all he has gotten is a wet eel by the tail.'[71]

There were those who stressed the benefits of marriage. In a ballad of about 1630, a husband defends marriage against attack, listing the advantages of having married: he has left off unthrifty games, given up drinking, feels better on the home cooking his wife provides, is able to discuss problems with her, rises in credit after the christening of his child, and gets pleasure from playing with the infant.[72] In a later eighteenth-century model letter, a gentleman urges his friend to

---

[68] I.W., *Speedie Post*, sig.D; More, *Utopia*, 103; Burleigh's advice in Percy, *Advice*, 38. [69] Hill, *Life of Johnson*, ii, 461.

[70] Brand, *Popular Antiquities*, i, 53; Milton, *Works*, iii, 194.

[71] *The Husbandman's Practice*, 171; Harrison, *Jacobean Journal*, 13.

[72] Rollins, *Pepysian Garland*, 357–8.

marry, arguing that there is no other lawful way of peopling the world; that children establish immortality of a kind; that 'there is nothing more comfortable than to live with a woman who has resigned herself to your protection'; that all decisions are jointly taken; that a 'husband may possess himself in perfect ease, by leaving the care of his domestic concerns to a frugal and good housewife'; that children are a delight, the 'effects of his love, and who will be hereafter the supports of his old age'. Thus 'single life, in man, can no where find the real consolation and assistance that are met with in the society of a woman.'[73]

Two centuries earlier a model letter book had urged similar advantages: the 'decay of his house if he be not married, or the continuance of a solitary, loose, and bad kind of living'; the 'dying of his wealth and name at one instant' if he should be without heirs; the institution of marriage by God to encourage propagation; the 'love and mutual society and comfort between man and wife . . . the sweet pleasures, cares, and delights interchangeably passing between them', each seeking the 'others contentment, solace, and pleasing'; the 'joy of procreation' wherein the infant's noises shall be 'an incredible delight'.[74] A similar picture of marital harmony and mutual love had led Bartholomaeus Anglicus to argue that 'no man hath more wealth than he that hath a good woman to wife.'[75]

People in many societies in the past would have ended the argument there. Marriage is not only natural, it is highly desirable. The gains so far outweigh the losses that there is really no need to balance benefits and costs: there is really no choice. Marriage is inevitable, it is the gateway to adulthood, posterity, power and prosperity. Yet in the English evidence it is clear that there is a choice to be made, and there are serious costs to be weighed against the benefits. Even those who were amongst the firmest defenders of marriage had to admit this. Thus Fuller, while encouraging marriage, warned people not to be over-optimistic. One should 'expect both wind and storms sometimes', and 'make account of certain cares and troubles which will attend thee'. He warned his readers to 'remember the nightingales', which stop singing when their young are hatched, 'as if their mirth were turned into care for their young ones'. Nearly

---

[73] *The Court Letter Writer*, 156–7.   [74] Day, *Secretorie*, 139.

[75] Anglicus, *Properties*, i, 309. For further discussion of the criteria of choice in marriage in the fifteenth to eighteenth centuries, see Houlbrooke, *English Family*, 73–8.

two centuries later Cobbett admitted that 'the cares and troubles of the married life are many', but justified his preference for this state by asking 'are those of the single life few?'[76] He may be consciously alluding to Dr Johnson's earlier attempts to weigh up the pros and cons, in a dialogue between Rasselas, Prince of Abyssinia, and his sister Princess Nekayah. The princess points out the many inconveniences of marriage, yet she concludes that 'marriage has many pains, but celibacy has no pleasures.' She continues, 'I know not . . . whether marriage be more than one of the innumerable modes of human misery.' To this the prince replies, 'you seem to forget . . . that you have, even now, represented celibacy as less happy than marriage. Both conditions may be bad but they cannot both be worst.' The real problem, as Nekayah proceeds to show, is that of lesser evils: every course has disadvantages.[77]

There was an extensive literature warning people of the dangers and disadvantages of marriage. In Chaucer we find common expressions of scepticism about marriage. The merchant told the tale of a man who had 'wept many a tear', since he had married, and found in marriage only 'cost and care'. Chaucer's advice concerning marriage was:

> Bet is to wedde than brenne in worse wyse,
> But thou shalt have sorwe on thy flessh, thy life,
> And ben thy wyves thral, as seyn these wyse.

Therefore it was almost better to die than to fall into the 'trap' of marriage.[78]

In the mid-sixteenth century the fictional Jack of Newbury claimed he was unwilling to marry because he had too little wealth, because 'many sorrows follow marriage, especially where want remains', and because it was hard to find a constant woman.[79] A little later, the same model letter in which we saw arguments for marriage gave as many reasons against it. First there was the loss of liberty, both in no longer being able to do what one liked and in having to be content with one person. This was bad enough if the partner was perfect, but if the woman proved to be a 'scold, wayward, self-willed, malicious, frowning or suspicious, what a hell then is he driven into whose

---

[76] Fuller, *Holy State*, 208; Cobbett, *Advice*, 197.
[77] Johnson, *Works*, iii, 374, 379, 384.   [78] Pollard, *Chaucer Works*, 207, 633.
[79] Deloney, 'Jacke of Newberrie', 9.

serpentine and more than adder like disposition be such as would terrify a thousand Devils.' She may be wanton or proud; if she is cleverer than the man, then she is arrogant; if she is foolish, 'then a mocking stock'; if she is fair, 'then a spectacle to gaze on, if foul then a simpering poppet to wonder on, if she be rich: presumptious, if poor, then becometh she odious'. Whatever her personality, she brings an 'intolerable charge' with her for apparel, diet, household and servants. Then there is the cost of 'provision for children, furniture for house, daily continual and never resting cark [load, burden] and toil for her and hers'.[80] Half a century later another model letter pointed out further disadvantages: 'Beauty may breed jealousy, and wit may be a wanton: again, a fool and a foul one are couple of fretting companions: riches may breed pride, and poverty charge: if she be noble you must make courtesy to all her kindred: if base, you must maintain a nest of beggars.'[81]

It was widely joked that marriage was not what it seemed. 'Marriage is now become a miriage, matrimony a matter of money.'[82] 'Marriage is a desparate thing. The frogs in *Aesop* were extremely wise; they had a great mind to some water, but they would not leap into the well, because they could not get out again.' As a character in *The Country Wife* put it, 'Well, Jack, by thy long absence from the town, the grimness of thy countenance, and the slovenliness of thy habit, I should give thee joy, should I not, of marriage?' 'To be married, I find, is to be buried alive.'[83] One of the most vitriolic of the many attacks on marriage was Aphra Behn's *Ten Pleasures of Marriage*. As the author frankly put it, 'for my part, I believe that of all the disasters we are subject to in our life-time, that of marriage takes preference from all the rest.' The 'tortures of marriage' lead to 'a thousand vexations and a thousand torments'. The moral was 'therefore oh you that are yet so happy as to have kept your selves out of this dreadful estate of marriage, have a horror for it.' As Dryden wrote:

> Love, like a scene, at distance should appear
> But Marriage views the gross-daubed landscape near.[84]

---

[80] Day, *Secretorie*, 140–1.   [81] I.W., *Speedie Post*, sig.C4v.

[82] Fleming, 'Notebook', fol.21v.

[83] Singer, *Table-Talk*, 90; Wycherley, *Country Wife*, Act I, scene 1; *The Court Letter Writer*, 174.

[84] Behn, *Pleasures*, 133, 130; quoted in Schucking, *Puritan Family*, 130.

Such were the disadvantages, that it was a popular theme to ask why anyone should enter this trap. Aphra Behn mused: 'the nuptial estate trailing along with it so many cares, troubles and calamities, it is one of the greatest admirations, that people should be so earnest and desirous to enter themselves into it.'[85] Johnson told Boswell, 'you will recollect my saying to some ladies the other day, that I often wondered why young women should marry as they have so much more freedom, and so much more attention paid to them, while unmarried than when married.' Pepys at a wedding thought it 'strange to see what delight we married people have to see these poor fools decoyed into our condition, every man and wife gazing and smiling at them.'[86] It was a matter of decoys, of false expectations, many thought. That 'most maids account it a great misfortune to live long unmarried', the Duchess of Newcastle thought, was probably because 'they know not, or will not believe the cares and troubles that accompany a married life.' Basically, as Bartholomaeus Anglicus had put it, if it worked well, it increased happiness; if it worked badly, it was a disaster. Or as an eighteenth-century observer wrote, 'the pleasures and pains of a single life, are both less than of a married state.'[87] The verse in the Bible that enjoins that man and woman should cleave to each other and be one flesh, is the great knot-tier of matrimony, according to Milton: 'this is that grisly porter, who having drawn men, and wisest men, by subtle allurement within the train of an unhappy matrimony, claps the dungeon-gate upon them, as irrecoverable as the grave.'[88]

In the early eighteenth century, Dudley Ryder was undecided whether to marry. He discussed the matter with a friend.

> I said though I had often upon consideration thought that the miseries and inconveniences that attended that state were much greater than the advantages of it and a man runs a vast hazard in entering upon it, yet at the same time I could not suppose myself capable of being completely happy here without it. I cannot but be uneasy to think that my life shall terminate with myself.

Later in the same year he talked it over with his cousin, and 'agreed in this that the sorrows and cares and burdens to which it exposes a

[85] Behn, *Pleasures*, 1.
[86] Hill, *Life of Johnson*, ii, 471; Latham, *Pepys*, vi, 338–9.
[87] Cavendish, *Letters*, 379; *Characters*, 189.   [88] Milton, *Works*, iii, 337.

man don't seem to be sufficiently balanced by the joys and pleasures one can expect from it.' Yet he was unable to overcome his emotion with his reason. But then his cousin pointed out that 'for a young man not in business that had 2 or £3,000 to marry a woman of perhaps 1 or £2,000 it would keep him low all his life.' Ryder reconsidered his current relationship: 'why should I think of having her when it would expose us both to want?'[89]

The pros and cons were also weighed by Boswell. He contrasted the bachelor, who was like a feather and had many connections, to the married man who has his 'affections collected by one great attachment'. Marriage, he wrote, could be regarded in two ways.

> If you think of that weariness which must at times hang over every kind of society, those disgusts and vexations which will happen in the intercourse of life, you will be frightened to take upon you the serious charge of the father of a family. But if you think of the comforts of a home where you are a sort of sovereign, the kind endearments of an amiable woman who has no wish but to make you happy, the amusement of seeing your children grow up from infancy to manhood, and the pleasing pride of being the father of brave and learned men . . . then marriage is truly the only condition in which true felicity is to be found.[90]

To marry, many pointed out, was an irrational act. For men it meant loss of liberty, expense, discord; for women, loss of independence, pain and possible death in childbirth. Furthermore, information was imperfect and the risk high: the consequences of making a mistake were enormous. Looked at from the cool perspective of a business enterprise, it was not sane behaviour, for almost all the advantages of marriage could be bought in the market – from sex to housekeeping and friendship. Hence, Halley observed in 1693, 'the growth and increase of mankind is not so much stinted by anything in the nature of the species, as it is from the cautious difficulty most people make to adventure of the state of marriage, from the prospect of the trouble and charge of providing for a family.'[91] Yet people continued to flock to get married, and did so for many reasons.

---

[89] Matthews, *Ryder Diary*, 224; ibid., 309–10.
[90] Brady, *Boswell in Search*, 25.
[91] Quoted by Habakkuk in Glass, *Population*, 275, cf. also Goode, *Family*, 83.

Some marry for heirs to disappoint their brothers, and others throw themselves into the arms of those whom they do not love, because they have found themselves rejected where they were most solicitous to please ... some marry because their servants cheat them, some because they squander their own money, some because their houses are pestered with company, some because they will live like other people, and some only because they are sick of themselves.[92]

Yet there was one force which turned all the equations to nothing. Half-blind Cupid threw confusion into the cold calculations with his mysterious darts. This 'instituted irrationality' at the heart of the system continues to bring people together. Just as it had drawn Paris to his doom, and Abelard to the feet of Heloise, so the elderly Richard Baxter, the late seventeenth-century scourge of matrimony and banner of Nonconformity, suddenly found himself in love with his eighteen-year-old pupil. Amidst the mockery of his enemies and against all his principles, he succumbed and lived in marital bliss.[93] The loneliness which Milton, Donne, Shakespeare and others diagnosed at the heart of love led many to marry. The examination of this emotion, impulse, inclination, will provide us with a final indication of the way in which people were propelled into marriage through these centuries. The marriage contract was something more than other contracts. In an extraordinary way, what began as an artificial exercise of will, an almost random linking of two bodies, minds and personalities, became the most important and, paradoxically, the most natural of relationships.

But marriage, as an institution, was a very unnatural state. Asked whether matrimony was natural to man, Dr Johnson replied, 'Sir, it is so far from being natural for a man and woman to live in a state of marriage, that we find all the motives which they have for remaining in that connection, and the restraints which civilized society imposes to prevent separation, are hardly sufficient to keep them together.'[94] Yet this unlikely state generated the deepest bond in a person's life. Culture was turned to nature: a decision by an individual replaced all the relationships of blood and status. Men and women to this extent could shape their own destinies, even if an error would lead to disaster. At least the frogs were free to jump or not to jump, and who knew what life was like at the bottom of the well?

[92] Johnson, *Works*, iv, 293.   [93] Baxter, *Breviate*.
[94] Hill, *Life of Johnson*, ii, 165.

9

Romantic Love

I n contrast to most other recorded societies, it has been noted that Americans do 'not merely build their households on the husband–wife relationship, but build their whole value system and morality on it'. Whereas in industrial Western societies the emotional relationship between man and wife is primary, it is not the pivot of social structure in the majority of societies.[1] As we have noted, the relationships that are most important are often those between parents and children, with the marital bond as a poor second. 'In Eastern countries with their ancient civilization there exists even now comparatively little of that tenderness towards the woman which is the principal charm of our own family life,' wrote Westermarck.[2]

The transition from a situation where the marital relationship is subordinated to others, to the prevalent Western view of it as the deepest and most enduring relationship of life, brings numerous consequences, changing the nature of marriage and women's and men's roles. One consequence is the demographic one. The substitution of the husband–wife relationship for wider kinship links and parent–child ties, decreases the pressure to have children. The couple are sufficient to each other: children become a luxury, not a necessity. Effective contraception makes it possible to choose whether to indulge in a few or many. Hence the strengthening of the husband–wife bond is part of that emotional and economic nucleation which certain demographers like Caldwell see as leading to a state of affairs propitious for the demographic transition to lowered fertility.[3] It is thus essential to estimate when this situation – characterized by deep attraction and affection before marriage and an all-conquering

[1] Bohannan, *Social Anthropology*, 99; Goode, *World Revolution*, 14, 89.
[2] Westermarck, *Marriage*, ii, 24ff; ii, 28.   [3] Caldwell, 'Restatement', 354.

emotion within marriage – was established. As we have seen, this cultural premise was part of the Malthusian marriage pattern. Malthus assumed throughout his work that marriage was mainly for 'love' and that the marital relationship would, if entered into, be the most important in a person's life.[4] Though now very widely shared, at the time both assumptions were culturally idiosyncratic. How recent was this transformation?

We may start by looking at some of those who advised on how these things should be – moralists and philosophers. There is little need to elaborate the fact that by the eighteenth century they took it for granted that marriage was based on love. They might condemn or applaud, but there could be no denying that conjugal love was widespread. David Hume thought love arose from the mixture of three impressions, or passions: 'the pleasing sensation arising from beauty; the bodily appetite for generation; and a generous kindness or good-will'. The most common species 'is that which first arises from beauty, and afterwards diffuses itself into kindness and into the bodily appetite'.[5] Essayists commented: 'it is the very essence of love, to be free and unconstrained: love is the will improved into friendship and desire.' 'The friendship which a generous husband has towards his wife, is as much above the friendship which man bears to man, as the conversation of a courtship is more pleasing than ordinary discourse.'[6] Aphorisms and sayings were coined. 'Love is a strange passion: it puts a man into a great pain and uneasiness, and will not give him leave even to desire to be rid on't.' 'We are free agents in most things, but in love. For we can neither love where we have a mind; nor help loving where we would not.' It was assumed that 'love is the natural passion of youth', that the common people 'marry purely for love and for nothing else'. It was also assumed that the depth of emotion would continue into marriage. It is strange that women marry 'when one considers the excessive sorrow and lamentation some women make for the loss of their husbands and children.'[7]

Throughout the eighteenth century, numerous editions of the enormously popular *New Whole Duty of Man* laid out the nature of Christian marriage based on love and the primacy of the husband–wife relationship. Love was the essential prerequisite of marriage. 'No law obliges a man to marry; but he is obliged to love the woman whom

---

[4] Malthus, *Population*, i, 237.   [5] Hume, *Treatise*, 394–5.
[6] Steele, *The Englishman*, 41, 39.   [7] *Characters*, 186, 187, 166, 191, 189.

he has taken in marriage'; marriage 'cannot be enterprised with any hopes of felicity, without a real affection on the one side, and a good assurance of it on the other'; 'love is a tender plant, it must be kept alive by great delicacy.'[8] That love is the basis of marriage is shown by the marriage contract itself: 'the husband first promises to love his wife, before she promises to obey him: and consequently as his love is the condition of her obedience' she need only obey if he is loving. What is this love? It is 'being kindly affectioned to their persons'. The marital relationship was the core of stability and happiness.

> What avails all the pomp and parade of life, which appears abroad; if, when we shift the gaudy flattering scene, the man is unhappy, where happiness must begin, at home? . . . Abroad, we must more or less find tribulation; yet, as long as our home is a secure and peaceful retreat from all the disappointments and cares which we meet with in that great scene of vexation, the world, we may still be tolerably happy.'[9]

As the title of a book on the history of the modern family puts it, the home is 'a haven in a heartless world'.[10] The married couple are partners and companions; separated from kin, from children, from friends, yet united with each other, they form an indivisible and mutually supportive pair. Thus

> men should maintain their wives as becomes partners; they are friends and companions to their husbands, not slaves, nor menial servants; and are to be partners in their fortunes: for, as they partake of their troubles and afflictions, it is just that they should share their fortunes. For when a husband falls into decay, or any sort of calamity, he involves his wife with him; they are inseparable companions in misery and misfortune.[11]

It would be difficult to find a more succinct statment of the ideal of companionate marriage, constantly reasserted throughout the century.

In the seventeenth century the ideal was equally widely stressed and universally assumed. God made woman as a man's second self, as a complementary part. Not satisfied merely to describe woman as a help, God 'goes on describing another self, a second self, a very self

---

[8] *The New Whole Duty*, 227, 202, 220.   [9] Ibid., 227, 220.
[10] Lasch, *Haven*.   [11] *The New Whole Duty*, 229–30.

itself'.[12] Woman is thus the redeeming other half which completes a man; marriage turns an incomplete person into something whole.

In Paradise, Adam had pleaded with God for a partner, being alone,

> . . . defective, which requires
> Collateral love, and dearest amity

upon which God promised to give him 'Thy likeness, thy fit help, thy other self'. When he beheld Eve, Adam found

> Bone of my bone, flesh of my flesh, myself
> Before me: Woman is her name; of Man
> Extracted: for this cause he shall forego
> Father and mother, and to his wife adhere;
> And they shall be one flesh, one heart, one soul.

Adam is not attracted primarily by Eve's physical beauty or 'procreative' potential; her main appeal is described otherwise.

> So much delights me, as those graceful acts,
> Those thousand decencies, that daily flow
> From all her words and actions, mixed with love
> And sweet compliance, which declare unfeigned
> Union of mind, or in us both one soul;
> Harmony to behold in wedded pair . . .

The harmony is so close, the joining into one flesh so intense, that something very strange happens: Adam puts Eve before God.

In Genesis there is no indication as to why Adam should have taken the apple from Eve: 'she took of the fruit thereof, and did eat, and gave unto her husband with her; and he did eat.' Milton offers a motive for this cataclysmic decision. It was love and a desire to cleave to his partner that made Adam put Eve and possible doom before his Maker. Adam knows that Eve has eaten of the forbidden fruit and he wishes to share her fate. Though it may lead to destruction,

> However, I with thee have fixed my lot,
> Certain to undergo like doom: if death

[12] Milton, *Works*, iii, 334.

> Consort with thee, death is to me as life;
> So forcible within my heart I feel
> The bond of nature draw me to my own –
> My own in thee, for what thou art is mine;
> Our state cannot be severed; we are one –
> One flesh; to lose thee were to lose myself.

This heroic assertion that married love will conquer even death is reciprocated by Eve. She is moved to hear that Adam would rather risk God's vengeance than be parted from her

> . . . from whose dear side I boast me sprung,
> And gladly of our union hear thee speak,
> One heart, one soul in both; whereof good proof
> This day affords, declaring thee resolved,
> Rather than death, or aught than death more dread,
> Shall separate us linked in love so dear,
> To undergo with me, one guilt, one crime,
> If any be, of tasting this fair fruit.

Thus man's disobedience, the loss of innocence and Paradise, grew from too deep a love between man and woman. Conjugal love is the original myth of Milton's vision.

Milton's epic drew its inspiration from many sources. For instance, it consciously drew from the earlier work by the French Protestant writer Du Bartas, in the translation of whose work we find that

> . . . Man were but half a man,
> But a wild wolf, but a Barbarian,
> Brute, rageful, fierce, moody, melancholike,
> Hating the light; whom nought but nought could like:
> Born solely for himself, bereft of sense,
> Of heart, of love, of life, of excellence.
> God therefore, not to seem less liberall
> To Man, than else to every Animall;
> For perfect pattern of a holy love,
> To *Adams* halfe another halfe he gave . . .

Adam was not slow to recognize the excellence of what he had been given, and he reacted with delight:

> Kissing her kindly, calling her his Life,

His Love, his Stay, his Rest, his Weal, his Wife,
His other-selfe, his Help (him to refresh),
Bone of his Bone, Flesh of his very Flesh.
Source of all joys! sweet *He-Shee*-Coupled-One,

O Chastest friendship, whose pure flames impart
Two souls in one, two Hearts into one Heart![13]

This rapturous picture of man and woman as two halves of one whole, one flesh and one blood, is central to the modern concept of the deeply interdependent nature of the married couple. It is also reflected in the numerous characterizations of 'the good wife' and 'the good husband' with which this period abounds. Two examples may be given. Sir Thomas Overbury's *Characters* was published in 1614, though written earlier. He began his description of 'A Good Wife' thus:

[She] is a man's best movable, a scion incorporate with the stock, bringing sweet fruit; one that to her husband is more than a friend, less than trouble; an equal with him in the yoke. Calamities and troubles she shares alike, nothing pleaseth her that doth not him. She is relative in all, and he without her but half himself. She is his absent hands, eyes, ears, and mouth; his present and absent all . . . a husband without her is a misery to man's apparel: none but she hath an aged husband, to whom she is both a staff and a chair.[14]

Two years later Nicholas Breton published another set of character sketches, *The Good and the Bad*. The praise was even more exuberant: 'A good wife is a world of wealth, . . . She is the eye of warriness, the tongue of silence, the hand of labour, and the heart of love; a companion of kindness, a mistress of passion, an exercise of patience, and an example of experience . . . She is her husband's jewel, her children's joy, her neighbour's love, and her servant's honour.'[15]

This was not just an ideal, for it was clearly thought to reflect a widespread depth and intensity of companionly love. This was shown in the attitude to marital love conveyed by those who were trying to comfort or uplift their congregations. In a funeral sermon, Ralph

[13] Milton, *Paradise Lost*, 240–1, 242, 246, 281, 282; Du Bartas, *Weekes*, 57.

[14] Morley, *Character Writings*, 45.

[15] Ibid., 274. See also the affectionate portraits of husband and wife in Fuller, *Holy State*, 1, 7.

Josselin advised the sorrowing husband, 'you can consider, here I was wont to see my dear wife; here to enjoy her delightsome embraces; her counsel, spiritual discourses, furtherance, encouragement in the ways of God, I was wont to find her an help to ease me of the burden and trouble of household-affairs, whose countenance welcomed me home with joy.'[16] When Thomas Hooker was trying to find similes for Christ's ordinances, it was natural for him to turn to the deepest and most loving relationship:

> as a wife deals with the letters of her husband that is in a far country; she finds many sweet inklings of his love, and she will read these letters often, and daily: she would talk with her husband a far off, and see him in the letters, Oh (saith she) thus and thus and thus he thought when he writ these lines, and then she thinks he speaks to her again . . . so these ordinances are but the Lords love-letters.

Even more powerful is Hooker's description of how a loving husband feels towards his wife:

> the man whose heart is endeared to the woman he loves, he dreams of her in the night, hath her in his eye and apprehension when he awakes, museth on her as he sits at table, walks with her when he travels and parlies with her in each place where he comes . . . That the husband tenders his Spouse with an indeared affection above all mortal creatures: this appears by the expression of his respect, that all he hath, is at her command, all he can do, is wholly improved for her content and comfort, she lies in his Bosom, and his heart trusts in her, which forceth all to confess, that the stream of his affection, like a mighty current, runs with full tide and strength.[17]

As Morgan concludes, although these are metaphorical and abstract descriptions, this 'does not weaken the obvious authenticity of their language. Hooker was describing feelings that really existed.'

The necessity and presence of love were assumed in much of the popular pamphlet literature, both secular and 'godly', of the later sixteenth and early seventeenth centuries. Here a secular work describes the overpowering nature of love: 'The passions of love are so passing kind, as they subdue wheresoever they become, yea,

---

[16] Quoted in Macfarlane, *Ralph Josselin*, 107.
[17] Morgan, *Puritan Family*, 61–2.

assuredly they will either conquer or kill . . . Love is a pleasing gout
. . . He is a nettle that stings the heart with continual pleasure.': 'the
hearts of women are like unto wax that, tempered by the passions of
love, are ready to take the impression thereof.'[18] This passion was the
basis for what the author took to be the overriding relationship in a
man's or woman's life. We owe a duty to our parents, but it is
superseded by the duty arising out of marital love: 'I confirm that love
is a duty, himself binding to so great obedience, and tying with such
strong conveyances, as he removes all thoughts of lower duties; I
terming all duties lower, for that by commandment those duties must
be rejected in respect of the loving duty that of a Husband shall
require.' In a portrait of an ideal husband in *The Glasse of Godly Love*
we find the image of the supremacy of marital love. The husband is
the woman's ruler and protector, he owes her

> most fervent love and affection, all gentle behaviour, all faithfulness
> and help, all comfort and kindness, as to himself, his own flesh and
> body; so that under God there is no love, no affection, no friendship,
> no nearness of kin, to be compared unto this, nor any one thing under
> the Sun, that pleaseth God more than man and wife that agree well
> together, which live in the fear of God.

It is because of this that Christ and the Church and the 'holy body
of them both' are 'set forth for an example or mirror of the state of
wedlock, or conjugal love'.[19]

The godly treatises covering marriage were equally insistent on the
necessity for deep love and the primacy of the marital bond. Gouge
likened love to glue, which needed to be present from the start: 'If at
first there be good liking mutually and thoroughly settled in both their
hearts of one another, love is like to continue in them for ever, as
things which are well glued, and settled before they be shaken up and
down, will never be severed asunder; but if they be joined together
without glue, or shaken while the glue is moist, they cannot remain
firm.'[20] Whateley was equally adamant: 'Love is the life and soul of
marriage, without which it differs as much from it self, as a rotten
apple from a sound, and a carcase from a living body.' This love
supersedes all others: 'a man must love his wife above all the
creatures in the world besides . . . no neighbours, no kinsman, no

---

[18] Furnivall, *Tell-Trothes*, 39, 28, 57.   [19] Ibid., 57, 183.
[20] Gouge, *Domesticall*, 197.

friend, no parent, no child should be so near and dear.'[21]

Half a century earlier, Becon encouraged people to base their marriage on a deep and enduring love that would outweigh all others. A man should love his wife, 'even as himself, and as Christ loved his congregation.' Quoting St Paul, who had said that men ought to 'love their wives as their own bodies. He that loveth his wife loveth himself', several further reasons are given for loving one's wife, including the fact that 'she is flesh of his flesh, and bone of his bones.' The 'father' in Becon's dialogue asks, 'must the love of a married man toward his wife excel his love toward all other persons?', to which the 'son' replies, 'Yea, verily', quoting Matthew 19, 'for this cause shall a man leave his father and his mother, and shall be joined with his wife; and they shall become one flesh.'[22] In consequence of this love, it was the duty of a husband to protect and cherish his wife, not to be 'churlish and cruel toward her, but quiet, gentle, modest, patient, long-suffering, kind, and soft in all his behaviour toward her, and even such one as a gentle and tender father is toward his most dear and sweet child.' It was equally the wife's duty to

> truly, dearly, faithfully, and unfeignedly love her husband ... the married woman shall love her husband as herself, and think her own husband in her eyes to be most fair, most beautiful, most proper, most handsome, most amiable, most honest, most garnished with all virtues and qualities that become a godly husband; which opinion the husband also ought to have of his wife, that one may unfeignedly rejoice in another, and heartily love one another.[23]

It is clear that this widely established attitude to marriage was not something that sprang up at the Reformation. Books of advice written before the Reformation in England convey the same message. For example, Harrington's *Comendacions of Matrymony* first published in 1528 but written some time earlier, while scrupulously and ortho-doxly Catholic, took the same view. It points out, for instance, that the husband–wife bond should be stronger than that between parent and child: 'the husband ought to love his wife and the wife her husband above their father and mother.'[24] A detailed study of these books of advice before and after the Reformation, both Catholic and Protestant, has found no shift in this emphasis. 'There is enough

[21] Whateley, *Bride-Bush*, 31, 38.   [22] Becon, *Works*, 334.   [23] Ibid., 338, 341.
[24] Harrington, *Matrymony*, sig.Dii.

continuity in the advice ... to indicate that Puritan conduct books do not show any change to domesticity and affection as ideals of marriage. There was nothing new in such ideals,' concludes Kathleen Davies, for 'what is interesting about the Puritan conduct books is the fact of their very continuity.'[25]

As far back as we can easily go, there is evidence of the same insistence. If we leap back to the early thirteenth century we find in the encyclopaedia by Bartholomaeus Anglicus a similar emphasis on love, 'fellowship', affection, consideration. This was based on the same two important principles – first, that the conjugal relationship replaced all others: 'a man hath so great love to his wife that for her sake he adventureth himself to all perils; and setteth her love afore his mother's love; for he dwelleth with his wife, and forsaketh father and mother.'[26] The ultimate choice had been made. Mind and heart had conquered blood, choice had replaced necessity; or, adapting Sir Henry Maine, contract had replaced status in the heart of the couple. The second feature was the sharing, the companionship, the jointness of the relationship. A man made his wife his 'fellow at bed and board'.[27] The word 'fellow', as with Oxbridge fellows today, implies a communion of equals, a partnership, a mutuality of interests. Husband and wife were conceived of as having set up a small enterprise, to the exclusion of all others, which would last while both lived. If such a picture, derived from moralistic literature, is confirmed by other sources it suggests that the revolution to conjugality and companionate marriage, which is both unusual and so influential, had occurred at least by the time of Chaucer in England, if not long before.

The cultural premise of love is equally evident in other literature of the period between Chaucer and Malthus. The theme of the novel was the tension between love and duty, love and reason, love and fate, in the formally recognized novels of the eighteenth century as well as in the more fragmentary stories which preceded them.[28] Indeed the word 'novel' was defined by Dr Johnson in his *Dictionary* as 'a small tale, generally of love'. It is perhaps not a coincidence that a country which agonized so much about love should have produced some of the greatest novelists.

The same could be argued for drama. Anyone who has read the

---

[25] Outhwaite, *Marriage*, 78.   [26] Steele, *Medieval Lore*, 56.   [27] Ibid., 57.
[28] Wright, *Domestic Manners*, 274; Deloney, 'Jacke of Newberrie'.

plays produced in England between the early sixteenth and late eighteenth centuries will know that the tensions created by the conflicts of love are the most important single element dominating the plots. The passion of love in its myriad manifestations is brought into conflict with a thousand obstacles, and the resolution of these difficulties keeps audiences in the past and today in a state of suspense and enchantment. We cannot consider here these plays one by one, but only cite a very few of the images. Shakespeare's treatment of love in many of his plays is widely known, reaching exquisite perfection in *Romeo and Juliet*. The other Elizabethan and Jacobean dramatists also assumed the power of love: 'where both deliberate the love is slight: who ever lov'd, that lov'd not at first sight'; 'all her particular worth grows to this sum: she stains the time past, lights the time to come'; 'why, I hold fate clasped in my fist, and could command the course of times eternal motion, hadst thou been one thought more steady than an ebbing sea'; 'let storms come when they list, they find thee sheltered; Should any doubt arise, let nothing trouble thee. Put trust in our love for the managing of all thy hearts peace.'[29] The preoccupation with love continued with the Restoration dramatists – in Dryden's *All for Love*, Wycherley's *The Country Wife*, Vanbrugh's *The Provok'd Wife*, and many others. Love was a haven: 'Sure I have had the dream of some poor mariner, a sleepy image of a welcome port, and wake involved in storms!' Yet it could not be hurried 'You like nothing; your time is not come; Love and Death have their fatalities, and strike home one time or other.'[30] Better to have loved and lost: 'But say what you will, 'tis better to be left than never to have been loved. To pass our youth in dull indifference, to refuse the sweets of life because they once must leave us, is as preposterous as to wish to have been born old, because we one day must be old.'[31] These plays and novels took love as their central theme, a love intimately connected with marriage.

In poetry, too, love is the dominant concern. It reaches an apotheosis in Tennyson's *Princess*. Though written in 1847, it reads like a version of Milton or Du Bartas. Marriage is to be welcomed:

[29] Marlowe, Hero and Leander quoted in Cohen, *Penguin Dictionary*; Webster, *Duchess of Malfi*, Act I, scene 1; Ford, *'Tis Pity She's a Whore*, Act V, scene 5; Middleton, *Women Beware Women*, Act II, scene 1.

[30] Farquhar, *Beaux' Stratagem*, Act V, scene iv; Act II, scene 1.

[31] Congreve, *Way of the World*, Act II, scene 1.

> . . . seeing either sex alone
> Is half itself, and in true marriage lies nor equal,
>   nor unequal: each fulfils
> Defect in each, and always thought in thought
> Purpose in purpose . . . the two cells' heart beating
>   with one full stroke.[32]

This mention of love as a remedy, correcting a 'defect' or emptiness, takes us back two centuries to John Donne's *Extasie*:

> When love, with one another so
> Interanimates two souls,
> That abler soule, which thence doth flow,
> Defects of lonelinesse controules.

The Metaphysical poets – Donne, Herbert, Marvell, King and others – celebrated love with an intensity and seriousness which it would be difficult to believe could be surpassed. Here, surely, was a passionate outpouring on love within and outside marriage that could not be rivalled. This was the high point.

Yet if we move back fifty years the emotion is, if anything, more intense. As L. E. Pearson has concluded in her study, *Elizabethan Love Conventions*, 'never before or since has the world been so interested in love in this manner.'[33] Delight, longing, concern, anguish, jealousy, constancy – each is anatomized over and over again in the poems of Sir Philip Sidney, Edward de Vere, George Peele, Fulke Greville, Christopher Marlowe, Robert Greene, Nicholas Breton, Sir Walter Raleigh, and a host of others. Almost always there was the theme of love as the total union of flesh with flesh, mind with mind, heart with heart, soul with soul, until the separateness and loneliness were overcome and the two halves made whole.

> If thus we needs must go;
> What shall our one Heart do,
> This One made of our Two?
> Madam, two Hearts we brake;
> And from them both did take
> The best, one Heart to make.[34]

---

[32] Tennyson, *The Princess* (1st edn, 1847), 157.
[33] Pearson, *Elizabethan Love*, 297.   [34] *Some Longer Poems*, 433.

And towering above these giants are Spenser and Shakespeare. Of the former, C. S. Lewis writes, 'in the history of sentiment he is the greatest among the founders of that romantic conception of marriage which is the basis of all our love literature from Shakespeare to Meredith.'[35] Of Shakespeare, it is really superfluous to speak; universally applauded as the greatest of all love poets, he had 'represented in an inimitable and masterly manner all the phenomena and manifestations of love'. The love he describes is 'modern love in its full development'.[36] Genius that he was, Shakespeare did not spring forth unannounced as the inventor of modern love, singing to a world that did not comprehend him. Both his contemporary audience and his own life gave him ample illustration of romantic love, and his literary predecessors had also sung of love with vigour, if not with quite the same skill.

Chaucer's verse is filled with references to, and assumptions about, the prevalence of love. Love is frequently the theme of *The Canterbury Tales*. In 'The Miller's Tale', for instance,

> This Carpenter hadd wedded newe a wyf,
> Which that he lovede moore than his lyf

This turned out to be a mistake, since she was much younger than him, and he 'was fallen in the snare'. When the carpenter thinks his young wife will drown, he is beside himself with anxiety: ''Allas, my wyf! And shal she drenche? Allas, myn Alisoun!' For sorwe of this he fil almoost adoun.' 'The Merchant's Tale', set in Lombardy, is based on the cuckolding of an old man who had married a young bride for love. He had decided to wed in his old age so that he

> Might ones knowe of thilke blisful lyf
> That is bitwixe an housbonde and his wyf

His decision is welcomed by Chaucer, who proceeds to write in praise of marriage:

> For who kan be so buxom as a wyf?
> Who is so trewe and eek so ententyf
> To kepe hym, syk and hool, as is his make?

---

[35] Lewis, *Allegory*, 360. [36] Bloch, *Sexual*, 507, and Finck in the same.

> For wele or wo she wole hym nat forsake;
> She nys nat wery hym to love and serve,
> Thogh that he lye bedrede til he sterve.

A wife is God's gift to help man in his loneliness and nakedness:

> Heere may ye se, and heerby may ye preve,
> That wyf is mannes helpe and his confort,
> His Paradyse terrestre, and his disport;
> So buxom and so vertuous is she,
> They moste nedes lyve in unitee.
> O flessh they been, and o flessh, as I gesse,
> Hath but oon herte in wele and in distresse.

She is a helpmeet in husbandry and in sickness and the wise man should

> Love wel thy wyf, as Crist loved his chirche.
> If thou lovest thyself thou lovest thy wyf.

This picture of marriage is exactly like those of the seventeenth century, with the emphasis on mutual love, one heart and one flesh. In many of Chaucer's early poems too, love is celebrated. The whole of *The Dethe of Blaunche the Duchesse* is concerned with love, and *Troilus and Criseyde* is filled with passionate love. The *Legend of Good Women*, the *Parlement of Fowles*, the *Romaunt of the Rose* translation, all contain a very large element of love. There are numerous lines that could have been written at any time from the fourteenth to the seventeenth century:

> Thus am I slayn with Loves firy dart.
> I can but love hir best, my swete fo;
> Love hath me taught no more of his art
> But serve alwey, and stinte for no wo.[37]

Chaucer's poetry was part of a long tradition of love verse, clearly influenced by French poetry. But the object of affection appears to be of the same rank as the poet; she is not a distant and superior lady, nor is there any stress on the adulterous theme. There is reverence

[37] Pollard, *Chaucer Works*, 44, 48, 204, 205, 334. There is, of course, some irony in Chaucer's praise.

and respect, but not servility, and the love is attainable. In a poem from the Sloane manuscripts we have an attempt to define love, starting

> Love is soft and love is sweet, and speaks in accents fair;
> Love is mighty agony, and love is mighty care;
> Love is utmost ecstasy and love is keen to dare:
> Love is wretched misery; to live with, it's despair.

A particularly poignant set of love poems has survived by chance in one manuscript, Harley 2253, composed in the late thirteenth and early fourteenth centuries. The first secular poem begins:

> The heart of man can hardly know
> What secret love can do,
> Unless a lovely woman show,
> Who knows it through and through.

Another implores:

> All this year I've been in love, and I can love no more:
> My sighing for your grace was endless, lover I adore,
> But love is yet no nearer me, and that afflicts me sore.
> Sweet darling, I have loved you long, so hear me, I implore.

It concludes:

> From Lincoln, Lindsey, Lound, Northampton, round for
>   many a mile
> I've never seen a prettier girl who could my heart beguile.
> Sweet darling, let me beg you, be my lover for a while.

This is a far cry from the castles and the lord's wives of 'courtly love'; it suggests a peripatetic lover who had met a pretty girl and fallen in love with her. At the end there is a delightful duet between 'He' and 'She'. He implores her, 'with just a word from you, my love, my care and grief were past.' She calls him a fool and tells him to desist. He replies:

> The scandal would be yours if love for you were death of me;
> So let me live and be your love, and you my lover be.

She tells him to 'stop that din'. He reminds her that he is now full of woe, though once 'at your window fifty time we clung exchanging kisses.' She is finally convinced and proclaims him her love, 'so you be mine, and I'll be yours, and all your joy fulfil.'[38]

It would be possible to take these themes back even earlier, to the Anglo-Saxon 'Wife's Lament', for instance, based on the story of a woman separated from her husband. She tells of how

> . . . we have vowed
> Full many a time that nought should come between us
> But death alone, and nothing else at all.
> All that is changed, and it is now as though
> Our marriage and our love had never been . . .

Left alone,

> The absence of my lord comes sharply to me.
> Dear lovers in this world lie in their beds,
> While I alone at crack of dawn must walk
> Under the oak-tree round this earthly cave,[39]

That nothing should come between them, that the love of marriage superseded all, speaks for itself. And that other married couples are assumed to be 'dear lovers' who lie together in bed, is equally revealing.

It might be argued that most of this drama and poetry was written for and by a very small, educated, upper-class group, whose feelings may not accurately reflect those of the majority of the population. It is very difficult through poetry to penetrate to lower levels, for it is well known that many of the supposed 'folk' ballads that ordinary people sang and recited through the centuries are, in fact, merely adaptations or copies of the very poetry we have been considering. Many of the ballads which were sold in vast quantities from the sixteenth century onwards had been composed specifically by the self-same poets. Yet this fact is interesting in itself, suggesting that the love-soaked literature of the educated elite was attractive and meaningful to the rest. It is worth noting that a high proportion of the ballads printed by the great ballad collectors of the nineteenth century were concerned

[38] *Medieval English Verse*, 178, 101, 199, 209, 211–12.
[39] Quoted in Mount, *Subversive Family*, 101.

with love.[40] So many love ballads circulated that in Pepys' library there was a whole volume devoted exclusively to them. Such ballads explored every angle of love, seeing it as a strange, overwhelming passion which could strike anyone and which could lead to delight or disaster.

Although the artistic materials – poetry, drama, stories – all fit together and are entirely consistent with the moralistic and philosophical accounts, it could be contended that such evidence is not conclusive. First, art does not always necessarily reflect life. Secondly, much of it was based on classical or continental models, which means that what it reflects had complex roots. In order to pursue the question of whether love before and during marriage was necessary and widespread, we need to turn to other sources which are of a more personal kind, written by and about specific historic individuals. One such source is the letters written between or about men and women.

There are, of course, serious difficulties in using letters as a source. There are conventions in letter-writing which mean that we have to read behind what is said. Sometimes there is an unnatural formality and stiffness, which can be misinterpreted as absence of feeling; sometimes a fulsome sentimentality which misleads in the opposite direction. Furthermore, the letters that have been preserved tend to be those of middling to upper-class families.

The first point to notice about letters as a source for husband–wife relationships is the very fact that letters between spouses were so important. As we shall see, the absence of husbands from wives for more than a few days very often initiated a regular flow of letters from both directions. Such letters, as Hooker observed, gave delight to their receivers, and the contents illustrate how necessary it was for husband and wife to communicate emotions, thoughts and practical advice. It is no accident that England should have produced four of the greatest writers of love letters – Swift, Steele and Robert and Elizabeth Browning – or that we should have some fine letter collections to draw on. The extremes to which it could be carried are shown by Dudley Ryder, whose musings on the advantages and disadvantages of marriage we have already examined. We are told that he corresponded daily with his wife, she managing all the money matters as well as household affairs. The importance of letters between men and women, both before and after marriage, and the

40 Percy, *Reliques*.

depth of conjugal closeness that the letters were expected to exhibit, are well illustrated in the letter-writing manuals that were published in profusion from the later sixteenth century onwards.

The Revd Cooke's *Universal Letter Writer* of about 1841 devoted a quarter of its examples to 'Love, Courtship and Marriage'. Here was portrayed the Tennysonian image of marriage as the union of two souls, minds and hearts – a real, deep friendship. A girl writing to her cousin three months after her wedding about the advantages of marriage explained, 'to have a real friend to whom I can communicate my secrets, and who on all occasions is ready to sympathize with me, is what I never before experienced.' A widow thinking of remarrying 'would choose, as I advance in years, to have a friend to whom I might at all times be able to open my mind with freedom.' *The Court Letter Writer* of 1773 devoted 59 out of 122 model letters (excluding those by eminent persons) to 'love, marriage and the conduct of married life'. A model letter from an absent husband ran: 'were it possible for me to be happy when absent from you, I must be very much so at this time: but a husband may be believed, where a lover would be suspected. Indeed, nothing gives me a true satisfaction that you do not share with me.' People were warned that passion was necessary for a successful marriage. One woman advised another not to marry an old miser: 'romantic ideas of love are what you and I have long disclaimed; yet let me tell you there should be a sufficient stock of the *belle passion* to counterbalance those little anxieties which naturally arise in the married state.' A gentleman advised his sister that 'unhappily esteem alone will not constitute a happy marriage; passion also must be kept alive'; he then quoted with approval Madame de Maintenon's advice – 'Let your husband be your best friend, your only confidant.'[41]

Moving back 120 years, another model letter book devoted equal space to love, married and unmarried, 105 pages out of 279 being filled with letters on amorous themes. Many were from lovers, but some were between husband and wife. One, 'To her dearest husband' addresses him as 'My only life', and is clearly from a woman who is in some sort of captivity, ending 'your ever loving wife in distress'. Another, 'To his loving wife, B. G.', makes excuses for 'tarrying too long from a wife'.[42] An earlier manual, *The English*

---

[41] Cooke, *Universal Letter Writer*, 73, 76, and cf. 77; *The Court Letter Writer*, 107, 166, 180–1.   [42] S.S., *Secretaries Studie*, 84, 97.

Secretorie of 1586, contained a number of letters concerning love and marriage. An especially striking model letter was one written to comfort a woman who had recently lost her husband. It was assumed here that she had lost her very best and strongest friend and was suffering deep grief. The writer, being 'informed with what great extremity you have entertained the news of his loss', the widow being in so 'great a storm of grief' and having been in tears since hearing the news a month before, attempts to reason the woman out of the excesses of lamentation. He admits that she has every reason to be sorrowful, 'having lost the chief and principal jewel of all your worldly love and liking, the favoured companion of all your pleasant and youthful years, the entire comfort and solace of your present happiness, and such a one who above all worlds, or any earthly estimation at all, accounted, honoured, and entirely more than any others received and loved you', yet he tries to persuade her to mitigate her lamentations and control her grief.[43]

The model letter books stand intermediate between art and life, and their accuracy can only be tested by looking at real letters, many of which they themselves quoted as 'models'. The letters of the eighteenth century – by Swift, Steele, Lady Montagu, William Pitt – are well known and show an elevated conception of married love. Many seventeenth-century letters show the same features, even though they are almost all written by members of the upper gentry whose marriages, we have seen, were under heavy pressure from economic considerations. Sir William Mainwaringe wrote in 1645 a letter, 'For my dearest and best Love, These', starting 'My only Joy, your letter was welcome to me.' He then counselled her, 'Be ruled and advised by this bearer who is able, and will advise you every way for the safest and the best; and dearest my love, let your greatest care be to look after your own health, and next that we may but live together, our being asunder being (next never seeing one another again which God of Heaven forbid) the greatest curse and vexation can happen to me.' He ended, 'Thy most constant, faithful, and ever affectionate, tho' poor, W. Mainwaringe'.[44]

The Civil War separated many husbands and wives, sometimes for good. In 1651 Sir Timothy Fetherstonhaugh wrote his wife a letter, before his execution, which included a passage advising her on the children's education: 'they sucked nothing but virtue from thy womb

[43] Day, *Secretorie*, 211–12. [44] *The Topographer*, i, 70–1.

and in the presence of God I speak it thou hast been to me an unparalleled wife and a mother to my children.'[45] A number of the affectionate letters which Lady Brilliana Harley wrote to her husband in the 1620s have survived and been published. The start of one, written to 'my dear husband Sir Robert Harley', will indicate their tone. 'Dear Sir – your two letters . . . were very welcome to me: and if you knew how gladly I receive your letters, I believe you would never let an opportunity pass.' Having commented on the weather and that she hoped to see him soon, she continued, 'you see how my thoughts go with you: and as you have many of mine, so let me have some of yours. Believe me, I think I never missed you more than now I do, or else I have forgot what is passed.' She then gives her news of the family, says she has sent him a hamper of books, food and drink, ending 'your most faithful affectionate wife, Brilliana Harley'.[46]

The letters of the royalist Knyvett family are equally eloquent testimonies of domestic affection. As the editor of the letters states,

the careful preservation of these missives by his wife, his frequently expressed impatience to return to her side and to 'sleep in her arms', the warmth and passion of the letters as well as their banter, their commendations and occasional playful scoldings, their varied but always affectionate addresses and subscriptions, the careful study of fashion and choice of presents for his wife, the delicacies sent by her to him on his travels – all these are eloquent of a mutual understanding and affection.

We may quote just one letter:

Sweet heart I am forced yet to send the shadow of my self, the true affection of a substance that loves you above all the world. My business I hope will be effectually despatched presently and god willing I will be with thee before you are aware. I have been to look for stuff for your bed and have sent down patterns for you to choose which you like best. They are the nearest to the pattern that we can find. If you lack anything except my company you are to blame not to let me know of it, for my self being only yours the rest do follow. Thus in haste entreating thee to be merry and the more merry to think thou hast him in thy arms that had rather be with you than in any place under heaven; and so I rest. Thy dear loving husband for ever, Tho: Knyvett.[47]

[45] Bouch, *Prelates and People*, 265. [46] *Letters of Harley*, 3.
[47] Schofield, *Knyvett Letters*, 23, 56–7.

One of the great letter collections of the seventeenth century, that of the Buckinghamshire Verneys, shows plenty of evidence of this depth and commitment between husband and wife. For instance, the loss of his wife by Sir Ralph Verney was an enormous blow. An early editor of the letters comments: 'the reality of Ralph's grief for the loss of his wife was shown by his life-long widowhood and his undying remembrance of her throughout the succeeding forty-six years ... the references to her in his letters are as true as they are touching.' To take one example, Sir Ralph wrote to Dr Denton: 'My mind runs more after Italy; not to delight myself with anything there, for since my dear wife's death I have bid adieu to all that most men count their happiness ... Ah, Dr., Dr., her company made every place a paradise unto me, but she being gone, unless god be most miraculously merciful, what good can be expected by your most afflicted and unfortunate servant.' His son, John Verney, was equally uxorious, it would appear. He married a girl of fifteen, some twenty-five years younger than himself, and, the editor tells us, 'never ceased to be her lover during the six short years of their married life'. He had her portrait painted and 'during their rare separations, their letters reveal the depth of tender sentiment which underlay the cautious reserve of the worldly-wise man of affairs.' Part of one letter will have to suffice as evidence:

> Dearest Dear, I wrote you this morning by the Coach since which I have received your pretty lines under the 22nd and for your tender expressions there is nothing but a reciprocal love can make you returns, and that be confident you have ... I thank you for your ten thousand kisses and wish I had one half dozen from you in the mean time; but for this vacancy we'll have the more when I return to you whom God preserve. I rest your Truly loving and most affectionate Dear, John Verney. I have had my hair cut.[48]

As we move back beyond the seventeenth century, there is a tendency for archaic language and a certain formality of style to come between us and the writers. The letters often seem more constrained, their contents more practical. Allowing for a change in style, we nevertheless find a similar undercurrent of closeness. In the sixteenth century, several collections of letters only survived because they were confiscated and hence preserved in the Public Record Office. One

[48] Verney, *Verney Memoirs*, ii, 422; ii, 423; iv, 251–2; iv, 252–3.

such collection is that of the merchant family Johnson, whose extensive correspondence of the period 1542–1552 was sent to the Privy Council when the firm went bankrupt. The correspondence that has survived has been the basis of *Tudor Family Portrait* by Barbara Winchester. The author clearly expected to find little affection or love. Until Elizabeth's reign, we are told, 'Tudor Englishmen were not of a noticeably romantic disposition . . . In that world, romantic love played little part; . . . love and marriage were poles apart.' Yet what do these letters, of a mainly businesslike kind, reveal? They reveal a marriage, after extensive and costly courtship, based on mutual attraction between John Johnson and Sabine Saunders. Before marriage 'it seems that Sabine was seldom out of his thoughts', and constant presents were sent to her. Once married, love increased.

> Several years of marriage did not change the lover into the husband. There is no doubt that John and Sabine loved each other passionately. They were blissfully happy in each other's company, and utterly miserable when apart. During his enforced sojourns abroad at the Staple, they wrote each other long and loving letters, not once in a while, but many times a week.

In her letters to him 'love and cheeses are wonderfully mixed'; as for him, 'his affection and contentment increased with time. Sabine was the one person in the world with whom he could truly be himself, take off the mask.' Their letters to each other are full of news of children, of friends, of domestic matters, of business affairs. 'Sometimes they tease each other, write nonsense, long passionately for the other to be with them.' As time wore on, their affection increased, if anything. At news of his sickness, 'she grew into a fever of impatience to be with him and set off in a cold November to join him in Calais.' The passion and tenderness are present from start to end.[49]

Another similar chance occurrence, the treason trial of Arthur Plantagenet, Lord Lisle, has preserved for us an even more extensive collection. Some 1,900 letters written between 1533 and 1540 (almost exactly contemporaneous with the Johnson letters) have now been edited. Lord Lisle was in Calais like Johnson, but as Lord

[49] Winchester, *Tudor Portrait*, 61, 65, 67–8, 69, 73.

Deputy. Here, at a higher level, marriage was even more constrained, so that we might expect less spontaneity and affection. In the introduction to the abridged version of the letters we are told, 'whether the alliance was originally entered into by both parties as the usual Tudor business arrangement we do not know.' As with the Johnson collection, the editor clearly expected arranged marriage and little love. Yet the letters contradict this; 'what we do know, from the letters they wrote as husband and wife, is that either before or after their marriage they fell as whole-heartedly in love with each other as the most romantic modernist could wish.' This 'extraordinary' depth of love is revealed despite the conventions of phrasing. 'The letters they exchanged when absent from each other in 1538 and 1539, are, as a group, incomparable: the sixteenth century has nothing else of the kind to touch them. The intimacy of the writing is intensified rather than obscured by the formal phrasing.' 'In the midst of what is apt to seem to us the bewildering and terrifying brutality of the age, these letters make, as it were, a point of rest, reassuring us of ultimate values.' Even cynical friends could write to Arthur and Honor Lisle: 'because ye be both but one soul though ye be two bodies, I write but one letter.' Lord Lisle addressed his wife as 'Mine Own', 'Sweetheart', and signed himself 'your loving husband'. His wife replied, 'Mine own sweet heart'. She told him of her safe voyage home, that she was well, but 'should have been much merrier if I had been coming towards you, or if you had been with me.' She concluded, 'I shall think every hour X till I be with you again', and signed herself, 'By her that is both your and her own, Honor Lyssle'.[50] Thus these two major collections of confiscated letters mirror each other.

If we move back into the pre-Reformation period, the surviving letter collections are even fewer. The Plumptons', a Yorkshire gentry family, suggest, at least in the forms of address, a similar affection. In 1502 Robert Plumpton sent a letter 'To my entirely and right heartily beloved wife, Dame Agnes Plumpton', starting 'My dear heart . . .' and ending 'By your own lover Robert Plumpton, Kt'. That neither of them were stock or formal terms of address is shown by the variation in the next letter printed, which was addressed 'To my right heartily and mine entirely beloved wife', started 'Best beloved . . .', and ended 'by your loving husband . . .'[51] Another collection, the Cely letters,

[50] St Clare Byrne, *Lisle*, 2–3, 3, 3, 307, 310–11.
[51] Stapleton, *Plumpton Letters*, cx, cxiii-xiv.

are almost exclusively concerned with trade and there are none between husband and wife, though it is revealing that when one brother is encouraging another to marry, he recognizes the necessity for love: 'I pray God that it may be imprinted in your mind to set your heart there.'[52]

One of the two largest published collections of medieval letters are those of the Stonors, an Oxfordshire gentry family. Again the editor expects arranged marriage and lack of affection, and again is pleasantly surprised. 'Parental rule at the time was generally strict, but the Stonor Letters give us on the whole a uniform impression of family affection. This is the more remarkable since matrimony was very much a matter of business.' Thus we find that Elizabeth Ryche, who was married for the second time, to William Stonor, in 1475, 'wrote often to him with a manifest affection'. She addressed him as 'Right entirely and best beloved husband' and signed herself as 'your own to my power'. Again these were not stock phrases, for later she addressed him as 'Right reverent and worshipful and entirely best beloved husband', ending 'by your own wife'. A further letter was addressed 'To my most entirely beloved husband', and started 'Right entirely and my most special beloved husband'. The contents of the letters, showing concern, interest, overlapping lives, are entirely consistent with these intimate, warm salutations. Only one letter of courtship survives in these collections – from Thomas Betson to the young girl of about thirteen whom he would later marry. It is a delightful letter, playful, affectionate, enclosing a ring as a token of affection. For instance, he asked her to eat well so that she would 'wax and grow fast to be a woman', which would 'make me the gladdest man of the world, by my troth'.[53]

The most extensive collection of late medieval letters are those of the Norfolk gentry family of Paston. These show an interesting blend of the practical and the romantic, the economic and the psychological, which fits very well with the contemporary attempts to combine a marriage of two equals in fortune with something beyond the merely arranged. There is the love affair of Margery Paston and Richard Calle, commemorated in only one surviving letter from Calle, in which he asserts the primacy of their love and marriage bond over all others.[54] Despite bitter opposition from her mother, their marriage

[52] Hanham, *Cely Letters*, 106–7.

[53] Kingsford, *Stonor Letters*, i, xliii; i, xxviii; ii, 42; ii, 66–7; ii, 7.

[54] Gairdner, *Paston Letters*, ii, 350.

was solemnized and supported by the Church. What is equally interesting is the number of cases where marriages which had been preceded by extensive negotiations about property were also obviously accompanied by depth of feeling. The mother of the bride wrote to the groom that although he had promised not to break the matter of matrimony to her until other things had been settled, 'ye have made her such advocate for you, that I may never have rest night nor day, for calling and crying upon to bring the said matter to effect &c.' The mother points out that 'upon Friday is Saint Valentine's Day, and every bride chooseth him [*sic*] a mate', and encourages the suitor thus to come over and finalize the match. The bride herself then wrote to her 'right wellbeloved Valentine', asking to hear of his health, adding that 'I am not in good health of body, nor of heart, nor shall be till I hear from you.' She continues by quoting some snatches of love poetry, and imploring her suitor not to forsake her because her portion is inadequate: 'But if that ye love me, as I trust verily that ye do, ye will not leave me therefore; for if that ye had not half the livelihood that ye have . . . I would not forsake you.'

The marriage finally took place and the subsequent letters show the same concern, interest and affection that we have seen in later letters. Shortly after the wedding, Margery ended one letter: 'I pray that you will wear the ring with the image of Saint Margaret, that I sent you for a remembrance, till you come home; you have left me such a remembrance, that maketh me to think upon you both day and night and even when I would sleep.' In one letter she reprimanded her husband: 'I marvel I hear no word from you, which grieveth me full evil.' In the next she addresses him, 'Mine own sweet heart'. The love clearly lasted, as subsequent correspondence shows. For instance, Margery ends a letter seven years later: 'I am sorry that you shall not be at home for Christmas. I pray you that you will come as soon as you may. I shall think myself half a widow, because you shall not be at home. God have you in His keeping. Written on Christmas Even, By your, M.P.'[55] Of course, by definition, it was the more affectionate letter-writing couples whose letters we have. Yet the evidence is very suggestive.

The final major source we shall consider takes us down even deeper, behind most of the artifices, conventions and formalities, to what people really felt and thought during these centuries about love

---

[55] Ibid., iii, 169–70; iii, 215; iii, 293, 294; iii, 315.

and the marital relationship. These are the autobiographies and diaries which have survived from the sixteenth century onwards. One defect of this source is that it starts relatively late – we cannot really go back before the mid-sixteenth century. Furthermore, like most of our sources, diaries and autobiographies tend to be concentrated among the top, literate part of the population. Though we shall find a few written by yeomen, apprentices and others, we are mainly still confined to the middling upwards. This bias, however, is somewhat counteracted by the fact that it is precisely in such groups that marriage was under most pressure from economic and status considerations.

Many diaries and autobiographies illuminate all facets of the marital bond, and it would require a separate book to deal with their portrayal of the close and companionly relationship. Perhaps the most accurate single index we may use is the reaction to the actual or likely death of a spouse. Death concentrates the mind and emotions and jolts people into a conscious awareness of what they have lost, or are likely to lose. It is impossible to interpret silence or a short mention as evidence of lack of emotion; there are a thousand reasons why a person might not commit his real feelings to paper. But in certain cases people did attempt to describe their feelings, and this provides us with insights into the degree to which marriage was based on a deep interweaving of mind and heart.

Even though it is abridged in published form, the diary of Thomas Turner, a Sussex shopkeeper in the 1750s, gives a poignant account of a man who had lost his 'other half'. Earlier he had at times been deeply miserable in his marriage, but when his wife looked likely to die he wrote, 'quite destitute of father and mother, and am in all probability like to lose my wife, the only friend, I believe, I have now in this world, and the alone centre of my worldly happiness.' In her illness he lamented, 'Oh, my poor wife is most prodigious bad! No, not one gleam of hope have I of her recovery. Oh, how does the thought distract my tumultuous soul! What shall I do? – what will become of me!' His 'beloved wife' then died. 'In her I have lost a sincere friend, a virtuous wife, a prudent good economist in her family, and a very valuable companion.' Six weeks later he was 'almost distracted with trouble: how do I hourly find the loss I have sustained in the death of my dear wife! What can equal the value of a virtuous wife? I hardly know which way to turn, or what way of life to pursue. I am left as a beacon on a rock, or an ensign on a hill.' All that was 'serene and in order' became 'noise and confusion', and the memories of his dead wife continued to overwhelm him. Three years later he was still lamenting 'my present irregular and very unpleasant way of life' compared to 'what I used to lead in my dear Peggy's time. I know not the comfort of an agreeable friend and virtuous fair.' He graphically portrayed the loss of time, and the lack of the friend who had helped to overcome loneliness. 'Oh! how pleasant was the even spent, after a busy day, in my dear Pegg's time; but now it's all unpleasant – nothing to sooth the anxious mind, no pleasing companion, no sincere friend, no agreeable acquaintance, or at least amongst the fair sex.' So he started to look for a second wife, out of loneliness.[56]

Numerous seventeenth century diaries and autobiographies record the great grief of husbands at the loss of their wives.[57] We are forced to select just a few instances. Elias Pledger of Essex described how in losing his wife he had 'lost the companion of my life, one that was in every respect a meet help'. After the death of his wife, Sir John Bramston 'every day grew more sensible of her loss in regard of my children', and recalled how 'she was a very observant wife. I scarce ever went a journey but she wept.' Elias Ashmole lost his wife in childbearing: 'my dear wife fell suddenly sick about evening, and died (to my own great grief, and the grief of all her friends).' He then noted, 'She was a virtuous, modest, careful and loving wife, her affection was exceeding great toward me, as was mine to her, which caused us to live so happily together.'[58]

Richard Baxter married late but lived, according to his accounts, a life of devotion and shared hardship for nineteen years: 'we lived in inviolated love and mutual complacency, sensible of the benefit of mutual help.' At his wife's death, 'in depth of grief I truly wrote her life . . . In the same passion I published some *Poetical fragments*.' A marble monument of his wife having been destroyed some years before, 'I hope this paper monument, erected by one that is following, even at the door, in some passion indeed of love and grief, but in sincerity of truth, will be more publicly useful and durable than that marble stone was.' Written under the 'power of melting grief', it

[56] Turner, *Diary*, 46, 47–8, 50, 51, 54, 68, 70–1.

[57] Grosart, *Lismore Papers*, 102; Holles, *Memorials*, 195, 231; Fishwick, *Thomas Jolly*, 23; Parson, *Diary of Slingsby*, 74.

[58] 'Diary of Pledger', fol. 83v; Bramston, *Autobiography*, 111; Gunther, *Diary of Ashmole*, 18.

records the deep mental, spiritual and social ties that bound them. Margaret ran his finances, and came to share prison with him, making it a place of happiness. Indeed, this author of many notable works including the famous *Saint's Everlasting Rest*, one of the greatest spiritual counsellors of his century, found her advice on difficult spiritual cases exceeded his own: 'her apprehension of such things was so much quicker, and more discerning than mine . . . she was better at resolving a case of conscience than most divines that ever I knew in all my life.'[59]

An exact contemporary of Baxter, and like him a Nonconformist minister, Oliver Heywood provides an equally moving account of his marriage and his wife's death. The first mercy that he thanked God for was that He had 'given me a pious, provident, prudent, sweet natured wife, whom I love entirely and she loves me dearly, and is exceeding tender of me, almost to an excess.' God had 'knit my heart to my sweet wife by many invincible bands of cordial love, both natural, moral, and spiritual'. She 'was as loving a wife as ever lay in any mans bosom, if she offended in any way it was through vehemency of affection . . . never had couple so much comfort in each other and so little discontent, as we had in that six years we were together.' Heywood gives two accounts of her death. One is a painful description of the death scene itself, of her last words to the assembled family, which cover four printed pages. Then follows further reflection. The loss of his 'dear and precious wife . . . was the heaviest personal stroke that ever I experienced'. Her loss was of the deepest kind: 'I want her at every turn, every where, and in every work. Methinks I am but half my self without her.' Heywood's short 'Life' of his wife is very tender – for instance, describing her as 'the mirror of patience and subjection in her relation, as a child as a wife, and of tenderness and care as a sister, and as a mother'. His diaries show that her memory did not fade. Seventeen years later he recorded the anniversary of her death, as he did fifty years after the event, when he was 'something affected'.[60]

Unfortunately, English autobiographies and diaries are very rare before 1600, and it is therefore impossible to take this analysis much further back. An exception is the diary of another Puritan clergyman,

---

[59] Lloyd-Thomas, *Autobiography of Baxter*, 274, 249; Baxter, *Breviate*, 149, 61, 127.

[60] Turner, *Heywood*, iii, 270; i, 169–70; i, 62; i, 66–9; i, 176–7; i, 176–7; i, 61; ii, 64; iv, 258.

Richard Rogers of Essex, in the 1580s. His reaction to the possible death of his wife in childbirth lays out clearly some of the threads which we have seen bound men and women in marriage. His list of what he would lose if she died reads: 'First, the fear of marrying again, dangerous as 2 marriages are. Want of it in the mean while. Forgoing so fit a companion for religion, housewifery, and other comforts. Loss and decay in substance. Care of household matters cast on me. Neglect of study. Care and looking after children. Forgoing our borders. Fear of losing friendship among her kindred. These are some.'[61] It is a rich mixture of the practical and emotional needs that a wife fulfilled.

These reactions of husbands indicate one side of the loss, and we can complement them with some reaction by wives, all of them from the seventeenth century. Lucy Hutchinson was so deeply involved with her husband that in her widowhood she wrote a lengthy *Memoirs of the Life of Colonel Hutchinson*. At the start she addressed her children. She was under the command of her husband at his death 'not to grieve at the common rate of desolate women', and thus was studying ways 'to moderate my woe, and if it were possible to augment my love, can for the present find out none more just to your dear father nor consolatory to myself than the preservation of his memory'. She thanked God for the 'excess of love and delight' she had received from him, and proceeded to describe his person and his virtues. These were legion, and among them was his conjugal love.

> For conjugal affection to his wife, it was such in him, as whosoever would draw out a rule of honour and kindness, and religion, to be practised in that estate, need no more, but exactly draw out his example; never man had a greater passion for a woman, nor a more honourable esteem of a wife, yet he was not uxorious, nor remitted not that just rule which it was her honour to obey . . . he governed by persuasion, which he never employed but to things honourable and profitable for herself; he loved her soul and her honour more than her outside . . . all that she was was *him*, while he was here, and all that she is now at best but his pale shade . . . so constant was he in his love, that when she ceased to be young and lovely, he began to show most fondness, he loved her at such a kind and generous rate as words cannot express.[62]

[61] Knappen, *Puritan Diaries*, 74.
[62] Hutchinson, *Memoirs*, i, 29–30, 31, 45–6.

These are a few phrases from a paean of praise to his virtues lasting for sixteen printed pages, which Mrs Hutchinson was so dissatisfied with that she attempted to re-write the whole section. Then follow the 650 pages of his *Life*.

Alice Thornton's *Autobiography* likewise describes a deep relationship with her husband, though she had at first been reluctant to marry him. She wrote a long 'relation of the last sickness and death of my dear and honoured husband William Thornton, esquire'. Out of the 'vale of tears and shadow of death' she tried to reconcile his death with God's will. The first news of his sickness led her to 'a great trembling, with excessive grief and fears upon me for his life and safety'. She nearly fainted several times, hoping to do so as an alternative to losing her 'joy and comfort'. On hearing that he was worse, 'my faintings renewed with my exceeding sorrows, for the fears of being deprived of this my sole delight in this world next under God.' She then heard news 'of my most terrible loss that any poor woman could have, in being deprived of my sweet and exceeding dear husband's life'. They had 'lived a dear and loving couple, in holy marriage, almost seventeen years'. Her 'sorrows and laments cannot be weighed for him which parted with the great and sole delight and comfort I esteemed of my life.' She recounted how 'often had I petitioned Heaven to spare him, and to call me to Himself, when I have seen him in his palsie fits. But my dear would reprove me, and say that I offended God in too much loving him, and not to be willing to part with him.'[63]

Like Lucy Hutchinson, Anne, Lady Fanshawe decided to write a life of her husband in order to assuage her grief and to describe to a child what his father had been like. The extraordinary and turbulent life they led during the Civil War was based on an intense personal relationship which Lady Fanshawe described to her son as follows.

Now you will expect I should say something that may remain of us jointly, which I will do, though it makes my eyes gush out with tears, and cuts me to the soul, to remember and in part express the joy I was blessed with in him. Glory be to God we never had but one mind throughout our lives, our souls were wrapped up in each other, our aims and designs one, our loves one, and our resentments one. We so studied one the other that we knew each other's mind by our looks; whatever was real happiness, God gave it me in him. But to commend

[63] Jackson, *Thornton Autobiography*, 172–3, 175, 176, 173.

my better half . . . methinks is to commend myself, and so may bear a censure.

The whole text is filled with little vignettes showing this deep love and affection. After their marriage, her husband had to go to Bristol. 'As for it was the first time we had parted a day since we married, he was extremely afflicted even to tears, though passion was against his nature.' When they met again, her husband greeted her with a hundred pieces of gold, saying, 'I know that thou keepest my heart, so wilt keep my fortune, which from this time I will ever put into thy hands.' On another occasion she tried to pry into her husband's delicate political affairs as a member of the Council. 'Going to bed I asked him again, and said I could not believe he loved me, if he refused to tell me all he knew; but he answered nothing but stopped my mouth with kisses.' Later the next day she tried again to put pressure on him, to which, taking her in his arms, he replied, 'My dearest soul, nothing upon earth can afflict me like that [i.e., hurting her], and when you asked me of my business, it was wholly out of my power to satisfy thee; for my life and fortune shall be thine, and every thought of my heart . . . but my honour is my own, which I cannot preserve if I communicate the Prince's affairs.' It is no surprise that his death should ring from her a cry of piercing agony to God, calling for help 'to my disquieted soul and now sinking under this great weight'.[64]

One final, brief vignette, this time of the agony of actual parting, comes from the autobiography of the Quaker Mary Pennington. Describing the death of her first husband, she wrote: 'At last he called to me – 'come my dear, let me kiss thee before I die!' which he did with that heartiness, as if he would have left his breath in me. Come once more, said he, let me kiss thee and take my leave of thee; which he did in the same manner as before; saying now no more, no more, never no more.' He was writhing in agony: 'Oh! this was a dreadful sight to me; my very heart strings seemed to me to break, and let my heart fall into my belly.' Her friends asked her to leave the bedside, saying that while she was there he could not die: 'which word was so great, so much too big to enter into me; that I like an astonished, amazed creature, stamped with my foot, and cried, die! die! must he die! I cannot go from him.'[65]

[64] *The Memoirs of Fanshawe*, 5–6, 31, 34, 36, 195.
[65] 'A Brief Account', 33, quoted in Delany, *British Autobiography*, 159.

I have selected only one aspect of the close relationship shown in many of the autobiographical works that have survived. It would need a longer and more sustained analysis to show how in many husband and wife relationships there was a companionate sharing of tasks and interests that strikes us as very modern. The sort of work that could be done is shown in the analysis of the diary of Ralph Josselin, which indicates a marriage where the couple were constantly involved with each other, their mutual ties being by far the most important for both of them.[66]

The widespread presence of 'romantic love', both before and within marriage, from at least the time of Chaucer is reflected in many other sources. Wills frequently mentioned the 'loving wife'.[67] Astrologers were besieged by clients asking about love: 'an incessant stream of servant girls asking about their future husbands'. So great were the numbers that the astrologer Forman in the later sixteenth century drew up a questionnaire for male clients, which included the question concerning a prospective wife, 'Was she really in love?' Michael MacDonald summarizes the results of his extensive research on the notebooks of the astrologer Napier:

> Almost 40% of the men and women who described their anxieties and dilemmas to Napier complained about the frustration of courtship and married life. Their tales make nonsense of historians' confident assertions that romantic love was rare in seventeenth-century England or that it was unimportant in choosing marital partners. Passionate attachments were very common among the astrologer's clients. Lovers' quarrels, unrequited love, and double-dealing accounted for the emotional turmoil of 141 persons, about 40 patients mentioned that they had been in love before they were married. These young people suffered the unmistakeable pangs of romantic love.[68]

Many others became ill because of it. From the mid-sixteenth century, when Andrew Boorde recognized that men and women might have the serious illness of 'love-sickness', through the seventeenth, when Robert Burton in his *Anatomy of Melancholy* described the symptoms and cures of love, to the eighteenth when Dr Buchan wrote that love was the strongest passion, it was widely known

---

[66] Macfarlane, *Ralph Josselin*, 105–10.
[67] For a particularly detailed example, see LPS, 8 (Spring 1972), 65.
[68] Thomas, *Religion*, 314; MacDonald, *Mystical Bedlam*, 88–9.

that love was the cause of much sickness and depression.[69]

In the only detailed contemporary analysis we have of an English parish before the eighteenth century, Richard Gough's *Antiquities and Memoirs of the Parish of Myddle*, there are frequent references to people falling in love and to loving couples.[70] When Robert Loder in the early seventeenth century noticed a strange loss in his accounts of over £5 for making malt, he mused: 'what should be the cause hereof I know not, but it was in that year when R. Pearce and Alice were my servants, and then in great love (as it appeared too well), whether he gave it my horses . . . or how it went away, God only knoweth.'[71] The walls of many churches in the seventeenth and eighteenth centuries were covered with memorial inscriptions by husbands for wives and vice versa: 'his late loving, loved wife'; 'she left behind her an affectionate but inconsolable husband'; 'her constant and passionate affection to her dear husband (who sorrowfully undergoes the great affliction of her loss)'; 'constant each to other'; 'sweet society of the best of wives', and so on.[72]

A particularly revealing set of sources are the depositions and examinations taken in matrimonial causes before ecclesiastical courts. Reaching down into the lower levels of society, they are also unique in stretching back to the fourteenth century. This was the time when people explained the feelings that had led them to make marriage vows. The sixteenth-century evidence speaks plainly of romantic love. To select just a few instances: a woman refused to marry a suitor in Elizabethan Essex because 'she could not find in her to love him'; two servants were described by the clerk of the court as 'falling in love together'; a woman 'being in love with a fellow of that parish' tried to prevent him from marrying another.[73] A Leicestershire man addressed his future spouse, 'Rosa, so it is that we have been in love together a long time.'[74] In a case in Essex in 1636, what was expected of a couple is particularly well revealed. A girl's sister deposed that 'John Smith did carry him self very lovingly towards her as a suitor for her marriage and did intreat her that she would grant him her love, and that if she and her father would consent he would be her husband.' She had often heard John say 'that he did entirely love and affect' her

[69] Boorde, *Breviary*, fol.62; Buchan, *Domestic Medicine*, 119.

[70] Gough, *Myddle*, 84, 105. [71] Lodge, *Account Book*, 127.

[72] *The Topographer*, iv, 94; ii, 35; ii, 154; iii, 176; ii, 143.

[73] ERO, D/AED/1, fol.18; ibid., fol.7v; D/ACA/42, fol.49.

[74] Moore, 'Marriage Contracts', 296.

sister, and other witnesses had noted his 'loving carriage and demeanour'.[75]

On the basis of a very detailed study of Wiltshire material, Martin Ingram concludes that 'something very close to our idea of "romantic love", with all its heartaches and inconstancies, emerges quite strongly from the pages of depositions in matrimonial suits.' Likewise Ralph Houlbrooke, who has concentrated on Norwich material, comes to a similar conclusion for the period 1450–1750. 'Cases in the church courts reveal that passionate attachment was a common experience further down the social scale and suggest that the ideal of romantic love was deeply rooted in popular culture in the first half of our period.'[76] Nor is there any sign that this was new in the sixteenth century. A Canterbury court book for 1456 reports: 'She said to him, 'There is something I would like to say if it is not displeasing'. And the man said, 'Speak'. And then she said, 'There is no man in the world whom I love more'. And he said, 'I am grateful to you. And I love you'.' In a second case, heard at York in 1407, the church authorities supported love against the wishes of parents. We are told that 'Agnes Nakerer met and fell in love with a travelling minstrel named John Kent. He married her clandestinely, apparently without her parents' knowledge and certainly without their consent.' The parents then tried to contract her to another, but the court upheld the validity of the marriage.[77]

So what was this love deepened into passion, matured into companionship and friendship, often leading to the knitting together of two minds, bodies and hearts? It was a compound mixture, a bundle of connections, perhaps never better analysed than by a woman who was pining deeply after her husband's death. She explained their relationship thus:

> my love to my husband was not only a matrimonial love, as betwixt man and wife, but a natural love, as the love of brethren, parents, and children, also a sympathetical love, as the love of friends, likewise a customary love, as the love of acquaintances, a loyal love, as the love of a subject, an obedient love, as the love to virtue, an uniting love, as the love of soul and body, a pious love, as the love to heaven, all which several loves did meet and intermix, making one mass of love.[78]

[75] ERO, D/ABD/8, fols 141–3v.

[76] In Outhwaite, *Marriage*, 50; Houlbrooke, *English Family*, 78.

[77] Helmholz, *Marriage Litigation*, 7, 133.   [78] Cavendish, *Letters*, 394.

Without taking into account this powerful, widespread, and impelling passion at the heart of the marriage system,[79] it is impossible to make sense of the other features. To channel, mitigate and encourage this force was a difficult task. The rules and customs which constrained people in their expression of it will be our next concern.

[79] For further recent evidence, and conclusions of a similar kind, see Houlbrooke, *English Family*, 102–5.

PART IV

THE RULES OF MARRIAGE

10

The Duration and Durability of Marriage

Where one of the major aims of marriage is to increase the store of children, it is an obvious strategy to encourage women to have children as early in their reproductive lives as possible. In most human societies, therefore, women have entered first marriages around puberty, at about fifteen or so. This gives them roughly twenty years of effective reproduction, in which they can produce at least ten live-born children. Usually the culture strongly enforces such statistical tendencies; marriages are organized by kin to occur as soon as possible, and it is extremely important to marry off a girl when she becomes nubile. Indeed, to have unmarried, sexually mature women around is dangerous to her family. In Muslim, Hindu and some south European Catholic cultures, they are an embarrassment and shame to their parents and a vulnerable potential threat to the honour of the family. In contrast, we have already seen that England through the centuries up to the industrial revolution seems to have had a very late age for women at marriage. Already we have begun to examine some of the reasons why this might have been the case. Clearly among the pressures were the contemporary legal and popular ideas as to when people were ready to marry.

One source for the study of this topic is medical textbooks, which considered the gynaecological implications of childbearing. There seems to have been a widespread view in such works of the sixteenth to eighteenth centuries that 'early' marriages could be dangerous. An early sixteenth century text argued: 'Many great sicknesses do spring thereof; young mothers also have no just strength, neither to nourish nor to bring forth the fruit . . . Likewise the children which were born of children, became sick and feeble.'[1] Here were a number of

---

[1] Coverdale, *Matrimony*, fol.16v.

separate arguments rolled into one, each of which was repeated elsewhere. Over-young marriages could have several harmful effects. They would weaken the man: he was still growing up and would be drained by sexual activity; part of his vital fluid, his sperm, would flow out of him. This was a view based on theories of bodily humours and fluids inherited from Avicenna and the classic philosophers. In the imagery of the period, just as a young fruit tree was stunted if it was allowed to bear fruit too soon, so a young man might become stunted. The effects on a growing woman were even worse, for she was subjected to the strains of childbearing at too young an age. She might well be damaged for life by beginning to breed too soon. Thirdly, the effects on the offspring of such children were harmful: they would be stunted and sickly because their parents had been immature. Analogies were drawn with the supposed damage produced by the mating of immature animals. Even those who, like Sir William Petty, were very keen to raise the birthrate, argued that 'no youth under 18, and girl under 16, meddle with each other', and others put the age higher.[2]

A second contemporary argument was economic. Foreshadowing Malthus, people had long argued that individuals should be economically as well as physically mature before they married. The bar on marriage before economic independence was institutionalized into many vocational training schemes. One of the major reasons for a mid sixteenth century Act forbidding the admission of anyone to the freedom of the City of London before the age of 24, and forbidding the taking on of apprentices whose time would end before that age, was said to be the likely distress caused to the city: 'one of the chief occasions [i.e., of poverty] is by reason of the overhasty marriages and over soon setting up of households by the young folk of the city . . . be they never so young and unskilful.'[3] Apprentices and servants, as we have seen, were forbidden to marry, and this often took both men and boys to their late teens or early twenties before they could consider marriage.

A particularly forthright account of the necessity of waiting until one had accumulated before marrying is provided by Defoe. Only after Robinson Crusoe's final position has been fully secured by a further voyage does the hero marry.[4] In his *Complete Tradesman*,

[2] Landsdowne, *Petty Papers*, ii, 50.
[3] Quoted in Tawney, *Agrarian Problem*, 106, note.
[4] As noted by Watt, *Rise of Novel*, 75.

Defoe put forward both theoretical arguments and case histories to show the improvidence of early marriage. He lamented that the convention which had once prevented apprentices from marrying was beginning to lose its power – 'custom has taken the edge off it since' – for he agreed with the rule about non-marriage during apprenticeship expressed in the saying, 'they should not wed before they had sped', meaning 'that a young beginner should never marry too soon.' Not only should a person not marry during apprenticeship, but even after it had ended and the young man had set up a shop, he should wait a few years. He noted that 'as the custom now is, generally speaking, the wife and the shop make their first show together: but how few of these early marriages succeed!' Defoe described specific cases where early marriage had led to ruin – the young man 'cripples his fortune, stock-starves his business, and brings a great expense'. A person should save for a while, laying up profits until he is in a state to obtain a wife with a good position. He should not marry 'till, by a frugal, industrious management of his trade in the beginning, he has laid a foundation for maintaining a wife and bringing up a family.'[5]

Defoe put into words the view of many over the sixteenth to eighteenth centuries. For instance, in the early seventeenth century Whateley warned that only 'those of a sufficient estate' should marry; even those who could easily afford it 'do best to forbear matrimony, as I suppose'. They should accumulate a surplus or have good prospects because 'very many after marriage, be put into the close stocks of misery, want, and necessity, not having wherewithall to provide convenient food and rayment for themselves . . . to provide diet and attire for a wife, for many small children, for some servants.'[6]

The basic premise of the many discussions about the relationship between economics and marriage seems to have been that the individual should have obtained economic independence before or by the time of the marriage. Right up to the Second World War in England it was assumed that clerks in banks, junior employees of foreign companies and others would not marry until they had reached a moderately high position in the hierarchy. For they might be sacked from the job if they married on their first home leave. Marriage, in a sense, was a sign of status, something now replaced by the large

[5] Defoe, *Complete Tradesman*, 87, 88, 92, 91–2, 98.
[6] Whateley, *Care-Cloth*, sig.A5, 56; cf. also Gouge, *Domesticall*, 180; Stubbes, *Anatomie*, fols 55–55v.

company car or executive flat. To marry as an undergraduate or even graduate student was still considered foolish and improvident in British universities in the 1950s..

A third argument was that not only should individuals be physically and economically mature, their 'growing' process over, but they should be socially mature. That is to say, their personalities, minds, character, should have left the turmoil of youth behind, and they should have reached some settled plateau. Of course, the time at which this is thought to be achieved is largely culturally determined. In some cases, as with the tribal Lepchas of Sikkim, a person was thought to be capable of adult work and the responsibilities of adulthood at twelve, and frequently married at that age.[7] In other situations, because of race or filial status, a man never gets to be called a 'man', or remains a 'boy' until late in his life.[8]

It would appear from both general statements of the sixteenth to eighteenth centuries and from the self-perceptions of individuals that the English tended to see 'maturity' as both necessary for marriage and as occurring relatively late in life. Thus the late sixteenth-century autobiographer Thomas Whythorne learned from Sir Thomas Elyot that 'after the age of childhood (which continueth from the infancy until fifteen), beginneth the age named adolescency, which continueth until twenty and five.'[9] Interestingly, the *Oxford English Dictionary* still defines 'adolescence' as 'ordinarily considered as extending from 14 to 25 in males, and from 12 to 21 in females'. Thomas Cogan in the sixteenth century, following Galen, divided human life into five periods: childhood (0–15), 'adolescence' (15–25), 'lusty juventus' (25–35), middle age (35–49) and old age (50 onwards).[10] If it was generally thought that men were adolescent and immature to 25 and women to 21, it is easy to see how this both reflected and checked the age at marriage. There is, indeed, some contemporary evidence that people thought that marriage below the age of 20 for men was too early. Thus a Quaker, aged twenty, when under a certain amount of pressure to marry, replied that 'I was but a lad, and I must get wisdom', while Thomas Whythorne, when asked by a gentlewoman whether he was married, replied 'that I had need to be wise first. 'For I thought myself too young and unfurnished of

---

[7] Gorer, *Himalayan Village*, 307.   [8] Arensberg, *Irish Countryman*, ch.iv.
[9] Osborn, *Whythorne Autobiography*, 11 and note.
[10] Cogan, *Haven of Health*, 191–2.

experience and wealth to take such a care upon me.'[11] In the later seventeenth century the autobiographer William Stout described the marriage of a man of nineteen to a girl of the same age, commenting that 'they being both so young, I had no hopes they would do well.'[12] Not everyone was so pessimistic, but exceptionally young marriages would attract attention. Thus Gough noted that a couple 'when they were married were so young, that they could not make passing thirty years between them, and yet neither of them were constrained by parents to marry, but they going to school together fell in love with one another, and so married.'[13]

On the whole, people were thought to escape from adolescence in their twenties. Yet why was it essential that they should be socially mature in order to marry? This again flowed from the nature of marriage. The married couple would usually be separate from their families of origin, would manage a separate economy and would largely bring up and socialize their children using their own skills and resources. It was therefore essential that they be self-sufficient and competent. They needed to have ended their education and training, often a long process. Furthermore, they needed to have reached a point where their characters were 'stabilized'. It was no good setting up a contract which would become permanent and unbreakable if the partners to the contract were still uncertain of their long-term aims and desires. There would then be a danger that as their characters continued to change and evolve, the young pair would grow apart. As we have seen, the marital relationship was the most important private, personal relationship of a person's life, one that, it was assumed, needed to be based on an intense bond of liking or love between husband and wife, if it was to succeed. It would be foolish for people to be married before they knew their own minds. This lies behind the seventeenth-century English proverb that 'to marry children together, is the way to make whoremongers and whores.'[14] Marriage was a contract entered into between two consenting, mature, adults.

If we attempt to summarize all the views, the following pattern emerges. There was a low legal threshold, a minimum age for valid marriage of 12 for girls and 14 for boys.[15] For the next six years for each sex, marriage was possible but there was restraint. There was

---

[11] Watkins, *Puritan Experience*, 192; Osborn, *Whythorne Autobiography*, 23.

[12] Marshall, *Stout Autobiography*, 178.   [13] Gough, *Myddle*, 105.   [14] Ibid., 73.

[15] Swinburne, *Spousals*, 47; Gouge, *Domesticall*, 180.

then a period when 'adolescence' still prevailed – between 18 and 20 for women, 20 and 25 for men – when they could marry, but there were probably still some pressures of an economic or social kind against marriage. From 20 and 25 onwards women and men were 'ripe' for marriage, and during the following ten years both sexes would be most likely to marry. As girls reached their early thirties, and men their late thirties, the likelihood of marriage began to decline and they might join the considerable portion of the population who never married. Thus the peak marrying period, between twenty and thirty, was late and there was no specific age which would suddenly bring a crop of marriages.[16] The swings of fertility between the fifteenth and nineteenth centuries can almost all be accounted for by changes in women's age at first marriage, varying between 22 and 26. Anywhere within this range would be considered late in most civilizations. As a contemporary traveller observed, 'the Turks at this day repute them old women, or past the age of love, who are come to the age of 25 years.'[17]

We may also wonder whether there was an age after which it was considered too late to marry. The answer seems to be that there was no absolute cut-off point. Men and women married at any age. This was obviously the case in the numerous remarriages, but even first marriages could be very late. Whole families sometimes married late. Thus the astrologer Forman noted with some surprise that none of his brothers or sisters or he himself married below the age of 34.[18] There is little evidence of condemnation or even surprise at such late marriages. Thus when Oliver Heywood's son decided to marry, Heywood did not comment unfavourably, but wrote that 'I looked upon this as an answer of my prayer, he having been above 20 years chaplain at Wallin-wels, and being 42 years of age.'[19]

An examination of the ages at first marriage of men and women in Earls Colne shows that the mean age at first marriage for women between 1580 and 1750 was 24.5 and the most frequent or modal age was 22 (463 women). For men it was 26 and 22 respectively (317 men). The gap between mean and mode shows that there were a number who married much above the mode. Of the 463 women, 54 married for the first time at between 30 and 39. Most interesting are

---

[16] See Hajnal in Glass, *Population*, for a survey of the usual ages at marriage in various societies. [17] Moryson, *Itinerary*, iii, 435.

[18] Halliwell, *Diary of Forman*, 2. [19] Turner, *Heywood*, iii, 300.

those women who married for the first time at over 40, with little chance of childbearing. There are ten of these, including two women of 45, one of 47 and two of 48. Men show no later age at marriage, even though they could go on procreating longer: only four were aged 40 or over. In Kirkby Lonsdale township, of those who appear in the listing of 1695 the mean average age of first marriage for men was 28, the modes 26 and 28, the range from 20 to 50. For women the mean average was 28.6, the mode 26 and the range from 18 to 48. Thus there was a maximum chance of marriage in the twenties, gradually diminishing but not ending until about 50 for either sex. There seems no confirmation of the idea that men remained attractive longer. Unlike the situation in some African societies, the idea that marriage was pointless when childbearing was unlikely does not seem to have been strongly held.[20]

Cultural views on marriage therefore absorbed many of the economic and other arguments which were later deployed by Malthus. The right age at which to marry was not precisely defined. There was no pressure to force girls to marry straight after puberty. Indeed, there was a gradually lessening social pressure against marriage as an individual grew up. It was as if society was gradually unwinding the constraints as the person emerged as an autonomous, independent being. In such a context it is not difficult to see how the balances could be shifted by changes in the economy, making entry into the risky enterprise more or less attractive. Thus, in that curious way which is at the heart of the puzzle, a link was formed between apparently spontaneous, individual and psychological motives, and regular, structured, general economic pressures.

The notice in an English registry office now states that 'marriage according to the law of the country is the union of one man with one woman voluntarily entered into for life to the exclusion of all others.' There are four assumptions in this definition, each of which is rather unusual. That concerning the necessity of consent – the 'voluntary entry' – we have already discussed. The other three bear on the nature and durability of marriage, and the first of these concerns the rule that marriage should only be between one man and one woman – monogamy. The second is that marriage was 'for life', that it should not – and at times could not – be broken by the will of one or both partners. The third is that it is 'to the exclusion of all others': that

---

[20] Lorimer, *Human Fertility*, 284, 286.

adultery, concubinage and so on were not to be tolerated.

This set of rules about the exclusiveness and durability of marriage is of significance in determining the attitude towards marrying. As observers pointed out at the time, unlike all other decisions this one was irrevocable. In the majority of societies there is not this possessive exclusiveness. With the possibility of adding further wives or husbands, with full divorce by consent and a permissive attitude towards adultery and concubinage, an error of judgement is not fatal. In England, a decision often made in passion would determine the rest of a person's life. Lord Burleigh warned that people should exercise great care in choosing a spouse, for 'from thence will spring all thy future good or evil.'[21] A single man or woman could change career, house or friends. In marriage the rule was one partner, for life, to the exclusion of all others. This limitation clearly lay behind the late age at marriage and the large proportion who never took the risk at all. Marriage was not to be ventured on lightly, as the marriage service solemnly warned, but 'reverently, discretely, advisedly, soberly, and in the fear of God'.

Concentrating firstly on the nature of marriage, we need to be precise about the words used to describe multiple marriage. English lawyers distinguished between polygamy, which meant marrying more than one spouse at a time, and bigamy, trigamy, and so on, which meant marrying more than once, a previous spouse having died. Thus, polygamy – 'to marry a second Husband or Wife, the former Husband or Wife living' (as Sir Edward Coke put it) – was first made a felony by an Act of 1603.[22] Anthropologists have further distinguished between the two forms of 'polygamy': where one man marries more than one woman – polygyny; and where one woman marries more than one man – polyandry.

The rule of monogamy is unusual. Westermarck surveyed the distribution of monogamy and polygamy and found that most societies allow the latter.[23] As Jack Goody writes, 'as far as human cultures are concerned, it is monogamy that is rare, polygyny common.' Monogamy has largely been confined to Europe in the past, and recently it has been one of the major exports from the West.[24] The prevalence of permitted polygyny in most other societies attracted attention as soon as Europeans became aware of the

---

[21] In Percy, *Advice*, 38.   [22] Coke, *Institutes*, 3rd, 88.

[23] Westermarck, *Marriage*, iii, chs xxvii-xxix.

[24] Goody, *Production*, 51; Kiernan in Goody, *Family and Inheritance*, 376.

European peculiarity. Montesquieu, characteristically, related it to the climate. In hot climates, women were married off very young, at eight or nine. Montesquieu thought this was because they aged very quickly. 'It is, therefore, extremely natural that in these places a man, when no law opposes it, should leave one wife to take another, and that polygamy should be introduced.' In temperate climates people marry later, there is a greater equality between the sexes, and 'in consequence of this, the law of having only one wife'. Thus, 'the law which permits only one wife is physically conformable to the climate of Europe, and not to that of Asia.'[25]

This is a theme that others elaborated. A century after Montesquieu, Lord Avebury put forward almost identical views to his concerning age at marriage and polygyny.[26]

> Thus in all tropical regions girls become marriageable very young; their beauty is acquired early, and soon fades, while men, on the contrary, retain their full powers much longer. Hence, when love depends, not on similarity of tastes, pursuits, or sympathies, but entirely on external attractions, we cannot wonder that every man who is able to do so provides himself with a succession of favourites.

He did not take up the second theme in Montesquieu's arguments – the unequal relations implicit in polygyny – but it was a strand which had also attracted the attention of the Scottish philosophers. Lord Kames argued that 'polygamy sprang up in countries where women are treated as inferior beings: it can never take place where the two sexes are held to be of equal rank.' This would account for its absence from northern Europe: 'Crantz, in his history of the Saxons, affirms that polygamy was never known among the northern nations of Europe; which is confirmed by every other writer who gives the history of any of these nations.'[27] In his essay 'Of Polygamy and Divorces', David Hume recognized that 'the laws may allow of polygamy, as among the *Eastern* nations; or of voluntary divorces, as among the Greeks and Romans; or they may confine one man to one woman, during the whole course of their lives, as among the modern Europeans.' The 'advocates for polygamy' recommended it as the only way of regaining male superiority. In reply, while recognizing the connection of polygamy with male dominance, Hume argued that

[25] Montesquieu, *Spirit*, i, 251–2.
[26] Avebury, *Origin*, 150–1.   [27] Kames, *Sketches*, i, 359.

'this sovereignty of the male is a real usurpation, and destroys that nearness of rank, not to say equality, which nature has established between the sexes.' Men are, 'by nature, their lovers, their friends, their patrons'; to introduce polygamy would destroy that closeness.[28]

Recent anthropologists have broadened the analysis of the functions of polygyny. Summarizing the reasons for polygyny in a South African tribe, Raymond Firth includes the following functions. First there is sexual satisfaction, an overcoming of the difficulties for the man caused by long post-partum sexual taboos. Secondly, 'plurality of wives increases the probability of offspring, desired by both men and women.' As Winwood Reade had earlier put it, in Africa 'propagation is a perfect struggle; polygamy becomes a law of nature.' Furthermore, the 'barrenness of a wife, or the birth of female offspring only, is a very common reason for the choice of another partner in addition to the former one.'[29]

There are also economic advantages in areas where the main problem is to increase the labour supply. A man with many wives can avoid heavy labour, and increase his hospitality and prestige. But there may also be advantages for women: the younger wives may take the strain off the older ones, and polygamy may deal with the 'problem' of how to deal with surplus women. Thus it has been suggested that the move from polygamy to monogamy reflects and causes many of the deeper structural features we are concerned with. It is linked to the decreasing desire for children and the decreasing need for kinsfolk. It is connected to the growth of the view of marriage based on companionship, equality and romantic love, where the husband–wife tie becomes the most important one.[30] As Jacqueline Sarsby points out, 'monogamy is more suited to the notion of the meeting of twin souls than either polygyny or polyandry.'[31] It would be interesting to try to rewrite the great English love poems in a polygamous mode. In a study of recent trends in African marriage, the decline in polygamy is related to the growth of Western 'love marriages': to have 'a plurality of wives is no longer the way to increase influence and status.' The connection between 'notions of romantic love and the social aspirations of educated young West Africans', we are told, 'largely explains the contemporary popularity of monogamous marriage.'[32]

[28] Hume, *Essays*, 108, 109 (Essay xviii).

[29] Firth, *Human Types*, 108; quoted in Westermarck, *Marriage*, iii, 80; ibid., iii, 75.   [30] Westermarck, *Marriage*, iii, 105.   [31] Sarsby, *Romantic Love*, 39.

The fact that throughout the period under consideration marriage was monogamous is hence a powerful indicator of the attitude towards women and children. It might be argued that this is not necessarily the case because the main reason for monogamy was Christianity. Although there is an element of truth in this, it does not explain why Christians, on the whole, were monogamous. As Westermarck pointed out, 'although the New Testament assumes monogamy as the normal or ideal form of marriage, it does not expressly prohibit polygyny, except in the case of a bishop and a deacon.' He goes on to say that polygyny 'was frequently practised by the Merovingian kings', and later Lutheran clergy were to approve the bigamous marriages of Philip of Hesse and Frederick William II of Prussia.[33] Even Abraham, who was a 'perfect Christian', had had two wives. After the Thirty Years War, in order to encourage population growth the Frankish Krestag at Nuremberg passed the resolution that every man should be allowed to marry two women simultaneously.

There continued to be a deep ambivalence on the issue, with a strong underground tradition in the Christian Church that polygamy should be allowed. This has been surveyed by John Cairncross, who shows that many prominent figures, including Milton and perhaps Newton, as well as the Christian communities of Munster Anabaptists and Mormons, adhered to the theory that polygamy was consistent with Christianity.[34] Sir Thomas Browne was not prepared to condemn polygamy out of hand: he would not disallow ' in all cases, of Polygamy, which considering some times, and the unequal number of both sexes, may be also necessary'. Likewise, William Petty approved of it in certain situations.[35] In fact there was a continual and often brisk discussion of whether polygamy should be made legal and encouraged, and there is an extensive bibliography of the arguments for and against it.[36] The proscribing of polygamy was thus not a unanimous view, flowing out of the teaching of Christ and the agreement of the early fathers. But it was a majority view,

[32] Little, 'Modern Marriage', 414, 422.   [33] Westermarck, *Marriage*, iii, 50.

[34] Cairncross, *After Polygamy*.   [35] Browne, *Religio Medici*, 79; Landsdowne, *Petty Papers*, ii, 523.

[36] Hill, *Puritanism and Revolution*, 316–17, 390; Thomas, 'History and Anthropology', 16; Thomas, 'Women', 337; Howard, *Matrimonial Institutions*, i, 406; Cairncross, *After Polygamy*.

maintained through the centuries, despite considerable pressures from the realities of power and passion. Its origin and persistence are thus a puzzle.

There are two major views as to the origins of the proscribing of polygamy. Kames, we have seen, linked it to the culture of the northern Europeans, particularly the Saxons. Sir Henry Maine saw it as a peculiarity inherited from Rome. He argues that the 'monogamy of the modern and Western world is, in fact, the monogamy of the Romans',[37] who drove out the polygamy they found in Celtic societies. He does not seem to consider the early evidence referred to by Kames, and supported by Caesar's and Tacitus' observations on the Germans, that the people who conquered Rome shared the basic premise of monogamy. Thus the argument between the Roman and Germanic schools becomes a false one. In fact, for reasons unknown, both of these cultures had the unusual system of monogamy, and the two systems coalescing were strong enough to form a foundation which has lasted for over fifteen hundred years in the West and is now the dominant one in the world.

Thus, despite the arguments and a deep ambivalence, monogamy was the rule in England from Chaucer to Malthus. Consequently, both in the ecclesiastical courts and, at times, in the secular courts under the Statute of 1603, we find people presented and prosecuted for this offence. Thus a person who married more than one person at a time could before 1604 be presented for polygamy in the church courts.[38] After 1604, polygamy was made a felony, punishable by death. The basic rule was only one spouse at a time, a rule which England shared with the rest of the Continent. It was a rule that was consistent with equality of the sexes, with an emphasis on the deep bond between husband and wife, and with a relatively low demand for children. Its link with these features was strengthened by a second unusual feature, the practically indissoluble nature of marriage.

Maine had pointed out that the effects of Roman monogamy had been emphasized by a second rule introduced by Christianity that forbade the changing of partners during life. The Romans practised monogamy, but they allowed easy divorce and hence enabled people to practise 'serial polygamy'. But from this system 'the license of divorce had been expelled by Christian morality.'[39] A detailed outline

---

[37] Maine, *Early Institutions*, 60.   [38] ERO, D/AED/1, fols 6–9; Emmison, *Morals*, 168ff, ERO, Q/SBa/2, fol.55; Gough, *Myddle*, 51.

[39] Maine, *Early Institutions*, 60; Howard, *Matrimonial Institutions*, ii, ch.1.

of the history of divorce has been provided by Howard, who shows how Christianity imposed this new rule. Relatively easy divorce, based on the wishes of either or both partners, seems to have been a feature of early Germanic societies, for instance Anglo-Saxon England.[40] Thus up to the tenth century most European countries permitted easy divorce, and in doing this they conformed to the pattern of the majority of human societies. Hobhouse, Wheeler and Ginsberg in their survey found that of 271 tribal groups, only 4 per cent forbade divorce, while 72 per cent permitted it on the grounds of mutual consent based on incompatibility or whim. A survey of divorce laws around the world suggests a relaxed attitude in most societies, with wide grounds for divorce, though there are a few where divorce is unknown.[41]

The possibility of divorce with remarriage is often related to the desire for children. If a couple are childless, they separate and each may try again with another partner. A marriage is not complete without children. Thus a society or civilization that forbids full divorce with the right to remarry, that views marriage, with or without children, as indissoluble, reveals certain attitudes towards the purposes of marriage. Such a view also has considerable implications for marriage. Once married, always married, makes the initial decision even more important. As Westermarck and Howard agreed, it was Christianity that made marriage practically indissoluble. 'Christianity revolutionized European legislation with regard to divorce.' For the first time, divorce became widely prohibited. 'A consummated Christian marriage is a sacrament and must as such remain valid for ever. It represents the union between Christ and the Church, and is consequently as indissoluble as that union.' Only in the tenth century in England did the easier freedom of divorce in Anglo-Saxon societies become crushed by the Church.[42] In England one then sees almost a thousand years of the regime that forbids divorce with right to remarry. It was not until 1857 that civil divorce was made possible.

The medieval Church distinguished between two forms of 'divorce': divorce *a vinculo*, from the 'chains' of marriage, and divorce *a mensa et thoro*, from bed and board. Neither of them exactly parallels

---

[40] Pollock and Maitland, ii, 392–3; Howard, *Matrimonial Institutions*, ii, 39; Whitelock, *English Society*, 150; Lancaster, 'Kinship', i, 246–7.

[41] Quoted in Hoebel, *Primitive World*, 215; Westermarck, *Marriage*, iii, xxxii; ibid., iii, 269. [42] Westermarck, *Marriage*, iii, 327; iii, 328; iii, 333.

our own contemporary divorce. The first was total annulment: the marriage was decreed never to have existed at all because there had been some impediment from the very start, such as the pre-contract of one partner or an affinity between the partners which placed them within the prohibited degrees. Since there were many grounds, there was in practice 'a very wide liberty of divorce in the Middle Ages, though it existed mainly for those who were able to pay the ecclesiastical judge.' As a consequence, as Maitland pointed out, 'in the middle ages marriages, or what looked like marriages, were exceedingly insecure', for they could be shown retrospectively never to have existed at all.[43] The second form of divorce was merely separation from bed and board, with no possibility of the partners marrying anybody else.

It is ironic that the Protestant Reformation should have had the effect in England of making divorce with the right to remarry even more difficult. Marriage was no longer a sacrament, a symbol of Christ's relations with his Church, but reverted to being a covenant or contract between two individuals. As Kathleen Davies points out, 'if matrimony was a covenant, and not a sacrament, then adultery destroyed the basis of the contract, and it was therefore dissoluble.'[44] This is what should have happened, and indeed some of the radical Protestant theologians on the Continent took this attitude.[45] The law very nearly changed in England. The new Protestant doctrines were expounded in the *Reformatio Legum Ecclesiasticarum*, submitted in 1552. This dismissed separation *a mensa et thoro* and spiritual affinity as a cause of divorce. But it did advocate complete divorce from the 'chains' of marriage 'in cases of extreme conjugal faithlessness; in cases of conjugal desertion or cruelty; in cases where a husband, not guilty of deserting his wife, had been for several years absent from her', provided there was reason to believe him dead, and in cases of 'such violent hatred as rendered it in the highest degree improbable that the husband and wife would survive their animosities and again love one another.' 'Divorce is denied where both partners are guilty of unfaithfulness; and when one is guilty, only the innocent spouse is permitted to contract another marriage.'[46]

The report prepared by the commissioners of the *Reformatio* never received the approval of the king, perhaps because of his premature

[43] Howard, *Matrimonial Institutions*, ii, 56; Pollock and Maitland, ii, 369.

[44] Outhwaite, *Marriage*, 74.   [45] Howard, *Matrimonial Institutions*, ii, 60ff.

[46] Quoted in ibid., ii, 78, 79.

death. No change was made to the canon law. But the principles the *Reformatio* embodied seem, for a short time, to have been followed in the ecclesiastical courts. Thus, for the period 1552–1602, 'marriage was not held by the Church, and therefore was not held by the Law, to be indissoluble.' Through Elizabeth's reign, 'new marriages were freely contracted after obtaining divorce from unfaithful partners.' A number of cases arising from this attitude are recounted for Elizabethan Essex by F. G. Emmison.[47]

Then in 1603, following canons of 1597 and a celebrated case in Star Chamber, there was re-enacted the pre-1552 position. Divorce with remarriage became impossible. The situation was, however, even stricter than it had been before the Reformation, because now the elaborate series of causes – namely, pre-contract, spiritual affinity and so on, which had enabled some at least of the population to obtain annulments – were removed. Between 1603 and 1837, English marriage was almost indissoluble. As Jeaffreson wrote, after 1603 'our ancestors lived for several generations under a matrimonial law of unexampled rigour and narrowness. The gates of exit from true matrimony had all been closed, with the exception of death. Together with the artificial impediments to wedlock, the Reformation had demolished the machinery for annulling marriages on fictitious grounds.'[48]

Three narrow exits did remain. First, judicial separations, from bed and board, remained possible, but with no right to remarry. Secondly, from the later seventeenth century divorce by Act of Parliament became possible. But the grounds were extremely limited and the process was 'enormously expensive', so that only a little over 300 such divorces were granted in the whole period up to 1857, and only about half a dozen of them at the suit of women.[49] There may also have been two tactics employed by the majority of the population who did not have access to such parliamentary Acts. The first was to avoid marriage at all: from the later seventeenth century, there are signs of the rapid growth of 'clandestine' unions, of people merely living as 'common law' husband and wife.[50] This may in part have been a response to the impossibility of divorce. A second tactic was a popular practice which grew widespread from the time when, in the

[47] Ibid., ii, 79, 81; Emmison, *Morals*, 164–8. [48] Jeaffreson, *Bridals*, ii, 339.
[49] Westermarck, *Marriage*, iii, 337; Thomas, 'Double Standard', 201.
[50] Hollingsworth, *Historical Demography*, 21; Laslett, *Family Life*, 131.

mid-eighteenth century, Hardwick's Marriage Act made clandestine and common law marriage less easy. This was an act whereby a couple could divorce themselves – it was known as 'wife-selling'.

The function of these 'wife sales' as an alternative to an Act of Parliament was delightfully pointed out by a judge at the Oxfordshire Assizes in 1855. Trying a 'bigamy' case in which a man showed how, although his wife had cohabited with another man for 16 years, he could not obtain a divorce, the judge addressed the plaintiff thus:

> I will tell you what you ought to have done ... You should have instructed your attorney to bring an action against the seducer of your wife for damages; that would have cost you about £100. Having proceeded thus far, you should have employed a proctor and instituted a suit in the Ecclesiastical Courts for a divorce *a mensa et thoro*; that would have cost you £200 or £300 more. When you had obtained a divorce *a mensa et thoro*, you had only to obtain a private Act for divorce *a vinculo matrimonii* ... altogether these proceedings would cost you £1000. You will probably tell me that you never had a tenth of that sum, but that makes no difference. Sitting here as an English judge, it is my duty to tell you that this is not a country in which there is one law for the rich and another for the poor. You will be imprisoned for one day.[51]

The alternative available to the less than rich was to undergo a ritual whereby a woman was taken to a public place, perhaps with a halter round her neck, and 'auctioned'. The highest bidder, usually by some pre-arrangement, would 'buy' her, thereby becoming the husband. Thus divorce and remarriage were effected all in one act. Although it was never legally sanctioned, there seems to have been a widespread *de facto* acceptance of this popular method of divorce; Menefee, who has provided an extensive account of the institution, lists some 387 known 'cases', and there were probably many more.[52] They almost all occurred in the lowest quarter of the socio-economic hierarchy, as in the famous description of a wife sale in Hardy's *Mayor of Casterbridge* in the early nineteenth century. Even for this group, the humiliation for the woman and the ambiguous legality of the method were discouragements. For the majority of the population, who lay between the tiny group at the top who could obtain a divorce through parliamentary Act and the group at the bottom who after the early

---

[51] Quoted in Menefee, *Wives for Sale*, 25.   [52] Ibid., 211–59.

eighteenth century employed wife sales, there was no way out. Despite the eloquent pleas for a humane attitude to divorce by Milton, the Anglican Church 'maintained continuity over this question', and the Catholics in England were equally rigorous.[53] Any group that permitted easy divorce was shunned. The Jews were a case in point. We are told that 'the right of the husband to divorce his wife at his pleasure is the central thought in the entire system of Jewish divorce law.' But it was the laxity in this respect that was found, even in the Puritan Interregnum of 1655, to be 'one of the strongest arguments against their proposed admission to the rights of citizenship'.[54]

There thus arose a situation whereby divorce with right to remarry became more and more difficult. Moderately easy until the tenth century, increasingly difficult in the medieval period, just possible in the later sixteenth century, the net closed tighter and tighter. A few escaped through Acts of Parliament or 'wife sales', but for the rest who found that marriage had been a mistake, the best that could be hoped for was to live apart. To be fully divorced was too expensive and too scandalous, especially for women. Many accounts describe people who were so unhappy that they contemplated separation.[55] Many may have secretly thought what only Lady Montagu dared say in a letter, that 'the best expedient for the public, and to prevent the expense of private families, would be a general act of divorcing all the people of England.'[56]

One of the interesting features of this situation was that the grounds for divorce never included the infertility of the partners. While inability to perform the sexual act, or non-consummation, was from very early on a ground for annulment of marriage, neither the pre- nor post-Reformation authorities ever considered barrenness or infertility as a sufficient cause for divorce. Sex was necessary to constitute a marriage, but children were not. Despite the demographer Petty's urging that divorce for infertility be introduced to encourage population growth, there is no evidence either in law or in actual cases in court that such grounds were accepted.[57]

The indissolubility of marriage, assumed by Malthus and others,

---

[53] Milton, *Works*, iii, 169–461; Davies in Outhwaite, *Marriage*, 74.

[54] Westermarck, *Marriage*, iii, 307; Inderwick quoted in Howard, *Matrimonal Institutions*, i, 421.

[55] E.g. Turner, *Diary*, 4; Eyre, 'Dyurnall', 53; Gunther, *Diary of Ashmole*, 60.

[56] Wharncliffe, *Letters of Montagu*, ii, 211.   [57] Landsdowne, *Petty Papers*, ii, 50.

was clearly one of its principal costs. To marry was a high-risk strategy. The risk was particularly pronounced for women, because even the palliative of a separation was likely to prove hard in relation to their links to their children and their livelihood. It is generally the case in other societies that after a divorce or separation a woman is entitled to family support: she rejoins her kin group where she and her children may be welcome. Her dowry may well revert with her.[58] Yet the position in England seems less favourable. There was no kin group to return to: no brothers, parents or more distant kin had any responsibility to shelter and maintain her and her children. Marriage had cut the last strong links, and she was alone. Furthermore, she was still married and hence, to a certain extent, under the 'couverture' and power of her husband. A bleak picture of the situation in the sixteenth to eighteenth centuries is painted by Keith Thomas.

> The wife was seldom able to claim a separation from her husband. The reasons for this were economic; she would probably be unable to support herself during such a separation, because, although separated, she was still subject to all the legal disabilities of a married woman. In other words, she was now in a state of virtual outlawry, for her husband retained all his rights over her property, including even the wages she might earn after her separation; she was incapable of conducting a legal action by herself, and she could not even claim access to her children.

As for maintenance, 'all she had was a small allowance in the shape of alimony and the payment of this was often difficult to enforce.'[59] There are a number of separate issues here. It is clear that if a man and woman were separated, the woman did remain in a certain sense 'married'. Thus she had the advantages of a common law right to a third of the man's freehold estate, or 'dower', as well as the disadvantages of being a legal minor. She lost this dower if she eloped. Dower was also, of course, lost if a full divorce from the 'chains' of marriage was granted, since technically there had never been a marriage.[60] What in effect happened in a judicial separation was that the couple were still 'man and wife' but had agreed to live apart, separated in sleeping and eating, bed and board. In order to

---

[58] E.g. Obeyesekere, *Land Tenure*, 43; Friedl, *Vasilika*, 59.
[59] Thomas, 'Double Standard', 200.   [60] Blackstone, *Commentaries*, ii, pt 1, 130; Burn, *Ecclesiastical Law*, ii, 458; Pollock and Maitland, ii, 394.

make this possible, the court which granted the separation would allocate a 'reasonable' maintenance for the woman from their joint estate. The husband was obliged, as in marriage, to provide as much for her as for himself, and if she contracted debts he must pay them. This obligation did not hold if she eloped with another.

There was a view current that women sometimes did quite well out of alimony rules. Thus William Lawrence argued that judicial separations in the later seventeenth century had grown quite 'frequent' because of alimony payments which were larger than the interest from the capital which wives had brought to the marriage.[61] In other words, like the alleged alimony suits of modern filmstars, to trap a man, then make his life intolerable and claim alimony, was an attractive strategy. We are told that when Moneylove threatened a separation in Rawlinson's *Tom Essense* (1677) his wife responded, 'Fret on sir, yet 'twill not do, for your promise is good, the Portion must be paid, and Divorce when you will the Prerogative Court will give me alimony, and the Chancery separation money, enough to maintain a gallant.' It was hence stated that 'cuckoldom is the liberty, and a separate maintenance the property, of the freeborn woman of England.'[62]

Yet this jaunty attitude, perhaps reflecting the position of affluent merchants' and gentry wives in London, conceals a host of difficulties for women. It has always been hard to ensure the regular payment of alimony from an unwilling partner, and there is also the problem of children. Many a miserable wife, and many husbands, must have been aware that one or other would be likely to 'lose' the children, even if the parents remained amicable. In a survey of the question of custody throughout Europe, Westermarck concluded that 'in England great discretion is given to the court.'[63] The court is principally concerned with the welfare of the children and may determine the custody in either direction; but if the woman has eloped, she is very unlikely to be given the children. Although, as Maitland argued, early on the 'law had not even been careful to give the father a right to the custody of his children', except his heir apparent, it appears that the right of the husband in this, as in other matters, grew over time.[64] By the early nineteenth century at common law, we are told, 'the father was entitled to the custody of his

[61] Lawrence, *Marriage*, 94.   [62] Thompson, *Women*, 184, note 72.
[63] Westermarck, *Marriage*, iii, 363.   [64] Pollock and Maitland, ii, 444.

legitimate children until they reached the age of 21.' His rights would only be lost 'if to enforce them would probably lead to the physical or moral harm of the child'.[65] Only through a series of Acts in the later nineteenth century and up to the present were wives given equal rights to husbands. Even if the principle that 'the innocent party shall suffer as little as possible', so that 'as a general rule the custody of the children is always given to the innocent petitioner, whether husband or wife', was frequently followed, there was a considerable risk that the husband would claim and obtain the children.[66] Thus separation for a woman with children was a hazardous business: she was still in the 'covered' position of a married woman, but her maintenance was precarious and she might lose her children. Often it was better to endure an unsatisfactory marriage.

The dilemma facing Christian societies is well expressed by David Hume. On the one hand there is Milton's view that marriage is no longer marriage when its central essence, the dignity and companionship of mutual love, has departed: 'nothing can be more cruel than to preserve, by violence, an union, which, at first was made by mutual love, and is now, in effect, dissolved by mutual hatred.' Such marriage is the worst of prisons. On the other hand, if easy divorce is permitted there are, Hume maintains, three 'unanswerable objections'. First, what will happen to the children? Secondly, the heart of man 'naturally submits to necessity, and soon loses an inclination, when there appears an absolute impossibility of gratifying it.' Make divorce impossible and marriages will, on the whole, be happier. Thirdly, if we are going to join people closely, we must make the 'union entire and total'. For the 'least possibility of a separate interest must be the source of endless quarrels and suspicions.' Thus a society which places marriage in such a central position, as the deepest of all relationships, must pay the price.[67]

We have in England a controlled experiment. The Christian way was attempted and marriage seen as life-long. We now have widespread divorce and remarriage. It is difficult to assess the relative cost of each solution. All that can be stressed here is that one of the central features underlying the Malthusian marital regime, and which differentiated it from the present, is that it fitted into a system which for a number of centuries made marriage practically indissoluble. The only legitimate way of ending it was to prove that it had never

---

[65] Bromley, *Family Law*, 268.   [66] Geary, *Marriage*, 406.
[67] Hume, *Essays*, 111–12 (Essay xviii).

existed. This resolved the tension: marriage is for life in the ideal, so those that are not for life are not marriages, by definition.

It might have been supposed that with such a negative attitude towards remarriage after divorce, and a total ban on multiple marriage, it would follow that remarriage after the death of one of the partners would also be either prohibited or at least strongly discouraged. It has been noted that there is usually opposition to remarriage in 'stable agrarian societies' for a number of reasons.[68] Another marriage complicates the economic and social situation: the two groups who have been joined through the initial marriage are now linked to a third group. The children of the first marriage are now in competition with the children of subsequent marriages. How are these new tensions and conflicts to be dealt with? One way is to assume that a woman marries a group and not an individual: if her husband dies, then she remains 'married' to him, though her husband's brother is the one who actually procreates with her. This 'widow inheritance' or levirate is widespread, being recognized in well over a third of known tribal groups; it protects the widow and her children as well as resolving the difficulties of property and kinship alliance.[69] Thus once married, always married: the problem of widowhood is abolished. Consequently E. E. Evans-Pritchard 'found great difficulty in making the Nuer understand that in our country it is possible for a widow to remarry.' Widow inheritance was a system which occurs in the Old Testament and was found in ancient India.[70] Where the kin group will not absorb the widow, her position is often anomalous and sometimes intolerable: in the extreme form, her life is extinguished at the same time as her husband's on the funeral pyre, as in India in the past, through *suttee*.

If there is a pressure against remarriage after the death of a spouse, this will have effects on a society's demographic pattern. Mortality rates in England were much higher than today, particularly for women in childbirth. Perhaps up to a half of those who married in their mid-twenties would find themselves without a partner before they reached the age of 60.[71] If remarriage was forbidden, there

---

[68] Davis, 'Fertility', 228.

[69] Lowie, *Primitive Society*, 30; Lienhardt, *Social Anthropology*, 111; Westermarck, *Marriage*, iii, 216ff.

[70] Evans-Pritchard, *Nuer Kinship*, 112; Maine, *Early Law*, 100ff.

[71] For figures in India, see Myrdal, *Asian Drama*, ii, 1438; for the nobility see Hollingsworth article in Glass, *Population*, esp. 369; for France, Goubert, *Beauvais*, 37–8.

would be numbers of young widowers and widows, who would have been taken out of the reproductive pool. If, on the other hand, remarriage was allowed and even encouraged, considerable numbers of those who were marrying would be entering unions which were not their first.

We can find hints of a negative attitude towards remarriage in the past. Among some of the Germanic peoples described by Tacitus there seems to have been a popular dislike, if not legal proscription, of remarriage for a widow, and this tradition continued in the Christian Church. Vives in his treatise on marriage advised people not to remarry, though it was not forbidden.[72] Remarriage after the death of a spouse, as we have seen, was technically known as 'bigamy'; thus marriage to a widow or widower was bigamy. Such remarriage at one time lost a person 'benefit of clergy', though this was later restored.[73] There are also hints of a popular disapproval, for which there seem to have been three major grounds. First, there was thought to be an element of adultery, or overlap of sexuality, about the affair, even though the first spouse was dead. There was something indelicate about it. Thus Cobbett was particularly opposed to the remarriage of women: 'a second marriage in the woman is more gross than in the man, argues great deficiency in that delicacy, that innate modesty.' All the practical reasons for remarriage he thought 'not worth a straw'.[74] It was believed by some that the womb of a woman was like a clay mould: it would be shaped by the first child, and all subsequent children would bear the imprint of the first. This theory of 'telegony' was espoused by the great English doctor, William Harvey. As John Aubrey related his views:

> he that marries a widow makes himself Cuckold. *Exempli gratia*, if a good Bitch is first warded with a Cur, let her ever after be warded with a dog of a good strain and yet she will bring curs as at first, her womb being first infected with a cur. So, the children will be like the first Husband (like raising up children to your brother). So, the Adulterer, though a crime in law, the children are like the husband.[75]

But I have not come across such views expressed by ordinary people.

[72] Howard, *Matrimonial Institutions*, i, 277.

[73] *Oxford English Dictionary* and Coke, *Institutes*, 3rd, s.v. 'Polygamy', and Burn, *Ecclesiastical Law*, s.v. 'Bigamy'.

[74] Cobbett, *Advice*, 207.   [75] Aubrey, *Brief Lives*, 213.

A second form of opposition came from those who would suffer from remarriage, particularly those children who might lose part of their inheritance and suffer from a step-parent. A number of diaries and autobiographies illustrate the bitterness and apprehension of children when a parent contemplated remarriage.[76] The difficulties were immense for the parental generation, for step-parents and children, and for step-siblings. Hume speculated on why the remarriage of a mother was even more disastrous for children than that of a father, and decided that it partly lay in the fact that the wife now had divided loyalties – to her former husband and children by that marriage and to the new relationship.[77] As *The New Whole Duty of Man* argued when explaining why children might sue their parents, 'when a new affection intervenes, then the prospect is disturbed, and the new wife is supposed to make herself acceptable to her new choice, by carrying with her all the advantages of fortune she can get, and in such cases often forgets her children and former love.'[78] For this reason, as Sir Thomas Overbury argued, the virtuous widow would not remarry, 'for she married that she might have children; and for their sakes she marries no more.' Thus Bramston waited until his children were grown up before he remarried.[79] For others, the institution of leaving home early for service was both a reflection and a safety valve in these difficulties.

A third form of pressure against remarriage lay in the rights and economic position of women. The jointure of a woman, either as arranged in a marriage contract or in the common law dower of freehold property for life which women were entitled to, does not seem to have been affected by marriage. But on certain manors a woman might lose her rights in the customary lands of her late husband if she remarried or even if she had sexual intercourse; the rights lasted for her chaste widowhood.[80] It might not, therefore, be in the economic interest of a woman to remarry. Left a good estate by her husband, free of husbandly domination, some widows would indeed be merry.

---

[76] E.g. Bourcier, *D'Ewes Diary*, 65, 121; Halliwell, *D'Ewes Autobiography*, i, 134; Brady, *Boswell in Search*, 240ff; Gunther, *Diary of Ashmole*, 31; e.g. Hutchinson, *Memoirs*, i, 76.

[77] Hume, *Treatise*, 355.   [78] *The New Whole Duty*, 203.

[79] Morley, *Character Writings*, 81; cf. also *Letters of Harley*, 117; Bramston, *Autobiography*, 34.

[80] See E.P.Thompson in Goody, *Family and Inheritance*, 351ff; Campbell, *English Yeoman*, 128.

Yet, despite our expectations, the outstanding impression for the whole period from the fourteenth to the nineteenth century is that this was a society which tolerated, even encouraged, remarriage. This 'serial polygamy', with the numerous family difficulties it must have caused, is a central feature of the Malthusian marriage regime.

The high mortality rates could lead to some extreme cases: the Dutch woman who had just married her twenty-fifth husband, the Essex man who had buried eight wives, and Defoe's famous account of the debilitating fevers of the Essex marshes which led people to have 'fourteen or fifteen wives'.[81] Josselin noted: one of these 'repeaters' a man who had had six wives and 32 children; while another cleric noted that in a small village 'there are 4 who have had 4 wives apiece and 1 who has had 5.'[82] It was not just men who married frequently: there are numerous instances of women remarrying again and again. From the famous widow of Bath with her five marriages and her remark that while God had advised us to leave father and mother to marry, 'But of no nombre mencioun made he, of bigamye, or of octogamye', through Lady Margaret Hoby who was thrice married before the age of 26, to the woman who survived eight husbands, to be buried by the ninth. Very often a woman who had survived several husbands must have married a widower.[83] The ensuing complexity of kin relations would have been very great, as it is today with widespread marital breakdown.

The sort of remarriage figures one might obtain are shown for the parish of Clayworth by a listing of 1688. At that date there were 72 husbands in the village, of whom 21 were recorded as having been married more than once, with one married five times. Of the 72 wives, nine had been previously married.[84] The very great amount of remarriage that occurred is well illustrated in Gough's description of Myddle.[85] That this was an old-established pattern in England can be seen from medieval evidence, and indeed Bloch has argued that in the eleventh to twelfth centuries in Europe generally, remarriage was 'almost universal'.[86]

[81] Bray, *Evelyn Diary*, 19; Moryson, *Itinerary*, iii, 437; Defoe, *Tour*, 55.

[82] Macfarlane, *Josselin Diary*, 9 November 1644; Gill, *Rector's Book*, 88.

[83] Pollard, *Chaucer Works*, 155; Muncey, *Parish Registers*, 85; Meads, *Hoby Diary*, 10.

[84] Summarized in Laslett, *Lost World*, 104.

[85] Gough, *Myddle*, e.g.49–50; Hair, 'Bridal Pregnancy', 64, for fuller figures.

[86] Titow, 'Differences', 7; Bennett, *Pastons*, 35; Bloch, *Feudal*, i, 136.

Several features of widespread remarriage strike us as odd. The first is the speed at which it happened, though there were some slight restrictions on women. By Roman law, remarriage 'within the year of mourning' was forbidden. This was for two reasons: to prevent uncertainty concerning paternity, and 'because a reverential mourning and pious regard to the memory of her deceased husband is in decency expected.'[87] But remarriage within the year was not prohibited by common law or canon law in England, and consequently had no force. People might disapprove of too rapid remarriage as unseemly – as Josselin did of a marriage after only four months, and Whateley wrote critically of how people can nowadays 'bury and marry, and all in a month' – yet it is clear that people often waited for only a short period.[88]

Some extreme cases can be found: the husband who buried his wife on 28 October and remarried on 5 November, or the gentleman who 'carried his wife to London last week and died about 8 at night, leaving her £500 a year in land. The next day before 12 she was married to a journeyman woollen draper that came to sell mourning to her.'[89] But these were unusual. The study of Earls Colne shows that there was a tendency for men to remarry more frequently and more speedily than women after a bereavement, and there is no significant change in this pattern over the period 1580–1740. Of all women who married there, 13.5 per cent were widows, and 19 per cent of men who married were widowers. Of those who remarried, 60 per cent of the men did so within a year, while only 14 per cent of the women did so. The men waited on average five months if they remarried within the year, women on average eight months. In nine cases out of the 78 males the remarriage occurred within three months, but none of the 36 females remarried within six months of their husband's death. We may wonder how much the factor of having young children influenced the situation. With men, there is only a slight difference between the speed of remarriage of those with children and of those without. With the women, none of the five who remarried within a year had children, but over half of the rest who remarried after a longer period had. If anything, young children were an impediment to remarriage, which leaves open the question of how

---

[87] Burn, *Ecclesiastical Law*, ii, 416.
[88] Macfarlane, *Josselin Diary*, 15 January 1657; Whateley, *Care-Cloth*, 50.
[89] Ellis, *Smyth Obituary*, 70; Rye, 'Gawdy', 172.

a widowed mother managed to support herself and her children.

This frequent and often rapid remarriage clearly indicates a widespread tolerance, even zest, for it. As an Italian visitor noted in the later fifteenth century, 'it is not considered any discredit to a woman to marry again every time that she is left a widow, however unsuitable the match may be as to age, rank and fortune.'[90] Though preachers might occasionally condemn remarriage,[91] the general populace showed little opposition. Those who went to astrologers in the sixteenth and seventeenth centuries often asked how many husbands they were likely to have.[92] However, an ambivalence towards remarriage, both on the part of the unmarried who felt that certain sections of the population were taking an unduly large share of the eligible spouses, and on the part of those who sympathized with the children of an earlier marriage, was shown in certain forms of popular disapproval. Thus 'rough music' or charivari was often employed in Europe against those who remarried.[93] Yet it would appear that little 'rough music' was to be found in England, and what took place was not directed against those who remarried. This is an interesting omission. Indeed, from very early on, as J. Z. Titow has shown, there was a pattern of almost instituted remarriage; an older woman would marry a younger man, who then in older age married a younger woman.[94] Part of this pattern included the enthusiastic pursuit of rich widows.

There was a whole tradition of jokes, proverbs and advice about the advantages of marrying a widow. As Ralph Roister Doister remarked, 'Is she a widow? I love her better therefore.' Each widowhood improved a woman. 'Rich widows are not unlike some books of the 2d or 3d edition . . . always come out with additions and amendments.'[95] Thus a bachelor explained why he wished to marry a widow rather than a virgin. It was not her wealth, but her 'matronlike modesty' arising from experience, that made him woo her: 'for that you know better both what belongs to a man, as also to use thriftely what I get.'[96] As a popular joke put it, 'Tis princelike to marry a Widow, for 'tis to have a taster.' It is significant that no similar literature exists in

[90] Sneyd, *Relation*, 27.   [91] Latham, *Pepys*, i, 60.   [92] Thomas, *Religion*, 283.

[93] Pitt-Rivers, *People of Sierra*, 175; see Burguiere in Wheaton, *Family*.

[94] Ingram, 'Ridings', *passim*, especially 86–7, 90–2; Titow, 'Differences', *passim*.   [95] Gassner, *Medieval Drama*, 272; *Characters*, 177.

[96] Furnivall, *Tell-Trothes*, 63; for other advice to marry a widow, see Rollins, *Pepysian Garland*, 229–32.

relation to widowers, perhaps because they were less appealing. 'A widower is like a 2d hand book; takes not half the price.'[97] It would seem that whatever social pressures existed on men and women as to the choice of marriage partner decreased over time: a widow with her own estate was unlikely to be under any formal pressure from parents or kin, though this may not have been the case amongst the upper gentry and above.[98] The consent of parents was still desirable, but certainly not necessary.[99] Even more than in first marriage, the partners could decide for themselves. This does not mean that friends and others did not try to persuade the individual either to marry or to stay single. Thus Mrs Venables as a widow wrote that she was 'very unwilling to change my condition', despite pressure from friends. Friends would often try to encourage a lonely widower to remarry a widow,[100] but it was largely up to the individual whom he or she chose.

In societies where there has been a large transfer of wealth from one group to another at marriage, then the wife's remarriage choice is likely to be circumscribed. She may have to marry or be absorbed by another of the kin group of her husband.[101] If she dies, she may be replaced by a sister. But there are no signs of preferential or prescribed kin remarriage in the English evidence. Indeed, Sir Henry Wotton's father explicitly wished to avoid remarriage to a kinswoman, and he also wished to avoid a woman who had children or one who was involved in law suits. Falling in love, Wotton's father disregarded all his own good advice and married a person who had all these characteristics.[102] Men mentioned a number of motives for remarriage, including the need for a good housekeeper to avoid being cheated by servants, loneliness, and the need for a deep 'friendship' and companionship of the sort to which they had grown accustomed.[103] It seems likely that both men and women had become used to the marital state, liked or 'needed' it, and tried to remarry. Although some men and women were happier and freer released from the bond of matrimony, many found the task of running a home, earning a living and bringing up children overwhelming.

---

[97] Fleming, 'Notebook', fol.29v; *Characters*, 190.

[98] E.g. Bramston, *Autobiography*, 18–19.   [99] Perkins, *Oeconomie*, 151.

[100] 'Diary of Venables', 23; Hutchinson, *Memoirs*, i, 15.

[101] Cf. Murdock, *Social Structure*, 270.   [102] Wotton, *Reliquiae*, sig.b4.

[103] Wright, *Autobiography*, 144; Turner, *Diary*, 50ff; Fishwick, *Thomas Jolly*, 109; Thale, *Place Autobiography*, 254–8.

The pattern whereby more marriages were broken by death then than today and many people remarried quite soon after the death of a spouse might be thought to influence, or at least to indicate, the nature of a marital relationship. If marriages were relatively vulnerable and partners often replaced, does this tell us anything of the depth of the emotion involved? The problem is a complex one, for swift remarriage can be interpreted in two ways: as evidence of lack of affection – or as the opposite. Autobiographical material and advice of the time imply that the latter interpretation is more accurate. As Dr Johnson put it, a man who remarries 'pays the highest compliment' to his first wife, by showing that marriage has been attractive; or as a widower said a century and a half earlier, 'having loved and lived with my love ... so well liked I of my last loss, as my former good hap breeds an assured hope of the like good fortune.'[104] Although a man mourned deeply for his first wife, 'yet that long dropping grief did but soften his heart for the impression of a second love.' It was possible for a person to marry under six months after the death of a 'dear wife', though others found it was a long time before they could 'fancy a second marriage; but at the length, finding it many ways convenient', they did remarry.[105]

The natural repugnance that the grieving spouse might feel was something that friends might consider it their duty to try to overcome. Thus in one model letter in which a widow was advised to remarry, the writer started by saying that he had been unable to bring up the subject before because of 'the extreme grief wherein my self was a partaker with you, of the death of your late husband.' But now she was strongly advised 'for your estate' to consider remarriage, and asked whether she thought 'it profiteth at all the deceased ghost of him that loved you ... to live thus solitary?'[106] Indeed, it was not just friends who saw no inconsistency between past love and remarriage – the dying partner might exhort his or her spouse to remarry. Sir Walter Raleigh in a letter to his wife just before his execution wrote: 'thou art a young woman and forbear not to marry again, it is now nothing to me, thou art no more mine, nor I thine ... take care thou marry not to please sense, but to avoid poverty and to preserve thy child.'[107] It is clear that Oliver Heywood and his wife loved each other

---

[104] Brady, *Boswell in Search*, 332; Furnivall, *Tell-Trothes*, 57.

[105] Hutchinson, *Memoirs*, i, 61; Hodgson, 'Diary of Sanderson', 37–8; Holles, *Memorials*, 195.

[106] Day, *Secretorie*, 122, 124. [107] Hadow, *Sir Walter Raleigh*, 177–8.

deeply and he mourned her with passion. Yet his wife, being weakly, 'sometimes spoke of my second marriage desiring me to keep gods way as I did before, and god would provide well for me again: she mentioned not only some characters but persons to me, that she apprehended might be suitable to me and helpful to my children.'[108] Whereas today marriage is fragile through separation and divorce, and yet we still enter it with hope and base it on affection, likewise in the past it was fragile through death. We can infer nothing automatically from this demographic fragility.

Here then is a pattern whereby marriage was with one person, for life, but only for life. One final rule may be briefly mentioned, which is also implied in the definition which we began with – namely, that marriage is 'to the exclusion of all others'. The exclusive, or possessive, nature of marriage is again something that we tend to take for granted. Yet through institutions such as concubinage or 'adultery' there might well have been practical alternatives to monogamy. Nowadays, we know, marriage is certainly not exclusive in this way. Even in the 1950s about half of white married males in the United States had engaged in an adulterous relationship, and the figures now must be much higher.[109] We may therefore wonder what the incidence and attitude was in the historical past in England.

Concubinage is a widespread institution in human societies,[110] but apart from a few notorious cases such as that of Charles II, there is little sign of it in England. Thus, when she visited Vienna, Lady Montagu was surprised to find that 'tis the established custom for every lady to have two husbands, one that bears the name, and another that performs the duties.'[111] In England, marriage was to the exclusion of all others. Permanent liaisons were not encouraged and even temporary affairs were forbidden.

Lord Kames noted that the attitude to and treatment of adultery varied from society to society. In places 'where wives are purchased, and polygamy is indulged, adultery can scarce be reckoned a crime in the husband; and, where there are a plurality of wives, a sound sense makes it but a venial crime in any of them.'[112] On the other hand, 'matrimony between a single pair, for mutual comfort, and for procreating children, implies the strictest mutual fidelity.' Modern anthropological research supports Kames in showing a variation in

---

[108] Turner, *Heywood*, i, 65.   [109] Kinsey, *Human Male*, 585.
[110] Cf.'Concubines and co-wives' in Goody, *Production*.
[111] Wharncliffe, *Letters of Montagu*, i, 296.   [112] Kames, *Sketches*, ii, 45.

attitudes, from societies such as the Todas of South India where there is no disapproval of adultery, to those where the punishment is extremely harsh.[113]

In accordance with the extreme emphasis on the conjugal bond, adultery, which threatens that bond, has been a serious moral offence from the time of Tacitus' first description of the Germanic peoples up to the nineteenth century.[114] Proven adultery was grounds for separation, and there was clearly often communal disapproval manifested in the widespread hanging up of cuckolds' horns on deceived husbands' houses during the sixteenth to eighteenth century in England.[115] There were frequent exhortations to increase the severity of the penalties, to make it an offence for which the culprits should be hanged or have their eyes gouged out.[116] For a short period in the seventeenth century, it was indeed made a capital offence.[117]

Yet for nearly all of the period from Chaucer onwards, the penalties were, on the whole, surprisingly light. Contemporaries distinguished between 'double' and 'single' adultery. In the former, both of the offenders were married, but not to each other, and within 'single' adultery only one of the parties was married. There was also a further distinction between cases where an unmarried woman became pregnant and bore a child and those where there was no offspring. Analysis of ecclesiastical courts and local records suggests that, on the whole, the offence was regarded quite lightly. Often there was a vagueness in the presentments which obscured the distinction betwen adultery and sexual relations between unmarried persons. Often both were called 'fornication', or some other general term. There is little evidence of informal physical assault by kin or neighbours.[118] As contemporaries observed, from Anglo-Saxon times onwards the English had had a curiously lax attitude towards adultery.[119] It was often punished in other countries with death or branding, but in England it was considered to be a moral offence

[113] Note referring to the work of W.H. Rivers in Hoebel, *Primitive World*, 219; Evans-Pritchard, *Nuer Kinship*, 120; for table see Murdock, *Social Structure*, 270; Westermarck, *Moral Ideas*, ii, ch.xlii.   [114] Tacitus, *Germania*, 117.

[115] ERO, Q/SR/88, 71, 84; D/AEA/28, fol.32v.

[116] *Sermons or Homilies*, 11th Homily, 12; Landsdowne, *Petty Papers*, ii, 213.

[117] Thomas, 'Puritans and Adultery', *passim*.

[118] Macfarlane, 'Marital Relationships', 126–9.

[119] Lancaster, 'Kinship', i, 246; Moryson, *Itinerary*, iv, 291; *The New Whole Duty*, 225–6.

which concerned God, and hence was dealt with by the ecclesiastical court. The usual punishment was public confession and humiliation, but these could be avoided by a monetary payment. However, if an unmarried woman bore a child as the result of an adulterous union, the civil courts became involved. The putative father would be obliged to support the child, if he could be found. The mother was generally whipped, half-naked, through the streets and then confined in the house of correction for a year. Her offence was principally that she had offended the parish by bringing the extra charge of a bastard child to be supported by her neighbours. Here there was a double standard.

In this context of strong formal condemnation combined with only moderate sanctions and an apparent general disinterest in the offence by most of society, it is possible that adultery was quite common. It is, of course, impossible to be certain, since the fairly numerous cases presented in the ecclesiastical courts are likely to constitute only a tiny fraction of what went on. Yet even these cases suggest widespread and tolerated adultery. For instance, in a three-year period in Earls Colne, 1587–9, ten people were presented for suspected adultery.[120] Josselin thought adulteries were very common in the parish of which he was vicar, and the Homily against 'Whoredom' argued that 'that vice at this day reigneth most above all other vices.'[121] This seems to be a continuation of an earlier tradition,[122] for England seems to have had something of a reputation for adultery. In the fifteenth century the poet Hoccleve suggested that there was no worse land under the sun for the sin of adultery. A Scots lady explained to Burt in the early eighteenth century that the English 'often take liberties after they are married, and seldom before; whereas the Scots women, when they make a Trip, it is while they are single, and very rarely afterwards.'[123]

The frequency and tolerance of adultery are shown in a number of the classic diaries of the seventeenth century, particularly Pepys. It seems often to have been a matter for jest. Hence the joke about the country man who told his wife that 'there was a law to come forth, that all cuckolds should be thrown into the river, Husband (quoth she) can you swim?'[124] Or there was the vicar who, having kissed a woman who

---

[120] Cf. the description in Macfarlane, 'Historical Anthropology', 16–17.

[121] Macfarlane, *Josselin Diary*, 1 March 1668; *Sermons or Homilies*, 11th Homily, 5.

[122] Britton, *Community of Vill*, 34; Du Boulay, *Ambition*, 104.

[123] Hoccleve, *Works*, iii, 64; *Burt's Letters*, i, 107.

[124] Fleming, 'Notebook', fol.19.

remonstrated that he already had a wife, replied that 'change of pasture made calves fat and a bit abroad was worth two at home.' Some were even said to try to justify their behaviour. Thus in an Essex ecclesiastical case in 1588 a man was presented for having said 'that there is no sin if his own conscience doth not oppress him to have carnal company with a man's wife if the husband be asleep. And that he taketh the prophet David, or some part of the word of god to be author.'[125]

By English law, all children born of a marriage were automatically the legitimate offspring of the couple, even if everyone knew they had been procreated by another father.[126] Where such a view of legitimacy prevails, it can mean a tolerant attitude to adultery, for people are often most concerned to have children, whoever the genitor. Hence, for example, the 'Nuer do not attach great importance to physiological paternity. Men prefer to beget their own sons, but it is not ignominious to nurture children begotten by others.'[127] In England, adultery was seen as a form of theft, particularly a theft of the exclusive and monopoly rights in a partner's sexual and companionly services. *The New Whole Duty of Man* stated that 'the corrupting of a man's wife, enticing her to a strange bed is by all acknowledged to be the worst sort of theft, infinitely beyond that of goods.'[128] This suggests that essentially marriage was about a physical and emotional relationship between the couple: adultery damaged this, and it added insult to injury if a child was conceived, whereas among the Nuer it lightened the offence.

This line of thinking explains the well known 'double standard' whereby adultery by a woman was regarded as worse than adultery by a man. The argument was succinctly put in the eighteenth century: 'let a Man have never so many children, the wife is certain that none can be mother'd on her, but what are really her own. But the poor husband . . .'[129] As Lord Kames wrote:

> adultery . . . in the wife, is a breach of the matrimonial engagement in a double respect: it is an alienation of affection from the husband, which unqualifies her to be his friend and companion; and it tends to bring a

[125] ERO, D/ABD/7, fol.127v; D/AZ/1/9; D/ACA/16, fol.64v.

[126] Lawrence, *Marriage*, 72–73.   [127] Evans-Pritchard, *Nuer Kinship*, 120.

[128] Quoted by Thomas, 'Double Standard', 210; cf. also Coverdale, *Matrimony*, 42; Whateley, *Care-Cloth*, 38.   [129] Cf. Thomas, 'Double Standard', *passim*; Pitt-Rivers, *Fate of Shechem*, 74ff; *Characters*, 176.

spurious issue into the family, betraying the husband to maintain and educate children who are not his own.[130]

A similar point was made by Dr Johnson, when he argued that adultery was criminal because 'it broke the peace of families and introduced confusion of progeny.'

> These constitute the essence of the crime, and therefore a woman who breaks her marriage vows is so much more criminal than a man. A man, to be sure, is criminal in the sight of God, but he does not do his wife a very material injury if he does not insult her; if, for instance, from mere wantonness of appetite, he steals privately to her chamber-maid. Sir, a wife ought not greatly to resent this. I should not receive home a daughter who had run away from her husband on that account.[131]

By 'confusion of progeny', Johson seems to have been referring to a genetic or moral confusion: there was no legal confusion, for during marriage the offspring were all the pater's. Even Cobbett accepted that 'to be sure, infidelity in a man is less heinous than infidelity in the wife.' He believed that there was absolutely no situation in which a man could continue to live with an adulteress, though he admitted that many women were driven to this offence by bad husbands.[132]

This 'double standard' was attacked by a number of writers, more, it must be admitted, in an attempt to reduce the tolerance of husbands' adultery than to lighten the condemnation of women.[133] In fact, while evident in the propertied classes and in the law, these anxieties are not so obvious at the level of the mass of the population. For instance, there is no evidence of a singling out of wives rather than husbands for especially severe treatment in the ecclesiastical courts.[134] It is often extremely difficult to detect paternity, and it may be that at a time when it seems to have been assumed that once married a woman would continue to bear children, there was no overriding concern with it. The practical argument which Kames and Johnson put forward would finally vanish only in the twentieth century, with the spread of artificial contraception.

A further possible reason for the ambivalence towards adultery may

---

[130] Kames, *Sketches*, ii, 47.   [131] Brady, *Boswell in Search*, 166.
[132] Cobbett, *Advice*, 187, 193.   [133] Gouge, *Domesticall*, 219.
[134] Macfarlane, 'Marital Relationships', 129.

lie in the strictness of the marriage regime. With monogamy and practically no divorce, it may have been implicitly recognized that adultery was a kind of safety valve. Those who were unhappily married could hope to find satisfaction elsewhere, and there may have been a certain recognition that this was both inevitable and to be tolerated. Many of those who committed adultery would probably, in other societies, either have added spouses to create a polygamous union, or have obtained a divorce. High prostitution and adultery rates may have been the price the English paid from the sixteenth to the nineteenth century for the rigid marriage code.

11

Status Rules Concerning Marriage

The most powerful and widespread set of rules that have determined marriage in the majority of societies arise from kinship. An individual's marriage 'choice' is already largely determined on the day of his birth on the basis of the kinship relations of his parents. We are told that 'in Africa a marriage is not simply a union of a man and a woman; it is an alliance between two families or bodies of kin',[1] and this is historically the case in Asia, South America and elsewhere. In such a situation it is essential that individuals marry the 'right' person, belonging to an appropriate category defined by kinship. They must avoid certain close kin and positively marry into certain other categories. Even if there is no formal rule, there may be customary pressures which lead to a marked preference for certain kin marriages. Such systems, where the formal rules stating whom one must, or whom one should not, marry are observable in kinship terminology and in patterns of marriage, are termed 'elementary systems' by Claude Lévi-Strauss.[2] Such 'elementary' systems are predominant historically and occur in societies where kinship is the central pivot of political, economic and social life. Where such a situation obtains, Darwin would not have had to draw up a cost-benefit analysis. Not only would it have been known from birth that he would marry, but it would also have been apparent that he would marry within a certain range of kin.

'Elementary' structures are 'those systems which prescribe marriage with a certain type of relative, or alternatively, those which, while defining all members of the society as relatives, divide them into two categories, viz: possible spouses and "prohibited spouses".'

---

[1] Radcliffe-Brown, *African Kinship*, 51.
[2] Lévi-Strauss, *Elementary Structures*.

Lévi-Strauss describes the other major systems, 'complex' structures, as those 'which limit themselves to defining the circle of relatives and leave the determination of the spouses to other mechanisms, economic or psychological'.[3] In such 'complex' systems there is a range of negative rules about whom one must not marry. Often these are very limited, as in present-day north-western Europe or North America. One has to marry 'out' of the close family, but after that whom one marries is not dictated by kinship relations. The effect of a minimal rule of exogamy ('out-marriage') and no rule of endogamy ('in-marriage') is to 'send people shooting off in all directions at once.'[4] There are, of course, still constraints on choice, but these are related to class, status, education or religion rather than to the language and norms of kinship.

It is obvious that the majority of Western Europeans and North Americans now have a 'complex' system. It seems clear that this was also the case in the first half of the nineteenth century, when Malthus and Darwin were writing. We may wonder when and how it originated. Is there any evidence in the period from the fifteenth to the nineteenth century of a transformation from the marriage system based on kinship rules, to the free-floating marriages based on psychology and economics which exist today? In answering the questions concerning the curious link between economics and demography raised by Malthus and Wrigley, we need to pursue this further. A marriage system embedded in kinship is close to biological restraints: marriage for women will very often be at or near puberty. Marriages will not adjust sensitively to economic changes, since they are mainly determined by kinship. Nor will there be space for personal psychological pressures. Likes and dislikes, love and passion, have no formal place where the decision about whom to marry is encoded in the kinship structure.

The situation concerning the rules of out-marriage, exogamy, may be briefly summarized. Basically, with one small exception, the rules concerning which kin one may or may not marry are the same in England today as they were in 1540.[5] The exception is that in 1907 it became legal to marry a deceased wife's sister. Otherwise there have been no changes from a situation which allows marriage of all but very

---

[3] Ibid., xxiii.   [4] Fox, *Kinship*, 223.
[5] For details see Holdsworth, *English Law*, iv, 491–2; Burn, *Ecclesiastical Law*, ii, 407; Coke, *Institutes*, 2nd, 682.

close relatives. Essentially one may marry all except members of the nuclear family and all those, including uncles and aunts, nephews and nieces, in the ascending and descending generations. First cousin marriage is now, as it was from 1540, legal, if often disapproved of. At marriage the couple became 'one blood'. Thus a man was forbidden from marrying the same range of wife's kin as of his own blood relatives. For instance, he could not marry his wife's aunt even though she was not a blood relative. The prohibitions continued after the spouse's death. Hence marriage with a deceased wife's sister was forbidden.

In the three centuries before 1540 the prohibitions were wider. By the decision of the Fourth Lateran Council of 1215, impediments of consanguinity and affinity were set at the fourth degree, according to the canonical computation. Thus a person could not marry his own or his wife's third cousin, or any nearer relative.[6] Furthermore, wide rules of spiritual affinity prevented those related by godparenthood from marrying. On the other hand, dispensations were easily available, for a price, from the Church. There was a very limited prohibition in early Anglo-Saxon England, then a widening of the ring of prohibited persons, and then a narrowing again, so that England in 1540 returned to the situation that had prevailed in the seventh century.[7] The change at the Reformation was important, but it was neither unprecedented nor indicative of a shift from 'elementary' to 'complex' structures. Indeed, by allowing all to marry first and second cousins without dispensation, the Reformers, if anything, encouraged a move towards the possibility of an elementary system. It is difficult to see how preferential kin marriages can have been enormously attractive and common when the whole weight of the Church forbade them.

More important in assessing the presence of kinship pressures are the positive rules. To prevent estates going out of the family, or to consolidate social, political and other ties, most societies are organized so that strong pressures are put on the individual stating which kin he should marry. To find a person standing in the right kinship relationship is one of the central tasks of an elaborate kinship vocabulary, as well as of the 'marriage brokers' who exist in many societies. The necessity and function of such kin marriages are nicely

---

[6] Howard, *Matrimonial Institutions*, i, 353.
[7] Goody, *Family and Marriage*, *passim*.

illustrated by William Lawrence in 1680, contrasting such a situation with his own in England. 'The Arabians, [Ancient] Brittons, and other nations, to the intent that one family might not by marriage gifts rob another, always married in the same family, and brothers and sisters married, making that religion to marry in the family which others made incest; and that incest to marry out of the family, which others made religion.'[8] The presence of prescribed or strongly preferred kin marriages can be detected in three ways. First, the very terms used in referring to and addressing relatives may indicate who the preferred and forbidden partners are. Thus, for example, in the Gurung tribe of the central Himalayas where I worked, the word *nyelshaw* had the double meaning of mother's brother's daughter and also 'sweetheart' or 'preferred marriage partner'. A second set of rules is detectable by questioning the people concerned. When asked, a person will give a list of those categories of relatives he should and should not marry. Thus in the Yanomamo tribe of Amazonia, 'a male must marry a woman of the category called *suaboya* meaning "wife" . . . To state it more precisely, Yanomamo society is characterized by a rule that enjoins a man to marry a woman of a specific kinship category; he has no choice with respect to the category.'[9] Finally, there is the actual pattern, the proportion of persons who do actually marry relatives.

We might well come to the English evidence expecting some degree of preferential kin marriage. It is often thought that geographical mobility was so much lower in the past that villages would be filled with kin. Hence people would often find themselves marrying relations. This is assumed by W. G. Hoskins when he wrote of Wigston Magna, Leicestershire, in the later seventeenth century that 'as all these families persistently inter-married with each other (rarely going outside the village for a bridegroom or a bride) the degree of inter-relationship must have been beyond belief, and the number of "cousins" beyond accurate computation.' He continues, in words which recall the findings of anthropologists, that marriage is 'an alliance between two families or bodies of kin', that 'in this blood-brotherhood lay another of the great hidden strengths of the peasant community. By one marriage whole dynasties of peasant families were brought into relationship with each other.'[10] If this is

[8] Lawrence, *Marriage*, 117.   [9] Chagnon, *Fierce People*, 56.
[10] Hoskins, *Midland Peasant*, 196.

generally the case, it would be even more pronounced, it would seem, as we move back into the medieval period. Thus, a historian of the medieval manor stated that the lord's concern to restrict marriages to within the manor aggravated a difficult situation. H. S. Bennett approvingly quotes G. G. Coulton's belief that 'at least half the bond-men in a normal village had probably some common great-great- grandfather with any prospective bridegroom or bride', and hence were forbidden to marry. He goes on to say that 'we have only to look at the earliest parish registers to see how intermarried village communities became.'[11] Looking at it in a simple way, we might expect some sort of evolution, from kin-marriages, predominant up to the sixteenth and seventeenth centuries, then dropping away with the impact of the increased mobility of the industrial and urban revolutions of the eighteenth and nineteenth centuries.

From the start of adequate records, there is almost no evidence for such preferential or prescriptive rules. One area where we might have expected to find evidence is in literary and popular sources: in rhymes, proverbs, sayings and the general 'traditional' wisdom of the period. Yet there is nothing here that advised the young to marry certain kin. Nor in the extensive 'Advice' to young sons and daughters, or in the moralistic pamphlet literature, is any interest shown in the question of pre-existing kinship. We have already examined a great deal of this material in relation to the question of marriage choice, and nowhere have we seen any emphasis on the need to marry along kinship lines. Thus there is very little evidence in literary sources of any trace of an 'elementary' system from the time of Chaucer onwards.

Nonetheless, it could be that in practice there is evidence of that extensive intermarriage of kin. In order to find patterns, we would need to reconstruct from all sources a profile of each family and its relationships over time, and this has seldom been done. We need to know not only who married cousins and other relatives, but also who did not marry such cousins, though they were available.

For Earls Colne we have reconstructed the kinship network of forty of the largest families. These include several hundred marriages where we know something of the bride's and groom's kin. Because of the very high geographical mobility, it is seldom that we can be certain of the names and marriage destinies of all first cousins. But it seems

---

[11] Bennett, *English Manor*, 245.

likely that we know either matrilocal or patrilocal cousins' names frequently enough to be able to see if there was any systematic marriage with such cousins, either first or second.

There is absolutely no evidence of this. There are, in fact, three cases of kin marriages traceable in the records. One is with a mother's brother's daughter, another with a maternal grandfather's brother's daughter, the third with a patrilineal parallel second cousin. There is also a case where two brothers married girls who were third cousins to each other. This is the total that we could find for a parish of about 800 persons over two centuries. Probably, a few more cases would surface if the records were more complete, but there would still only be a handful, perhaps no more than in a modern population of the same size. Thus the evidence from Earls Colne provides no support for the view that from the sixteenth century, at least, close kin intermarriage occurred frequently.

Partial reconstruction of kinship networks in several other Essex villages, and in the nine chapelries of the Westmorland parish of Kirkby Lonsdale, suggests that Earls Colne is in no way exceptional. Several recent studies by other historians of parishes in Essex, Cambridgeshire and Shropshire have laid no stress on kin intermarriage.[12] This is not to say that such marriages never occurred. Clearly they did. But it is difficult to detect any systematic preference. Nor is there any evidence of a major change in the sixteenth to eighteenth centuries suggesting a transformation occurring during, or just before, the period when records are adequate to test the hypothesis. There is no hint from any of the extensive manorial court rolls for Earls Colne in the fifteenth century of frequent close intermarriage. It is difficult to use manorial records to discover such tendencies, but it is perhaps significant that recent detailed studies of late medieval court rolls have not commented on such marriages either.[13]

Until evidence to the contrary is brought forward, it seems reasonable to conclude that English marriage at the popular level conformed to a 'complex' structure from the later Middle Ages at least. Amongst the causes for this situation is mobility, social and geographical. As Robin Fox suggested, 'clearly the extent of both territorial and class mobility affects this deeply.'[14] Specifically, a high

---

[12] Wrightson, *Terling*; Spufford, *Contrasting Communities*; Hey, *Myddle*.
[13] Razi, *Medieval Parish*; Raftis, *Tenure*.   [14] Fox, *Kinship*, 237.

degree of geographical and social mobility will prevent the population from becoming fixed into isolated pools of related persons. When such pools occur, each marriage is heavily circumscribed negatively and positively by previous marriages. When there is great mobility, previously existing kinship links are relatively less important. We now know that both kinds of mobility were very high in late medieval and early modern England.

The consequences of the early development of a 'complex' system are considerable. Goode has argued that 'only if kin lines are unimportant, and this condition is found in no society as a whole, will entirely free choice be permitted.'[15] Throughout most of the population of England, over at least five hundred years, kin constraints on marriage were limited. Thus, while choice was not completely free, it was determined by factors other than kinship, and marriage could be left far more to individual selection. The individual was not constrained by the strategies of his kin, manipulated by language, into fitting his marriage into a pre-existing kinship structure.

As societies become the densely settled, partly literate, partly urbanized systems that we broadly term 'peasantries', status broadly determines marriage, but in a way that supplements and partly supersedes kinship. Birth now determines a position in a hierarchical society. Over-simplifying, there are two major systems: Indian caste systems, and the 'estates', sometimes combined with slavery, of China, much of medieval Europe and parts of Africa and South America. It is well known that, in general, castes in India subscribe to rules of endogamy. Although there may be specific exceptions, usually the situation is very fixed. It would have been unthinkable for a sweeper to marry a Brahmin; marriage rules are strong and reinforce the gaps between the four *varna* of priests, rulers, farmers and others. Intermarriage of the wrong kind would lead to pollution and cannot be allowed.

In general 'estate' systems have erected barriers almost as strong. As De Tocqueville wrote, 'amongst aristocratic nations, the different classes are like vast enclosures, out of which it is impossible to get, into which it is impossible to enter. These classes have no communication with each other.'[16] Thus slaves may not marry free

---

[15] Goode, 'Love', 47.
[16] De Tocqueville, *Democracy*, 248.

persons; the non-noble may not marry the noble. The social strata are hence consolidated and hedged in by legally enforced rules about intermarriage. Such laws are given added force and dimension by custom and convention. The literate townsman or churchman would not marry an illiterate country-dwelling peasant. Such societies are frozen into three or four endogamous blocks: nobility, the 'bourgeois' or city folk and administrators, the free peasants and, sometimes, slaves. Whom one marries will be heavily circumscribed by which rank one is born into.

It has been widely observed as one of the major features of modern 'democratic' and supposedly egalitarian societies in the West that this is no longer the case. 'Modern civilization tends more or less to lower or pull down the barriers which separate . . . the various classes of society. It has therefore made the endogamous rules less stringent and less restricted, it has widened the limit within which a man or woman may marry and generally marries.'[17] Although there may be lack of opportunity and considerable social pressure, there is no formal rule enshrined in law or custom preventing anyone from marrying whom he chooses. A commoner may marry into the titled ranks; the poorest and lowliest manual worker's daughter may marry a bishop's son, and so on.[18] This curiosity, when set against the system of estate barriers of *ancien régime* France, was early noted for England. In the nineteenth century De Tocqueville, referring back to the eighteenth century, laid enormous emphasis on this peculiarity and its consequences.

> Wherever the feudal system established itself on the continent of Europe it ended in caste; in England alone it returned to aristocracy. I have always been astonished that a fact, which distinguishes England from all modern nations . . . has not attracted still more than it has done the attention of philosophers and statesmen, and that habit has finally made it as it were invisible to the English themselves . . . England was the only country in which the system of caste had not been changed but effectively destroyed.

What was the major cause of this difference and in what did it find its best expression? It was in the absence of the rules forbidding

[17] Westermarck, *Marriage*, ii, 68.
[18] Though see the contrasted view of Stone, *Open Elite*.

intermarriage. 'The nobles and the middle classes in England followed together the same courses of business, entered the same professions, and, what is much more significant, intermarried. The daughter of the greatest noble in England could marry without shame a 'new' man.' Marriage is the supreme expression of estate fixity or flexibility, and to explain its patterns one is taken into an examination of social mobility.

> If you wish to know whether caste, its ideas, its habits, and the barriers which it creates among a people, are definitely destroyed, look at the marriages. There alone you will find the decisive feature that you want. Even in our own days in France after sixty years of democracy you will often seek for it in vain. The old and the new families, which seem blended in every other respect in France, still avoid as far as possible intermingling in marriage.[19]

De Tocqueville's views are corroborated by Sir Henry Maine late in the nineteenth century. 'In France, in spite of all formal institutions, marriages between a person belonging to the *noblesse* and a person belonging to the *bourgeoisie* (distinguished roughly from one another by the particle 'de') are wonderfully rare, though they are not unknown.'[20] Many people take it as a basic consequence of the fact that all men are born equal that they therefore have an equal right to marry whom they choose. When did such a view begin, and for what reasons? We have seen that Malthus isolated as the central determinant of when people married and hence the preventive check, the question of social mobility. As he put it, using the metaphor of a ladder, people were afraid of slipping down and anxious to climb up. In his view, a person could slip from near the top to near the bottom very easily. A rash marriage, too many children, and, as Darwin endorsed, a man might be forced to hard work – and even to poverty. The middling, respectable artisan or small landholder could be forced into the position of the pauper. There was, so to speak, no safety barrier on the ladder, no rigid brake which would prevent an individual falling too far, or prevent others rising past him. In such a situation, marriage was one of the most important strategies in improving one's life chances.

De Tocqueville pointed out the recentness of this phenomenon,

---

[19] De Tocqueville, *L'Ancien Régime*, 88–9.
[20] Quoted in Westermarck, *Marriage*, ii, 64.

originating from a precocious development which he traced from England. He concentrated on the absence of a barrier between nobility and commoner, and suggestively pointed towards an answer that lay in the nature of the social structure as a whole. 'It has often been remarked that the English nobility has been more prudent, more clever, more accessible than any other. The truth is that for a long time past properly speaking there has no longer existed a nobility in England, if the word is taken in its old and circumscribed sense that it has everywhere else retained.' One central feature of the definition of nobility is that the nobility are of a different blood and different legal status from commoners, thus rendering intermarriage impossible. When did this great change occur? De Tocqueville does not know; 'this singular revolution is lost in the darkness of past ages.'[21] Equally important for our purposes is the absence of two other major barriers, which have been central to all other 'estate' societies. These are the barrier between the 'free' and the 'unfree' – notably slaves and the rest – and the barrier between the 'bourgeois', the town-dwelling administrators and traders, and the 'peasants', the illiterate, soil-working country folk. By Malthus' time there were no apparent formal or strong barriers lower down the social hierarchy. Just as the middling could marry up, so they could marry down. Slavery and serfdom were abolished; an educated tradesman could well marry a country girl, daughter of a small yeoman farmer.

A first index of the changing position is the laws of the land. One of the interesting absences in the laws of England, as surveyed by the great English lawyers and legal historians from Bracton to Maitland, is any hint of a legal barrier to marriage between 'nobility' and 'commoners'. From at least the thirteenth to the twentieth century there was no law whereby such marriages could be opposed. If a person had obtained the rights of wardship and marriage, and these were abused in some way, then a case of 'disparagement' could be brought. But this was concerned with property rights and did not rest on the status distinction between noble and commoner. The real test is what happened to an individual commoner, perhaps very wealthy, who married a titled person, at both partners' own, voluntary, decision. Such marriages were as valid as any other, and the heirs of such a union were in no way disqualified. There is no law and no custom to forbid them. This absence of a barrier of blood, of a

---

[21] De Tocqueville, *L'Ancien Régime*, 89.

hereditary 'caste', is a peculiarity that goes back very early and is part of the general, curious absence of a true hereditary nobility in England based on a special legal status. Marc Bloch suggests that, whereas on the Continent a true hereditary nobility was established from the thirteenth century, England followed a different path. 'On English soil the ordinary free man was in law scarcely distinguishable from the nobleman.' Status was based not on blood and law as in France, but on wealth and land. The nobility was more a social than a legal class. 'In England knighthood, transformed into a fiscal institution, could not serve as the focal point for the formation of a class founded on the hereditary principle.'[22] That difference which De Tocqueville and Maine had noted in the nineteenth century was already established in the thirteenth.

It is clear that there were no legal barriers to marriage within the broad middling ranks, between townsmen and countrymen, between different occupational groups. None of the law books or collections of customs suggest any such barriers. The one possible restriction is that between the 'free' and the 'bond', or serfs. But whatever such barriers may have been, they no longer had any effects from the start of the sixteenth century, and it is doubtful whether there was a true legal barrier even before that. Maitland discusses the various 'impediments to marriage'. No mention is made of impediments arising from birth status. Indeed, nowhere, either in his chapter on marriage or in the section on the 'unfree', does he make any reference to a legal bar to marriage between 'free' and 'unfree'.[23] A detailed discussion of what should be the status of children born of a union between a 'bond' and 'free' partner implies that such unions were permitted and perhaps common. Although the lord would need to give a licence for the marriage of a bondwoman, no special licence, it would seem, would be needed for the marriage of a bondman to a free woman. There is no evidence that the church courts would have recognized the barrier between free and unfree as a ground for annulling a marriage or breaking a contract to marry.

As with the nobility, this absence reflected a particular feature of English society – namely, that there was no legal status of totally unfree. There was nothing equivalent to slavery in England from at least the thirteenth century. Maitland has outlined very clearly the

[22] Bloch, *Feudal*, ii, 331; ii, 330.
[23] Pollock and Maitland, book 2, ch.7, and book 2, ch.2, sect.3.

legal position of the medieval serf. Summarizing Bracton, he states that 'serfdom with him is hardly a status; it is but a relation between two persons, serf and lord. As regards his lord the serf has, at least as a rule, no rights; but as regards other persons he has all or nearly all the rights of a free man: it is nothing to them that he is a serf'; 'in relation to men in general, the serf may have lands and goods, property and possession, and all appropriate remedies.'[24] This 'freedom' is essential, for only between free persons can a contract such as marriage take place. As we have seen, a servant who is also a bondwoman would need permission to marry,[25] as servants would continue to need permission through the centuries. But otherwise, marriage was a private contract between two individuals, and a bondman or bondwoman could legally enter it with free persons. Thus even in the thirteenth century there was no strong legal barrier. By the fifteenth century, whatever minimal control lords had over their serfs had virtually disappeared, and we are in the 'open' situation where blood and hereditary status have little influence.

As for informal pressures and advice, we have already seen that throughout the centuries those who gave advice on marriage stressed that, if possible, partners should be roughly of the same social standing. But they also, as we have seen, laid equal stress on things other than blood and birth – namely, on wealth, education, personality, beauty and godliness. There is nothing in the advice to suggest that a person must absolutely not marry out of a rigid social rank. Indeed there was a mass of literature encouraging people to trade off birth against wealth. Particularly for younger sons, it was advised that they should use their good breeding and titled background to marry a wealthy tradesman's daughter. Fuller relates in the seventeenth century that it was a strategy for an impoverished younger brother to meet a girl who 'disdaineth her marriage should be contracted in an exchange, where jointure must weigh every grain even to the portion.'[26] In reverse, the younger daughters of the gentry might marry wealthy yeomen. In advising a gentleman how to deal with the problem of having many sons and daughters, an author explained in the early seventeenth century that 'your daughter at home will make a good wife for some good yeoman's eldest son, whose father will be glad to crown his sweating frugality with alliance to such a house of Gentry.'[27] Meanwhile, of two daughters

---

[24] Ibid., i, 415; i, 419.　[25] Anglicus, *Properties*, i, 305.
[26] Fuller, *Holy State*, 44.　[27] Furnivall, *Tell-Trothes*, 174.

apprenticed in the city – 'if they can carry it wittily, the City affords them variety.' They will ensnare the young tradesman and foreman of the shop.

Thus city and country, gentry and yeomanry, exchanged new-found wealth for older 'breeding' in that way that has been characteristic of England for many centuries. The considerable extent of marriage between the landed gentry and city wealth has struck historians of eighteenth-century England.[28] Many lamented the consequences: the preference of wealth over blood was to be deplored, as a late-sixteenth-century commentator argued. He noted that 'men will sooner match their daughters with any young master, a rich cobbler's son, though they be their heirs, than with a Gentleman of a good house, being a younger brother.'[29] This was to be condemned, for 'hereby comes the decay of ancient gentility, and this the making of upstart houses', bringing 'that corruption of blood which you, with your corruption of money, hath made'.[30] Yet the very disapproval is evidence of the widespread phenomenon, which we find in numerous collections of letters and other sources from the fifteenth to the nineteenth century.[31] As Mildred Campbell writes, 'a yeoman also frequently numbered his grandchildren among the gentry by successfully marrying his daughter into that rank. Such marriages were a commonplace.' Contemporary documents are 'filled with references to negotiations over such matches'.[32] The contrast between England and Germany in this respect was noted by the early-seventeenth-century traveller, Fynes Moryson, who saw with surprise that in Germany 'a gentleman never so poor, will not marry the richest merchant's daughter.'[33]

Statistics can be provided to support the view that intermarriage between different ranks of society was very common: thus, for example, in the period from 1570 to 1599, the proportion of 'titular peers and their heirs male' marrying within the peerage 'fell to a third'.[34] An analysis of Lincoln marriage licences between 1612 and 1617 undertaken by Laslett showed that of fifty bridegrooms and over sixty brides who were described as 'gentry', 'almost a third of the men and two-fifths of the women married outside their social order.'

[28] Habakkuk, 'Marriage Settlements', 23, but cf. Stone, *Open Elite*.

[29] Furnivall, *Tell-Trothes*, 98.   [30] Ibid., 99.

[31] Kingsford, *Stonor Letters*, i, xxviii; Verney, *Verney Memoirs*, iii, 296; Stone, *Aristocracy*, 590ff.

[32] Campbell, *English Yeoman*, 48.   [33] Moryson, *Itinerary*, iv, 325.

[34] Stone, *Crisis*, 286.

Nearly a quarter of the women and over 15 per cent of the men married into yeomen or artisan families.[35] Lower down the social scale there is evidence in village studies of considerable marital mobility. The son of a poor labourer often married the daughter of a rich butcher or yeoman. Thus different branches of the same family could soon end up a long way apart. Families did not move in social standing as a block, the marriage of one child dependent on the birth position and marriages of the others. Rather, there was room for individual mobility. In three generations one branch of a family could end up amongst the wealthiest and most powerful in the land, while misfortune or mismanagement plus a disastrous marriage could bring another branch down to the level of beggars. In such a situation of easy movement and basic instability, it is not surprising that there should be such concern about marrying at the right time and with the right person. One of the basic preconditions of the Malthusian marriage system – namely, the desire and possibility of social climbing through marriage – seems to have been apparent from very early on in England.

If it does indeed turn out to be the case that though people tended to marry people of roughly the same status and wealth, wealth and status were to a large extent interchangeable, this is of great significance. In most societies birth status – either kinship position or legal status – sets very rigid limits on marriage choice and divides the society into strict endogamous enclosures. Where this is not the case, although kinship and social status are still among the considerations, they merely set vague outer parameters. A great deal depends on achievement and personal initiative. The final outcome is a marriage based on a man's and a woman's decision to join forces, and not on status or pre-existing relationships based on birth.

Archetypically, as in Hogarth's illustrations of the popular theme 'Industry and Idleness', we have two brothers. The industrious one earns his master's favour, marries his master's daughter, builds up wealth and prestige, and ends up as Lord Mayor of London. Perhaps his children will become earls or prime ministers. The idle one is sent to sea, fails to marry, consorts with prostitutes and thieves, and ends up executed on Tyburn Tree. Any unfortunate offspring may well end up as the poorest of poor illegitimates. Thus, although all do not have an equal chance at birth, all do have a chance of some kind. In

[35] Laslett, *Lost World*, 202.

the nineteenth-century version, take a beggar from the pavements of Covent Garden, put her in a fresh dress and give her elocution lessons, and using charm and beauty she will have a chance to marry into the highest circles, as Shaw's satire *Pygmalion* shows. Of course, this is not just an English phenomenon, as Lampedusa's *The Leopard*, or Balzac's works, show. But it was carried to an extreme in England. The chances of such breaks is made much easier in a very geographically mobile society where adventurers and adventuresses can move to a distant city and meet anyone. In the eighteenth century the growing Empire emphasized the chances of mobility, allowing successful clerks to come back and found great families, but the eighteenth-century experience is merely an extension of an earlier tendency. Thus three great-granddaughters of the West Country cloth merchant, William Stump, became through marriage Countesses of Rutland, Suffolk and Lincoln.[36]

In a classic essay, J. H. Hexter has shown for the gentry and 'middle classes' that the roots of this phenomenon go back as far as the evidence allows us to investigate. For the fifteenth century, the 'Pastons, with their perpetual negotiations for London heiresses, Sir William Stonor with his successful marriage to a rich City widow, are but instances of the general truth that before the Tudor period country families had discovered the tonic effect on their more or less blue blood of a transfusion of *aurum potabile* from the City.' Hexter then traces the same processes back 'through the centuries, as far as the record will take us'.[37] As a fourteenth-century author lamented, the time when 'boys of no blood, with boast and pride, shall wed landed ladies, and lead them at will', is already nigh.[38] It was a medieval saying that 'a dog hath but a day, a good marriage will recover all together.'[39] The widespread existence of a large, wealthy, part-landed, part-mercantile, 'middling' stratum in England, from the Middle Ages onwards, made such marriage mobility both desirable and relatively easy.

The innuendoes and contradictions of the play between wealth, blood and personal desire were a central theme in much of the social commentary and literature through the centuries. Moreover, the fortunes of various groups were constantly changing over time, which made the situation even more interesting. There were, in fact, a series

[36] Hexter, *Reappraisals*, 76. [37] Ibid., 78–9. [38] Quoted in ibid., 81.
[39] Furnivall, *Meals and Manners*, 126.

of different ladders, propped side by side, and people could climb from one to the other. There are no signs of occupational endogamy, as taken to the extreme in the caste system of India. There was very open intermarriage between occupational and professional groups. It was, as it were, a game of snakes and ladders, with different-length ladders; as one reached near the top of one, it made it easy to move over to the next. But the ladders themselves were, as a whole, moving up and down. A well known instance is the position of clergymen. In a famous passage, Macaulay showed how the clergy had slipped rapidly down, from the Reformation onwards. Once wealthy and respected, they had sunk and sunk. By the end of the seventeenth century 'a waiting woman was generally considered as the most suitable helpmate for a parson.' Later, Swift was to advise the waiting-maid in large households that she had a choice of lovers: 'I would first advise you to choose the steward; but if you happen to be young with child by my Lord, you must take up with the chaplain.'[40]

Thus we see that the marital pattern, in terms of status, was closely linked to the many peculiarities of the English social structure. And it cannot be understood without reference to the widespread use of money, markets, the penetration of city life, the intermingling of town and city, and the easy conversion of wealth into blood and vice versa. It was an insecure situation, since the game had very few definitive and absolute rules, and there was only a choice between lesser evils, a preference for minor advantages. It is only by appreciating this early open system that we begin to understand the late marriage pattern and the pressures on marriage choice which have been revealed by demographers.

Any marriage, and particularly a wrong marriage, could lead to disaster. Marriage was thus not determined by 'status', that is, by a fixed position allotted by birth either in a kinship system or in a fixed rank in society. It was a contractual arrangement, which both symbolized social rank and allowed complex conversions and exchanges to take place. It was a game which, as we have already seen, had slightly different ends for men and for women. Their concerns about wealth and status could also be different. Within this complex framework of calculation and weighing of advantages, the powerful force of romantic love often played havoc with the cool assessment of

[40] Swift, *Works*, ix, 237.

advantages. Yet even passion had to be constrained and guided, for the couple must not only love but live. In order to set up an appropriate marriage they needed an assured income and other property. Before considering these financial constraints we may consider one final set of rules that often circumscribe marriage.

In many peasant and tribal societies there are customs that require a person to marry either inside a particular small area or outside it. In England it is impossible to discover explicit rules during the sixteenth to eighteenth centuries. Yet there were statistical tendencies. Local studies have shown that the majority of people married over a short distance, usually within a radius of ten miles. Eversley summarizes the findings as follows: 'generally speaking, marriages between persons resident in the same parish, and those involving a partner from an adjoining parish or one within a five-mile radius, account for 75–80 per cent of all marriages, and if we extend the radius to fifteen miles, we are likely to include all except an insignificant fraction of places of origin of partners.'[41] This is hardly surprising. In the absence of computer-dating or arranged marriage and with mobility circumscribed by how far people could travel by foot or on horse, it was inevitable that most people would be living near each other at the time of their wedding. Only thus could they get to know each other sufficiently well. This is still the case in supposedly highly mobile urban societies. We know, for instance, that partners in the United States tend to live no more than a mile apart just before they marry. Usually they live only a few blocks away.[42]

It is important to remember, however, that there is a difference between marrying someone who has always lived a mile or two away, and marrying someone whom one has only known for a year or two because he or she has recently moved from elsewhere. As already mentioned, we know from recent studies that there was extensive geographical mobility in early modern England. Much of this movement of servants, apprentices and even gentry occurred between puberty and marriage. The kind of mobility that is concealed behind marriage registers and licences is nicely illustrated at the gentry level by Sir John Gibson in an autobiographical poem he wrote in 1655. It is quite likely that Sir John and his wife were registered as of London

---

[41] Hair, 'Bridal', 238; Hey, *Myddle*, 201; Eversley in Wrigley, *Demography*, 21–2; see also Hollingsworth, *Historical Demography*, 181.

[42] Goode, *World Revolution*, 29; Bell, *Marriage*, 133.

at the time of his marriage. In fact,

> Crake it had my infancye,
> Yorke did my youth bringe up,
> Cambridge had my jollitie,
> When I her breestes did sucke.
> London brought me into thraule
> And wed me to a wife . . . [43]

Thus while marriage licences or parish registers would suggest proximity at the time of marriage, tracing back the lives of the individuals would often show that they had not always lived near each other. As we saw earlier, linking baptisms and marriages in Earls Colne suggested that only a small proportion of those who were married to a person of the same parish had been born and brought up in the same parish as their partner. This may well have been the case in other parts of England.

Thus we see that while marriage was governed by pressures of an economic, social and psychological kind, the absence of an 'elementary' marriage structure, and of closed endogamous ranks, made individuals free, making them able to choose whom and when to marry. Yet in making such choices they also had to balance their desires against the probable consequences of an improvident marriage. In setting up the 'enterprise' of marriage, it was generally believed that capital and income were needed. We will now consider the rules and customs which determined these financial settlements.

[43] Hodgson, 'Sir John Gibson', 124.

12

Economic Arrangements at Marriage

In order to set up a successful marriage in the years between the fifteenth and nineteenth centuries, it was felt necessary to have four types of asset. First, one needed somewhere to live – preferably, as we have seen, a house of one's own. Secondly, it was necessary to have the furnishings for house and body: furniture, cooking utensils, bedding and clothes. Thirdly, it was essential to have prospects of an assured income over the years ahead. This could take numerous forms: income from land, interest from investments, a profession or trade. In some of these activities it was necessary to have the stock and tools with which to derive the income. Finally, it was advisable to have some ready cash – to cover the initial costs, to help with the early expensive years of child-rearing, and in case of accident and sickness. In a joint family system, all these things would have been part of the joint estate, and a person married at puberty would have had access to them. The interesting situation in England was the way in which each asset was accumulated and contributed by the partners and their parents. We may start by looking at what a bride was expected to bring to the marriage, and her rights in the objects that she brought.

The most conspicuous part of the contribution made to the 'conjugal fund' on the part of the woman and her family was the marriage portion. The word portion appears to have had a double meaning. It meant the share that the wife contributed to a marriage, and it also meant that part of a parent's estate, the share, that a girl would receive as her inheritance; this portion, it was assumed, could be used for marriage. The dictionary gives under 'portion', as two of the separate meanings: 'the part or share of an estate given or passing by law to an heir, or to be distributed to him in the settlement of the estate', and 'dowry; a marriage portion'.[1]

---

[1] *Oxford English Dictionary*, s.v. 'portion'.

The overall value of this portion varied enormously, both between social levels and over time. Among the upper gentry the sums involved were very considerable: Evelyn mentions portions of £3,000 and £8,000 going with brides, and Thomas Isham, a Northampton-shire gentleman, paid a total of at least £4,000 with his three daughters.[2] At both this level and that of the aristocracy, the sums seem to be equivalent to about three years' income from the man's estate.[3] The same sort of ratio seems to have occurred at the level of wealthy yeomen, traders and the 'middling' sort. Thus Josselin gave his three daughters portions varying between £240 and £500 apiece, the clergyman–yeoman Giles Moore gave his daughter about £300, and a northern yeoman states that he had £300 with the girl he married.[4] With annual incomes of between £50 and £100 in the seventeenth century, these were probably again roughly equivalent to three years' income. At the husbandman level, as far as we can yet see, a sum of between £10 and £50 was considered reasonable. Between 1550–1720, in Lupton, near Kirkby Lonsdale, where most of the inhabitants were husbandmen, out of 39 portions mentioned as being given to daughters (though not specifically tied to marriage), 33 were under £20. In Earls Colne between 1550 and 1800, of thirteen portions the mode (four cases) was between £40 and £50. The rest were widely distributed. These seem smaller sums in relation to annual income – probably one or two years' on average. Likewise, though it is very difficult to find evidence, the portion of a labourer's child was probably even smaller, perhaps one to five pounds at the most. The really poor would probably have no portion.

The size of the portion is affected by changes in the cycle of an individual family: thus later-marrying daughters, as in Josselin's case, may get a larger portion as the estate expands.[5] Variations also occurred according to the number of children who were sharing the estate. There were also secular trends over time; Stone and Habakkuk have pointed to the rapid rise in the size of marriage portions among gentry and aristocracy at the end of the seventeenth century, linking this to the state of the marriage market, which was mainly determined by the ratio of men to women.[6]

[2] Bray, *Evelyn Diary*, 375, 386; Finch, *Families*, 27.

[3] Stone, *Aristocracy*, 790. For estimates of yearly income from Gregory King, see Laslett, *Lost World*, 37.

[4] Macfarlane, *Ralph Josselin*, 93–4; Blencowe, 'Giles Moore', 117; Marshall, *Stout Autobiography*, 199.

[5] Macfarlane, *Ralph Josselin*, 94.   [6] Stone, *Crisis*, 288ff.

Thus it was expected that at marriage a girl would bring a portion varying from a few pounds to thousands, depending on her rank. The actual composition of the portion is important in determining the effect of such expectations. If, as is elsewhere the case, the portions consist mainly of land or of housing, the effects are different from portions mainly in goods or cash, which are movable. There was a mixture of constituents in English portions, with an emphasis on movable wealth: the two major items brought by girls as their portions were household furniture and ready cash. In other words, they were expected to contribute two of the four necessaries. Thus a Staffordshire yeoman's daughter, married in 1601, had the following 'marriage goods':

> one joined bedstead, a press, one feather bed and one flock bed, two bolsters, two pillows, a (quilt), two blankets and (twilled covering), five pairs of sheets, and two 'pillow beers', one tablecloth and a half-dozen tablenapkins, two pairs of candlesticks, nine pieces of pewter, a salt, one brass pot, and one brass pan . . . nine knitchen of hemp and five of flax. In addition she was allowed ten pounds in 'ready money' for taking care of other needs as they arose.[7]

Another contemporary list, this time of a merchant's daughter, shows the same preponderance of linen and furnishings. The general emphasis on household linen is shown in the contemporary 'chest' or 'chist', a large storage box which would carry the articles to the new house and then be a useful piece of furniture.[8] Alongside the furniture was the money, in cash, bills or bonds. It is likely that this formed the largest single item brought by the girl. Medieval portions for the gentry and for ordinary villagers show a similar emphasis on cash and furnishings.[9]

Since the portion was both an anticipation of inheritance and a marriage gift, it is helpful to look at wills for our two sample parishes to gain a further insight into the nature of portions. In the chapelry of Lupton, most often the portion mentioned was a lump sum of money. Fairly frequently in the later sixteenth century a single piece of livestock – a calf or cow – would be added to the money, and sometimes bedding and chests. Nowhere are agricultural tools

---

[7] Quoted in Campbell, *English Yeoman*, 240.

[8] Winchester, *Tudor Portrait*, 66.

[9] Gairdner, *Paston Letters*, iii, 180, and for ordinary villagers, Homans, *Villagers*, 140.

included, and only very occasionally, when there were no sons, would a house or land be mentioned as part of the portion. In Earls Colne likewise, money constituted the vast bulk of portions, with occasionally a house and land if there were no sons and the parents were dead. In Earls Colne livestock and agricultural tools were never mentioned.

What is perhaps most notable about the portions is the absences; unlike the dowries of many Mediterranean societies, the girl was not expected to provide a house, nor did she usually bring tools or livestock. Land, as we shall see, was an optional extra. She brought movable, fluid assets which could easily be transferred into the new enterprise. In other words, she provided capital for the venture. The question then becomes, how – if it was difficult to marry before a reasonable sum was provided by the bride – had such capital been accumulated? The answer will affect the question of age at marriage, and the degree of parental control over marriages.

In many societies the girl is expected to weave and embroider her own trousseau, the wedding outfit, the sheets and some of her clothes.[10] This may have been the case in England as well, though there is little evidence to show that it was indeed so. But what we are really concerned with is the raising of a sum equivalent to a year or two's income. Where did the money for buying the furniture and the ten or twenty pounds of cash come from?

It is clear from the descriptions of wedding contracts, from court cases, from wills and from other documents that, as in Josselin's case, a girl would often receive a lump sum as her portion or part of her parents' estate. While sons would have to wait for this until the parents' death, daughters would receive their share at or before marriage. It was recognized that this would put a strain on parents. There was a contemporary saying, 'Children are careful comforts, though good, daughters when marriageable, especially.'[11] The situation was particularly difficult, as one diarist observed, if a poorer family married into a richer one; the poorer family might well have difficulties trying to provide an adequate portion for their daughters.[12] This is exactly how a check on marriage would occur. If a daughter wanted to marry young, she would have to forfeit a chance of a large portion. Her parents could not stop her marrying, but they

---

[10] Stirling, *Turkish*, 59, 181.   [11] Schucking, *Puritan Family*, 92.
[12] Nichols, *Halkett Autobiography*, 7.

could point out that not much capital had been accumulated and she would thus be able to bring less to the marriage. The likelihood was that she would not obtain a good 'match', unless outstanding beauty, temperament or chance aided her. If her parents had married at 25, it was likely that only in their late fifties would they have accumulated enough to marry off their daughters. To give them each a good portion at the age of 15 (the mean age at marriage in many traditional societies) would have left them deprived of a substantial part of their estate. The giving of portions to daughters, therefore, often coincided with the start of a gradual retirement of parents; having been married for twenty-five to thirty-five years, they began to hand over advance shares to their daughters in their sixties.

What happened when parents were only just able to make a living and unable to give their daughter a portion? One very common solution was suggested by Richard Gough in relation to Myddle in Shropshire. He described a girl who was 'a comely good humoured young woman, but her father having no portion to give her she was constrained to betake herself to service.'[13] We have already seen that servanthood and apprenticeship were very widespread institutions in England from at least the fourteenth century. We have also seen that in these activities, and in other forms of wage labour, it looks as if the children kept the profits of their labour. Consequently it was they who were able to make some savings.[14] Roughly, there would be about ten years between starting paid labour and marrying. Assuming that a girl at this level needed about ten pounds in ready cash (a year's wages) at her wedding, she might well be able to save that sum during this period. This, of course, is crucial in understanding the relative weakness of parental control. An active labour market provided an alternative to inherited wealth.

As well as the efforts of the girl herself, 'friends' were asked to contribute pieces to furnish the house – the tradition of the wedding present. Thus in a church court case, the mother of the groom asked a witness 'to give them [i.e., the young couple] because they should be but young beginners some household stuff and that she trusted the rest of her friends also would give him some one thing and some another.' The cost of the wedding celebrations could be raised by a church 'ale' or 'bridal', where the food and drink was contributed by

[13] Gough, *Myddle*, 124.
[14] Cf. Anderson, *Family Structure*, 86.

friends and neighbours and a profit might be made.[15] Indeed, if the community approved and a man had solid friends, such presents themselves might stand as a good alternative to a portion; thus Ralph Josselin mentions a wedding in Earls Colne where the company 'offered freely; he took about 56 pounds.'[16]

The difficulties in cases where poor maids had no portions were widely recognized in the leaving of bequests to charities for paying 'poor maids' portions', which one can still sometimes see commemorated on church walls.[17] When a girl had been working as a servant or apprentice, it may well often have been the master, rather than the parent, who provided the bulk of any portion. It is to this that the Italian visitor to England (mentioned in chapter 5) was referring in the 1480s when he described the way in which individuals would make their marriages without depending on parents. Children of both sexes, he explained, would be sent away from home very early on as apprentices and servants, and would never return home, and then 'the girls are settled by their patrons, not by their fathers, they also open a house and strive diligently by this means to make some fortune for themselves.'[18]

Thus the girl's portion could come from six different sources. Part might come from her parents, if they could afford it; part from what she had saved over a period of years; and part as an extra gift from her employer. The community, through charity, might contribute something; friends would give presents, and, finally, neighbours would assemble on the day and contribute further presents and perhaps money. When we consider that the portion of a girl in the lower half of the population would probably be of the order of money and goods worth between £10 and £30, we can see that over time an enterprising girl could save a reasonable amount. She might even be able to do so without the help of her parents. Clearly, where hundreds of pounds were involved, as with wealthy yeomen, this was more difficult. There is thus a fine balance: marriages should not occur without a reasonable portion, and this would take time to accumulate, for both parents and bride.

When were such portions paid over? We know that dowry in other parts of the world is often paid slowly over a number of years by parents to children – for instance, in parts of Ireland. Payments may

[15] Houlbrooke, 'Courts and People', 127; Jeaffreson, *Bridals*, i, ch.xvi.
[16] Macfarlane, *Ralph Josselin*, 98.   [17] Stow, *London*, 139.
[18] Sneyd, *Relation*, 25–6.

start at the wedding, but terminate much later.[19] An instance of this can be seen in the huge aristocratic payments of the period: thus the £17,000 portion paid with Lady Anne Clifford was only finally paid off after ten and a half years of marriage.[20] On the other hand, one of the interesting things about the English situation seems to have been that the portion was often paid very quickly indeed. In describing the 'Fashions at our country weddings' for Yorkshire in 1641, Henry Best explained how about a month after the actual wedding the bride is fetched 'and the portion is paid that morning that she goes away.' An ecclesiastical court case for Essex described how in 1599 a man went to get the 'woman's portion' from her friends before he married her.[21] Josselin, also, seems to have paid over his daughters' portions within a few months of marriage. In the case of the Tudor merchant family of Johnson, the money was paid even before the young couple were wed.[22] Gough described a marriage portion in Myddle of £1400 which was all paid on the day of the wedding. On the other hand, wills and other sources show that sometimes the money was paid over a few years: in the case of the northern yeoman James Jackson, over a period of three years.[23] On the whole, however, the paying of the portion was usually not a long, dragged-out affair perpetuating the financial link between parents and children. It was specifically to set up the marriage, and the money was transferred as quickly as possible to get the new venture going.

This makes sense when we consider five of the six possible sources of cash – friends, neighbours, employer, charity authorities and the individual bride. But what is perhaps most interesting is the situation with parents. Here we may examine what happened at the village level. If we analyse material for our sample parishes, where portions are mentioned they are usually stated to be paid off when the girl is 18 or 21, irrespective of marriage. Executors were directed to pay the girl her 'share' of the estate when she reached that age. If this occurred both before parents' deaths and after, then it would alter the situation. If portions were paid automatically and irrespective of marriage, then the connection between marriage and payment would be partly broken. The situation does not seem as simple as this. First, it may be

---

[19] Connell, 'Peasant Marriage', 505.   [20] *The Diary of Anne Clifford*, 104.

[21] Best, *Rural Economy*, 117; Hale, *Precedents*, 221.

[22] Macfarlane, *Ralph Josselin*, 93–4; Winchester, *Tudor Portrait*, 77.

[23] Gough, *Myddle*, 128; Grainger, 'Jackson's Diary', 115, 121; see also 'Joyce Jeffries Diary', fol. 27v.

that parents acted differently when facing death than at other times. There was no strong incentive to delay paying portions after death, and they merely left instruction to wait until a girl came into her majority. If a portion had already been largely paid, the executors merely topped it up to the full amount.[24] The second qualification is that the customs probably varied considerably over the country.

The fact that the portion was raised from a number of different sources, and did not exclusively come from the family estate, may help to account for another curious feature of the system. We have seen that daughters' marriages put a strain on parents' estates: 'when the son of a house is married, the family is reckoned to be a gainer: when a daughter is married, quite the contrary.' It is clear that from the wealthiest to the poorest – such as the parents who had 'sold all our kine to make money for my daughter's marriage' – there were difficulties in raising the portion.[25] The situation was a complex one because parents needed to deal fairly with their children. This is particularly well expressed in the fifteenth-century Paston letters. A boy's mother wrote to the girl's mother: 'for, madam, though I would he did well, I have to purvey for more of my childer than him, of which some be of that age, that they can tell me well enough that I deal not evenly with them to give John Paston so large and them so little.' This was countered by the bride's mother who was 'right loath to bestow so much upon one daughter, that the other her sisters should fare the worse.'[26] Such worries were often suggested in diaries – for instance, Dudley Ryder was concerned at his brother's impending marriage. 'It gave me a great deal of concern to think of their marriage, for I don't know how my father will be able to give him down a £1,000.'[27]

It is well known that the large, set dowries which have to be paid in most peasant societies are a major cause of debt. Money cannot be raised out of current income, the family mortgages land to a money-lender or sells off property, and the downward spiral is precipitated. This is well known to be the case in India,[28] but so it also was in Europe. In Scotland, for instance, the English officer Captain Burt wrote home that the reason given for the mortgages and encumbrances on Scottish gentry estates 'seems to be something

[24] Macfarlane, *Ralph Josselin*, 94.

[25] *Characters*, 169; Deloney, 'Jacke of Newberrie', 27.

[26] Gairdner, *Paston Letters*, iii, 197, 177. [27] Matthews, *Ryder Diary*, 341.

[28] Bailey, *Caste*, 71.

extraordinary'. The reason was not the poverty of tenants or other disadvantages; but they ascribed it to 'the fortunes given with their daughters', the portion or *tocker*.[29] Yet in the English evidence – in ordinary wills, lists of debts in inventories, court cases (in Chancery and elsewhere), diaries and letters – this cause of indebtedness does not loom at all large. So it appears that parents were not prepared to cripple themselves to pay marriage portions to daughters. Basically, the child could only have a portion of what was already available. Hence there was a distinct advantage in a child waiting. The more delayed the marriage, the larger the portion was likely to be. Parents did not mortgage the future in order to marry their daughters as soon as possible.

As well as the portion itself, there were three other contributions that a wife might make. The first of these was that her parents would probably be expected to contribute the major share of the actual wedding expenses. It would seem that the probable cost in the seventeenth century was roughly of the order of £25–£200 for a gentry wedding, £5–£50 for a yeoman or middling trader, £1–£25 for a husbandman, and 5s–£5 for a labourer.[30] Such costs were not enough to make weddings impossible to undertake without parental support, and it was always possible to avoid much of the cost by marrying without a large church wedding. Thus the clergyman Moore invited only seven guests to his daughter's wedding, laying out nine shillings in all for the occasion, apart from the fees. For those whose parents were too poor to raise the money, the 'bride-ale', where guests would bring their own food and drink, provided an alternative. The church might even lend special jewellery for the occasion.[31]

A second contribution by the bride is of a much more general kind. It was the potential earning power, skills, energy and good health which a wife would bring to a marriage. Much of a woman's energies for the first fifteen years after marriage would be devoted to giving birth to and rearing children. Even so, a great deal of the labour devoted to agricultural and artisan work would come from wives. They would cook, knit, churn, thresh, help with harvesting. They could earn cash from the numerous part-time occupations available

[29] *Burt's Letters*, i, 254.
[30] Blundell, *Diary*, 14, 246; Emmison, *Tudor Food*, 32; Macfarlane, *Ralph Josselin*, 97; Turner, *Brighouse*, 151; Wright, *Autobiography*, 98.
[31] Cox, *Churchwardens*, 315.

through the centuries. There seems very little segregation of labour at the lower levels of society, and women filled in with most tasks. In such a situation, though they were perhaps not physically as strong as men, their earning potential was often very considerable indeed. There is no sense that their portion was merely meant to be a lump sum to keep them fed and clothed while they reared children.

Finally, a girl might bring 'real estate', that is, land and housing, as well as the movable property which constituted the portion. Thus Josselin gave his daughter Mary a house and land worth £400 as part of her portion, and several other daughters brought such estates in Earls Colne. Aphra Behn refers to a good portion: 'though it consist in immovable Goods, as in Houses, orchards, and lands that be oftentimes in another shire.'[32] Looked at from the point of view of strategies of marriage, a man might well consider that an only daughter or widow with large landed estates would bring him a very handsome portion, and that it was these estates that were most attractive. The difference between such property and the normal portions becomes very apparent when we consider how differently a wife's real estate was treated in comparison to her 'chattel estate', or goods and money.

English law made a strong distinction between 'real estate' and 'chattel interests'. Marriage portions consisted essentially of the latter. Law and custom were clear as to what happened to the chattels so brought – they went straight into the control of the husband, to do with as he thought best. As Blackstone wrote, 'the sole and absolute property rests in the husband, to be disposed of at his pleasure, if he chooses to take possession of them.' Of goods 'in possession', as they were known – that is, clothing, money, household goods, furniture – 'the husband hath therein an immediate and absolute property devolved to him by the marriage . . . which can never again revert to the wife.' 'The marriage transfers the bride's chattels to the husband.'[33] The one exception was what was known as the wife's 'paraphernalia', which signified 'the apparel and ornaments of the wife suitable to her rank and degree'. At the husband's death, the wife had the right to claim an equivalent amount in jewellery, clothing and so on from her husband's estate as she had brought to the marriage, and such a claim was settled before any other. Thus the position at

---

[32] Macfarlane, *Josselin Diary*, 10 April 1683; Behn, *Pleasures*, 27.
[33] Blackstone, *Commentaries*, ii, pt 2, 435; Pollock and Maitland, ii, 427.

common law was that all the chattel goods of the wife, including the portion, went to the husband or his kin.[34] Among ordinary families up to the end of the eighteenth century there is little sign of a development noted by Taine for the mid-nineteenth century: this was a form of protection for the woman, whereby

> nearly always the wife's dowry is put into the hands of 'trustees' who take responsibility for its management and pay only the income to the couple in question . . . Her fortune thus becomes a sort of endowment, safe from anything which may happen to the husband (or his business). This precaution is taken because the law assimilates all a wife's property in her husband's.[35]

Two other kinds of property also fell into a special category. One was debts upon bond, contracts and other assets that were 'in action', which a wife might bring to the marriage. If the husband recovered these at law, then they became like money or clothing – his to dispose of by will at his death. If he did nothing about them, then they would revert automatically to his wife at his death, and he could not dispose of them. Similarly with what were known as 'chattel real', that is, leases for terms of years: with these leases held by the bride, a 'husband shall receive all the rents and profits of it, and may, if he please, sell, surrender, or dispose of it during the couverture [i.e., marriage].' Yet if he failed to do any of these things during his lifetime, he lost his opportunity, and the leases reverted to his wife, even against his written will.[36]

It is clear that the portion attracted by a son's inherited estate might well be conceived of as partly the property of his siblings. Particularly in the case of the elder son, who had received the bulk of the property, a way of evening out the inheritance without breaking up the estate was to use the cash he had been able to bring in to match his property to provide portions for the other children. It was therefore particularly helpful to have movable property, cash, which could be easily circulated. Thus Pepys described Lady Pickering's plans for her son: 'his mother would fain marry him to get a portion for his sister Betty, but he will not hear of it.' It was generally stated of the upper groups in England that 'the young children are disposed

---

[34] See Chamberlayne, *State of Britain*, 178.   [35] Taine, *Notes on England*, 79.
[36] Blackstone, *Commentaries*, ii, pt 2, 434.

goods and chattels, and commonly the eldest son's wives' portion.'[37]

The way in which this worked as a way of evening out the effects of male primogeniture, the eldest son receiving the bulk of the land and the daughters sharing the cash which his land had attracted as a marriage portion, is well illustrated in a contemporary Chancery case from Kirkby Lonsdale.

> Francis Baines of London stated that his father 'married and had with his wife a dower and marriage portion of the sum of £60 of lawful money . . . which . . . was paid down upon her marriage day or within a short time after . . . unto his father in consideration that he [i.e., father] should procure an estate to be made to her for her life which was done accordingly. Which said money, which was paid to your orator's mother, as portion, was presently distributed by your orator's father unto his sisters for their legacies formerly bequeathed by your orator's grandfather's will.'[38]

This is in conformity with Blackstone's description. Such money became automatically the husband's, and he might dispose of it to his sisters if he so wished. His wife could not stop him, as long as she was maintained by her husband at an adequate level. Thus a Jacobean wife explained that the way to raise daughters' portions was to get the maximum by the marriage of the eldest son, then 'dichotomize the whole portion of his wife into several shares betwixt your other children'.[39]

Real estate – that is, freehold land or housing, or land held by other tenures such as copyhold by a woman at her marriage – was very different. Unless she formally transferred this to her husband, it remained ultimately in her ownership. As Blackstone put it, the husband only 'gains a title to the rents and profits during coverture: for that, depending upon feudal principles, remains entire to the wife after the death of the husband, or her heirs, if she dies before him.' In other words, he cannot sell the land; he cannot leave it to another by will. It remains his wife's, though he can have the use of it. Since it was not absorbed by the groom, real estate might not be part of the portion, or 'dower'. Only if the property was explicitly transferred to the husband in the terms of the marriage contract, that is, if it was effectively given to him and hence passed out of the woman's hands,

[37] Latham, *Pepys*, i, 295; Chamberlayne, *State of England*, 305.
[38] PRO, C.2, B11/34, 1Charles.   [39] Furnivall, *Tell-Trothes*, 144.

could he dispose of it. The exclusion of the man in this respect was one of the bastions of the liberty of women. Such a defence was also, needless to say, attacked frequently, but equally vigorously protected.

A particularly awkward situation occurred when a wealthy heiress with large estates died before her husband. She could leave the land to her own heirs; it was hers to bequeath and had merely been managed by her husband. But was he to be ousted from the house and lands straight away? Here English law was extremely 'courteous', or generous, to the husband, protecting him against the next generation and against his wife's heirs. This shows the enormous support given to marriage, when intact or when broken by death; it was protected against wider kin, children and any others. The way in which the 'courtesy' worked illustrates the extreme lengths to which the law would go to disentangle all possible eventualities.

A first distinction was made between freehold and copyhold land. It would appear that in the latter the man had no 'curtesy', that is, no automatic rights after his wife's death in the land she held in this way. 'There is no tenancy by curtesy of copyhold lands, unless there be a special custom for it.'[40] In both Kirkby Lonsdale and Earls Colne there were frequent transfers whereby the wife would come into court and surrender her rights, with husband and wife then jointly taking the land, which would remain with the longer liver. This would clearly not be necessary if there had been the special custom of courtesy. With freehold, there was an automatic right on the part of the husband to enjoy his wife's freehold estate for his life under certain conditions. Such a right existed in other countries, but what distinguished the English law and made it especially 'courteous' was that the right existed for the man's whole life, whether he remarried or not. In Normandy it had merely been for the period that a man remained a widower. In Scotland, the rights lay only in land the wife had inherited, not land which had been given to her. In England, it was 'an estate for his whole life in the whole land'.[41] Thus a second husband could keep a son of the first marriage from his inheritance during his life. But there was one important condition. There had to be a live-born issue of the marriage during the life of the wife.

Much concern about the 'liveborn' was expressed. A usual definition was that it must have been heard to cry. It was also essential that the woman be alive when the child was born. The test case was a

---

[40] Jacob, *Law-Dictionary*, s.v. 'curtesy'.   [41] Pollock and Maitland, ii, 416, 420.

caesarean operation. As Blackstone put it,

> the issue also must be born during the life of the mother; for if the mother dies in labour, and the Caesarean operation is performed, the husband in this case shall not be tenant by the curtesy: because, at the instant of the mother's death, he was clearly not entitled, as having had no issue born, but the land descended to the child, while he was yet in his mother's womb; and the estate being one so vested, shall not afterwards be taken from him.

This was the case in the majority of English tenures, but 'in gavelkind lands, a husband may be tenant by the curtesy without having any issue.'[42]

Viewing the contribution of the wife as a whole, some concluding points can be made concerning the flexibility of the system. First, the nature of the portion (usually movable property) meant that women could be geographically and socially mobile. Secondly, the size of the contribution from the woman was flexible. There were norms for any group at any time, but these were negotiable. The portion was only one of the assets of women: good blood, a pleasant character, beauty, could all be weighed alongside the portion. Thirdly, the sums needed for a marriage, particularly by the three quarters of the population at the husbandman or small artisan level and below, were not so great that it was impossible for a person to accumulate them by his or her own efforts. All this combined with the fact that there were numerous sources for financing marriages, made it possible for a person to marry without parental support. The goodwill of parents would be a useful asset, but they could only partially control marriages. On the other hand, the fact that a portion was thought to be needed helped to hold back marriage.

In terms of the central problems concerning the homeostatic devices that subtly influenced the proportion marrying and the age at marriage, it is possible to see how a continued period of increased wages and widening opportunities for labour, especially for servants and young women, might lower the age at marriage. After ten years of saving, a girl might well find she had accumulated enough, and that her friends were well enough off to help her to marry, in a situation where, in another period, she might not have been able to do so. Others benefited from the fact that their parents had saved enough

---

[42] Blackstone, *Commentaries*, ii, pt 1, 127. 'Gavelkind' was a custom whereby the youngest son was the heir.

over a period of rising real incomes to release their marriage portions while they were still relatively young. The fact that portions were accumulated over a period of years – ten to twenty years on the part of parents, five to ten for the children – may partly help to explain the curious time-lag of twenty or so years that Wrigley and Schofield have discovered between fluctuations in the level of real wages and marriage rates. One bumper harvest or a sudden upturn in wages would not immediately convert itself into earlier marriages; it was cumulative.

This was just the kind of delayed response which Malthus advocated, providing that breathing space which would allow acceleration and growing investment. The particular pattern of women's marriage finance is a crucial feature in the delicate mechanism. Furthermore, we have seen how delaying marriage had a number of economic advantages. A child would have saved more, parents would be in a better position to pay over a portion, and the pressures from other siblings would be less intense. In wealthy families, the marriage of the heir might also ease the situation for other children. Thus the portion system was a delicate device for adjusting marriage to economic prosperity. If a girl wished to 'marry well' she would be advised to bide her time. Often her economic attractiveness increased at the very point when her physical charms were diminishing. The mid-twenties were perhaps an ideal point when the two combined to an optimum degree.

One other economic advantage of the system may be noticed. The flow of portions allowed a flexible interchange of wealth between social strata, between town and country, and between tradesmen and agriculturalists. 'Marriage was a business partnership – the wife's portion was often the means of setting her husband up as a master' in his own business.[43]

While the contributions provided by the bride bear a resemblance to what is described as dowry by anthropologists in other cultures, what is clearly absent in England throughout the centuries is anything resembling the other major type of marriage transaction, the 'bridewealth' or 'brideprice'. As described in anthropological litera-ture, this is a payment made by the groom's kin to the bride's kin which is used to compensate them for the loss of their daughter to

---

[43] George, *London Life*, 171; cf. Winchester, *Tudor Portrait*, 77; Chambers, *Population*, 52.

another kin group.[44] Where an individual is being transferred from one defined group to another, particularly in agnatic societies where the woman moves to her husband's group, certain 'wealth' flows back to fill the vacuum left by the departing individual. There are hints of some kind of payment to the bride's kin in Anglo-Saxon England,[45] but in none of the sources from the fifteenth century on do we find any such gifts or payments. The flow of wealth, such as there is, is down to the next generation, to the young couple. Nor is there evidence of a variant of this – the practice of 'groom service', whereby a prospective groom 'pays' for his bride by working for his in-laws, instead of paying them in cattle or other movables. The nearest one might come to this in England was the apprentice or servant who finally married his master's daughter. This is explicable in terms other than groom service, however. It seems as plausible to argue that a man was encouraged to marry his master's daughter not as a reward, but because, having worked in the business for some years, he would be able to help the daughter to mind it.

In marriage a small enterprise was set up in which the woman brought the furnishings, liquid capital and her skills. What would the man contribute? The two main elements that he would need to provide for the conjugal fund were shelter, that is, a house to live in, and a means of earning a living. The latter would characteristically consist of land with its necessary tools and livestock, or a small business of some kind with its assets and stock, or a skill or profession which placed him on a ladder of increasing wealth – for example, training as a lawyer or doctor. In other words, a man had to have the prospects of a 'living'. To this he would, with his wife's help, devote his labour and earn enough to bring up their children and provide for old age.

It was the pervasive social rule that a man should not marry until he was able to earn an independent 'living' sufficient to maintain his family at a reasonable standard, that acted as a brake on marriages. It operated in the same way as the portion for women. A man could marry young, but by doing so he was probably consigning himself and his family to downward mobility. The longer he delayed his marriage, the greater his chance of a comfortable middle and old age. Against

[44] E.g. Goody and Tambiah, *Bridewealth and Dowry*; Westermarck, *Marriage*, ii, xxiii.

[45] Howard, *Matrimonial Institutions*, i, 263; Goody, *Family and Marriage*, App. 2.

this he had to balance the loss of sexual and social satisfaction caused by deferring marriage. To marry before his training was over, whether as apprentice or university student, was disastrous, but to wait too long was difficult. The optimum point was again probably in the mid- to late twenties. But the intersection of economics and psychology was subject to fluctuations caused by a number of external pressures.

On the one hand, a period of economic growth would translate itself into a slackening of the pressures against marriage. The demand for labour would increase, people would find themselves moving faster up career structures and hence earlier attaining that level where it would be considered reasonable and 'safe' to marry. On the other hand, such growth might also raise levels of expectation. What would be considered a 'reasonable' level of maintenance in one generation might not be so for the next. An ever-upward moving scale of wants, the acquisitive spiral which is at the heart of capitalism and which Malthus recognized as essential to his marriage system, was intimately linked to marriage. This was recognized by Adam Ferguson in the eighteenth century. People could not marry until they had 'the necessary of life', but this is 'a vague and relative term . . . it has a reference to the fancy and to the habits of living.' As wealth increases, a person may leave 'a scene overflowing with plenty, because he has not the fortune which his supposed rank, or his wishes, require.'[46] Not only do general expectations rise, but the desire for upward social mobility may cause an individual to defer marriage for a few years longer, by which time he has reached a higher level of wealth which can then be cemented by a 'better' marriage. One expression of this never-ending upward accumulative spiral can be seen in the question of housing.

The man was expected to organize the acquisition of a house. As we have seen, people preferred to have their own, rather than live with parents or lodge, and being able to afford this was one of the determinants of marriage. Except among the very wealthy, it was unusual for parents to provide the house. If we look at contemporary seventeenth-century diarists – Josselin, Heywood, Pepys and others – there is little sign that their parents provided them with a house, or that they did so for their own children. For the majority of the population it was up to the couple themselves, and it seems likely that

[46] Ferguson, *Essay*, 142–3.

it was a joint enterprise. Some of the wife's portion might go towards it, just as she would provide furnishings. The man, also, through savings, would contribute to the purchase of the lease. Others might also contribute: the parents could give gifts, as could masters and friends. Ultimately, the sum had to be raised from a number of sources and the decision and purchase were in the hands of the couple themselves, and particularly the husband. The standard of what was acceptable as housing was culturally determined and was therefore subject to ever-upward redefinition. As today, the luxuries of one generation soon became the necessities of the next.[47] In the absence of a fixed standard, people found that increases in the wealth of the society, instead of making marriage easier to enter into, might have the effect of raising the threshold. The differences between standards amongst the English and the Irish poor, we have seen, was noted by Arthur Young as a major cause of the difference in marriage patterns.[48]

Whatever was actually given to the son by his parents was a free, unconstrained, gift. It was also, like the portion, seen as an advance share on whatever he might receive after their death. The amount the parents could give him at marriage would thus, as with daughters, depend on the number of other children, the position of his marriage in relation to siblings' marriages, how long he delayed his marriage. In many ways, younger sons were in the same position as daughters. They were often given cash portions like their sisters, and on these they must make their way. Only the eldest son, except in areas of partible inheritance, would receive the major estate, with which he might attract a rich portion and which in turn would help to contribute to the marriages of his younger siblings of both sexes. In Kirkby Lonsdale parish there was a great difference between the oldest son, who might inherit the parental home and land after his mother's death, and the younger sons. The latter were treated as exactly equivalent to daughters, receiving cash portions of exactly the same size. In Earls Colne also, it would appear that younger sons and daughters were treated as equal.

The main economic contribution about which there were negotiations at marriage did not concern sums of money or property provided by the man at the marriage itself, but rather a commitment to provide an income for life for the woman. There was a reasonable likelihood

[47] Hoskins, 'Rebuilding', *passim*.   [48] Hutton, *Young's Tour*, ii, 119–20.

that a woman would survive her husband, and she and her children needed to be provided for in that event. We have seen that in England the 'courtesy', and the way in which a man absorbed his wife's portion, protected against her death, but how were women to be protected? Here the analogy with a joint stock company was very close indeed because, in effect, the English marriage set up such a company. The articles of the marriage settlement were directly parallel to company articles. The main formal mechanism was the 'jointure', as it was called. This was the setting up of a 'joint estate', held by husband and wife, within some part of the estate brought by each partner, to be left to the longer liver of the two, thus excluding other heirs. As Sir Edward Coke defined it, a jointure was 'a competent livelihood of freehold for the wife, of lands and tenements; to take effect, in profit or possession, presently after the death of the husband; for the life of the wife at least'.[49] The essence of a jointure was that a man promised that his future wife would have a certain sum of money each year from his estate after his death.

There has been a great deal of research into the size of such 'jointures' and the inflation of their value in the sixteenth to eighteenth centuries at the level of the gentry and aristocracy.[50] Much of this is concerned with the ratio of the size of the 'jointure' to the size of the woman's marriage portion. John Evelyn mentions a marriage portion of £4,000 which was matched with a jointure of £500 per annum; Blundell speaks of a £2,000 portion bringing a jointure of £200; Pepys mentions a portion of £500 to a jointure of £40.[51] The ratio was very roughly 1:10 in the later seventeenth century – very approximately the profit one could expect from land or other capital at that time. In a sense, then, the jointure could be seen as an assured estate for the wife, arising from the capital she had brought to the marriage. At the start of the seventeenth century the ratio had been more favourable to women, with £600 of portion characteristically bringing £100 per annum of jointure. Habakkuk dismisses the argument that the fall in the rate of interest was the main cause of change, and argues that the alteration reflects a change in terms of marriage settlements in favour of husbands. He agrees with contemporaries that this was mainly due to the greater

[49] Quoted in Blackstone, *Commentaries*, ii, pt 1, 137.

[50] Habakkuk, 'Marriage Settlements'; Stone, *Crisis*; Cooper in Goody, *Family and Inheritance*.

[51] Bray, *Evelyn Diary*, 499; Blundell, *Diary*, 12; Latham, *Pepys*, iii, 176.

competition in the marriage market caused by a growing number of daughters of wealthy merchant families who were competing for husbands.[52] Much less work has been done below the level of the gentry, and we still do not know whether there were similar changes.

One point that needs to be stressed here is that the jointure may have been unnecessary in a number of cases, for there was, under English common law, an automatic right of 'dower' whereby a woman was seized of one third of her husband's freehold estate for life. This could not be taken from her, waived or undermined, and it needed no specification or contract to protect it. A form of dower existed in England from Anglo-Saxon times until 1833, when it was abolished.[53] The aim of the contractual jointure was merely to provide more generous terms for the wife, over and above the common law dower. This common law right of a woman to one third of a deceased husband's freehold estate was specifically 'for the sustenance of the wife, and the nurture and education of the younger children'.[54]

Dower was a right which the widow held against the other heirs. A woman was automatically entitled to her third, even if she was separated from her husband for adultery, though, of course, if the marriage was annulled she would not receive it. A woman was automatically given this right whether she was endowed at the church porch – in other words, had been through a church wedding (*ad ostium ecclesiae*) – or not (*dos rationabilis*). If she was endowed at the church of more than a third, she could choose whether to have the contracted amount, or fall back on the common law dower. As regards the family house, after her husband's death she had forty days of 'quarantine' during which she could live there while the heir worked out her dower and substitute lodging; she would become the heir's tenant if she remained in the house. The dower was for life, and not merely for her 'chaste widowhood'. As Maitland explained, a widow might enjoy her third even though she married again.[55] What did not happen in England was the Scottish practice whereby the wife's third went back, on her death intestate during her husband's lifetime, to her own kindred, rather than to her husband. In this case, also, English law was courteous to husbands.[56]

---

[52] Habakkuk, 'Marriage Settlements'.

[53] Whitelock, *English Society*, 152; Pollock and Maitland, ii, 365ff.

[54] Blackstone, *Commentaries*, ii, pt 1, 129.

[55] Ibid., ii, pt 1, 133; Pollock and Maitland, ii, 419.

[56] Pollock and Maitland, ii, 431.

These rules of jointure and dower applied to the freehold estate. But among the majority of the population much of the property was held of manors by customary tenures, for example by copy of court roll, or in boroughs by burgage tenure. What were the rights of the wife in this? Blackstone speaks of 'copyhold dowers, or free-bench', one of the main names by which the institution was known in England. The other term was 'widowright', and we are told that 'widows' rights seem to have been by far the most durable and firmly established of all inheritance customs.'[57] Yet it was clearly the case that 'copyhold estates are not liable to dower, unless by the special custom of the manor, in which case it is usually called the widow's free-bench.' Although a wife would be automatically guardian to a child until he or she was fourteen, and might thus have temporary security after her husband's death, she might nevertheless lose his non-freehold estates.[58] A jointure was one way out of this problem, assuring her a steady income, but there were also others.

In order to see how widespread free-bench was, it would be necessary to undertake a systematic survey of the customs of all the manors and boroughs in England, and of particular customs such as gavelkind in Kent. Thus, for example, in London there was a specific custom concerning the 'widow's chamber', giving a widow rights in the room where she had customarily slept.[59] No systematic survey has ever been done and there are no national or regional collections of customs, or custumals. We are therefore forced to look at specific instances.

The diversity of customs is well ilustrated for the county of Westmorland, within which Kirkby Lonsdale was situated. The customs for the barony of Kendal, including Kirkby, were described by Isaac Gilpin who had kept the courts at Kendal until the age of 80. He described the customs in the early seventeenth century as follows:

Within the Barony of Kendal if a tenant die and leaves a widow this widow by the custom there will have all the whole tenement or tenements be they never so many, which her husband died seized of during her widowhood. That is so long as she keeps her self a pure widow and the heirs can have no benefit during that time. But if she marry or miscarry then she loseth all her interest in her husbands

[57] Blackstone, *Commentaries*, ii, pt 1, 129; Faith, 'Inheritance', 91.
[58] Blackstone, *Commentaries*, ii, pt 1, 132; *The Order of a Court Leet*, 36.
[59] Blackstone, *Commentaries*, ii, pt 2, 517.

tenements neither can the husband by his last will and testament hinder his widow of her widows estate.

The same author points out that the customs in the other baronies were different: often the widow only had a half or a third during her 'pure widowhood'.[60] We can see this, for example, in the Furness district, where in Hawkshead the custom was a third. Then in Broughton-in-Furness there was a half for the first wife and one third for subsequent ones. In Ulverston, one part of the manor had a custom whereby the free-bench was in 'that part of land which the husband died seized of', while in another part of the manor, it 'attaches on marriage'. The variations were such that Gilpin wrote that 'a man might almost say that there are as many several customs as manors or lordships in a county, yea and almost as many as there are townships or hamlets in a manor.'[61] In the township of Lupton we can see from the wills that people made reference to their wives having all the tenement during the widowhood, 'according to the custom of the lordship'. But if a woman remarried, then she would lose the tenement. This is likely to have contributed a pressure against remarriage, unless there were ways of avoiding the threat of loss. By excluding a son from the whole estate until his mother died or remarried, the custom must also have helped to encourage late age at marriage. This is consistent with the very large number of bachelor sons aged over 25 which the listing of inhabitants in Lupton for 1695 reveals.

The differences within the southern county of Essex were equally great.[62] The customs could also change quickly over time, with old customs being abolished and new ones invented, even though there was supposed to be continuity. We can see this happening in Earls Colne. In the Earls Colne court roll of 7 June 1552 it was stated that a widow came into court and claimed one third of the customary holding as her 'reasonable dowry', and 'because it is testified by the homage that the custom of this manor is not to the contrary she is admitted the lord's tenant of the third part of the foresaid messuage ... in the name of her dowry.' This was during the time the manor was held in the relatively loose grip of the Earls of Oxford. Later it was bought and run by a resident landlord, Harlakenden. In June

---

[60] Bagot, 'Manorial Customs', 238, 243.   [61] Ibid., 228.
[62] E.g. see Benham, 'Manorial Customs', 83–4.

1595 the topic was specifically discussed:

> At this court the Steward of the manor by virtue of his office commanded an inquisition to be made whether women are indowerable of the third part of the customary lands of their husbands at any time during the marriage between them. And now the homage present that they have not known in their memory nor by the search of the rolls that women ought to have any dowry in the customary tenement of their husbands but they say that in times past diverse women have pretended their dowries but have always been denied and therefore they think there is no such custom.

In fact, if we look back through the voluminous court rolls from 1400 to 1600, which have now been published in full, we can see that the 1595 judgement was correct. There is little unequivocal evidence of an automatic right of dower, though occasional references to a possible right. It looks as if it was in 1552 that the change was attempted. Yet there were also ways to get round these difficulties, as evidenced by the very earliest court rolls. After his wedding a man would come into court and surrender his customary holding, and the husband and wife would then receive it back jointly to the longer liver of them. This happened very often in the courts – further evidence of absence of automatic widowright – and these courts came to be known as 'pairing courts'.[63]

In considering the contribution of the wife, we stressed that her skills and energies were among the most important assets. The same was equally true of men. It was their prospective earning power that was their major contribution. This would, of course, vary according to their occupation. A landed gentleman might live off his estate from an early age. But for the bulk of the population, including younger sons in landed families, it was necessary to achieve a level of income and of future expectations that would make the maintenance of a married household a real possibility. Those who needed an apprenticeship would have had to finish their training and to have established their trade. Among artisans or merchants this might take seven or more years, just as professionals who had perhaps been to university would need some years to establish themselves as doctors, lawyers or clergymen, before they could 'afford' to marry. For some years men would save and reinvest in their chosen occupation, and it was only

---

[63] Macfarlane, *Josselin Diary*, 20 October 1646.

when they reached a certain threshold that they could contemplate marriage. The waiting, as Tawney long ago pointed out, might be least for labourers, who reached their maximum earnings early on.[64] But even labourers might feel that they needed to save for a house and have a little in reserve, though many of them would start in rented houses.

A consideration of the capital deployed at a marriage suggests that it should come from both sides – in the form of a mixture of cash, housing, land, furnishings, tools, furniture, skills and labour. The contributions, as we have seen, would be fairly balanced, with perhaps the man providing the larger capital sum or earning potential, while his wife provided a larger immediate cash sum and the potential of bringing his children into the world. Wider kin were not much involved in raising the capital, which largely depended on the judicious efforts of the couple themselves, their 'friends' (which might or might not include kin) and neighbours and parents. In particular cases, of course, since wealth was only one consideration, it was possible for one side or the other to lower its contribution: it could substitute blue blood, beauty, excellent prospects or other advantages for wealth. The economic rules that lay behind setting up a marriage were obviously very much influenced by subsequent rules about what happened to the contributions, both before the marriage and once it was under way. We are thus led into a brief examination of the rules of marital property.

We may first consider a continuum of marital property systems that has been established for France in the work of Yver.[65] The central question here is the degree to which there is a 'community of goods' between husband and wife in English marriage. In the French case we have two extremes. At the 'community' end of the continuum were, for instance, the Norman and Walloon systems. At the 'lineage' end lay the area of Roman law in southern France.

In between the two extremes lay many parts of France – for instance, the Paris region. In the 'community' areas, the wife and husband no longer have separate rights after marriage; they become totally blended together, one legal person. It is impossible for either to have separate heirs. We might envisage the situation as a fully integrated company in which, when it ends, the partners have no

---

[64] Tawney, *Agrarian Problem*, 104–6.
[65] E.g. Goody, *Family and Inheritance*, as summarized by Le Roy Ladurie.

separate rights; body, blood and estate become one. In the 'lineage' situation the two partners remain autonomous and separate, there is a temporary 'alliance' of their properties, but ultimately the wife's kin retain their stake in her property, and the husband's kin in his. When the marriage ends, in whatever way, property reverts to his and her heirs respectively. The marriage is a temporary joining of estates. Where does England fit into this picture?

The issues, which have been revitalized by Yver, Ladurie and Goody, were discussed long ago by Maitland. At first sight it would seem quite obvious that England had a 'community' system during the centuries up to the industrial revolution. After all, as Blackstone implied, there seemed to be a complete merging of property at marriage. The 'chattels personal' of the wife are completely absorbed by the husband.[66] 'This depends entirely on the notion of an unity of person between the husband and wife; it being held that they are one person in law, so that the very being and existence of the woman is suspended during the coverture, or entirely merged or incorporated in that of the husband.' Terms such as 'unity of person', 'merged', 'incorporated', would immediately lead us to think of a full community identity. Yet if one looks a little closer, the situation becomes more complex. First, 'community' implies two-way rights, a woman having rights during the marriage in her husband's assets, as well as the other way round. This is conspicuously absent. Secondly, in true 'community', the pooling is for ever and can never be undone; it annihilates the separate identities. Yet in England Blackstone specifically uses the phrase, 'during the coverture', that is, during the marriage. So it is at best a temporary 'community'. After the marriage ends, the wife will reassert herself as an independent actor. In fact she has not been absorbed but, in the revealing phrase, she is a *'femme couverte'*, that is, a 'covered woman'. The image of being covered is linked to that of feudal tenant: she becomes a tenant or 'man' to her lord. This is very different from becoming absorbed into him, for a tenant has an independence of his or her own. The fact that there is no community, even in goods, was noted by Maitland: there is 'no community of goods, no *compagnie* between husband and wife; the bride's chattels become the bridegroom's.'[67]

A third reason why it is misleading to talk of community becomes apparent when we turn from personal or movable property to real

[66] Blackstone, *Commentaries*, ii, pt 2, 433. [67] Pollock and Maitland, ii, 447.

estate. As Blackstone and others point out, the husband only has rights in the *usufruct (sub modo)* of the wife's real estate. The two properties are not merged, but kept carefully distinct, unless the wife agrees to specifically surrender her land to her husband or to their joint estate. Marriage, in itself, does not set up this community. This was not only the case under common law in relation to freehold properties, but also under customary laws relating to manorial properties. Thus, for example, it was stated that 'when land descendeth on the mother's side, the heir on the mother's side shall inherit, and not the heirs of the father's side' and vice versa.[68] Thus, for example, if A married B, a woman with property, and they both died childless, in no circumstance could A's kin inherit, nor could children by an earlier marriage of A. In other words, there is a strong hint of a sort of lineage system, with rights continuing to flow down male and female lines.

Rather than seeing the wife as joining a 'community' in which she lost her identity entirely (along with her name),it is more accurate to see her as temporarily submerged, *couverte* but retaining her separate identity. When she became a widow she re-emerged relatively free and independent.

'The fundamental principle', as Maitland stated it, was that the husband, during marriage, became his wife's guardian. She became neither subsumed into him, nor merely his 'thing' or chattel. In law, Maitland states, 'we do not treat the wife as a thing . . . we treat her as a person', even if she is like a servant to a master, a subject to a king, a child to a parent, an inferior in that particular relationship. The rejection of that idea of community which, Maitland argues, was accepted by Scottish law and flirted with by the English, was decisive in many ways for the nature of English marriage. 'Scottish law has believed, or tried to believe, in a 'community of goods' between husband and wife, which English law has decisively rejected.'[69]

The rejection of community had many effects. One consequence of the fact that England was a country where 'long ago we chose our individualistic path', was that it gave women, *de facto*, considerable power.[70] Here was a paradox. It might be thought that community, by giving total mutual property between spouses, would raise the

[68] *The Order of a Court Leet*, 41.

[69] Pollock and Maitland, ii, 406, 400; for a more recent account of the rejection of the idea of 'community', see Holdsworth, *English Law*, iii, 521–4.

[70] Pollock and Maitland, ii, 433.

position of women and protect them in a much better way than a system where they were 'covered'. Thus many people commented on the apparently low *de jure* status of women in England when compared to women elsewhere.[71] But such commentators also argued that women seemed *in practice* more in control, more confident and more independent in England than anywhere else in Europe. This was not just a result of the fact that women's rights under customary law and under equity were much better than their common law position; it seems also to flow from the fact that, like subjects and servants, though subordinate they had separate rights. England was a society where the law recognized their inalienable property rights, even within marriage.

One of the difficulties in coming to grips with the curiously balanced but unusual system which seemed to extend to neither of the extremes of lineage or community, is how to separate the meanings of 'unity' and of 'community'. On the one hand, the unity of the married couple is constantly stressed. It is shown in the submerging of names: by a strange irony, in England, while the real estate of the woman is kept apart, she loses her maiden name, which becomes subsumed with that of her husband. In France and Scotland where there is complete community of property (at least in certain areas), the woman keeps her maiden name.[72] But even more important than naming is the way in which descent and affinity are conceived of. As we have already seen in our discussion of forbidden marriage, husband and wife were seen to become as 'one flesh' by the Church. They became identical, the ultimate community. As Maitland wrote, 'all my wife's or my mistresses' blood kinswomen are connected with me by way of affinity. I am related to her sister in the first degree, to her first cousin in the second . . . But if I and my wife are really one, it follows that I must be related by way of affinity to the wives of her kinsmen.'[73] Logically, one would not be related at all except through blood. The fact that a relationship was held to be established by marriage suggests that 'one flesh and one blood' was to be taken literally. A marriage created some kind of metamorphosis or blood transfusion. Husband and wife had become equivalent, identical; a man reckoned his kin as if he were his wife, and vice versa. The separateness of two persons was destroyed: the rib had been

[71] Chamberlayne, *State of Britain*, 178–9. [72] *Burt's Letters*, i, 64.
[73] Pollock and Maitland, ii, 388.

restored and the body made whole.

Such a conception of marriage helps to explain how marriage, and the physical union of two bodies through sex, became the pivot and heart of the social system. Our system is not one where marriage is merely an alliance between two groups, mediated through two representatives who become allies. Rather, a new entity is created – the conjugal couple. The obliteration of the wife's name and separate identity in kinship was somehow combined with her preserved separateness and individuality as a property-owner and as a citizen. She could, in the equity courts, bring cases against her husband; she could not be deprived of her real estate or of life and limb. Thus the system maintained a precarious tension between separateness of property and legal person on the one hand, and a very close emotional, psychological and spiritual identification. The kind of tension of identity and opposition that one finds in any system of hierarchy – of ruler and subject, of lord and tenant, of master and servant, of teacher and pupil, of parent and child – was central to the marriage relationship as well.

The combined elements of community and lineage in the English system are an important contributory factor in explaining the other features of marriage and family pattern. Goody, following Berkner, has suggested that the 'community' variant 'allows for earlier marriage, earlier transfer (of wealth) and more stem households', whereas the lineal system 'may well lead . . . to a high rate of celibacy, late marriage and (less certainly) a low incidence of stem households' – that is, households where parents lived with one or more married children.[74] To this extent the absence of 'community' is linked to the demographic patterns we are concerned with. On the other hand, we do not have extreme lineality with all its implications, among them the fact that the two families of origin are in opposition and the marriage is often a tense and short-lived fusion in which man and woman are pawns in an 'alliance'. Somehow, the English managed to combine an emotional fusion, making marriage the centre of the social structure, with the preservation of the autonomy and separateness of the partners. Some compromise had been achieved between the demands of love and market, of heart and mind, of pleasure and profit. How people actually negotiated this compromise through the ceremonies of courtship and wedding will be the concern of the next chapter.

[74] In Goody, *Family and Inheritance*, 25.

13

Courtship and Wedding

I n previous chapters we have examined marriage from a static and structural point of view. It has been argued that marriage was a matter of individual contract rather than a result of relations of social status. Each marriage was the outcome of the calculation of costs and benefits, principally by the couple themselves, but also by their friends and close relatives. The two major pressures which came to bear on marriage were the individual desire to marry and mate, and the recognition that if this ocurred at the wrong time or to the wrong person there would be serious consequences in terms of socio-economic position and personal happiness. Thus biology and psychology, sex and loneliness, fused into 'love', which pushed from one side; while economic and social factors, the desire for wealth and prestige, pulled from the other. The resolution of these forces was seen in the marriage strategies of millions of individuals. In order to understand how the pressures resolved themselves in action, it is necessary to view marriage as a process or a drama, or a game.

As we have seen, in the run-up to a marriage two sets of negotiations tended to go on simultaneously. One concerned the financial details that had to be settled, and here the same care had to be taken as in the setting up of any company. The words used to describe the marriage were also used in business: 'forming a connection', 'enterprise', 'match'. As in many other European societies past and present, a sort of joint stock company was being established.[1] The aim was to obtain the best possible terms for each side; not to be over-greedy, but also not to be duped. It was well known that much deception was practised, and books of advice

---

[1] Friedl, *Vasilika*, 54ff, or Nivernais marriage described by Sabean in Goody, *Family and Inheritance*, 108.

warned children of the dangers.[2] Subtle attempts to deceive and trick are frequently alluded to in both fictional and real accounts.[3] Particularly with the gentry and above, very large sums of money and the interests of other children were at stake.

In numerous sets of letters from the fifteenth century onwards we find lengthy discussions of the financial contract to be established.[4] Similarly, many diaries and autobiographies record in graphic detail the stages in the financial negotiations.[5] Legal records, both of central courts such as the Court of Requests and of ecclesiastical courts, are filled with echoes of such negotiations.[6] Henry Best in 1640 described how in Yorkshire, as soon as the young couple were 'agreed and contracted', their parents met 'to treat of a dower, and likewise of a jointure'.[7] In England, alongside the necessary financial details another kind of exchange was simultaneously occurring – concerned with psychological adjustments. Sometimes the two interests clashed; ideally they supported each other, and pleasure and profit were united as firmly as the couple. The two activities are delightfully portrayed in both words and pictures in Aphra Behn's *Pleasures of Marriage*, in the scene where the friends of the young couple are arguing and negotiating along 'rational', monetary, market, business lines while in the adjacent room the couple are 'kissing and slobbering', overcome with passion in pursuit of bodily and mental fulfilment.[8]

In earlier discussions we have roughly distinguished those societies where marriage is a contract between two individuals who have chosen each other on the basis of mutual attraction, from those where marriage is arranged as one aspect of the relationship between groups. In the former, individualistic, situation, courtship is largely the concern of the two main protagonists, and tends to be fairly long and elaborate. It is a period for making sure that one has chosen right, for testing or tasting the wares and comparing them to others available in the general market. Prolonged courtship, 'in giving time

[2] Percy, *Advice*, 93.

[3] Behn, *Pleasures*, 156; Stapleton, *Plumpton Letters*, 126–7.

[4] Kingsford, *Stonor Letters*, i, 127; St Clare Byrne, *Lisle*, 90; Verney, *Memoirs*, i, 417ff.

[5] Halliwell, *D'Ewes Autobiography*, i, 309ff; Bray, *Evelyn Diary*, 374–5; Matthews, *Ryder Diary*, 367; Jackson, *Thornton Autobiography*, 78–80.

[6] E.g. Campbell, *English Yeoman*, 48; Moore, 'Marriage Contracts', 293.

[7] Best, *Rural Economy*, 116.   [8] Behn, *Pleasures*, 14.

for the sentiment of love to mature and thus to absorb the sex impulses into a wider and more stable system tends . . . in general to civilize love'.[9] Courtship is basically a game between prospective partners, with some interested spectators and perhaps an umpire to decide who has broken the rules if something goes wrong. The players are the couple who are considering a permanent union, the rules are customary rules, and the stakes are marriage or non-marriage.

In contrast, there are the majority of human societies where the individuals are merely pawns in a wider game. What the young couple feel is largely irrelevant, and they are expected to play a minimal role. Marriage is a team game, and the couple, especially the girl, are often kept out of harm's way until the actual wedding day. 'Courtship' or 'getting to know you' is largely irrelevant. The very concept of an exquisite, yearning, intense period during which two personalities are supposed to blend into one is incomprehensible, ridiculous or indecent. Love is one thing, marriage another. The idea that the power of individual physical attraction, of psychological and social compatibility, should be harnessed and channelled into marriage is strange and sometimes repellant, for it places the individual above the group. An example of the clash of the two views is delightfully provided by Dudley Ryder. While suffering from the passion of love and involved in arduous courtship, he read Pitt's account, 'The Mohametan Religion', where 'there is no such thing as courting or wooing. A match is made up without so much as the young man's seeing his wife as is to be, by the father of the woman.'[10]

Two of the major functions of courtship behaviour in the Malthusian marriage system were to provide sufficient emotional momentum for the couple finally to agree to the irrevocable decision to marry, and to give as much information as possible on which to base the decision. In the open, non-pressurized, marriage system we have described, the impetus came mainly from the individuals, drawn like magnets to each other. Certain customary signals and codes had been developed over the centuries to stimulate and arouse the necessary ardour, and to allow the couple to test out parts of their characters. Although it was traditional to point out that people took

[9] Morris Ginsberg in *Encyclopedia of Social Sciences* (1931), 539–40, s.v. 'courtship'.

[10] Matthews, *Ryder Diary*, 329.

less care in inspecting partners than in selecting livestock, there is ample evidence that considerable attempts were made to establish that the prospective partner was compatible, and even delightful. As with the financial negotiations, this was a game filled with deceit, superficial trickery and blandishments. Yet it was necessary to try to uncover the frauds and to make sure that the 'other' was indeed the person who through the long years would remain one's closest friend.

This required a relatively long and careful observation. As a seventeenth-century manual advised, 'he therefore which will know all his wives qualities: or she that will perceive her husband's dispositions, and inclination, before either be married to the other, had need to see one the other eating, and walking, working, and playing, talking, and laughing, and chiding too.'[11] Malthus argued that that would mean that young people should be able to converse intimately without it being supposed that they intended marriage or an intrigue, and 'a much better opportunity would thus be given to both sexes of finding out kindred dispositions, and of forming those strong and lasting attachments without which the married state is generally more productive of misery than of happiness.'[12] In fact, the history of courtship behaviour in England shows that, to a consider-able extent, Malthus' hopes were fulfilled. Courtship combined the arousal and strengthening of passion with the possibility of mutual physical and psychological exploration.

The first notable feature of courtship in England was that it was usually initiated either directly or indirectly by the individuals themselves. Where marriage is urgently desired and arranged early, there arises a set of institutions for bringing together suitable mates. In most peasantries, whether in China, India or Europe, there are professional marriage 'brokers' or 'match-makers'.[13] Such people are experts in finding suitably endowed partners: they know the field, and who is a good 'investment'. They may arrange meetings and terms, and generally act as a kind of matrimonial agency.

In England, any such instituted role seems absent. There are hints of such activity, particularly among the gentry and nobility, where a powerful and well placed man like Lord Burleigh could act as a match-maker. But even at these upper levels it was usually family

---

[11] Dod, *Godlie Forme*, 109.   [12] Malthus, *Population*, ii, 162.
[13] E.g. Spence, *Woman Wang*, 77; Beals, *Gopalpur*, 29; Lofgren, 'Family', 30. In general see Mullan, *Mating Trade*, ch.2.

friends or kin who tried to help to find suitable matches.[14] There are also hints that amongst rich merchant families there were those whose temporary success in introducing a couple might lead them to try to do it more often. Thus the Duchess of Newcastle stated that 'women do fee her to get them husbands, and men to get them rich wives, so as she is become the huckster, or broker of males and females . . . indeed she is a matrimonial bawd.[15] No doubt, as today, individuals could advertise for partners, but it was significantly they themselves who would put in the 'lonely hearts' advertisements, and it was they rather than the parents who would try the services of a matrimonial 'bawd'. Furthermore, below the level of the upper gentry and merchant families, there is little evidence of marriage brokers. They are not mentioned in ecclesiastical court cases about broken engagements, they are not visible in accounts of courtship in diaries, they do not appear in letters, they are not referred to in accounts of courtship. Courtship was a game that, on the whole, people played for themselves.

The second feature of English courtship was its length. Although it is only possible to obtain literary, non-statistical evidence, it would appear that it was normal to court for almost exactly the same time as in modern America or Western Europe. In one study of modern America, for instance, the gap between first meeting and the wedding usually falls between six months and two years.[16] This is exactly in line with the historical evidence. Henry Best described the average marriage as involving a period of about six months between the first sounding out of the bride's family and the betrothal. If we add the period before the couple approached their parents, and between betrothal and marriage, nine months to a year would be about right.[17] This fits with the periods recorded in a number of diaries and autobiographies.[18] It also fits with the length described in breach of contract cases in the church courts. For instance, a mother deposed that 'by the space of a year and a half, there hath been good will in the way of marriage between her son and another.'[19] Of course there

---

[14] E.g. Bourcier, *D'Ewes Diary*, 123; Searle, *Barrington Letters*, 113; Stapleton, *Plumpton Letters*, 123.

[15] Cavendish, *Letters*, 210.   [16] Bell, *Marriage*, 131.

[17] Best, *Rural Economy*, 116.

[18] Gunther, *Diary of Ashmole*, 13; Grainger, 'Jackson's Diary', 115; Macfarlane, *Ralph Josselin*, 96.

[19] Hale, *Precedents*, 170.

were extremes, from the vicar who met and married his bride within six weeks to the couple who courted each other for sixty years and finally married, when all external opposition was ended, at the age of eighty.[20]

Since marriage was usually initiated on the basis of personal choice, it is important to know where and when the courtship began. Literary and autobiographical evidence shows that love's capricious darts could strike in any surroundings. Wherever men and women met, a courtship could start. Church was a favourite place: Ralph Josselin fell in love when he saw a girl in church, and dramatists satirized churches as marriage market places.[21] The numerous fairs and markets which took place almost daily in many districts were occasions for the institution of courtship.[22] Or again, there were the various village celebrations, where groups of young men and women would meet together.[23] What is clear from particular autobiographical accounts – for instance, the delightful description of the courtships of the Lancashire apprentice, Roger Lowe – is that courtship was a continuous activity.[24] It started when people worked together as servants or apprentices, when they worshipped together, when they traded together, and even when they went to court together as litigants. Although dancing and games, the alehouse and the village sports, were occasions of more than usually feverish courtship activity, they were only the peaks. As girls and boys passed through the ten years between puberty and marriage, they were constantly aware of solicitations and invitations, constantly examining their feelings. Starting with mild flirtations, many passed through a series of affairs before finally settling on a particular partner.

The numerous and varied occasions where courtships began and took place are partly to do with high geographical mobility. Often when children were living away from their parents, their activities brought them into contact with members of the opposite sex. This

[20] Smith, *Ecclesiastical History*, 190; Jeaffreson, *Bridals*, i, 72.

[21] Macfarlane, *Josselin Diary*, 1639; Farquhar, *Beaux' Stratagem*, Act II, scene 2; Middleton, *Women Beware Women*, Act I, scene 1.

[22] Malcolmson, *Popular Recreations*, 55, 77; Thompson, *Working Class*, 444; Defoe, *Tour*, 77; I.W., *Speedie Post*, sig.E3v.

[23] Turner, *Heywood*, i, 240; Strutt, *Sports and Pastimes*, 351–3; Brand, *Popular Antiquities*, i, 212ff.

[24] For Roger Lowe's intimate account of courtship, see Sachse, *Lowe Diary*, *passim*; Wotton, *Reliquae*, sig.b4.

frequency of opportunity is also related to something more intangible, but equally important – namely, the apparently relaxed attitude towards young men and women spending time together, often in the absence of any kind of chaperone. Where marriage is arranged and at an early age, it is usually accompanied by strict segregation of the sexes, a form of purdah which prevents boys and girls forming any kind of deep emotional or physical attachment. Thus, traditionally in Hindu and Islamic societies, unmarried and unrelated members of the opposite sex of marriageable age are absolutely forbidden to communicate. Even betrothed couples in a Turkish village are not meant to see each other, while in a Greek village 'unmarried village boys and girls do not talk to each other in public unless they are related.'[25] The 'honour and shame' complex, as it is known, means that women's purity is constantly thought to be threatened by unrelated men, and the family's honour to be under assault. Playfulness, flirtation, kissing, joking and all those amorous dallyings which cement passion into love and allow an exploration of the character of the other, are totally unthinkable. Yet, as Malthus argued, companionate marriage cannot work well without a relaxed and unsuspicious familiarity, an easy and open relationship between young men and women.

There is a great deal of evidence to show that such a relaxed atmosphere prevailed for the majority of people, from the time when it was delightfully documented by Chaucer up to the present. Both the necessity of such freedom for companionate marriage to succeed, and its precocious development, were noted by Frenchmen who visited England in the nineteenth century. Taine wrote, 'I have already made it clear that young people of both sexes meet and mingle freely and without surveillance: they are thus able to study and get to know each other as much as they like during four, five months, or longer, ride and talk together throughout several seasons running, in the country.'[26] La Rochefoucauld wrote in 1784 that 'to have a wife who displeases you must, in England, make your life most unhappy. One therefore seeks, rather, to know her before marrying her; she feels the same.' This is related to late age at marriage, he argues, and is made possible because 'it is much easier for people to know each other before marriage, for young people are in the world of society from their infancy; they always accompany their parents. Young

[25] Stirling, *Turkish*, 180; Friedl, *Vasilika*, 56.   [26] Taine, *Notes on England*, 78.

unmarried girls form part of the company, and talk and amuse themselves with as much freedom as if they were married.'[27] Both observers were commenting here on the gentry, where undoubtedly throughout the centuries control and chaperonage were strictest, as today. In earlier times there is evidence that at this level, and in certain occupational groups such as the clergy, there was some surveillance.[28] But for the bulk of the population the impression is of tolerant neighbours and kin.

There is evidence in diaries that young people were left alone for long periods to talk and embrace.[29] Particularly graphic are the accounts of the relaxed attitude toward affairs shown in the numerous ecclesiastical court cases which arose from broken marriage contracts. A good instance of the general climate is shown by a witness in an Essex case in 1576, who described how

> [he] hath seen great familiarity between the same William Kennett and the same Agnes and hath seen them sit dallying and kissing together by the space of two or three hours, and also hath seen them lie together alone by the space of two or three hours, her father being at London two or three sundry times, upon one bed in their clothes in the night time in her said father's house, none then present but this deponent being in bed by them too, of the which this deponent did think no offence for that they minded to marry together.[30]

Although contemporaries might warn their children against the danger of 'wanton embraces, sitting on the knee, bearing in arms, and such like',[31] such customs were widespread. Indeed, since marriage was to be a total emotional and physical relationship, it was essential that there be a prolonged and sustained effort to achieve ardent closeness. The difficulty was to have sufficient nearness without over-exposure, either to the irrevocable step of full sexual relations or to a plateau of frustrated boredom. The courtship patterns were further complicated by the very great stress laid on betrothal, or engagement, a contract which has now lost much of its force and meaning but which cast an ambiguous shadow over the second half of a courtship.

[27] Quoted in Flandrin, *Families*, 168–9.

[28] Hutchinson, *Memoirs*, i, 94; Barnard, *Country Gentleman*, 59; *The Diary of Anne Clifford*, 11.

[29] Sachse, *Lowe Diary*, *passim*; Wright, *Autobiography*, 36.

[30] ERO, D/AED/1, fol.24, see also Moore, 'Marriage Contracts', *passim*; ERO, D/AEA/15, fol.146v.   [31] S.S., *Secretaries Studie*, 145.

Anthropologists have noted that the marriage itself in many societies is a gradual process. A series of rites are enacted over time so that groups of people, as well as the individuals themselves, can gradually alter their relationships.[32] One major stage is the formal betrothal, or making a public promise. After this, the couple are, so to speak, neither married nor unmarried. For example, children born after the betrothal ceremony but before the wedding are often considered fully legitimate.[33] It is therefore no surprise that betrothal, or 'spousals' as they were known, should have carried more weight in the past than an engagement does today. It is clear that many people regarded the young couple as virtually married, after spousals.

The history and changing legal status of the betrothal is a subject of considerable complexity which merits longer treatment.[34] It will suffice to say here that in the Middle Ages and earlier the spousal probably constituted the main part of the marriage contract. By the sixteenth century it had come to mean different things in different contexts. An example of these multifarious meanings can be seen in the most famous work on the subject, Henry Swinburne's *Treatise of Spousals or Matrimonial Contracts*, written in the late seventeenth century.

Albeit this word *Sponsalia* (Englished *Spousals*) being properly understood, doth only signify Promises of future Marriage, yet it is not perpetually tied to this only Sense, for sometimes it is stretched to the signification of *Love Gifts and Tokens* of the Parties betrothed ... Sometimes it is taken for the *Portion of the Goods* which is given for and in consideration of the Marriage to be Solemnized; and sometimes for the *Feast or Banquet* at the Celebration of the Marriage, and of other it is otherwise used.

Swinburne pointed out that the church authorities distinguished between two types of spousal: *de futuro* (the ceremony carried out in words in the future tense, for example, 'I will take thee to be my wedded wife'), and *de praesenti* ('I take thee to be . . .').[35] The problem for many was that canonical lawyers 'oftentimes ... make no difference, or very little, betwixt the natures and effects of spousals *de praesenti* and of Matrimony solemnized and consummate'. Even after the Reformation this traditition was maintained. A *de praesenti*

---

[32] Cf. Van Gennep, *Rites*, 118ff. [33] Gorer, *Himalayan Village*, 318.
[34] Howard, *Matrimonial Institutions*, i, 270ff. [35] Quoted in ibid., i, 378.

betrothal was totally binding; it could not be dissolved except by proper divorce.[36] In a sense, 'the betrothal was a true marriage while the nuptials merely its confirmation.'[37]

As a result of the ambiguity of the law, the church courts were filled with matrimonial litigation. It is from these cases that we learn a great deal about courtship and about popular views of spousals. Two examples from Essex give the flavour. In 1576, a Romford informant described how he had overheard a man speaking to a woman. '[He] demanded of her if he and she were not before god lawful man and wife together, and that either of them had given to the other their faith and troth together by giving of hands in her father's entry, to the which she . . . answered they had so done.' Likewise, another married couple said that 'they had given their faith and troth the one of them to the other and also their hands and that they were as man and wife before god together.'[38] It is clear that some people thought that after the betrothal the couple could sexually consummate the match.[39]

If we revert to the market analogy, the betrothal or spousal was like a promise made between trading partners. Each agreed that he or she would now undertake to assemble the goods and bring them together in a joint venture. The contract could not be broken, even if a more tempting offer came along in the meantime. But the actual wedding, or the exchange of goods, had not yet occurred and might not occur for some months. Particularly in this period of uncertainty, but also in the run up to the engagement, the couple were expected to express their commitment to each other. One of the most interesting expressions was the exchanging of gifts. As many poems and songs illustrated, the giving and receiving of presents was a central feature of courtship:

> I give to you a packet of pins,
> And that is how our love begins . . .

Henry Best in Yorkshire described the giving of rings, gloves and a series of other trifles to mark the various stages of a relationship.[40] Articles like carved knitting sticks, spindles and bobbins were often given as love tokens. Marriage litigation confirms how important was

[36] Whateley, *Care-Cloth*, 31; cf. Howard, *Matrimonial Institutions*, i, 372–3.

[37] Howard, *Matrimonial Institutions*, i, 374.

[38] ERO, D/AED/1, fol.12; D/AED/2, fol.107; see also Hale, *Precedents*, 170.

[39] Laslett, *Lost World*, 150ff.   [40] Best, *Rural Economy*, 116.

this practice in sealing a bond. Sometimes the whole decision as to whether an engagement had taken place or not would hinge on whether the suitors had exchanged silver rings, whistles, handkerchiefs and other small 'tokens of love'. For instance, in a set of ecclesiastical depositions in 1639 it was stated that a woman had received from a man 'a piece of money and a pair of gloves with silver fringe as tokens of his love and affection towards her, at the receiving whereof as also of divers other times she the said Susan Marchant hath made many serious protestations of the continuance of her love and affection to him the said Thomas Cullen and that she would never forsake him as long as he lived.'

Sometimes the 'gifts' were gained by force, or so it was alleged. Thus, in Essex in 1576, a woman deposed that 'the silver ring mentioned, he suddenly taking her purse hanging by her side did by strong hand take the same ring from her which was in her purse and as for the silver whistle he requested this respondent to show it him he swearing that he would forthwith give it her again . . .'[41] The 'fairings' which young people brought back for their loved ones, the gifts of flowers and clothing, with their colour and symbolism, marked the attachment and, hopefully, discouraged others, as does the present-day engagement ring. A nice account of what happened if the courtship ended runs as follows: 'concerning Love Presents, in case marriage ensue not, between the parties, when tis affirmed, that if the man hath had a kiss for his money, he loseth one half of that which he gave. But that, as to the woman, whether kissing or not kissing; whosoever she gave, she may ask and have it again.' Thus Simon Forman, the astrologer, received back all his 'rings and jewels' from a girl he had been courting. The exchange of courtship gifts is a continuous practice from Chaucer onwards.[42]

One of the most acceptable 'gifts' from a lover was a letter. The love letter is a particularly interesting phenomenon, both for itself and in what it contains. Clearly, if marriage is arranged by parents or kin, the love letter is unnecessary. Yet such letters seem to have been a widespread institution in England from at least the sixteenth century. Indeed, so widespread were they that, as we have seen, a special genre grew up of 'model' love letters. These were often humorous parodies,

[41] ERO, D/ACD/5(separate folder); D/AED/1, fol.11; Deloney, 'Jacke of Newberrie', 13.

[42] BL, Harleian MS 980, fol.144; Halliwell, *Diary of Forman*, 26; Pollard, *Chaucer Works*, 46; Anglicus, *Properties*, i, 308.

but even as such they take much for granted about courtship practices. A mid-seventeenth-century example is introduced thus: 'A fair virgin being solicited by some very rich but exceeding old gentleman, and resolving not to be incorporate with rheums and catarhs, sends him her final resolve, thus.' The letter follows:

> Decrepit Sir:
> Your doting years have made you think your self very wise in fishing with a golden bait, presuming that your gold hath as much power for the renovation of your aged corpse, as *Medeas* enchanting spells in reference to Jason . . . Alas, you are much mistaken in our sex in this particular; for though gold be welcome to enrich our train, yet are we not so far in love with it, as for to neglect the chief of all, the person of a man; should we permit the flowers of our youth to be nipt by ages snowy winter, and so bereave our selves of all those joys that nature hath conferred on our sex, and barter our blooming youth for earth and dirt, no . . . which is the unalterable resolution,
>
> Of a younger than you.[43]

Another example suggests rustic jealousy – 'A letter of quarrel from one country youth to another', warning him against pursuing a sweetheart:

> Neighbour Robin you do me wrong, and that more than I mean to bear at your hands: for I hear that you are suitor to Margery my sweet-heart, and that upon the last holiday you danced with her upon the green and like a saucy fellow slapt her on the lips, when you parted from her: If I had been there, and it had been so, I would have told you a little of my mind, but never be the less, I give you warning henceforth, to be quiet, and to meddle with your own business, and let me be alone with mine, and come no more to the common where she goes a milking; for if I catch you there, I will so clapper-claw your cocks-comb, that you shall have small mind of wooing: and furthermore, I charge you, by these presents, that if you see her at the Market, that you speak not to her, and specially, that you go not with her into any alehouse, to drink and talk with her. For indeed to tell you the truth I lack but her consent to make her my wife, for I have loved her above these three weeks, though she know not so much: but she do shortly: and therefore I wish you in good will to forbear, otherwise you and I are two, and so will continue: and so I rest.
>
> Yours as you use me R.I.

[43] S.S., *Secretaries Studie*, 6–7.

To which Robin then replied in like manner, claiming that Margery was his sweetheart, and he would see her as often as he liked: 'I will go to the Common, and give her a green gown, and help her home with the milk, and see her every day.'[44] These letters, published in 1629, are a townsman's caricature of the country bumpkin. Nevertheless they take for granted many of the features already alluded to – easy meeting between the sexes, on the green, in the alehouse and at the market, and an open and physical relationship.

Special linguistic devices were used in courtship. Singing, of course, is a widespread technique, as is poetry – both rather stylized forms of communication. Ordinary conversation also seems to have taken on various particular forms, one being heightened praise or flattery. John Evelyn advised gentry lovers that 'you must improve all occasions of celebrating her shape, and how well the mode becomes her, though it be n'er so fantastical and ridiculous; that she sings like an angel, dances like a goddess, and that you are charmed with her wit and beauty.' The language became one of sugary compliment. Thus a wooer trying to seduce another's wife addressed her, 'what do ye, hony-comb, sweete Alisoun, my faire bryde, my sweete cynamome?' While flattery and sweetness was one thread, playful nonsense was another. 'There never can be more nonsense talked than there is betwixt a man and a woman in courtship.'[45] The exchanges included a strong element of teasing. The Duchess of Newcastle wrote, 'I have heard that the way or manner of courtship among the inferior sort of people in E is scolding, they scold themselves into matrimony, or at least, make love in a rough, rude style.' What is clear is the effort to discourse, exchange views, communicate and 'converse'. The shared enterprise that was being contemplated was paralleled with the effort to build up a shared world of thought.

The economic and mental fusion of the couple took place alongside the equally important sexual union. Marriage was the joining of spirit, mind and body, and there was a particular stress on the sexual 'conversation' of the partners. The late age at marriage together with a total ban on sexual relations outside marriage put a particular strain on individuals. Add to this the fact that members of

---

[44] I.W., *Speedie Poste*, sig.E3v.
[45] Hunt, *Love*, 226; Pollard, *Chaucer Works*, 51; *Characters*, 172.

the opposite sex were not segregated, and courtships were lengthy and little chaperoned. This was further aggravated by the nature of the marriage system. We have seen that the young couple were expected to get to know each other intimately, including their respective psychologies and physiologies. It was accepted at most levels that they should be allowed to spend time alone together and indulge in some physical play. Only in this way could they gradually test each other, become more and more bound to one another, and at a certain point make up their minds to share the rest of their lives together. But even after such a decision had been reached, they should wait until the wedding before they engaged in sexual relations. Thus physical passion might be encouraged; but it was not to overwhelm the partners. This was indeed tightrope walking. To permit too little or too much sexual intimacy could be disastrous for the girl: too much or too little ardour would lose a man a potential wife.[46]

An added cause of ambivalence was the Church's view, which condemned pre-marital intercourse, yet laid an enormous stress on the sexual relationship within marriage. Sexual satisfaction was a large component of the monogamous marriage system: the marriage could be annulled if it could be shown that it had not been consummated. In order to avoid further frustration or adultery, it was essential that the young couple not only found each other mentally, morally and spiritually attractive, but also physically so. The burning physical desire which poets and others celebrated was an essential feature of 'romantic love'. Yet the full pleasures should not be experienced until the marriage was solemnized. Much of the physical side of courtship was thus an attempt to discover the undiscoverable, to gauge the apple by nibbling at the skin. Kissing and fondling hence developed into important and elaborate acts which are not universal in human societies.[47] Of course, the pleasure of the sport of wooing was enhanced in many ways by the very inhibitions and rules, the forbidden and mysterious areas.

The situation was further confused by the ambivalence about what constituted a valid marriage. We have seen that it was really only in

---

[46] Cavendish, *Letters*, 87; Furnivall, *Tell-Trothes*, 51ff; Deloney, 'Jacke of Newberrie', 9.

[47] For the absence of erotic kissing outside Indo-European cultures, see e.g. Malinowski, *Sexual Life*, 278ff; Sumner, *Folkways*, 459–60; Crawley, *Mystic Rose*, i, 338; Henriques, *Love in Action*, 121ff.

the middle of the sixteenth century that the betrothal, which constituted the 'real' marriage, was joined to the nuptials or celebration of that marriage. Consequently, during the Middle Ages and up to the eighteenth century it was widely held that sexual cohabitation was permitted after the betrothal:

> contracted persons are in a middle degree betwixt single persons and married persons: they are neither simply single, nor actually married. Many make it a very marriage, and thereupon have a greater solemnity at their contract than at their marriage: yea many take liberty after a contract to know their spouse, as if they were married: an unwarrantable and dishonest practice.[48]

Howard summarized the position thus: 'until far down into the eighteenth century the engaged lovers before the nuptials were held to be legally husband and wife. It was common for them to begin living together immediately after the betrothal ceremony.'[49] The depositions in the church courts in the sixteenth and seventeenth centuries thus show people defending pre-marital sexual intimacy on the grounds of betrothal. An illustration from late-sixteenth-century Essex shows both the degree of intimacy allowed and the attitude of friends and neighbours.[50] Furthermore, by comparing the names of those whom we know were pregnant when they married with those who were presented in the church courts, we can see that there was scarcely any overlap. (Pregnancy can be detected by finding out how many months after marriage a child was born.) In the villages of Little Baddow and Boreham in Essex in the later sixteenth century, between 10 and 20 per cent of brides were pregnant at marriage, a figure in line with national figures for that period. Of the eleven pregnant brides in these two parishes, none were known to be presented in the church courts, an indication of the tacit acceptance of the activity.[51]

Up to about 1700, roughly one in ten brides was pregnant at marriage, though the figures varied over time and region, with much higher figures, reaching about a quarter, in the north and west.[52] During the first half of the eighteenth century the proportion rose enormously, so that for the eighteenth and nineteenth centuries

---

[48] William Gouge, quoted in Laslett, *Lost World*, 150, 152–3; cf. also Whitforde, *Householders*, sig.E.iii(verso).

[49] Howard, *Matrimonial Institutions*, i, 374. [50] ERO, D/AED/1, fols 13v, 17ff.

[51] More generally, see Hair, 'Bridal', esp. 237; Macfarlane, 'Marital Relationships', 112. [52] Hair, 'Bridal', *passim*; Laslett, *Bastardy*, *passim*.

something like one third were pregnant when they married. Just as the age at marriage dropped and a larger proportion of people married, the invisible pressures against intercourse also slackened. None of the theories put forward to account for this are satisfactory. The 'frustration' theory – namely, that sexual intercourse was the safety valve for those who could not hold themselves back within the late age at marriage pattern – has to be modified considerably to account for the fact that instead of falling when marriage age dropped, pregnancy rates rose dramatically. A second explanation might be termed a variation of the 'shotgun' theory – namely, that the pregnancy was a way of forcing a decision on an unwilling parent or partner. There is some evidence for this strategy: for instance, a court case in Essex in 1622 in which a woman 'being in love with a fellow of that parish and he being asked to another woman, she reported herself to be with child by him, thinking by that means to move him to marry her.'[53] As A. W. Ashby suggested for the eighteenth century, 'an illicit pregancy was the sure way to a secure, if not honourable, married life.'[54] Yet, again, it is difficult to see why the shotgun should have to be employed so very much more often after 1700 than before.

A third hypothesis is concerned with courtship as a time of fertility-testing. Where marriage is primarily designed to produce children, it is essential that the couple be able to procreate together. Hence in a number of peasant cultures in Africa, Europe and elsewhere the testing of fertility has been instituted.[55] Despite some assertions that fertility-testing customs existed in the English past,[56] any such evidence is conspicuously absent. Most social historians have been unable to find this institution, sometimes colloquially known as 'bundling', in England. Thus either fertility-testing is omitted from their surveys, or its absence is noted.[57] The scant evidence that is produced in support is either very-late-eighteenth-century, from the Celtic fringe, or based on far-fetched interpretations of diary evidence. No foreign observer, no moralist castigating the sexual behaviour of the lower orders, no individual defending his or her behaviour against the church authorities, no diarist or

---

[53] ERO, D/AZ/2/24, fol. 49v.   [54] Ashby, *Poor Law*, 84.

[55] Shorter, *Modern Family*, 102–3; Lofgren, 'Family', 31–3; Goode, *World Revolution*, 329; Goody, *Production*, 44; Sumner, *Folkways*, 525ff.

[56] Stone, *Family*, 520; Henriques, *Love in Action*, 174ff.

[57] Laslett, *Family Life*, 110; Quaife, *Wanton Wenches*, 247.

autobiographer describing his courtship, speaks of the need to be sure that a partner could bear children before the couple could marry. This silence, given the vast amount of commentary on sexual matters, is strong evidence, but there is more.

First, the actual timing of the wedding. If there had been a widespread custom of waiting until the wife was pregnant, we would have expected a bunching of weddings at a point when the pregnancies became obvious, after three or four months. As it is, it is clear that the weddings are distributed, apparently randomly, over the full nine months of gestation. Furthermore, the whole nature of marriage points in another direction. For example, the custom of allowing sex between betrothal and nuptials is significant. In societies which place a stress on childbearing, such a tacit period of cohabitation before the final wedding would be used to see if the couple would have children, as a form of 'trial marriage'. If the wife did not conceive, the marriage would not be completed. In England it was otherwise. Once a betrothal, coupled with consummation, had taken place, the contract was binding. No excuse such as alleged infertility would have been recognized, nor does it seem that such a plea was ever put forward in the courts to nullify a contract. Just as barrenness within marriage was not a ground for separation or divorce, so the discovery that a contracted partner was infertile could not be used to terminate the relationship. Thus in courtship we see a very considerable stress on sexual compatibility, and an intense encounter which paralleled other deepening bonds. But we do not find a heavy emphasis on fecundity and procreation.

We may end this brief account of courtship by considering how far courtship customs seem to have changed between the later Middle Ages and the nineteenth century. Numerous ballads and poems attest to a continuity of fundamental features over these centuries.[58] The picture we have of wooing and courtship in Chaucer's verse and in other medieval poetry is not inconsistent with the world of Shakespeare, or the account by Henry Best in the seventeenth century. And all this fits in with the description of courtship written by Bartholomaeus Anglicus in the thirteenth century. We learn that

afore wedding, the spouse thinketh to win love of her that he wooeth with gifts, and certifieth of his will with letters and messengers, and

[58] Holloway, *Broadside Ballads*, 23, 50, 57, 75.

with divers presents, and giveth many gifts, and much good and cattle, and promiseth much more. And to please her he putteth him to divers plays and games among gatherings of men, and useth oft deeds of arms, of might, and of mastery. And maketh him gay and seemly in divers clothing and array. And all that he is prayed to give and to do for her love, he giveth and doth anon with all his might. And denieth no petition that is made in her name and for her love. He speaketh to her pleasantly, and beholdeth her cheer in the face with pleasing and glad cheer, and with a sharp eye, and at last assenteth to her, and telleth openly his will in presence of her friends, and spouseth her with a ring, and giveth her gifts in token of contract of wedding, and maketh her charters, and deeds of grants and of gifts.[59]

Like those of later centuries, this delightful portrait offers a mixture of financial and emotional negotiation, exchanging of gifts and compliments, showing off by the male, an attempt to 'win' love. The mutual concern of the pair is the other's pleasure.

Such a long-lived but unusual system of courtship is a necessary part of the companionate Malthusian marriage pattern. It is therefore not surprising that when such a system is exported to the Third World today, shockingly 'free' relations between young men and women before marriage are a feature of the change. As we have seen, for two people to enter a contract, they must have a chance to test and taste the wares available. Such behaviour is difficult to reconcile with arranged marriage systems, though it is possible that flirtation and arranged marriage can co-exist as separate activities.[60]

The flexibility such courtship practices allowed left many people never married; others were married too late or too soon. As in any market, information is never perfect, and it is particularly difficult when considerations of loyalty, pride, and biological urges to mate and reproduce enter into the equation. Such courtship practices are only possible where women are free and relatively equal before marriage. Thus David Hume pointed out that polygamy destroys equality between the sexes. Introduce polygamy and 'the lover is totally annihilated; and courtship, the most agreeable scene in life, can no longer have place where women have not the free disposal of themselves.'[61] The elaborate and widespread courtship system is hence both an expression and a contributory cause of the individu-

[59] Steele, *Medieval Lore*, 56.

[60] Though it can be achieved in tribal societies; a particularly striking example is described in Elwin, *Muria*, for India.　[61] Hume, *Essays*, 109 (Essay xviii).

alistic social system which had developed early in England.

In certain of the simplest societies, as well as in some of the most technologically advanced, the wedding has been minimized or made an occasion of very little obvious importance.[62] There is no elaborate symbolism, little or no ceremony. Yet in the majority of societies, and particularly in settled agricultural societies, the wedding is usually very heavily stressed. Many people attend the celebration, a great amount is eaten and drunk, many customary rituals occur. One consequence of this considerable elaboration is that wedding rituals are often examined by anthropologists as a way of gaining an insight into the structure of society and the meaning of marriage.[63] The degree of elaboration of the ritual and its nature, the threshold rites, the barring of the door, the wedding gifts, the use of noise, colour, space – all these are held to show what marriage means in the society. Marriage is a turning point in the individual's life cycle, the transition from dependent minor to adult, and this is signified for men and women in the celebrations. Marriage is often the transfer of a person from one group of kin to another, as well as being an alliance between two groups. In this case the transfer and alliance are symbolized by gifts and ceremonial. All those involved are brought together and their new relationships are rehearsed, a process which often overshadows the new relationship of bride and groom. The marriage ceremony becomes a drama in which, through playing their customary parts, people adjust to new relationships.

The customs associated with English weddings over five centuries merit a much lengthier treatment than we can give them. Even the two volumes devoted to the subject by Jeaffreson hardly do more than touch the surface of the subject.[64] But again we may briefly try to abstract some general principles from a hugely varied set of phenomena. Behind the English wedding as it developed over the centuries there lay two separate acts, one essential and one voluntary. In Anglo-Saxon England the 'wedding' was the occasion when the betrothal or pledging of the couple to each other in words of the present tense took place. This was in effect the legally binding act; it was, combined with consummation, the marriage. Later, a public celebration and announcement of the wedding might take place – the 'gift', the 'bridal', or 'nuptials', as it became known. This was the

---

[62] Von Furer-Haimendorf, *Apa Tanis*, 92–3.

[63] Westermarck, Marriage, ii, chs xxiv-xxvi; Crawley, *Mystic Rose*, chs xiv on; Van Gennep, *Rites*, 118ff.   [64] Jeaffreson, *Bridals*.

occasion when friends and relatives assembled to feast and to hear the financial details. These two stages remained separate in essence until they were united into one occasion after the Reformation. Thus the modern Anglican wedding service includes both spousals and nuptials.[65] An important feature of the first act was that it originally involved no religious or ritual element. It was a purely personal, private, civil contract, only to be entered into by the couple. There was no necessity for a clergyman to be present, or for any religious ceremony. A marriage was valid without banns or licence, at any hour, in any building. This continued to be the case from Anglo-Saxon times to Hardwick's Marriage Act of 1753. Gradually, however, the Church began to embrace marriage as something of concern to God. Early in the twelfth century the secular contract became an ecclesiastical ritual. Only at the Reformation was the service finally performed in the ecclesiastical building and did the priest become more than a mere witness.[66]

That the presence of priest and congregation remained an added feature is shown by the later history of the wedding. But during the Interregnum of the seventeenth century, the logic was followed and the religious accretion was purged. Purely civil marriage, taking place before a magistrate, was temporarily reinstated. The Puritans in New England likewise abandoned all ecclesiastical ceremonies.[67] Present registry office weddings are the reassertion of the basically civil nature of the wedding. God may be a witness, and the 'congregation' may be asked to celebrate, but in essence this was not a religious or ritual event, but a legal contract between two free, consenting, adults. Throughout the centuries a sizeable minority of the population married 'privately', sometimes by special licence with a clergyman, sometimes engaging in 'common law' marriage which required no church and no congregation.[68]

This essential nature of the wedding as a private, individual, contractual and secular affair is of great significance. As we shall see, there were many popular accretions which at times made popular marriages look like full-blown *rites de passage*, transition rituals

---

[65] Whitelock, *English Society*, 152; Howard, *Matrimonial Institutions*, i, 381.

[66] Pollock and Maitland, ii, 372; Sheehan, 'Choice', 27; Howard, *Matrimonial Institutions*, i, chs vii, viii; ibid., i, 291ff.

[67] Morgan, *Puritan Family*, 31.

[68] Cf. Hollingsworth, *Historical Demography*, 21, note; Marchant, *Church Under Law*, 66, 140; Wrigley in LPS 10(1973), 15ff.

involving all the panoply of noise and colour, the inverted behaviour and the suspension of ordinary concepts of time and space that we find in marriage ritual all over the world. Yet all these were optional, or, in the view of reformers, forms of 'corruption'. The dangers of common usage turning the event into an almost religious ritual were pointed out in the *Admonition to the Parliament* in 1572:

> as for matrimony that also hath corruptions, too many. It was wont to be counted a sacrament; and therefore they use yet a sacramental sign, to which they attribute the virtue of wedlock, I mean the wedding-ring, which they foully abuse and dally withall, in taking it up and laying it down:in putting it on they abuse the name of the Trinity, they make the new-married man, according to the popish form, to make an idol of his wife, saying 'with this ring I thee wed, with my body I thee worship', etc. And because in popery no holy action may be done without a mass, they enjoin the married persons to receive the communion . . . Other petty things out of the book we speak not of . . . divers other heathenish toys in sundry countries, as carrying of wheat-sheaves on their heads, and casting of corn . . . whereby they make rather a May-game of marriage than a holy institution of God.[69]

Thus the church service was only a ceremony, performed to celebrate and commemorate, rather than a ritual affecting the material world through mystical power. A church service was an optional extra, lending gravity to the occasion. Likewise, the popular customs and sports which often took place were additional frills. As such they could be adjusted to suit the purse and inclination of the couple and their friends.

It is clear that very many avoided the standard marriage in their parish church before relatives and neighbours, with the reading of 'banns'. There seems to have been a widespread feeling that ordinary marriage, with the calling out of the names of the intended couple before the assembled people, was immodest. Consequently large numbers of people married by special licence, either in their own church or in a particular church noted for such 'special' weddings.[70] This might also have the advantage of avoiding the interference of parents or the expense of a large wedding feast. The most famous of the special wedding areas was that around the Fleet in London,

---

[69] Quoted in Howard, *Matrimonial Institutions*, i, 410–11.
[70] E.g. Gough, *Myddle*, 65; Howard, *Matrimonial Institutions*, i, 457–8; e.g. Tate, *Parish Chest*, 81; Aubrey, *Wiltshire*, 75.

where many thousands of weddings were undertaken.[71]

An analysis of those who attended wedding celebrations helps to show the nature of marriage. In essence, as we have seen, no one was necessary except the couple themselves. No specific categories of persons – close kin, close friends or anyone else – had to attend. There were no social or ritual roles which had to be fulfilled to make it a valid wedding. To ask one's parents, especially if they were paying for the celebration, was clearly polite. But even then we find that fathers, mothers and other close friends and relations did not always attend.[72] Likewise, which friends and neighbours were invited was up to the couple and their close advisers. It seems clear that, as with any other celebration party, a wedding was often by invitation only; there seem to have been guest lists. Thus in 1576 in Essex, a witness stated that 'the day of marriage was appointed and that all things were prepared for the marriage and guests bidden as well by the same Thomas Spicer as by the same Joan Ellys.'[73] A feature of the wedding preparations portrayed by Aphra Behn in the later seventeenth century was to 'consult with the friends on both sides, who shall be invited to the wedding, and who not'.[74]

This optional element shows people mobilizing certain kin and neighbourly links, selecting a smaller or wider circle. It explains why wedding celebrations varied enormously in expense and size. Sometimes there were only half a dozen or so present, and the numbers may have been kept small especially at second and subsequent marriages.[75] A visitor to England in the later seventeenth century commented that among the middling 'one of the reasons that they have for marrying secretly, as they generally do in England, is that thereby they avoid a great deal of expense and trouble.' He described how marriages 'are usually *incognito*' and only involve groom, bride, their parents, and 'two bridesmen and two bridesmaids'.[76] On other occasions, particularly amongst the gentry, hundreds might attend.[77] Diaries do not suggest that kin outside the nuclear family had an automatic right or duty to attend. Many

[71] Howard, *Matrimonial Institutions*, i, 435ff.

[72] E.g. Macfarlane, *Ralph Josselin*, 122; Verney, *Memoirs*, i, 428; Trappes-Lomax, *Diary of Brockbank*, 256.

[73] ERO, D/AED/1, fol.18v.   [74] Behn, *Pleasures*, 20.

[75] Symonds, 'John Greene', 392; Blencowe, 'Giles Moore', 115; Jackson, *Thornton Autobiography*, 82; Turner, *Heywood*, i, 242.

[76] Jeaffreson, *Bridals*, ii, 110.

[77] Cox, *Parish Registers*, 90; Emmison, *Tudor Food*, 30.

'cousins' had their marriages reported in diaries, without the diarist attending. Obviously, geographical mobility affected who was available. The guests were not, as in many other societies, the *raison d'être* of the occasion, essential for the carrying out of a ritual of separation and aggregation. They were not actors taking part in a drama which re-aligned social and moral relations. They were guests at a party to honour the couple, wish them well, and express joy at their union. If the couple, for a variety of reasons, wished to reduce the affair to the essential individual contract, they could do so.

Yet, over time, a number of popular customs, superstitions or 'corruptions' became attached to the wedding, which are in themselves revealing in what they show about the nature of English marriage. A number of these customs are illustrated in three accounts of what happened at weddings. The first describes an aristocratic wedding, that of Sir Philip Herbert in 1604.[78] 'No ceremony was omitted of bride-cakes, points, garters, and gloves, which have been ever since the livery of the Court; and at night there was sewing into the sheet, casting off the bride's left hose, with many other petty sorceries.' Henry Best described the popular Yorkshire customs in 1641 as follows:

> the day of marriage, which may perhaps be about a fortnight or three weeks after [the settling of the jointure], and in that time do they get made the wedding clothes, and make provision against the wedding dinner, which is usually at the maids fathers. Their use is to buy gloves to give to each of their friends a pair on that day; the man should be at the cost for them; but sometimes the man gives gloves to the men, and the woman to the women ... they give them that morning when they are almost ready to go to church to be married. Then so soon as the bride is attired, and that they are ready to go forth, the bridegroom comes, and takes her by the hand, and saith, 'Mistress, I hope you are willing', or else kisseth her before them, and then followeth her father out of the doors; then one of the bridegroom his men ushereth the bride, and goest foremost; and the rest of the young men usher each of them a maid to church. The bridegroom and the brides brothers or friends tend at dinner; he perhaps fetcheth her home to his house about a month after, and the portion is paid that morning that she goes away. When the young man comes to fetch away his bride, some of his best friends, and young men his neighbours, come along with him ... and then is there the same jollity at his house, for they perhaps have

---

[78] Briggs, *Pale Hecate*, 166.

love wine ready to give to the company when they light, then a dinner, supper, and breakfast next day.[79]

Here we have an orderly affair, embodying many of the common features: the giving of presents to guests, the wearing of special clothes, the procession to the church, the double wedding feast. A number of extra elements are added by another description of northern customs, this time for the parish of Warton at the end of the seventeenth century:

> when there is a wedding, the school boys make fast the Church Doors or else the gates, and demand a piece of money of the bridegroom before he goes out: and if he refuses to be conformable to custom, they presently seize one of the bride's shoes, which I have seen done . . . In the evening of the marriage night, the boys and other young people of the village gather together before the house of the new married couple and *Shout* as they call it, or call out for something to drink, and this is said by one of our greatest antiquaries to be the remainder of the ancient custom of receiving Bedde-Ale or Bid-Ale . . . which was an assignation made for neighbours or poor people to meet and drink at the house of new married persons, and then for all the guests to contribute to the house-keepers.[80]

The use of noise, the competitions, the giving of gifts, the mock resistance – all have been subjects of considerable attention by historians and folklorists.[81] Many accounts show that a large amount of food and drink was provided, and that there was mixed dancing. All this would express the company's joy at the consummation of the game of marriage. It was an affirmation that marriage was to be encouraged, that it was a cause of delight to all. Now, rather than analysing all of these complex elements, we will concentrate on just one feature relevant to our theme – the question of fecundity and sexuality.

There is considerable evidence that the wedding itself was frequently, as today, an occasion for sexual symbolism. The innuendo could come in the food and in the conversation.[82] It was most explicit,

---

[79] Best, *Rural Economy*, 117.

[80] Ford, *Warton*, 36 and see the later excellent description in Atkinson, *Moorland*, 205ff.

[81] E.g. Jeaffreson, *Bridals*, and Westermarck, *Marriage*; Pearson, *Elizabethans*, 311–61.

[82] Fleming, 'Notebook', fols 24–5; Furnivall, *Meals and Manners*, 358.

however, in the custom of 'bedding the bride' and associated acts. A number of contemporary diaries, and particularly that of Pepys, indicate that there was a widespread custom of seeing that the bride and groom climbed into bed together.[83] There were many variants, including the ceremony of turning down the bed-clothes, observed, for instance, in the north in the nineteenth century.[84] In order to make the point about cohabitation even more strongly, the couple might be sewn into the sheet together.[85] Sometimes they were woken by the guests, who would come into the bridal chamber or sing outside their room.[86]

In the period leading up to the wedding, religious conventions forbade sexual intercourse between the courting couple. Desire must be subdued until the wedding. But once the signal was given and the wedding performed, sexual intercourse was no longer forbidden, but positively enjoined. By a curious reversal, the sexual act became a *sine qua non* of marriage. It was the words spoken plus the consummation that constituted the wedding. No consummation – no marriage, was the rule. As Howard explained, by 'the middle of the twelfth century the doctrine prevailed that *copula carnalis* is the supreme legal moment in marriage.'[87] So it was advisable, in order to prevent future disputes, to have witnesses. Short of a public viewing of the act of intercourse or an inspection of the couple or their bedding after the event, neither of which methods were adopted, the next best thing was to make sure that a *prima facie* case existed. This could be done by seeing that the couple reached the marital bed together. It was not necessarily an occasion for voyeurism or ribaldry. The straight-laced Alice Thornton spoke of 'those usual solemnities of marriage of getting the bride to bed, with a great deal of decency and modesty'.[88] The modern equivalent is the waving to the young couple as they set out, seated side by side, on their honeymoon journey.

While the sexual relationship was stressed, the ceremonies laid little emphasis on fecundity and childbirth. In those societies where marriage is ultimately the pathway to childbearing, this is stressed in a number of ways in the marriage rites. Westermarck has surveyed

[83] Latham, *Pepys*, i, 196; vi, 176; ix, 51; Bourcier, *D'Ewes Diary*, 69; Notestein, *English Folk*, 208.
[84] Atkinson, *Moorland*, 208.   [85] Brand, *Popular Antiquities*, ii, 174–5.
[86] Ibid., i, 175–6.   [87] Howard, *Matrimonial Institutions*, i, 335.
[88] Jackson, *Thornton Autobiography*, 233.

many of these rituals: prayers are offered for a fruitful union; the bride carries a mock baby on her back; the bride rides a mare on account of its fruitfulness; children are rolled back and forth on the bridal bed; a child is put on the bride's lap; special food, for instance an 'offspring dumpling', is eaten, and so on.[89] Interestingly, scarcely any of these or parallel rites occurred at English weddings. The exception, which has sometimes been interpreted as a 'fertility rite', is the sprinkling of objects – grain, fruit, cakes – over the couple and over the nuptial bed.[90] Clearly there can indeed be fertility symbolism in this action, as Westermarck, who documents its widespread occurrence, shows.[91] In England it was also common to break bread, or throw wheat, over the couple's heads. But Westermarck points out that the connection with fertility is not necessary, but accidental: 'in many cases they are said to be means of ensuring prosperity as well as offspring, or prosperity or abundance only.' Thus he relates that in 'Surrey, also, as old people have told me, the rice which is thrown on the bride means prosperity; and at Hackness in Yorkshire the casting of rice after the wedding-party when it comes out of church is a sign of the wish, "may plenty strew their path".'[92] Certainly, when people have tried to explain the custom, they do not seem to have linked it to fertility rites. Saltonstall, for instance, thought that the breaking of the bride-cake over the couple was done in remembrance of the old Roman custom of 'confarreation', or the making of marriage by the breaking of bread. Not only is it difficult to see any obvious reference to fecundity in biscuits and cake, but the very act of sprinkling small objects is difficult to interpret.[93] It would be a rash observer who interpreted the piles of confetti or rose petals outside registry offices today as evidence of an urgent desire on the part of friends and kin to ensure that the couple achieve their two-child family.

We thus see in English weddings a reflection of a number of features of English marriage. There is an emphasis on sexuality rather than procreation. There is often a stress on conviviality and

---

[89] Westermarck, *Marriage*, ii, 467–80; cf. also Westermarck, *Marriage in Morocco*, 348ff.

[90] Pearson, *Elizabethans*, 353.   [91] Westermarck, *Marriage*, ii, 478ff.

[92] Ibid., i, 480.

[93] More generally see Brand, *Popular Antiquities*, ii, 100–2, where there is no reference to fertility; indeed none of the customs described by Brand have a fertility aspect. Likewise, Jeaffreson, *Bridals*, i, ch.xv, does not link the ceremonies to fertility at all.

celebration, joy and mirth. Yet there is no obvious indication that the marriage was regarded as altering the whole social structure, calling for a re-alignment of all kinship and neighbourly roles, as a *rite de passage* for the individual and a great *perturbation sociale* for the society.[94] There is little hint of the rituals of severing and absorbing, of tying and untying status and kinship roles. This is all consistent with a situation where the break from home and kin had already probably been made, and the partners were often living as self-supporting adults away from their communities of origin. Marriage altered all of a person's legal and financial obligations, changed the relationship of the partners, licensed sexual relations, created legitimacy of children. The day of the wedding was supposed to be the high point of the increasingly intense relationship between a man and a woman. The moon of love had waxed and come to its full. Passion and tenderness, combined with practical partnership, could now express themselves in a complete union of mind, soul and body. In some ways the whole process of courtship led up to the wedding night and honeymoon. In the absence of any particular external pressure from kin, the atmosphere of delight and excitement, the conventions of courtship and the feasting, drinking and presents, were all necessary in order to bring people to such a pitch that they would take the irrevocable decision to commit themselves to each other for life. The water in the well had to be made to look sufficiently attractive for the frogs to jump in. For a moment the water was changed into the honey and wine of love, as at another famous marriage feast. Or, as Sir Walter Raleigh asked,

> Now what is love, I pray thee tell?
> It is that fountain and that well
> Where pleasure and repentance dwell.
> It is perhaps that sauncing bell
> That tolls all into heaven or hell;
> And this is love, as I hear tell.[95]

---

[94] Van Gennep in Westermarck, *Marriage in Morocco*, 345.
[95] Hadfield, *Elizabethan Love*, 28.

PART V

CONCLUSIONS

14

The Malthusian Marriage System in Perspective

We are now in a position to stand back from the details and to consider the answers to the questions posed in the opening chapters. First, we can see how the Malthusian marriage system worked in England to provide a boost to economic growth. The marriage structure was composed of a number of interlinked features, the most important of which was the fluctuating age at marriage. This allowed marriage age to rise to a late level in periods when population growth would have been a hindrance to capital accumulation, and to drop when labour was needed. Combined with this was a selective marriage pattern, producing at times a large proportion who never married, for whom there was an established role. Marriage was not automatic, it was a choice, the outcome of cost–benefit calculations for both men and women. This optional marriage was based on the absence of the normal strong positive or negative rules about whom one should or should not marry. The kinship, caste, class and geographical rules which circumscribe marriage in the majority of societies were weak. The one hard and fast rule was that the young couple should be able to form an independent unit at marriage. The funding of marriage meant that resources for this independence came both from the wider society, through job prospects, and from the savings of the couple and their parents. Marriage was viewed as something one 'saved up for', which one could only 'afford' at a certain point.

As we have seen, the major purpose of marriage was to satisfy the psychological, sexual and social needs of the individuals concerned. Children were a consequence rather than a cause of marriage, a by-product of the sexual union. To be 'married friends' was, for many, the ideal. Ultimately, therefore, marriage was based on a blending of, or compromise between, economic necessities on the one hand and psychological and biological pressures on the other. The union was held to be based on a personal attraction – physical, social and mental – to beauty of shape and beauty of temperament. Marriage was a game, with strategies, tactics, prizes and penalties. The courtship was elaborate – testing and drawing the couple together. Ideally 'love' would convincingly resolve the complex equations whereby individuals tried to balance a whole set of criteria – wealth, beauty, temperament and status – against which they would measure the prospective partner. The wedding and subsequent married life reflected the premises upon which the system was based, showing that the heart of the matter was the deep attachment of one man to one woman.

The influence of this pattern on the relation between economics and demography was considerable. Above all, the fact that marriage was not embedded in kinship or status, that it was a choice, and that it was ultimately about individual satisfaction, meant that marital age was flexible. There was an invisible threshold of expectations below which people were unwilling to risk marriage – a threshold which it was sometimes easier, sometimes more difficult, to reach. After a period of economic growth the controls relaxed, and some people might decide to turn the new affluence into marriage. Others decided to hold out and move up socially. There was, at the least, that lag between economic expansion and population growth that Malthus advocated and that demographic historians have now established did occur. Marriage had become divorced from biology and was an option, a weighing of costs. This is the 'Malthusian revolution', which formed one of the necessary background features for England's industrial progress in the past, and which is sweeping the world today. Industrialization and urbanization are often linked to the system, but there is no *necessary* connection between them. Hence, the Malthusian system can spread in areas which are neither urban nor industrial; similarly, as we saw in Ibadan, the presence of industry and urbanization does not necessarily bring about the Malthusian regime.

We can see how a particular demographic regime was produced by a peculiar marriage pattern, but we are then left with the elusive and equally complex question of what 'caused' the marriage pattern. A few hints and suggestions have been given in the preceding chapters. We may draw these together and advance others at a more speculative level. Probably the most convincing general theory is that the Malthusian marriage system 'fitted' perfectly with the particular socio-economic formation known as capitalism. About this Malthus himself was in no doubt. He wrote his work as a rebuttal of the Utopian Godwin, who had argued that the abolition of private property and the equalization of wealth would lead to a balanced and harmonious world in which trouble and strife would fade away. Put in later terms, he advocated the substitution of socialism for capitalism. Abolish the ethics and institutions of capitalism, and all would be well. Malthus' reply was that the central features of capitalism guaranteed stability and happiness. In the strange kind of metamorphosis that Bernard Mandeville has illustrated,[1] private 'vice' was transformed into public benefit; the private passions and the instituted inequalities of life were the only guarantee that war, famine and disease would not re-emerge. If Godwin gained the day, if wealth was redistributed, private property abolished, and the revolution ushered in, as Rousseau and others had urged, disaster would ensue. The 'natural passion between the sexes' would go unchecked, the productive tension between affluence and children would be destroyed, all would marry young, and soon mankind would be cast into misery as population outstripped resources.

Thus Malthus saw that the four essential underpinnings of this regime were an accumulative ethic which justified and glorified the endless pursuit of gain; the ranked, but mobile, society which meant that people were constantly scrambling up and down a ladder of fortune; private property, which was protected by government and law; and a generally elevated standard of living which would give people that taste for bodily comforts which would tempt them to forego immediate sexual gratification and delay marriage until they could afford it. The most important of these was that constant drive which has received many names from its critics: the 'acquisitive ethic' (Tawney), the 'spirit of capitalism' (Weber), 'possessive individualism' (Macpherson).[2] Malthus argued that if the four elements were present, his regime would automatically follow. If they were abolished, then, as in present-day China, the only way in which population could be held in check was through draconian and discriminatory laws and public control.

Put in another way, Malthus was saying that the marital and family system that he advocated was the natural corollary of what today

---

[1] Mandeville, *Fable*.

[2] Tawney, *Religion*; Weber, *Protestant Ethic*; Macpherson, *Possessive Individualism*.

would be called market capitalism. Where capitalism flourishes, he argued, so will the particular set of traits he analysed. Thus the system of marital choice, the weighing of costs and benefits, the battle between biology and economics, the constant striving and manoeuvring which dragged mankind painfully up the spiral of wealth – all these were the familistic dimensions of a particular economic and political system. In making this connection, of course, Malthus was not alone. While he justified capitalism as one of the only bulwarks against 'misery', just as Hobbes had justified Leviathan, so other writers saw the close 'elective affinity' between the particular kinship and marriage system and capitalism.

Marx highlighted the capitalistic assumptions in Malthus' work in a number of ways. He pointed out that in absorbing Malthus' ideas, Darwin extended to the whole of life the 'free' world of competitive capitalism. In a letter to Engels, Marx wrote: 'it is remarkable that Darwin recognizes among brutes and plants his English society with its division of labour, competition, opening up of new markets, 'inventions' and Malthusian 'struggle for existence'.[3] It is Hobbes' *bellum omnium contra omnes.* Or, as Bertrand Russell wrote more recently,

> from the historical point of view, what is interesting is Darwin's extension to the whole of life of the economics that characterized the philosophical radicals. The motive force of evolution, according to him, is a kind of biological economics in a world of free competition. It was Malthus' doctrine of population, extended to the world of animals and plants, that suggested to Darwin the struggle for existence and the survival of the fittest as the source of evolution.[4]

Given Darwin's private speculations and the way they exemplified Malthus, it is tempting to argue further that Darwin projected on to the animal kingdom the same kind of analysis he used in his own reproductive choice.

The connection between capitalism and the 'modern' marital system was made more explicitly by Engels. He pointed out that monogamy was a necessary if not sufficient cause of modern 'sex-love', as he called it, but that it took time to develop into modern individual-choice marriage. 'Before the middle ages we cannot speak

---

[3] Meek, *Marx and Engels*, 95, 198.   [4] Russell, *History of Philosophy*, 753.

of individual sex-love ... All through antiquity marriages were arranged for the participants by the parents, and the former quietly submitted.' The 'mutual love', presupposing equality and consent between the partners, and 'intensity and duration' were still a long way off. In medieval bourgeois society 'the question of fitness was unconditionally decided, not by individual inclination, but by family interests. In the overwhelming majority of cases the marriage contract thus remained to the end of the middle ages what it had been from the outset: a matter that was not decided by the parties most interested.'[5]

Then, in the late fifteenth century, the 'time of geographical discoveries', came 'capitalism'. This created a new world: 'by changing all things into commodities, it dissolved all inherited and traditional relations and replaced time hallowed custom and historical right by purchase and sale, by 'free contract'.' But to make 'contracts', people must be 'free' and 'equal', and hence 'the creation of these "free" and "equal" people was precisely one of the main functions of capitalist production.' Engels argued that while marriages became 'contracts', legal affairs, the principle of freedom to contract inevitably placed the decision in the hands of those who would have to honour the contract – the couple themselves. 'Did not the two young people who were to be coupled together have the right freely to dispose of themselves, of their bodies, and the organs of these?' So the 'rising bourgeoisie', especially those in Protestant countries, recognized the 'freedom of contracting a marriage'. 'In short, the love match was proclaimed as a human right.'[6] Another irony was that the richer people were – that is, the higher their social class – and the more property at stake, the less room for manoeuvre there really was. Yet the majority of the population began to base their marriage on 'love'. Thus romantic marriage is a by-product of the rise of capitalistic, contractual and individualistic societies. Since this occurred, according to the Marx–Engels chronology, in north-western Europe from the later fifteenth century, this is where we shall find the phenomenon. The Malthusian marriage system emerged triumphant between the sixteenth and eighteenth centuries in one part of Europe, and then spread outwards. This is the view that is now implicitly accepted by many investigators. For instance, we are told that romantic love 'entered middle-class life by the seventeenth

[5] Engels, *Origin of the Family*, 84, 92, 95.   [6] Ibid., 96, 97, 98.

century . . . when industrialization caused the middle class to grow rapidly in size and power, its ideals of love and marriage began first to colour and then to dominate western thinking.'[7]

The connection between the marriage system and capitalism has been developed in other ways. One argument is that by a curious paradox the central emotional feature, 'love', is a necessity where capitalist economic structures have developed most fully. At first sight, sexual passion and 'love' seem to be totally at variance with what is needed by capitalism. Max Weber observed long ago that 'being one of the strongest non-rational factors in human life', sexual drives are 'one of the strongest potential menaces to the individual's rational pursuit of economic ends'.[8] Yet, by a subtle shift, love and sex were domesticated, the force was channelled, and it became one of the central dynamic elements in the capitalist system. Weber saw that as societies became more bureaucratic and 'rational', so at the heart of such systems grew an impulsive, irrational and non-capitalistic emotion at the level of the individual. Just as he had caught the paradox of other-worldly mysticism leading to capitalistic accumulation, Weber hints at the way in which love-marriage lies at the heart of rational capitalism:

> the erotic relation seems to offer the unsurpassable peak of the fulfilment of the request for love in the direct fusion of the souls of one to the other. This boundless giving of oneself is as radical as possible in its opposition to all functionality, rationality, and generality. It is displayed here as the unique meaning which one creature in his irrationality has for another, and only for this specific other . . . The lover . . . knows himself to be freed from the cold skeleton hands of rational orders, just as completely as from the banality of everyday routine.[9]

Freed from the constraints of the wider world, from the power of family, class and custom, and moved to make a leap of faith where calculation is either impossible or discouraging, the lover selects his life-long mate. In a modern way, it could be argued that 'rational, profit-seeking individuals would never marry at all except for the "institutionalized irrationality" of romantic love.'[10]

---

[7] Hunt, *Love*, 266–7. [8] Watt, *Rise of Novel*, 74, paraphrases Weber.
[9] Gerth and Mills, *Max Weber*, 347.
[10] Greenfield's argument in Lasch, *Haven*, 144.

It is not difficult to see that although the passion of romantic love is 'irrational', it has many parallels with the 'irrational' passion for endless accumulation, the driving desire to possess, which is also at the heart of capitalism. Not only is there a linguistic congruence between the idea of wishing to 'purchase' objects in a market and the desire to completely 'own' or 'possess' another human being, but the emotions can be harnessed and inflamed by those trying to 'sell' other goods. Thus the 'selling' of consumer goods through mass advertising, and the passions between people, are used to reinforce each other. As Jules Henry puts it, 'without the pecuniary exploitation of romantic love and female youth and beauty the women's wear, cosmetics and beauty-parlour industries would largely disappear and the movies, TV and phonograph-record business would on the whole cease to be economically functional.'[11] Both romantic love and capitalistic activity are based on individual choice, possession, property and 'free enterprise', as Brain argues.[12]

Another way of perceiving the connection between market capitalism and the Malthusian marriage pattern is to examine the contrast between pre-capitalist and capitalist organizations of the domestic economy and their effects on attitudes towards childbearing. It has been pointed out that where we have a non-capitalist 'domestic mode of production', with the family farm or business as the basic unit of both production and consumption, there reproduction will often expand production and consumption. The fact 'that the family is the basic unit of work' in the Punjab, for instance, encourages fertility.[13] The peasant family is 'distinguished by a higher birth rate'. The 'very fact of giving birth to a child is regarded as a fact of significance to the farm as far as its future continuity is concerned.'[14] We are told that 'the objectives of the enterprise are primarily genealogical and only secondarily economic.'

But all this changes with the rise of capitalism. 'As the capitalist system of production has come to dominance a growing separation of the kinship from the economic order has prevailed.'[15] No longer were kinship and economics linked. No longer was it the larger families who were rich, as it had often been in peasant societies.[16] No more was it the case, as in the domestic mode, that wealth flowed

---

[11] Quoted in Haviland, *Cultural Anthropology*, 212.
[12] Brain, *Friends and Lovers*, 246. [13] Mamdani, *Myth*, 132.
[14] Galeski, *Basic Concepts*, 58, 63. [15] Franklin, *European Peasantry*, 1, 2.
[16] Galeski, *Basic Concepts*, 63.

automatically upwards, from children to their parents, through the concept of a joint fund. Now reproduction and production came into conflict: people had to make the kind of choice which Malthus and Darwin outlined. They had to balance their individual standard of living against their desire to have children. In this situation, many chose to restrain their fertility by marrying only when or if they could 'afford' to. The major change in many parts of the world 'has been that from family production to capitalist production within a labour market external to the family', for 'family-based production is inevitably characterized by high fertility; and a fully developed system of capitalist production . . . is ultimately just as inevitably characterized by low fertility.'[17] With the arrival of capitalism, the society is no longer held together by status, but by contract – that is, by the market, by an impersonal law, a centralized state. This provides a framework which permits a certain disengagement from the family, enabling free-floating individuals to enter the labour market early, and parents to maintain their independence and security through savings.

The association between the capitalist and Malthusian systems outlined by Malthus, Marx and Engels is attractive. Yet there is one major objection – namely, temporal incompatibility. Put bluntly, the marriage system emerged too early. This is not the place to detail the origins of the various features of the marriage system, but we can briefly sketch in some outside dates for the two phenomena. The 'capitalist revolution', by the standard chronology that we have inherited from Marx and Weber, is widely believed to have occurred sometime between the second half of the fifteenth century and the end of the seventeenth. Thus of the later fourteenth century, Marx writes, 'the mode of production itself had as yet no specific capitalistic character', and the 'capitalistic era dates from the sixteenth century.'[18] For Engels, as we have seen, it dates from the 'discoveries', that is, the end of the fifteenth century. Yet if we look at the various features of the marital system, none seem to have emerged in the period between 1450 and 1700.

If we look at the rules of marriage, most of them go back to before the fourteenth century. Age at marriage is difficult to estimate, but late marriage may be a very old characteristic indeed. Tacitus in describing the Germanic peoples in the first century AD wrote, 'the young men are slow to mate, and thus they reach manhood with

<hr>

[17] Caldwell, 'Education', 247, 225.   [18] Marx, *Capital*, i, 689, 669.

vigour unimpaired. The girls, too, are not hurried into marriage. As old and full-grown as the men, they match their mates in age and strength.'[19] Certainly, there is no strong evidence to show that women, in particular, married at or near puberty in the thirteenth and fourteenth centuries. Nor is there evidence of a revolutionary change to the wider West European marriage pattern in the sixteenth and seventeenth centuries. The rule of monogamy was demonstrably ancient. Again, the Germanic peoples who invaded England had long been monogamous,[20] and the Christian Church merely reinforced this cultural premise. One substantial change introduced by the Church was the forbidding of easy divorce, but this occurred well before the fifteenth entury. Such a block to divorce, combined with monogamy, may lie behind another change from the Germanic roots – the relatively tolerant attitude towards adultery. This, and the growing acceptance of the remarriage of widows and widowers, were features not present in Tacitus' description. But again they were clearly well established by the thirteenth century, at least.

Rules concerning whom one should not marry were probably also very early established. No substantial evidence has yet been produced to show that there were ever strong kinship rules, any form of 'elementary structure', concerning whom one *should* marry. Certainly by the thirteenth and fourteenth centuries such a structure, if it had ever existed, was gone. Likewise, evidence of rules forbidding marriage between different ranks in the social hierarchy is difficult to find from early on, and is certainly absent by the fourteenth century. The customs concerning marriage payments are particularly well documented. As Blackstone long ago noted, the custom of dower and jointure, of portion and gift, was derived from very early Teutonic customs.[21] The crucial system of balanced payments, the absence of 'bridewealth', and the curious intermediate system which lay between the extremes of full 'community' and full 'lineality', are very early established. They can be shown in Anglo-Saxon laws and customs and were certainly widespread in the thirteenth century.

The very ancient origins of these rules – at the earliest, with the Anglo-Saxon cultures that invaded England, at the latest by the fourteenth century – was related to the apparently early establishment of a particular view of marriage which was consistent with them. This

[19] Tacitus, *Germania*, 118.   [20] Ibid., 116.
[21] Blackstone, *Commentaries*, ii, pt 1, 128, note 24, also p.138.

view had four main elements. The first was that marriage was ultimately of concern to the couple themselves, that it was founded on the mutual consent of the bride and groom and did not depend on others for its arrangement. We have seen that this doctrine was formally accepted into the Christian view of marriage by the twelfth century, and maintained thereafter. In fact, it was probably based on earlier laws and customs: for instance, the laws of Canute in the early eleventh century made the consent of the bride necessary, while consent of the father or guardian was not.[22] So we probably have a blend of Teutonic and Christian traditions establishing freedom of marriage very early on. A second feature was the downgrading of marriage to second best, with celibacy as the higher estate. Marriage was thus not a necessary, universal stage, but a particular kind of 'vocation' to which not all were called. This view is well established in the writings of the early Christians, and was one of the major contributions of that religion to the later pattern. Unlike most world religions, Chistianity did not stress marriage and childbearing very heavily.

A third theme is that marriage is above all to be entered into for companionship's sake, as a partnership of mind and body. It follows from this that the husband–wife bond is the strongest of all relationships; this new contract overrides all the relations of blood – with parents, with siblings, with children – which in many societies are more powerful than the marital relationship. Here again we see a mingling of two traditions. On the one hand, Christianity emphasizes the conjugal bond. Man and woman become one flesh and one blood; Eve was created to be Adam's companion and helpmate; believers were advised by Paul to sacrifice their ties with their parents for the new tie with their spouse. This fitted well with the old uxoriousness of the Germanic peoples who colonized England and much of Europe. The practice of reciprocal marriage gifts 'typifies for them the most sacred bond of union'. Men and women will share their lives. Tacitus described them in the first century as follows.

> The woman must not think that she is excluded from aspirations to manly virtues or exempt from the hazards of warfare. That is why she is reminded . . . that she enters her husband's home to be the partner of his toils and perils, that both in peace and in war she is to share his sufferings and adventures . . . She takes one husband, just as she has

[22] Howard, *Matrimonial Institutions*, i, 278.

one body and one life. Her thoughts must not stray beyond him or her desires survive him.[23]

This almost sounds like the present-day marriage service, which is not surprising, for this service is based on the sixteenth-century wording, which in turn is taken from old Teutonic custom. As Maitland pointed out, the marriage rituals of the church 'have borrowed many a phrase and symbol from ancient Germanic custom'.[24] Certainly the companionate view of marriage was the formally and informally accepted one by the fourteenth century, and possibly before.

Finally there is the question of 'love' as a basis for marriage: the origins and rise of romantic love. There is considerable disagreement about this topic, but since it is so important to our argument it is worth examining some of the theories that have been put forward. One of the earliest locations for its emergence is southern Europe in the eleventh and twelfth centuries. Marc Bloch summarized the argument that romantic love started in the 'courtly love' traditions of southern France. This 'courtly love' had at first 'nothing to do with marriage, or rather it was directly opposed to the legal state of marriage, since the beloved was as a rule a married woman and the lover was never her husband.' But this 'all-engrossing passion, constantly frustrated, easily jealous, and nourished by its own difficulties', was nevertheless a 'strikingly original conception', an 'idea of amorous relationships, in which today we recognize many elements with which we have now become familiar.' It had little to do with religious values, and the 'Arab influence', Bloch thinks, is as yet unproven. Yet it 'made the love of man and woman almost one of the cardinal virtues . . . it sublimated – to the point of making it the be-all and end-all of existence – an emotional impulse derived essentially from those carnal appetites whose legitimacy Christianity only admits in order to curb them by marriage.' It flourished, Bloch tells us, in the lyric poetry which 'arose as early as the end of the eleventh century in the courtly circles of southern France'.[25] Love was somehow connected to the weakness of the Church and the strength of an heretical laity. This allowed the emergence of a new secular morality, of which 'courtly love' was a part. These themes have been expanded by subsequent investigators.

[23] Tacitus, *Germania*, 116–18. [24] Pollock and Maitland, ii, 370.
[25] Bloch, *Feudal*, ii, 309, 310.

While agreeing on the place and time, De Rougemont links courtly love more explicitly to heresy: 'it was not Christianity that caused passion to be cultivated; it was a heresy of Eastern origin ... Passionate love ... is rather a by-product of Manichaeism'; it is in Catharist heresy that love originated.[26] C. S. Lewis in *The Allegory of Love* is equally confident about the date and place, and equally unsure about the reasons. 'Every one has heard of courtly love', we are told, 'and every one knows that it appears quite suddenly at the end of the eleventh century in Languedoc.' There can be no doubt about its novelty: it was absent from classical antiquity and from the Dark Age literature. Thus 'French poets, in the eleventh century, discovered or invented, or were the first to express, that romantic species of passion which English poets were still writing about in the nineteenth century.' But as to the causes, Lewis admits himself baffled: 'the new thing itself, I do not pretend to explain', though it is one of the three or four 'real changes in human sentiment' in human history. None of the theories – Germanic, Celtic, Byzantine, Classical or Arabic – is satisfactorily proven. Lewis is not even sure whether the feeling came first and then the literature, or the other way round.[27]

Apart from the absence of any convincing explanation of the location of the phenomenon, there are a number of criticisms which have been made of a theory that links the modern love marriage to Provençal love poetry invented at the end of the eleventh century. One is that the dating is wrong. We are told that 'in recent years Peter Dronke and others have argued with much cogency that the sentiments reflected in the lyrics and romances of the twelfth century were not entirely novel.'[28] Secondly, the portrayal of 'courtly love' as being exclusively concerned with adulterous love and detached from marriage may be mistaken, as Sarsby argues, citing Chrétien de Troyes' *Erec et Enide* which celebrates newly married love.[29] The various criticisms of the courtly love interpretation have been summarized recently by Ferdinand Mount. He points out that adultery is not at the heart of courtly love, that 'courtly love' is in fact a vacuous concept, and that many of its themes can be found much earlier. Again citing Dronke's work, he shows that sexual passion and marital love are widely found in Anglo-Saxon and Celtic poetry.

[26] De Rougemont, *Passion and Society*, 326, 292.
[27] Lewis, *Allegory*, 2, 9, 4, 11, 22. [28] Brooke in Outhwaite, *Marriage*, 30.
[29] Sarsby, *Romantic Love*, 17ff.

Thus, the interpretation that courtly love was invented in the twelfth century is suspect.[30]

There had also been another difficulty, which was recognized by G. M. Trevelyan. If courtly love was the origin of modern love marriage, how was it transformed from its basically anti-marriage stance, into the foundation of marriage? Basing his account on C. S. Lewis, Trevelyan accepted that 'the great gift of the medieval poets to the Western world was this new conception of the love of man and woman as a spiritual thing.' But, he asked, 'could this thrice-precious concept of the medieval poets be allied, by a further revolution, to the state of marriage? Could the lovers themselves become husband and wife? Could the bond of young love be prolonged till age and death?' He believed that this 'further revolution' did, in fact, occur in England, 'in the gradual evolution of the idea and practice of marriage'. But the fact that 'in France, for instance, the arranged marriage is still [1944] normal' suggests that it 'was not an inevitable change'.[31]

Thus Trevelyan documents a second revolution which he believes occurred in the fifteenth and sixteenth centuries: 'among the poor, it is probable that marriage choice had always been less clogged by mercenary motives', and so for the common folk, among the peasantry in the Middle Ages, love matches were normal. It was among the higher groups that there had to be a softening, and here 'in the fifteenth century things were slowly moving.' Already in the popular ballad literature of the late fifteenth century, 'the *motif* of the love marriage was more and more making itself heard.' By the time we reach the 'age of Shakespeare', 'literature and the drama treat mutual love as the proper, though by no means the invariable, basis for marriage.' Yet parental compulsion continued, so that 'the slow and long contested evolution towards the English love match goes on throughout our social history, until in the age of Jane Austen and the Victorians free choice in love is accepted as the basis of marriage, even in the best society.'[32] In this chronology, love matches move upwards through the social ranks. What is lacking in Trevelyan's account is any explanation for the change. He points out that it is a revolution and a peculiar one, but then assumes in the best 'whig' fashion that it was bound to happen. Not only has Trevelyan posed

---

[30] Mount, *Subversive Family*, 93–103;
[31] Trevelyan, *Social History*, 67, 68.   [32] Ibid., 69–71.

yet not answered the problem of the transmission of courtly love, but he has also tacitly accepted something very important – namely, that for the 'common folk' love matches were normal for centuries before the Reformation. If this was so, it is something that needs explanation.

Finally, we may look at some of the economic and social preconditions which have been suggested as a background to the calculative attitude toward having children. It has been advanced that in England children, like marriage, were not essential. For most they were a luxury, and this fits in with those purposes of marriage that we have outlined. In contrast to most societies, where maximum childbearing is of benefit to the parents, children were a mixed blessing. It has been argued that this was due to a number of structural features in English society. One of these was that parents could not automatically absorb their children's surplus value, their earnings. Put in another way, children had protected property rights – in what they were given and in what they inherited or earned – even against their parents. Children were separate economic individuals. We have traced this feature back to the thirteenth century, but it is likely to go back even further, to Anglo-Saxon law. Since it is totally contrary to Roman law, it is difficult to see where else it could have come from. This was linked to another feature, namely, that property descends, but never ascends. Parents cannot automatically inherit their children's property. This is again an established principle by at least the thirteenth century. These aspects of the separate property of children become especially important when there is widespread wage labour outside the home. When children earn money outside the family, then they are faced with the real choice of whether to direct their income back to their parents and kin. Such a situation, based on the three institutions of servanthood, apprenticeship and wage labour, was established by the thirteenth century at the latest.

The separation of children and parents from an early age, which is embodied in these customs and institutions, led to a situation where the family no longer acted as an undivided unit of production and consumption. Before marriage, and particularly after marriage, children did not automatically invest their wealth back into a family fund from which they automatically inherited. Parents could disinherit children, while children could, in a sense, disinherit their parents, by refusing to maintain them. These separate, nuclear, neolocal patterns appear to have been established quite early, probably becoming widespread by the fourteenth century, if not long before. They were able to persist because the family was not the pivot of the political, economic or religious system.

A powerful, unified, political system had been built up by the later Anglo-Saxon kings and consolidated by the Normans and Angevins. This stable order meant that public peace and the control of violence were in the hands of chosen officials, rather than the family's. This was reinforced by the early adoption of the wide-scale use of money and the development of markets, which meant that many services usually provided by kin could be provided by others. This also is apparent by at least the thirteenth century, if not long before. In particular, one of the major functions of children – that of protection against risks of various kinds – had been largely eroded. Political risk was kept in check by the state and by a tough, early system of common law, aided by England's position as an island, which protected it from foreign invasions. Economic risk was minimized by early affluence and a relatively flexible monetized economy. The difficulties of old age were met not by stress on children's responsibility, but by a double response. First, through the medium of money, people could save for their old age and buy the services they needed from the profits of their accumulated capital. Secondly, for those who through accident or miscalculation had not been able so to provide, the Church, the guilds and the manor took on the responsibility for poverty. This non-familistic provision we also know stretches back into the thirteenth century and earlier.

No doubt the exact timing of many features of the system could be disputed, some placing them later, others earlier. What is difficult to see is that any of them could have changed radically in the period between 1450 and 1750. If the marriage system was a 'product' of capitalism, as is usually suggested, we would have expected a slight delay – with many of the transformations occurring in the later sixteenth and seventeenth centuries. There is little evidence of this.

Such a conclusion is not entirely negative. If capitalism is not a cause of the marriage system, as Malthus, Marx and Engels argued, then it may be tempting to suggest the reverse – that the individualistic family and marriage system, and its consequent 'rational' demographic pattern, was a necessary, if not sufficient, cause of capitalism. But if that was the case, what caused the marriage system? Can we accept that a particular religious ethic, combined with particular tribal customs, caused an explosive mixture which first led to a revolution in sentiment, and later provided the basis for a new socio-economic order? There may be something in this, but there is a modified alternative which fits better with the evidence and preserves what intuitively seems to be the extraordinary 'fit' between the marital system, capitalism and individualism. This emerges if we examine the hitherto assumed chronology of capitalism a little more closely.

We may take as three of the indices of the development of capitalism: the establishment of the concept of private, fully alienable, property; the widespread use of monetary values and the dominance of market forces; the wide-scale presence of wage labour. Elsewhere I have examined each of these at length and argued that all three can be traced back to the thirteenth century at least.[33] There is certainly little evidence for the supposed transformation from a basically communal-property, subsistence, agrarian 'peasant' society into a capitalist one in the sixteenth and seventeenth centuries, as suggested by the Marx–Weber chronology. If my argument is accepted, then we are in a better position to see that there is a much deeper and longer association between the Malthusian marriage system and other features of the society. They could both be seen as parts of that 'bourgeois arch, which stretches from the twelfth century to our own time'.[34] The absence of any signs of a real peasantry in the fourteenth and fifteenth centuries would thus be both cause and effect of the demographic and family system. Malthus and Marx would be right, but over a much longer period than perhaps the latter, at least, realized.

Once we re-date the capitalist revolution, or rather admit that there does not seem ever, in recorded history, to have been a sudden revolution at all in England, then the pieces fall into place. Taking Malthus' system's four central desiderata, we find that all of them were considerably developed in England by the end of the fourteenth century, and probably well before. A study of the activities and principles of traders, merchants and artisans as well as large and small landholders in the thirteenth and fourteenth centuries is enough to convince us that the central acquisitive ethic, the desire for profit, was widespread. The very extensive penetration of money and monetary values, and the desire to pursue economic gain largely as an end in itself, are very clear to all those who are not blinded by a desire to prove some vast contrast between post-Reformation England and its

---

[33] Macfarlane, *Individualism, passim.*   [34] Thompson, 'Peculiarities', 357.

Catholic past. This acquisitiveness fits with a system of widespread individual property, guaranteed by a developed system of law and powerful government which supported such an ethic. It also fits with a social structure in which there were many grades of status and wealth and in which it was relatively easy to move up and down. Malthus' 'ladder' for social climbing was already in place.

Finally, all this was set against a background of considerable and widely distributed affluence. The English were early noted for their rich diet, their opulent clothing, their leisurely ways, their comfortable houses and magnificent churches and cathedrals. Thus those economic, social and political preconditions for the Malthusian family system, that set of interrelated features which we label 'individualism' or 'capitalism', were already strongly developed. They had probably generated, and continued to maintain, that peculiar marital and demographic structure that was then 'exported' to North America and is now spreading to much of the world. Money, profit, contract, mobility, individualism, competition, had all asserted themselves. Behind the antique modes of speech and the different technology, there existed a recognizably 'modern' world.

History is hydra-headed; each problem we solve generates others. The implication of this argument is that we have a very old association between particular marital, demographic, political and economic systems that go back at least to the thirteenth century in England. Furthermore, it has been tentatively suggested that many of the roots lie much further back, in a particular amalgam of Christianity and Germanic customs. But if this was so, how was it that England, which was merely a small part of north-western Europe infiltrated by Christianity and Teutonic invaders in the fifth and sixth enturies, should have ended up so different from the rest of Europe? This again is a vast topic to which we can only give a brief, tentative, and superficial answer here.

Two points need to be established straight away. First, even in the seventeenth and eighteenth centuries, when the differences were probably most marked, there was much more in common between England, Holland and Belgium, Germany, northern France and Scandinavia, than there was to divide them. From a demographic point of view, for example, they were all part of that 'unique west European marriage pattern' to which Hajnal has drawn our attention. Delayed and selective marriages were part of a much wider pattern. Likewise, as has been pointed out by Laslett, the whole of this north-western area had a similar household structure, small and nuclear, consisting of parents, some unmarried children and possibly servants.[35] At a broader level, many of the deepest assumptions implicit in Christianity, and in particular a Protestant variety of it, united this part of Europe. Similarly, the economic ethics and institutions of England and Holland, for instance, largely overlapped. Thus from a perspective outside Europe, we are dealing in England with a phenomenon which is still very recognizably north-west European. On the other hand, as we have seen at the start, there were peculiarities about the English demographic regime and something must have led to the fact that it was in England that the first massive industrial and urban growth occurred. We cannot completely wipe away all differences. When Montesquieu visited England in 1729 he wrote, 'I am here in a country which hardly resembles the rest of Europe.' It is not difficult, if we look at other contemporary observers, to see what he meant.[36]

A second point to stress is that the differences may have been much smaller, if non-existent, earlier. De Tocqueville believed that the political and legal systems of the Middle Ages over the whole of France, England and Germany had a 'prodigious similarity', that 'in the fourteenth century the social, political, administrative, judicial, economic, and literary institutions of Europe' bore a close resemblance to each other.[37] In the light of certain deep differences that Marc Bloch, for instance, noted between England and France from at least the second half of the thirteenth century, it seems that De Tocqueville was in error about the timing of the divergence.[38] But his point about the 'prodigious similarity' of much of north-western Europe in the Middle Ages is undoubtedly valid. Both the similarities and one reason for the later divergence are suggested by Maitland in relation to legal changes.

It would be possible to argue that in the eleventh century the legal systems of the whole of the northern half of Western Europe were almost identical, based almost exclusively on the Germanic law of the conquerors. But during the twelfth to sixteenth centuries much of

[35] Laslett, *Family Life*, 15; see also the contrasts within France, as in Flandrin, *Families*, 72.

[36] Montesquieu, quoted in De Tocqueville, *L'Ancien Régime*, 89; see Macfarlane, *Individualism*, ch.7.

[37] De Tocqueville, *L'Ancien Régime*, 18.

[38] Summarized in Macfarlane, *Individualism*, 186.

northern Europe was reconquered by a renovated Roman law. As Maitland put it,

> Englishmen should abandon their traditional belief that from all time the continental nations have been ruled by the 'civil [i.e., Roman] law', they should learn how slowly the renovated Roman doctrine worked its way into the jurisprudence of the parliament of Paris, how long deferred was the 'practical reception' of Roman law in Germany, how exceedingly like our common law once was to a French *coutume*.[39]

By the thirteenth century, England was beginning to look distinctly different from the rest of Europe, not because England had changed, but because Roman law had made no conquest there: 'English law was by this time recognized as distinctly English.' This feeling of contrast was heightened because, although 'Roman jurisprudence was but slowly penetrating into northern France and had hardly touched Germany' by the thirteenth century, many Englishmen thought that the whole of Europe now had written Roman law, which 'served to make a great contrast more emphatic'.[40] Certainly, by the sixteenth century England was an island carrying an old Germanic legal system, and lying off a land mass dominated by Roman law. The contrast is obvious in relation to criminal law – the absence of judicial torture, the use of juries, process by indictment.

But the consequences for economics and kinship, and hence demography, are no less important. We may briefly mention one of these contrasts, the concept of property, which has been described by Peter Stein and John Shand:

> the civil law tradition, reflected in the Codes of France, Germany, Switzerland, Italy and even the Soviet Union, tends to identify ownership with the thing owned, and to limit its definition of things to movable or immovable property, as opposed to more abstract rights. The common law, on the other hand, has developed from the tenures of medieval feudalism and has been more ready to analyse ownership in terms of bundles of rights, obligations, and inter-personal relationships arising from the control and enjoyment of property.[41]

The more flexible English system enabled several individuals to have property rights in different parts of an asset. This difference was

[39] Pollock and Maitland, i, cvi.　[40] Ibid., i, 188.　[41] Stein, *Legal Values*, 216.

the basis for the early development of full private property. As the comparative jurist Sir Henry Maine argued, this was of fundamental importance. He believed that the modern concept of 'private property', held by the individual, the basis of the capitalist system, arose out of the difference. 'Nothing can be more singularly unlike than the legal aspect of allodial land, or, as the Romans would call it, land held *in dominium*, and the legal aspects of feudal land. In passing from one to the other you find yourself among a new order of legal ideas.'[42] The basis of this new system was the idea of the impartible, individually owned, estate which could be bequeathed to specific individuals.

In England there persisted over many centuries a concept of individual ownership that was not drowned by a resurgent Roman law. This meant that any individual – man, woman or child – could have absolute rights in their 'own' property, and the concept was fully established by the middle of the thirteenth century, at the latest. People could also have complete rights in themselves; in other words, they were not in the hands of the powerful Roman law concept of *patria potestas*. We have already seen the consequences of this for the marriage and demographic regimes. The separate property rights of children and their ability to enter into marriage contracts without parental permission were central to the Malthusian marriage pattern.

It was not that England changed, but that the laws and customs of its early conquerors were retained. Increasingly, this made it feel different, and this difference was compounded by two further factors. In Europe, Christianity was not a static phenomenon. During the crusades and monastic movements of the twelfth and thirteenth centuries, and during the resurgence known as the Counter-Reformation of the sixteenth, the Catholic Church established a deep hold on the political and social systems of much of Europe. The Roman Church was the ethical and spiritual counterpart to Roman law. Here again, England remained stranded. The establishment of a separate, Protestant, Church by Henry VIII was but one step in the distancing from a resurgent Catholicism. Through the work of Weber, Tawney and others, we know how this Protestantism shielded and even encouraged those capitalistic tendencies already present. Ultimately, it protected private judgement and independence of belief. The Inquisition, which destroyed huge trading networks and

[42] Maine, *Early Law*, 342.

corroded economic development throughout continental Europe, never took root in England.

A third and growing gulf was between the political systems. A dominating feature of English government, symbolized in Magna Carta and explained in Sir John Fortescue's *Learned Commendation of the Politique Laws of England*, written in 1461, was that England was a constitutional monarchy – the king was under the law. Ultimately the law was supreme: England was not an absolutist state. Despite the activities of Henry VIII and the attempts of James I and Charles I, it remained so. Sir Edward Coke's defence of English liberties, in which he appealed to the long tradition of limited monarchy, helped to prevent the development of the absolutist monarchies that spread over much of the rest of Europe. Like England, Holland kept the resurgent Catholicism and absolutism at bay, which helps to account for the great similarities between the two countries. But in Spain with Philip II, in France with Louis XIV, we see at its most extreme that growth of the absolutist state that has been charted by Perry Anderson.[43] In England alone, there was no large standing army, no centralized bureaucracy, no huge court, no theory that placed the king above the law. In England, consequently, there continued a tradition that had been widespread in earlier centuries over much of Europe.

Max Weber approvingly quoted Montesquieu's observation that there were deep connections between economic, religious and political developments in England. England had 'progressed the farthest of all peoples of the world in three important things: in piety, in commerce, and in freedom'.[44] This was even more obvious when the potential of a 'New England' had been realized in North America, where these connections were taken to their extremes. What is important for us is to realize that while the Malthusian marriage system was behind the peculiar demographic structure, behind that marriage system itself lay layer upon layer of political, legal, cultural and economic decisions which had by chance preserved some ancient features. Most dramatically, the success of the Armada in 1588 would have brought Roman law, Roman religion and absolutist monarchy. The subsequent course of world development would have been very different, for the major alternative to the English – the Dutch – might then also have been swamped. But enough of speculation. Let us

[43] Anderson, *Lineages*.   [44] Weber, *Protestant Ethic*, 45.

return to where we started, to Malthus.

Whatever the outcome of arguments about the origins of the system, there are also arguments about the necessary connections between capitalism and the Malthusian demographic pattern. Malthus, Marx and Engels agreed that there was a connection. The difference between them was that while Malthus believed there was a necessary causal connection, Marx believed that it was to a certain extent accidental. Malthus argued that to abolish part of the structure was to abolish the whole. If one destroyed capitalism, inevitably the iron law of population would take over. Man would be faced inevitably with a return to maximum breeding, and hence to famine, war and disease as the only checks. This theory was as direct and deadly a threat to Marx's communism as it had been to earlier theories. The undermining effects of Malthus' theories for those who sought to abolish capitalism were recognized by the Scottish philosopher Dugald Stewart as soon as the *Essay on Population* appeared. 'The reasonings of Mr Malthus, therefore, in so far as they relate to the Utopian plans of Wallace, Condorcet and Godwin, are perfectly conclusive, and strike at the root of all such theories.' Marx recognized that his was one of 'all such theories'. He admitted that 'if this theory is correct, then again I can *not* abolish the law [iron law of wages] even if I abolish wage labour a hundred times over, because the law then governs not only the system of wage labour but *every* social system.'[45]

Apart from abuse, the major answer to this threat by Marx and Engels was to argue that Malthus had merely established a specific, not a universal, connection. Writing to Marx in 1865, Engels argued, 'to us so-called "economic laws" are not eternal laws of nature but historic laws which arise and disappear.'[46] Thus the law of Malthus was 'a law of population peculiar to the capitalist mode of production; and in fact every specific mode of production has its own special law of population, historically valid within its limits alone. An abstract law of population exists for plants and animals only.'[47] So when Malthus '*asserted* the fact of overpopulation in all forms of society' his conception was 'altogether false and childish', because he turned a natural fact into a social fact, without appreciating all the intervening

[45] Stewart, *Works*, viii, 207.
[46] Marx, quoted in Meek, *Marx and Engels*, 118.
[47] Quoted in Meek, *Marx and Engels*, 20.

variables which meant that in each different 'mode of production', in Marx's sense, population would act in a different way.[48] Thus, the Marxist eliminates the historical and specific Malthusian predictions when he abolishes capitalism. It is capitalism and not deeper, 'natural' laws that cause overpopulation.

Despite the invective and a few debating points, Marx's counter-dismissal is not convincing, and Malthus still stands. *De facto* this has been recognized in China where, having for years declared that there is no population problem under socialism, in the 1970s the rulers were suddenly faced with soaring population, and recognized that there was indeed a problem. The Chinese were then forced into measures of law and repression which Malthus had predicted would be necessary if the balances of capitalism were not present; there ensued that suppression of childbearing through mass sanctions, laws and inducements which Malthus would have considered grossly immoral, not to say dictatorial. As William Petersen observes, 'when Marx's criticisms of Malthus' principles of population are examined, it becomes evident that neither Marx himself nor any Marxist has developed a population theory to replace the Malthusian one they rejected.'[49] A sneaking admission of defeat is contained in a letter from Engels to Kautsky: 'There is, of course, the abstract possibility that the number of people will become so great that limits will have to be set to their increase.'[50] This the Chinese have discovered.

Finally, it is important to stress that the Malthusian marriage system does not generate any particular population outcome. In England and North America in the nineteenth century it produced very rapid population growth as the equation between economy and personal emotions held at a certain level. Nor does the marriage pattern necessarily find itself linked to a particular technological system (industrialism), social system (urbanism), political system (democracy) or religion (Christianity). These tended to be associated by the nineteenth century in the mother country and to spread over Europe and North America. But the central ideology – a family pattern and individualistic philosophy – can float free. It can find echoes wherever people wish to pursue those ends which Malthus held up before them: equality of the sexes, physical comfort rather than misery, and responsibility for one's own decisions. In its wake

[48] Marx, *Grundrisse*, 605. [49] Petersen, *Population*, 93.
[50] Quoted in Cassen, *India*, 300.

come all the associated costs: the destruction of wider groups and communities, the corrosion of loyalties, the calculative, rational view of life, that 'alienation' which Marx documented, the 'anomie' that Durkheim analysed. If Malthus is right, there is only a choice between war, famine and disease on the one hand, and individualistic capitalism on the other. If Marx is right, we can both have our cake and eat it. The two prophets stand locked in battle today as they did in the nineteenth century. This history of the Malthusian family system and its components is intended to explain to us how we came to be as we are, and to help those who still have to choose to know what the choice implies.

Bibliography

This bibliography includes all the works referred to in the text. The abbreviation (author and short title) used in the footnotes is given first, followed by the full reference. The following abbreviations have been used:

Am.	*American*
Arch., *Arch.*	Archaeological, *Archaeological*
CWAAS	Cumberland and Westmorland Archaeological and Antiquarian Society
Econ., *Econ.*	Economic, *Economic*
Hist., *Hist.*	Historical, *Historical*
HMC	Historical Manuscripts Commission
Jnl	*Journal*
LPS	*Local Population Studies*
n.d.	no date
n.s.	new series
pt	part
Rev.	*Review*
Soc., *Soc.*	Society, *Society*
tr.	translated by
Trans	Transactions

Documents located in Record Offices (RO) in Essex (E), London (L), Westmorland (W) or Public (P) are given their archival number. Rare books in the British Library (BL), formerly British Museum, are given call numbers.

A General Abridgement. A General Abridgement of Cases in Equity . . . in the High Court of Chancery, By a Gentleman of the Middle Temple, 2nd edn, corrected 1734.

A Rational Account. A Rational Account of the Natural Weaknesses of Women, By a Physician (Edward Jorden?), 2nd edn, 1716, BL 1177.c.1.

A Treatise of Feme Coverts. *A Treatise of Feme Coverts: Or the Lady's Law* (1732), reprint New Jersey, 1974.

Anderson, *Family Structure*. Anderson, Michael, *Family Structure in Nineteenth-Century Lancashire*, 1971.

—, *Western Family*. *Approaches to the History of the Western Family 1500–1914*, 1980.

Anderson, *Lineages*. Anderson, Perry, *Lineages of the Absolutist State*, 1974.

Anglicus, *Properties*. Anglicus, Bartholomaeus, *On the Properties of Things*, 2 vols, tr. John Trevisa, 1975.

Arensberg, *Irish Countryman*. Arensberg, Conrad M., *The Irish Countryman*, 1959.

Ashby, *Poor Law*. Ashby, A.W., *One Hundred Years of Poor Law Administration in a Warwickshire Village*, Oxford Studies in Social and Legal History, vol. 3, 1912.

Ashley, *Stuarts*. Ashley, Maurice, *The Stuarts in Love*, 1963.

Atkinson, *Moorland*. Atkinson, (Revd) J.C., *Forty Years in a Moorland Parish*, 1891.

Aubrey, *Wiltshire*. Aubrey, John, *The Natural History of Wiltshire*, ed. John Britton, Wilts. Topographical Soc., 1847.

—, *Brief Lives*. *Brief Lives*, ed. Oliver Lawson Dick, 1949.

Avebury, *Origin*. Avebury, (Lord), *The Origin of Civilization and the Primitive Condition of Man*, 6th edn, 1911.

Aylmer, *Diary of Lawrence*. Aylmer, G.E. (ed.), *The Diary of William Lawrence (1662–1681)*, 1961.

Bacon, *Essayes*. Bacon, Francis, *The Essayes or Counsels Civill and Morall of Francis Bacon, Lord Verulam*, Everyman Library, 1910.

Bagot, 'Manorial Customs'. Bagot, Annette, 'Mr Gilpin and Manorial Customs', in Trans CWAAS, n.s. LXII, 1962.

Bailey, *Caste*. Bailey, F.G., *Caste and the Economic Frontier*, 1957.

Ballam & Lewis, *Visitors' Book*. Ballam, H., & Lewis, R., *The Visitors' Book, England and the English as others have seen them A.D. 1500 to 1950*, 1950.

Banks & Banks, *Family Planning*. Banks, J.A., & Banks, Olive, *Feminism and Family Planning in Victorian England*, 1964.

Barnard, *Country Gentleman*. Barnard, E.A., *A Seventeenth-Century Country Gentleman*, 2nd edn, 1948.

Baxter, *Breviate*. Baxter, Richard, *The Breviate of the Life of Margaret Baxter* (1681), 1928.

Bayne-Powell, *Travellers*. Bayne-Powell, Rosamund, *Travellers in Eighteenth-Century England*, 1951.

Beals, *Gopalpur*. Beals, Alan R., *Gopalpur. A South Indian Village*, New York, 1962.

Becon, *Works*. Becon, Thomas, *Works*, Parker Soc., 1844.

—, *Workes*. *Workes*, 1560, BL 3752 f.6.

Behn, *Pleasures*. Behn, Aphra, *The Ten Pleasures of Marriage*, Navarre Soc., 1922.

Bell, *Marriage*. Bell, Robert E., *Marriage and Family Interaction*, Illinois, 1963.

Benham, 'Manorial Customs'. Benham, W. Gurney, 'Manorial Customs in West Mersea and Fingringhoe', Trans Essex Arch. Soc., n.s. vol. XIII, 1915.

Bennett, *Pastons*. Bennett, H.S., *The Pastons and their England*, 1968.

—, *English Manor*. *Life on the English Manor*, 1962.

Berkner, 'Stem Family'. Berkner, Lutz K., 'The Stem Family and the Developmental Cycle of the Peasant Household: An Eighteenth-Century Austrian Example', *Am. Hist. Rev.*, vol. 77, 1972.

Best, *Rural Economy*. Best, Henry, *Rural Economy in Yorkshire in 1641*, Surtees Soc., vol. 33, 1857.

Blackstone, *Commentaries*. Blackstone, (Sir) William, *Commentaries on the Laws of England*, 4 vols, 18th edn, 1829.

Blencowe, 'Giles Moore'. Blencowe, Robert W., 'Extracts from the Journal and Account Book of the Rev. Giles Moore ... from 1655 to 1679', Sussex Arch. Coll., vol. I, 1847.

—, 'Burrell'. (ed.), 'Extracts from the Journal and Account Book of Timothy Burrell', Sussex Arch. Coll., vol. III, 1850.

Bloch, *Sexual*. Bloch, Ivan, *Sexual Life in England Past and Present*, 1938.

Bloch *Feudal*. Bloch, Marc, *Feudal Society*, 2 vols, trs. L.A. Manyon, 2nd edn, 1962.

Blundell, *Diary*. Blundell, Margaret (ed.), *Blundell's Diary and Letter Book 1702–1728*, 1952.

Bohannan, *Social Anthropology*. Bohannan, Paul, *Social Anthropology*, 1969.

Boorde, *Breviary*. Boorde, Andrew, *The Breviary of Health*, 1575.

Boserup, *Population*. Boserup, Ester, *Population and Technology*, 1981.

Bouch, *Prelates and People*. Bouch, C.M.L., *Prelates and People of the Lake Countries*, 1948.

Bourcier, *D'Ewes Diary*. Bourcier, Elisabeth (ed.), *The Diary of Sir Simonds D'Ewes, 1622–4*, Paris, n.d.

Bouverie, Manuscripts. Bouverie, Philip, Report on the Manuscripts of Philip Pleydell Bouverie Esq., HMC, 10th Report, App., pt VI.

Brady, *Boswell in Search*. Brady, Frank, & Pottle, Frederick (eds), *Boswell in Search of a Wife 1766–1769*, 1957.

Brain, *Friends and Lovers*. Brain, Robert, *Friends and Lovers*, 1977.

Bramston, *Autobiography*. Bramston, Thomas William (ed.), *The Autobiography of Sir John Bramston*, Camden Soc., no. 32, 1845.

Brand, *Popular Antiquities*. Brand, John, *Observations on the Popular Antiquities of Great Britain*, 3 vols, 1848.

Bray, *Evelyn Diary*. Bray, William (ed.), *Diary and Correspondence of John Evelyyn*, n.d.

Briggs, *Pale Hecate*. Briggs, K.M., *Pale Hecate's Team*, 1962.

Britton, *Community of Vill*. Britton, Edward, *The Community of the Vill*, Toronto, 1977.

Bromley, *Family Law*. Bromley, P.M., *Family Law*, 4th edn, 1971.

Brooke, 'Marriage'. Brooke, Christopher N.L., 'Marriage in Christian History', Inaugural Lecture, Cambridge University, 1978.

Browne, *Religio Medici*. Browne, (Sir) Thomas, *Religio Medici*, 1962.

Bruce, *Diary of Manningham*. Bruce, John (ed.), *Diary of John Manningham, 1602–1603*, Camden Soc., no. 99, 1868.

Buchan, *Domestic Medicine*. Buchan, William, *Domestic Medicine*, 11th edn, 1790.

Buckland, *Roman Law*. Buckland, W.W., & McNair, Arnold D., *Roman Law and Common Law*, 2nd edn, 1965.

Burn, *Ecclesiastical Law*. Burn, Richard, *Ecclesiastical Law*, 4 vols, 15th edn, 1788.

—, *Justice*. *The Justice of the Peace and Parish Officer*, 4 vols, 16th edn, 1788.

Burt's Letters. *Burt's Letters from the North of Scotland*, intro. R. Jamieson, 2 vols, 1876.

Cain, 'Extended Kin'. Cain Mead T., 'Extended Kin, Patriarchy and Fertility', International Union for the Scientific Study of Population, Seminar on Family Types and Fertility in Less Developed Countries, Brazil, Aug. 1981.

—, 'Children'. 'The Economic Activities of Children in a Village in Bangladesh', *Population and Development Rev.*, vol. 3, no. 3, Sept. 1977.

Cairncross, *After Polygamy*. Cairncross, John, *After Polygamy was Made a Sin*, 1974.

Caldwell, 'Rationality'. Caldwell, J.C., 'The Economic Rationality of High Fertility: An Investigation Illustrated with Nigerian Survey Data', *Population Studies*, vol. 31, no. 1, March 1977.

—, 'Fertility'. 'Fertility and the Household Economy of Nigeria', *Jnl of Comparative Family Studies*, vol. VII, no. 2, 1976.

—, 'Restatement'. 'Toward a Restatement of Demographic Transition Theory', *Population and Development Rev.*, vol. 2, nos 3 & 4, 1976.

—, 'Education'. 'Mass Education as a Determinant of the Timing of Fertility Decline', *Population and Development Rev.*, vol.6, no.2, June 1980.

Camden, *Elizabethan Woman*. Camden, Carol, *The Elizabethan Woman*, 1952.

Campbell, *Patronage*. Campbell, J.K., *Honour, Family and Patronage*, 1964.

Campbell, *English Yeoman*. Campbell, Mildred, *The English Yeoman Under Elizabeth and the Early Stuarts, 1942*.

Cassen, *India*. Cassen, R.H., *India: Population, Economy, Society*, 1978.

Cavendish, *Letters*. Cavendish, Margaret (Duchess of Newcastle), *CCXI Sociable Letters Written by the Thrice Noble, Illustrious, and Excellent Princess, The Lady Marchioness of Newcastle*, 1664.

Cellier, 'Royal Hospital'. Cellier, (Mrs) Elizabeth, 'A Scheme for the Foundation of a Royal Hospital' (1687), reprinted in *Harleian Miscellany*, vol. IX, 1810.

Chagnon, *Fierce People*. Chagnon, Napoleon A., *Yanomamo. The Fierce People*, 1968.

Chamberlayne, *State of England*. Chamberlayne, Edward, *The Present State of England*, 19th imp., 1700.

Chamberlayne, *State of Britain*. Chamberlayne, John, *The Present State of Great Britain*, 33rd edn, 1737.

Chambers, *Population*. Chambers, J.D., *Population, Economy and Society in Pre-Industrial England*, 1972.

—, 'Vale of Trent'. 'The Vale of Trent 1670–1800', *Econ. Hist. Rev., suppl. 3, 1957.*

Characters. *Characters and Observations, an Eighteenth-Century Manuscript*, foreword by Lord Gorell, 1930.

Clark, *Women*. Clark, Alice, *Working Life of Women in the Seventeenth Century* (1919), reprint 1968.

Clark, *Population Growth*. Clark, Colin, *Population Growth and Land Use*, 1968.

Coale, 'Malthus'. Coale, Ansley J., 'T.R. Malthus and the Population Trend of His Day and Ours', Encyclopaedia Britannica Lecture, 1978, University of Edinburgh.

Cobbett, *Advice*. Cobbett, William, *Advice to Young Men, and (incidentally) to Young Women*, 1837.

—, *Advice to a Lover. Advice to a Lover.* 1837.

Cogan, *Haven of Health*. Cogan, Thomas, *Haven of Health*, 1589.

Cohen, *Penguin Dictionary*. Cohen, J.M., & Cohen, M.J., *The Penguin Dictionary of Quotations*, 1960.

Coke, *Institutes*. Coke, (Sir) Edward, *Institutes of the Laws of England*, 2nd, 3rd & 4th Institutes, 1797.

Comenius, *Orbis*. Comenius, Johannes Amos, *Orbis Sensualium Pictus* (1672), facsimile reprint, Sydney, 1967.

Connell, 'Peasant Marriage'. Connell, K.H., 'Peasant Marriage in Ireland: its Structure and Development since the Famine', *Econ. Hist. Rev., 2nd series, vol. XIV, no. 3, April 1962.*

Cooke, *Universal Letter Writer*. Cooke, (Revd) T., *The Universal Letter Writer* . . ., n.d. (c.1840s).

Coulton, *Medieval Village*. Coulton, G.G., *Medieval Village, Manor, and Monastery*, New York, 1960.

Coverdale, *Matrimony*. Coverdale, Myles, *The Christian State of Matrimony*, a translation of Bullinger's work, 1575.

Cox, *Parish Registers*. Cox, J.C., *The Parish Registers of England*, 1910.

– *Churchwardens. Churchwardens' Accounts*, 1913.

Crawley, *Mystic Rose*. Crawley, Ernest, *The Mystic Rose*, 2nd edn, 1960.

Culpeper, *Midwives*. Culpeper, Nicholas, *A Directory for Midwives*, 1656.

Culpeper's Herbal. *Culpeper's English Physician and Complete Herbal*, arranged Mrs C.F. Leyel, 1961.

Davies, *English Village*. Davies, Maude F., *Life in an English Village*, 1909.

Davis, *Human Society*. Davis, Kingsley, *Human Society*, New York, 1948.

—, 'Fertility'. 'Social Structure and Fertility: An Analytic Framework', *Econ. Development and Social Change*, vol. 4, no. 3, 1956.

—, 'High Fertility'. 'Institutional Patterns Favouring High Fertility in Underdeveloped Areas', *Eugenics Quarterly*, vol. 2, 1955.

—, 'Population Policy'. 'Population Policy: Will Current Programs Succeed?', *Science*, vol. 158, no. 3802, 1967.

—, 'Theory'. 'The Theory of Change and Response in Modern Demographic History', *Population Index*, XXIX, 1963.

Day, *Secretorie*. Day, Angel, *The English Secretorie* (1586), 1967.

De Mause, *Childhood*. De Mause, Lloyd (ed.), *The History of Childhood*, 1976.

De Rougemont, *Passion and Society*. De Rougemont, Denis, *Passion and Society*, 1940.

De Tocqueville, *L'Ancien Regime*. De Tocqueville, Alexis, *L'Ancien Regime*, tr. M.W. Patterson, 1956.

—, *Democracy*. *Democracy in America*, abridged edn ed. Richard D. Heffner, 1956.

Defoe, *Tour*. Defoe, Daniel, *A Tour Through the Whole Island of Great Britain*, ed. Pat Rogers, 1971.

—, Complete Tradesman. *The Complete English Tradesman* (1745) 2 vols, facsimile reprint.

Delany, *British Autobiography*. Delany, Paul, *British Autobiography in the Seventeenth Century*, 1969.

Deloney, 'Jacke of Newberrie'. Deloney, Thomas, 'Jacke of Newberrie', in *Shorter Novels: Elizabethan*, intro. George Saintsbury, Everyman Library, 1929.

Demos, *Little Commonwealth*. Demos, John, *The Little Commonwealth*, 1971.

'Diary of Pledger'. 'Diary of Elias Pledger of Little Baddow, Essex', MS in Dr Williams Library, Gordon Square, London.

'Diary of Venables'. 'Diary of Mrs Venables', *Chetham Soc. Miscellany*, vol. IV, no. 83, 1872.

Dod, *Godlie Forme*. Dod, John, & Clever, Robert, *A Godlie Forme of Household Government*, 1612.

Dore, 'Fertility'. Dore, R.P., 'Japanese Rural Fertility; some Social and Economic Factors', *Population Studies*, vol. 7, no, 1, July 1953.

Du Bartas, *Weekes*. Du Bartas, *His Divine Weekes and Workes*, tr. Joshua Sylvester, 1633.

Du Boulay, *Ambition*. Du Boulay, F.R.H., *An Age of Ambition*, 1970.

Dube, *Indian*. Dube, S.C., *Indian Village*, 1967.

Earle, *Microcosmography*. Earle, John, *Microcosmography*, reprint of Dr Bliss's edn of 1811, n.d.

Ellis, *Smyth Obituary*. Ellis, (Sir) Henry (ed)., *The Obituary of Richard Smyth*, Camden Soc., no. 44, 1849.

Elwin, *Muria*. Elwin, Verrier, *The Muria and their Ghotul*, Bombay, 1947.

Emmison, *Tudor Food*. Emmison, F.G., *Tudor Food and Pastimes, Life at Ingatestone Hall*, 1964.

—, *Morals*. *Elizabethan Life: Morals and the Church Courts*, 1973.

Engels, *Origin of the Family*. Engels, Frederick, *The Origin of the Family, Private Property and the State*, Chicago, 1902.

Epstein, *Fertility*. Epstein, T. Scarlett, & Jackson, Darrell, *The Feasibility of Fertility Planning*, 1977.

Evans-Pritchard, *Nuer Kinship*. Evans-Pritchard, E.E., *Kinship and Marriage among the Nuer*, 1951

Eyre, 'Dyurnall'. Eyre, Adam, 'A Dyurnall, or Catalogue of All my Actions . . .' in *Yorkshire Diaries and Autobiographies*, Surtees Soc., vol. 65, 1877.

Faith, 'Inheritance'. Faith, Rosamond Jane, 'Peasant Families and Inheritance Customs in Medieval England', *Agricultural Hist. Rev.*, XIV, pt II, pp. 77–95, 1966.

Ferguson, *Essay*. Ferguson, Adam, *An Essay on the History of Civil Society 1767*, ed. Duncan Forbes. 1966.

Finch, *Families*. Finch, Mary E., *The Wealth of Five Northamptonshire Families*, Northants Record Soc., vol. XIX, 1956.

Firth, *Human Types*. Firth, Raymond, *Human Types*, revised edn, 1956.

Fishwick, *Thomas Jolly*. Fishwick, Henry (ed.), *The Note Book of the Rev. Thomas Jolly, 1671–1693*, Chetham Soc., n.s. 33, 1894.

Flandrin, *Families*. Flandrin, Jean-Louis, *Families in Former Times*, tr. Richard Southern, 1979.

Fleming, 'Notebook'. Fleming, Daniel, 'Manuscript notebook of jokes, stories etc.', WRO, WD/Ry.

Flinn, *Industrial Revolution*. Flinn, M. W., *Origins of the Industrial Revolution*, 1969.

Ford, *Warton*. Ford, J. Rawlinson, & Fuller-Maitland, J.A. (eds), *John Lucas's History of Warton Parish*, 1931.

Forde, *African Worlds*. Forde, Daryll (ed.), *African Worlds*, 1954.

Fox, *Kinship*. Fox, Robin, *Kinship and Marriage*, 1967.

Franklin, *European Peasantry*. Franklin, S.H., *The European Peasantry*, 1969.

Fretwell, *Family History*. Fretwell, James, *A Family History . . . in Yorkshire Diaries and Autobiographies*, Surtees Soc., vol. 65, 1877.

Friedl, *Vasilika*. Friedl, Ernestine, *Vasilika. A Village in Modern Greece*, New York, 1962.

Fuller, *Holy State*. Fuller, Thomas, *The Holy State*, 2nd edn, 1948.

Furnivall, *Tell-Trothes*. Furnivall, F.J. (ed.), *Tell-Trothes New Yeares Gift &
The Passionate Morrice . . .*, New Shakspere Soc., 1876.

—, *Meals and Manners*. *Early English Meals and Manners*, Early English Text
Soc., 1931.

Fussell, *Loder's Accounts*. Fussell, G.E. (ed.), *Robert Loder's Farm Accounts
1610-1620*, Camden Soc., vol. 53, 1936.

Gairdner, *Paston Letters*. Gairdner, James (ed.), *The Paston Letters 1422–
1509*, introductory vol. & 3 vols, 1900–1.

Galeski, *Basic Concepts*. Galeski, Boguslaw, *Basic Concepts of Rural Sociology*,
1972.

Gassner, *Medieval Drama*. Gassner, John (ed.), *Medieval and Tudor Drama*,
1968.

Gaunt, 'Retired Farmers'. Gaunt, David, 'The Property and Kin Relationships of Retired Farmers in Northern and Central Europe', in *Family
Forms in Historic Europe* ed. Richard Wall, Jean Robin & Peter Laslett,
1983.

Gay, *Beggar's Opera*. Gay, John, *The Beggar's Opera*, ed. Peter E. Lewis, 1973.

Geary, *Marriage*. Geary, Nevill, *The Law of Marriage and Family Relations*,
1892.

George, *London Life*. George, M. Dorothy, *London Life in the Eighteenth
Century*, 1966.

Gerth & Mills, *Max Weber*. Gerth, H.H., & Mills, C. Wright (eds), *From Max
Weber: Essays in Sociology*, 1967.

Gill, *Rector's Book*. Gill, Harry, & Guilford, Everard (eds), *The Rector's Book of
Clayworth, Notts (1675–1700)*, 1910.

Glass, *Population*. Glass, D.V., & Eversley, D.E.C. (eds), *Population in
History*, 1965.

Goode, *World Revolution*. Goode, William J., *World Revolution and Family
Patterns*, New York, 1968

—, *Family*. *The Family*, New Jersey, 1964.

—, 'Love'. 'The Theoretical Importance of Love', *Am. Sociological, Rev.*, vol.
24, pp. 38–47, 1959.

Goody, *Family and Marriage*. Goody, Jack, *The Development of the Family and
Marriage in Europe*, 1983.

—, *Production*. *Production and Reproduction. A Comparative Study of the
Domestic Domain*, 1976.

Goody, *Developmental Cycle*. Goody, Jack (ed.), *The Developmental Cycle in
Domestic Groups*, 1958.

Goody & Tambiah, *Bridewealth and Dowry*. Goody, Jack & Tambiah, S.J.,
Bridewealth and Dowry, 1973.

Goody, *Family and Inheritance*. Goody, J., Thirsk, J., & Thompson, E.P.,
(eds), *Family and Inheritance*, 1976.

Gorer, *Himalayan Village*. Gorer, Geoffrey, *Himalayan Village*, 2nd edn, 1967.

Goubert, *Beauvais*. Goubert, Pierre, *Beauvais et le Beauvaisis de 1600 à 1730*, Paris, 1960.

Gouge, *Domesticall*. Gouge, William, *Of Domesticall Duties*, 1622.

Gough, *Myddle.* Gough, Richard, *Antiquities and Memoirs of the Parish of Myddle*, Salop RO, n.d.

Graham, *Scotland*. Graham, H.G., *The Social Life of Scotland in the Eighteenth Century*, 1909.

Grainger, 'Jackson's Diary'. Grainger, Francis, 'James Jackson's Diary 1650 to 1683', in Trans CWAAS, n.s. XXI, 1920.

Greven, *Protestant Temperament*. Greven, Philip, *The Protestant Temperament*, New York, 1977.

Grosart, *Farmer MS*. Grosart, (Revd) Alexander, *The Dr. Farmer Chetham MS*, 2 vols, Chetham Soc., 1873.

Grosart, *Lismore Papers*. Grosart, A.B. (ed.), *The Lismore Papers*, 5 vols, 1st series, autobiography, notes and diaries of Sir Richard Boyle, 1st Earl of Cork, 1886ff.

Gunther, *Diary of Ashmole*. Gunther, R.T. (ed.), *The Diary of Elias Ashmole*, 1927.

Habakkuk, 'Marriage Settlements'. Habakkuk, H.J., 'Marriage Settlements in the Eighteenth Century', in Trans Royal Hist. Soc., 4th series, XXXII, 1950.

Hadfield, *Elizabethan Love*. Hadfield, John (ed.), *Elizabethan Love Lyrics*, 1969.

Hadow, *Sir Walter Raleigh*. Hadow, G.E. (ed.), *Sir Walter Raleigh, selections from his Historie of the World, his letters . . .*, 1926.

Hair, 'Bridal Pregnancy'. Hair, P.E.H., 'Bridal Pregnancy in Earlier Rural England Further Examined', *Population Studies*, vol. 24, no. 1, March 1970.

—, 'Bridal'. 'Bridal Pregnancy in Rural England in Earlier Centuries', *Population Studies*, vol. 20, no. 2, Nov. 1966.

Hale, *Precedents*. Hale, William, *A Series of Precedents and Proceedings in Criminal Causes*, 1847.

Hall, *Family Law*. Hall, J.C., *Sources of Family Law*, 1966.

Halliwell, *Diary of Forman*. Halliwell, J.O. (ed.), *Autobiography and Personal Diary of Dr Simon Forman*, 1849.

—, *D'Ewes Autobiography*. *The Autobiography and Correspondence of Sir Simonds D'Ewes*, 2 vols, 1845.

Halpern, *Serbian Village*. Halpern, Joel M., *A Serbian Village*, 1967.

Hanham, *Cely Letters*. Hanham, Alison (ed.), *The Cely Letters*, Early English Text Soc., 1975.

Harrington, *Matrymony*. Harrington, William, *The Comendacions of Matrymony*, 1528.

Harrison, *Jacobean Journal*. Harrison, G.B., *A Jacobean Journal*, 1941.

Haviland, *Cultural Anthropology*. Haviland, William A., *Cultural Anthropology*, 3rd edn, 1980.

Hawthorn, *Population*. Hawthorn, Geoffrey (ed.), *Population and Development*, 1978.

Helmholz, *Marriage Litigation*. Helmholz, R.H., *Marriage Litigation in Medieval England*, 1974.

Henriques, *Love in Action*. Henriques, Fernando, *Love in Action*, 1966.

Hexter, *Reappraisals*. Hexter, J.H., *Reappraisals in History*, 1961.

Hey, *Myddle*. Hey, David G., *Myddle Under the Tudors and Stuarts*, 1974.

Hill, *Puritanism and Revolution*. Hill, Christopher, *Puritanism and Revolution*, 1962.

Hill, *Life of Johnson*. Hill, George Birkbeck (ed.), *Boswell's Life of Johnson*, 6 vols, 1887.

'Historical Population'. 'Historical Population Studies', *Daedalus*, Spring 1968.

Hoccleve, *Works*. Hoccleve, Thomas, *Works*, ed. F.J. Furnivall, Early English Text Soc., extra series, 61, 72, 73, 1892–1925.

Hodgson, 'Diary of Sanderson'. Hodgson, J.C. (ed.), 'Selections from the Diary of Christopher Sanderson of Barnard Castle' in *Six North Country Diaries*, Surtees Soc., vol. 118, 1910.

—, 'Sir John Gibson'. 'Autobiography of Sir John Gibson, 1655' in *North Country Diaries*, 2nd series, Surtees Soc., vol. 124, 1915.

Hoebel, *Primitive World*. Hoebel, E. Adamson, *Man in the Primitive World*, 1st edn, New York, 1949.

—, *Primitive*. Man in the Primitive World, 2nd edn, New York, 1958.

Holdsworth, *English Law*. Holdsworth, (Sir) William, *A History of English Law*, 16 vols, 3rd edn, 1945.

Holles, *Memorials*. Holles, Gervase, *Memorials of the Holles Family 1493–1656*, Camden Soc., 3rd series, vol. 55, ed. A.C. Wood, 1937.

Hollingsworth, *Historical Demography*. Hollingsworth, T.H., *Historical Demography*, 1969.

Holloway, *Broadside Ballads*. Holloway, John, & Black, Joan (eds), *Later English Broadside Ballads*, 1975.

Homans, *Villagers*. Homans, G.C., *English Villagers of the Thirteenth Century*, New York, 1960.

Hoskins, *Midland Peasant*. Hoskins, W.G., *The Midland Peasant*, 1965.

—, 'Rebuilding'. 'The Rebuilding of Rural England 1570–1640', reprinted in *Provincial England*, 1964.

—, *Leicestershire*. *Essays in Leicestershire History*, 1950.

Houlbrooke, *Church Courts*. Houlbrooke, Ralph, *Church Courts and the People during the English Revolution 1520–1570*, 1979.

—, 'Courts and People'. 'Church Courts and People in the Diocese of Norwich, 1519–1570', Oxford University, D.Phil. thesis, 1970.

—, *English Family*. *The English Family 1450–1700*, 1984.

Howard, *Matrimonial Institutions*. Howard, George Elliott, *A History of Matrimonial Institutions*, 3 vols, 1904.

Huarte, *Men's Wits*. Huarte (Navarro), John, *The Examination of Men's Wits*, tr. R.C., 1594.

Hume, *Treatise*. Hume, David, *A Treatise of Human Nature*, ed. L.A. Selby-Bigge, 1928.

—, *Essays*. *Essays, Literary, Moral and Political*, n.d.

Hunt, *Love*. Hunt, Morton M., *Love*, 1960.

Hunter, *Thoresby Diary*. Hunter, (Revd) Joseph (ed.), *The Diary of Ralph Thoresby*, 4 vols, 1830, 1832.

Hutchinson, *Memoirs*. Hutchinson, Lucy, *Memoirs of the Life of Colonel Hutchinson*, 2 vols, 4th edn, 1822.

Hutton, *Young's Tour*. Hutton, A.W. (ed.), *Arthur Young's Tour of Ireland (1776–1779)*, 2 vols, 1892.

I.W., *Speedie Poste*. I.W. (N. Breton), *A Speedie Poste, with Certain New Letters*, 1629.

Ingram, 'Ridings'. Ingram, Martin, 'Ridings, Rough Music and the Reform of Popular Culture in Early Modern England', *Past and Present*, 105, Nov. 1984.

Jackson, *Thornton Autobiography*. Jackson, Charles (ed.), *The Autobiography of Mrs Alice Thornton of East Newton, Co. York*, Surtees Soc., vol. 62, 1875.

Jacob, *Law-Dictionary*. Jacob, Giles, *A New Law-Dictionary*, 1754.

Jeaffreson, *Bridal*. Jeaffreson, J.C., *Brides and Bridals*, 2 vols, 1872.

Johnson, *Works*. Johnson, Samuel, *Works*, new edn, 12 vols, 1810.

'Joyce Jeffries Diary'. 'Joyce Jeffries of Hereford, Diary, 1638–648', BL, Egerton MS 3054.

Kames, *Sketches*. Kames, (Lord), *Sketches of the History of Man*, 4 vols in 2, Basil, 1796.

Kaplan, *Fertility*. Kaplan, Bernice A. (ed.), *Anthropological Studies of Human Fertility*, Detroit, 1976.

Kardiner, *Psychological Frontiers*. Kardiner, Abram, *The Psychological Frontiers of Society*, 1945.

King-Hall, *Nursery*. King-Hall, Magdalen, *The Story of the Nursery*, 1958.

Kingsford, *Stonor Letters*. Kingsford, Charles Lethbridge (ed.), *The Stonor Letters and Papers 1290–1483*, Camden Soc., 3rd series, vol. 29, no. 1, 1919.

Kinsey, *Human Male*. Kinsey, A.C., Pomeroy, W.B., & Martin, C.E., *Sexual Behavior in the Human Male*, 1948.

Knappen, *Puritan Diaries*. Knappen, M.M. (ed.), *Two Elizabethan Puritan Diaries*, 1933.

Kunitz, 'Mortality'. Kunitz, Stephen J., 'Speculations on the European Mortality Decline', *Econ. Hist. Rev.*, 2nd series, vol. XXXVI, no. 3, Aug. 1983.

Kussmaul, *Servants*. Kussmaul, Ann, *Servants in Husbandry in Early Modern England*, 1981.

Lancaster, 'Kinship'. Lancaster, Lorraine, 'Kinship in Anglo-Saxon Society', *British Jnl of Sociology*, pt 1, vol. IX, no. 3; pt 2, vol. IX, no. 4, Sept., Dec. 1958.

Lansdowne, *Petty Papers*. Lansdowne, (Marquis of) (ed.), *The Petty Papers. Unpublished writings of Sir William Petty from the Bowood Papers*, 2 vols, 1885.

Lasch, *Haven*. Lasch, Christopher, *Haven in a Heartless World*, New York, 1977.

Laslett, *Lost World*. Laslett, Peter, *The World we have Lost*, 2nd edn, 1971.

—, *Family Life*. *Family Life and Illicit Love in Earlier Generations*, 1977.

Laslett, *Household*. Laslett, Peter, (ed.), *Household and Family in Past Time*, 1972.

Laslett, *Bastardy*. Laslett, Peter, et al. (eds), *Bastardy and its Comparative History*, 1980.

Latham, *Pepys*. Latham, Robert, & Matthews, William (eds), *The Diary of Samuel Pepys*, 11 vols, 1970–83.

Lawrence, *Marriage*. Lawrence, William, *Marriage by the Morall Law of God Vindicated*, 1680.

Lee, *Rose*. Lee, Laurie, *Rose for Winter*, 1971.

Leibenstein, 'Interpretation'. Leibenstein, Harvey, 'An Interpretation of the Economic Theory of Fertility', *Jnl of Econ. Literature*, vol. XII, no. 2, pp. 467–79, June 1974.

Lesthaeghe, 'Social Control'. Lesthaeghe, Ron, 'On the Social Control of Human Reproduction', *Population and Development Rev., vol. 6, no. 4, Dec. 1980.*

Letters of Harley. *Letters of the Lady Brilliana Harley*, intro. & notes by Thomas Taylor Lewis, Camden Soc., 1853.

Levi-Strauss, *Elementary Structures*. Levi-Strauss, Claude, *The Elementary Structures of Kinship*, 2nd edn, 1969.

Levine, *Family Formation*. Levine, David, *Family Formation in an Age of Nascent Capitalism*, 1977.

Lewis, *Allegory*. Lewis, C.S., *The Allegory of Love*, 1959.

Lienhardt, *Social Anthropology*. Lienhardt, Godfrey, *Social Anthropology*, 1966.

Little, 'Modern Marriage'. Little, Kenneth, & Price, Anne, 'Some Trends in Modern Marriage Among West Africans', *Africa*, vol. XXXVII, no. 4, 1967.

Lloyd-Thomas, *Autobiography of Baxter*. Lloyd-Thomas, J.M. (ed.), *Autobiography of Richard Baxter*, Everyman Library, 1931.

Locke, *Government*. Locke, John, *The Second Treatise of Government*, ed. J.W. Gough, 3rd edn, 1966.

Lodge, *Account Book*. Lodge, Eleanor C., *The Account Book of a Kentish Estate 1616–1704*, British Academy Records of Social and Econ. Hist., vol. VI, 1927.

Lofgren, 'Family'. Lofgren, Orvar, 'Family and Household among Scandinavian Peasants: An Exploratory Essay', *Etnologia Scandinavia*, 1974.

Long, *Oglander Memoirs*. Long, W.H. (ed.), *The Oglander Memoirs*, 1888.

Lorimer, *Human Fertility*. Lorimer, Frank, *Culture and Human Fertility*, UNESCO, 1954.

Lowie, *Social Organization*. Lowie, Robert H., *Social Organization*, 1950.

—, *Primitive Society. Primitive Society*, 1921.

MacDonald, *Mystical Bedlam*. MacDonald, Michael, *Mystical Bedlam*, 1981.

Macfarlane, 'Reproduction'. Macfarlane, A., 'Modes of Reproduction' in G. Hawthorn (ed.), *Population and Development*, 1978.

—, 'Marital Relationships'. 'The Regulation of Marital and Sexual Relationships in Seventeenth-Century England . . .' LSE M. Phil. thesis, 1968.

—, *Resources. Resources and Population, A study of the Gurungs of Nepal*, 1976.

—, *Ralph Josselin. The Family Life of Ralph Josselin*, 1970.

—, *Individualism. The Origins of English Individualism*, 1978.

—, 'Historical Anthropology'. 'Historical Anthropology', *Cambridge Anthropology*, vol. 3, no. 3, 1977.

—, 'Review'. 'Review of Lawrence Stone, "The Family, Sex and Marriage in England 1500–1800"', *History and Theory*, vol. XVIII, no. 1, pp. 103–25, 1979.

—, *Guide. A Guide to English Historical Records*, 1983.

—, *Reconstructing. Reconstructing Historical Communities*, 1977.

—, *Justice. The Justice and the Mare's Ale*, 1981.

—, *Josselin Diary*. Macfarlane, Alan, (ed.), *The Diary of Ralph Josselin 1616–1683*, 1976.

Macpherson, *Possessive Individualism*. Macpherson, C.B., *The Political Theory of Possessive Individualism*, 1962.

Maine, *Early Institutions*. Maine, (Sir) Henry Sumner, *Lectures on the Early History of Institutions*, 1875.

—, *Early Law. Dissertations on Early Law and Custom*, 1883.

Maitland, *Forms of Action*. Maitland, F.W., *The Forms of Action at Common Law*, ed. A.H. Chaytor & W.J. Whittaker, 1968.

Malcolmson, *Popular Recreations*. Malcolmson, Robert W., *Popular Recreations in English Society 1700–1850*, 1973.

Malinowski, *Sexual Life*. Malinowski, Bronislaw, *The Sexual Life of Savages in North-West Melanesia*, 3rd edn, 1932.

Malthus, *Population*. Malthus, T.R., *An Essay on Population*, 2 vols, Everyman Library, n.d.

Mamdani, *Myth*. Mamdani, Mahmood, *The Myth of Population Control*, New York, 1972.

Mandeville, *Fable*. Mandeville, Bernard, *The Fable of the Bees*, ed. Phillip Harth, 1970.

Marchant, *Church Under Law*. Marchant, Ronald A., *The Church Under the Law*, 1969.

Marshall, *Stout Autobiography*. Marshall, J.D. (ed.), *The Autobiography of William Stout of Lancaster 1665–1752*, 1967.

Marshall, *Natality*. Marshall, John F., & Polgar, Steven (eds), *Culture, Natality, and Family Planning*, North Carolina, 1976.

Martin, *Western Islands*. Martin, Martin, *A Description of the Western Islands of Scotland circa 1695*, ed. Donald J. Macleod, 4th edn, 1934.

Marx, *Capital*. Marx, Karl, *Capital*, 2 vols, 1974.

—, *Grundrisse*. *Grundrisse*, tr. Martin Nicolaus, 1973.

Matthews, *Ryder Diary*. Matthews, William (ed.), *The Diary of Dudley Ryder 1715–1716*, 1939.

Maudlin, 'Family Planning'. Maudlin, W. Parker, & Berelson, Bernard, 'Cross-Cultural Review of the Effectiveness of Family Planning Campaigns', in *Proceedings of the International Population Conference*, vol. 3, pp. 163–85, Mexico, 1977.

McKeown, *Population*. McKeown, Thomas, *The Modern Rise of Population*, 1976.

McNicoll, 'Institutional Determinants'. McNicoll, Geoffrey, 'Institutional Determinants of Fertility Change', *Population and Development Rev.*, vol. 6, no. 3, Sept. 1980.

Mead, *New Guinea*. Mead, Margaret, *Growing Up in New Guinea*, 1942.

Mead, *Cultural Patterns*. Mead, Margaret, (ed.), *Cultural Patterns and Technical Change*, New York, 1955.

Meads, *Hoby Diary*. Meads, Dorothy (ed.), *Diary of Lady Margaret Hoby 1599–1605*, 1930.

Medieval English Verse. *Medieval English Verse*, tr. Brian Stone, 1964.

Meek, *Marx and Engels*. Meek, Ronald (ed.), *Marx and Engels on the Population Bomb*, Berkeley, 1971.

Menefee, *Wives for Sale*. Menefee, Samuel P., *Wives for Sale*, 1981.

Milton, *Works*. Milton, John, *Prose Works*, 5 vols, Bohn's Library, 1848.

—, *Paradise Lost*. *Paradise Lost*, Bohn's Library, 1854.

Mitchell, 'Fertility'. Mitchell, J. Clyde, 'An Estimate of Fertility in some Yao Hamlets', *Africa*, vol. XIX, no. 4, Oct. 1949.

Mitterauer, *European Family*. Mitterauer, Michael, & Seider, Reinhard, *The European Family*, 1982.

Montesquieu, *Spirit*. Montesquieu, *The Spirit of the Laws*, 2 vols, tr. Thomas Nugent, New York, 1975.

Moore, 'Marriage Contracts'. Moore, A. Percival, 'Marriage Contracts or Espousals in the Reign of Elizabeth', *Associated Architectural Societies Reports and Papers*, vol. XXX, pt 1, 1909.

More, *Utopia*. More, Thomas, *Utopia*, tr. Paul Turner, 1965.

Morgan, *Puritan Family*. Morgan, Edmund S., *The Puritan Family*, 1966.

Morgan, *Ancient Society*. Morgan, Lewis H., *Ancient Society*, Chicago, n.d.

Morley, *Character Writings*. Morley, Henry (ed.), *Character Writings of the Seventeenth Century*, 1891.

Moryson, *Itinerary*. Moryson, Fynes, *An Itinerary*, 4 vols, 1907–8.

Mount, *Subversive Family*. Mount, Ferdinand, *The Subversive Family*, 1982.

Mullan, *Mating Trade*. Mullan, Bob, *The Mating Trade*, 1984.

Muncey, *Parish Registers*. Muncey, R.W., *The Romance of Parish Registers*, 1933.

Murdock, *Social Structure*. Murdock, G.P., *Social Structure*, New York, 1949.

Myrdal, *Asian Drama*. Myrdal, Gunnar, *Asian Drama*, 3 vols, 1968.

Nag, 'Children'. Nag, Moni, White, Benjamin, & Peet, R. Creighton, 'An Anthropological Approach to the Study of the Economic Value of Children in Java and Nepal', *Current Anthropology*, vol. 19, no. 2, June 1978.

Netting, *Balancing*. Netting, Robert McC., *Balancing on an Alp*, 1981.

Nichols, *Halkett Autobiography*. Nichols, John G. (ed.), *The Autobiography of Anne Lady Halkett*, Camden Soc., n.s. 13, 1875.

Nicoll, *Shakespeare*. Nicoll, Allardyce (ed.), *Shakespeare in his Own Age*, Shakespeare Survey 17, 1964.

Notestein, 'Population Change'. Notestein, Frank W., 'Economic Problems of Population Change', from *Proceedings of the Eighth International Conference of Agricultural Economists*, Oxford, 1953.

Notestein, *Four Worthies*. Notestein, Wallace, *Four Worthies, John Chamberlain, Anne Clifford, John Taylor, Oliver Heywood*, 1956.

—, *English Folk*. *English Folk*, 1938.

Obeyesekere, *Land Tenure*. Obeyesekere, G., *Land Tenure in Village Ceylon*, 1967.

Origo, *Merchant*. Origo, Iris, *The Merchant of Prato*, 1963.

Osborn, *Population*. Osborn, Frederick, *On Population, Three Essays*, New York, 1960.

Osborn, *Whythorne Autobiography*. Osborn, James M. (ed.), *The Autobiography of Thomas Whythorne*, 1962.

Osborne, *Advice*. Osborne, Francis, *Advice to a Son*, 5th edn, 1656.

Outhwaite, *Marriage*. Outhwaite, R.B. (ed.), *Marriage and Society*, 1981.

Page, 'Poor-Law'. Page, Frances M., 'The Customary Poor-Law of three Cambridgeshire Manors', *Cambridge Hist. Jnl*, vol. III, no. 2, 1930.

Parkinson, *Life of Martindale*. Parkinson, (Revd) Richard (ed.), *The Life of Adam Martindale*, Chetham Soc., vol. 1V, 1845.

Parson, *Diary of Slingsby*. Parson, (Revd) Daniel (ed.), *The Diary of Sir Henry Slingsby, of Scrivan, Bart*, 1836.

Pearson, *Elizabethan Love*. Pearson, Lu Emily, *Elizabethan Love Conventions*, 1933.

—, *Elizabethans*. *Elizabethans at Home*, Stamford, 1957.

Penney, *Sarah Fell*. Penney, Norman (ed.), *The Household Account Book of Sarah Fell of Swarthmoor Hall*, 1920.

Percy, *Advice*. Percy, Henry, *Advice to His Son*, ed. G.B. Harrison, 1930.

Percy, *Reliques*. Percy, Thomas, *Reliques of Ancient English Poetry*, ed. H.B. Wheatley, 3 vols, 1876.

Perkins, *Oeconomie*. Perkins, William, *Christian Oeconomie*, 1609.

Petersen, *Population*. Petersen, William, *The Politics of Population*, New York, 1965.

Pitt-Rivers, *Countrymen*. Pitt-Rivers, J. (ed.), *Mediterranean Countrymen*, Paris, 1963.

Pitt-Rivers, *People of Sierra*. Pitt-Rivers, J.A., *The People of the Sierra*, 1954.

—, *Fate of Shechem*. *The Fate of Shechem, or the Politics of Sex*, 1977.

Place, *Population*. Place, Francis, *Principle of Population*, 1967.

Poffenberger, 'Fertility'. Poffenberger, T., & Poffenberger, S.B., 'The Social Psychology of Fertility Behaviour in a Village in India, in J.T. Fawcett (ed.), *Psychological Perspectives on Population*, New York, 1973.

Pollard, *Chaucer Works*. Pollard, A.W., et al. (eds), *The Works of Geoffrey Chaucer*, 1965.

Pollock & Maitland, *English Law*. Pollock, F., & Maitland, F.W., *The History of English Law*, 2 vols, 2nd edn, 1968.

Pollock, *Forgotten Children*. Pollock, Linda A., *Forgotten Children*, 1983.

Pottle, *Boswell's Journal*. Pottle, F. (ed.), *Boswell's London Journal 1762–1763*, 1950.

Pound, *Census*. Pound, John F. (ed.), *The Norwich Census of the Poor, 1570*, Norfolk Record Soc., XL, 1971.

Power, 'Women'. Power, Eileen, 'The Position of Women' in G.C. Crump & E.F. Jacob (eds), *The Legacy of the Middle Ages*, 1926.

Quaife, *Wanton Wenches*. Quaife, G.R., *Wanton Wenches and Wayward Wives*, New Brunswick, 1979.

Quarles, *Divine Poems*. Quarles, Francis, *Divine Poems*, 5th edn, 1717.

Radcliffe-Brown, *African Kinship*. Radcliffe-Brown, A.R., & Forde, Daryll (eds), *African Systems of Kinship and Marriage*, 1950.

Raftis, *Tenure*. Raftis, J.A., *Tenure and Mobility: Studies in the Social History of the Medieval English Village*, Toronto, 1964.

Raine, 'Depositions'. Raine, James, 'Depositions and Other Ecclesiastical Proceedings from the Courts of Durham', *Surtees Soc.*, vol. 21, 1845.

Razi, *Medieval Parish*. Razi, Zvi, *Life, Marriage and Death in a Medieval Parish*, 1980.

Redfield, *Human Nature*. Redfield, Robert, *Human Nature and the Study of Society*, Papers of R. Redfield vol. 1, ed. Margaret Redfield, Chicago, 1962.

Reeve & Muggleton, *Epistles*. Reeve, John, & Muggleton, Lodowicke, *A Volume of Spiritual Epistles*, collected by Alexander Delamaine, 1820.

Rollins, *Pepysian Garland*. Rollins, H.E. (ed.), *A Pepysian Garland*, 1922.

Rosenberg, *Family*. Rosenberg, Charles E., *The Family in History*, Pennsylvania, 1975.

Russell, *History of Philosophy*. Russell, Bertrand, *History of Western Philosophy*, 1946.

Rye, 'Gawdy'. Rye, Walter, Report on the MS of the Family of Gawdy, Formerly of Norfolk, HMC, 1885.

—, *Isham Journal*. (ed.), *Journal of Thomas Isham of Lamport, Northants, 1671–1673*, 1875.

S.S., *Secretaries Studie*. S.S., *The Secretaries Studie: Containing New Familiar Epistles*, 1652.

Sachse, *Lowe Diary*. Sachse, William L. (ed.), *The Diary of Roger Lowe*, 1938.

Salisbury, *Stone*. Salisbury, R.F., *From Stone to Steel*, Melbourne, 1962.

Sarsby, *Romantic Love*. Sarsby, Jacqueline, *Romantic Love and Society*, 1983.

Schapera, *Married Life*. Schapera, I., *Married Life in an African Tribe*, 1956.

Schofield, *Knyvett Letters*. Schofield, Bertram (ed.), *The Knyvett Letters (1620–1644)*, 1949.

Schofield, 'Review'. Schofield, Roger, 'Review of McKeown, "The Modern Rise of Population"', in *Population Studies*, vol. 37, pp. 179–81, 1977.

—, 'Mobility'. 'Age-Specific Mobility in an Eighteenth Century Rural English Parish', *Annales de Demographie Historique*, 1970.

Schucking, *Puritan Family*. Schucking, Levin L., *The Puritan Family*, 1969.

Searle, *Barrington Letters*. Searle, Arthur (ed.), *Barrington Family Letters, 1628–1632*, Camden Soc., 4th series, vol. 28, 1983.

Semmel, *Papers of Malthus*. Semmel, Bernard (ed.), *Occasional Papers of T. R. Malthus*, New York, 1963.

Sermons or Homilies. *Sermons or Homilies, appointed to be read in Churches*. n.d.

Shanin, *Peasants*. Shanin, Teodor (ed.), *Peasants and Peasant Societies*, 1971.

Shapcott, *Rutherford Autobiography*. Shapcott, Reuben (ed.), *The Autobiography of Mark Rutherford*, 15th edn, n.d.

Sharp, *Midwives*. Sharp, (Mrs) Jane, *The Midwives Book*, 1671.

Sheehan, 'Choice'. Sheehan, M., 'Choice of Marriage Partner in the Middle Ages', *Studies in Medieval and Renaissance History*, n.s. 1, pp. 3–33, 1978.

—, 'Stability'. 'The Formation and Stability of Marriage in Fourteenth-Century England: Evidence of an Ely Register', *Medieval Studies*, 33, 1971.

Shorter, *Modern Family*. Shorter, Edward, *The Making of the Modern Family*, 1976.

Singer, *Table-Talk*. Singer, S.W. (ed.), *The Table-Talk of John Selden*, 1856.

Smith, *Wealth*. Smith, Adam, *The Wealth of Nations*, 2 vols, ed. Edwin Cannan, Chicago, 1967.

Smith, *Ecclesiastical History*. Smith, Harold, *The Ecclesiastical History of Essex*, n.d.

Smith, 'Nuclear Family'. Smith, Richard, 'The Nuclear Family and Low Fertility. A Spurious Correlation?' *International Union for the Scientific Study of Population*, Belgium, Aug. 1981.

—, 'Fertility'. 'Fertility, Economy, and Household Formation in England over Three Centuries', *Population and Development Rev.*, vol. 7, no. 4, Dec. 1981.

Smyth, *De Republica*. Smyth, (Sir) Thomas, *De Republica Anglorum*, reprinted 1970.

Sneyd, *Relation*. Sneyd, Charlotte Augusta (tr.), *A Relation, or Rather a True Account of the Island of England . . . about the year 1500*. Camden Soc., 1848.

Some Longer Poems. Some Longer Elizabethan Poems, intro. A.H. Bullen, 1903.

Spence, *Woman Wang*. Spence, Jonathan D., *The Death of Woman Wang*, 1978.

Spooner, *Population*. Spooner, Brian (ed.), *Population Control: Anthropological Implications*, Massachusetts, 1972.

Spufford, *Contrasting Communities*. Spufford, Margaret, *Constrasting Communities*, 1974.

St Clare Byrne, *Lisle*. St Clare Byrne, Muriel (ed.), *The Lisle Letters. An Abridgement*. 1983.

Stack, *Love-Letters*. Stack, V.E. (ed.), *Love-Letters of Robert Browning and Elizabeth Barrett*, 1969.

Stapleton, *Plumpton Letters*. Stapleton, Thomas (ed.), *Plumpton Correspondence*, Camden Soc., 1839.

Steele, *The Englishman*. Steele, Richard, *The Englishman*, ed. R. Blanchard, 1955.

Steele, *Medieval Lore*. Steele, Robert, *Medieval Lore from Bartholomew Anglicus*, 1966.

Stein, *Legal Values*. Stein, Peter, & Shand, John, *Legal Values in Western Society*, 1974.

Stewart, *Works*. Stewart, Dugald, *Collected Works*, (ed.), Sir William Hamilton, 11 vols, 1971.

Stirling, *Turkish*. Stirling, Paul, *Turkish Village*, New York, 1966.

Stone, *Family*. Stone, Lawrence, *The Family, Sex and Marriage in England 1500–1800*, 1977.

—, Crisis. *The Crisis of the Aristocracy 1558–1641*, abridged edn, 1967.

—, *Aristocracy. The Crisis of the Aristocracy 1558–1641*, 1965.

Stone, *Open Elite*. Stone, Lawrence, & Stone, Jeanne C. Fawtier, *An Open Elite? England 1540–1880*, 1984.

Stow, *London*. Stow, John, *The Survey of London*, Everyman Library, 1912.

Strutt, *Sports and Pastimes*. Strutt, Joseph, *The Sports and Pastimes of the People of England*, ed. William Hone, 1838.

Stubbes, *Anatomie*. Stubbes, Philip, *The Anatomie of Abuses*, 1585.

Sumner, *Folkways*. Sumner, William Graham, *Folkways*, 1934.

Swift, *Works*. Swift, Jonathan, *Works*, 13 vols, 1768.

Swinburne, *Wills*. Swinburne, Henry, *A Treatise of Testaments and Last Wills*, 1728.

—, *Spousals. A Treatise of Spousals or Matrimonial Contracts*, 1686.

Symonds, 'John Greene'. Symonds, E.M. (ed.), 'The Diary of John Greene', *English Hist. Rev.*, vol. XLIII, 1928.

Tabah, 'Population'. Tabah, Leon, 'World Population Trends, A Stocktaking', *Population and Development Rev.*, vol. 6, no. 3, Sept. 1980.

Tabarah, 'Demographic Development'. Tabarah, Riad, 'Towards a Theory of Demographic Development', *Econ. Development and Cultural Change*, vol. 19, no. 2, Jan. 1971.

Table Talk. Table Talk by Various Writers from Ben Jonson to Leigh Hunt, Everyman Library, 1934.

Tacitus, *Germania*. Tacitus, *The Agricola and the Germania*, tr. H. Mattingly, 1975.

Taine, *Notes on England*. Taine, Hippolyte, *Notes on England*, tr. Edward Hyams, 1957.

Takizawa, 'Germanic Love'. Takizawa, Masahiko, 'An Essay on Friendship; Tradition of Germanic Love', *Hitotsubashi Journal of Social Studies*, vol. 9, no. 1, May 1977.

Tate, *Parish Chest*. Tate, W.E., *The Parish Chest*, 1960.

Tawney, *Agrarian Problem*. Tawney, R.H., *The Agrarian Problem in the Sixteenth Century*, New York, 1967.

—, *Religion. Religion and the Rise of Capitalism*, 1926.

Thale, *Place Autobiography*. Thale, Mary (ed.), *The Autobiography of Francis Place (1771–1854)*, 1972.

The Court Letter Writer. The Court Letter Writer, 1773.

The Determinants of Population. The Determinants and Consequences of Population Trends, UN Population Studies, no. 17, New York, 1953.

The Diary of Anne Clifford. The Diary of the Lady Anne Clifford 1590–1676, intro. V. Sackville-West, 1923.

The Essays of Montaigne. The Essays of Montaigne, tr. E.J. Trechmann, 2 vols, 1935.

The Fifteen Joys. The Fifteen Joys of Marriage, tr. Elizabeth Abbott, 1959.

The Harleian Miscellany. The Harleian Miscellany; or, a Collection of . . . Tracts . . . in the late Earl of Oxford's Library, 12 vols, 1808.

The Husbandmans Practice. The Husbandmans Practice: or, Prognostication for Ever, 1685.

The Memoirs of Fanshawe. The Memoirs of Ann Lady Fanshawe 1600–1672, 1907.

The New Whole Duty. The New Whole Duty of Man, 24th edn, 1792.

The Order of a Court Leet. The Order of Keeping a Court Leet and Court Baron, (1650), facsimile reprint.

The Prayer-Books. The First and Second Prayer-Books of King Edward the Sixth, Everyman Library, 1913.

The Topographer. The Topographer, 4 vols, for 1789–91.

The Works of Aristotle. The Works of Aristotle, New improved edn, n.d. (early nineteenth century).

Thomas, *Natural World*. Thomas, Keith, *Man and the Natural World, Changing Attitudes in England 1500–1800*, 1983.

—, 'Puritans and Adultery'. 'The Puritans and Adultery. The Act of 1650 Reconsidered', in *Puritans and Revolutionaries*, ed. D. Pennington & Keith Thomas, 1978.

—, *Religion. Religion and the Decline of Magic*, 1971.

—, 'Women'. 'Women and the Civil War Sects', in Trevor Aston (ed.), *Crisis in Europe 1560-1660*, 1964.

—, 'History and Anthropology'. 'History and Anthropology', *Past and Present*, 24, April 1963.

—, 'Double Standard'. 'Double Standard', *Jnl History of Ideas*, XX, 2, 1959.

Thomas, *Polish Peasant*. Thomas, William I., & Znaniecki, F., *The Polish Peasant in Europe and America*, 2nd edn (abridged), New York, 1958.

Thompson, *Working Class*. Thompson, E.P., *The Making of the English Working Class*, 1970.

—, 'Peculiarities'. 'The Peculiarities of the English', in Ralph Milliband & John Saville (eds), *Socialist Register*, 1965.

Thompson, *Lark Rise*. Thompson, Flora, *Lark Rise to Candleford*, 1945.

Thompson, *Women*. Thompson, Roger, *Women in Stuart England and America*, 1974.

Titow, 'Differences'. Titow, J.Z., 'Some Differences between Manors and their Effect on the Conditions of the Peasants in the Thirteenth Century', *Agricultural Hist. Rev.*, vol. X, 1962.

Trappes-Lomax, *Diary of Brockbank*. Trappes-Lomax, R. (ed.), *The Diary and Letter Book of Rev. Thomas Brockbank 1671–1709*, Chetham Soc., n.s. 89, 1930.

Trevelyan, *Social History*. Trevelyan, G.M., *English Social History*, reprint 1948.

Turner, *Brighouse*. Turner, J. Horsfall, *The History of Brighouse, Rastrick, and Hipperholme*, 1893.

Turner, *Heywood*. Turner, J. Horsfall, (ed.), *The Rev. Oliver Heywood B.A., Diaries . . ., 4 vols, 1882–85*.

Turner, *Diary*. Turner, Thomas, *The Diary of a Georgian Shopkeeper*, ed. G.H. Jennings, 2nd edn, 1979.

Van Gennep, *Rites*. Van Gennep, Arnold, *The Rites of Passage*, 1960.

Verney, *Memoirs*. Verney, F.P. (ed.), *Memoirs of the Verney Family*, 2nd edn, New York, 1907.

—, *Verney Memoirs. Memoirs of the Verney Family During the Civil War*, (1892), facsimile reprint, 1970.

Von Furer-Haimendorf, *Apa Tanis*. Von Furer-Haimendorf, C., *The Apa Tanis and their Neighbours*, 1962.

—, *Merit. Morals and Merit*, 1967.

Wall, 'Leaving Home'. Wall, Richard, 'The Age at Leaving Home', *Jnl of Family History*, 1978.

Watkins, *Puritan Experience*. Watkins, Owen C., *The Puritan Experience*, 1972.

Watt, *Rise of Novel*. Watt, Ian, *The Rise of the Novel*, 1983.

Webb, *English Poor Law*. Webb, Sidney, & Webb, Beatrice, *English Poor Law*, pt 1, *The Old Poor Law*, 1927.

Weber, *Protestant Ethic*. Weber, Max, *The Protestant Ethic and the Spirit of Capitalism*, 1970.

Westermarck, *Marriage*. Westermarck, Edward, *The History of Human Marriage*, 3 vols, 5th edn, 1921.

—, *Marriage in Morocco. Marriage Ceremonies in Morocco*, 1914.

—, *Moral Ideas. The Origin and Development of the Moral Ideas*, 1906.

Wharncliffe, *Letters of Montagu*. Wharncliffe, (Lord) (ed.), *The Letters and Works of Lady Mary Wortley Montagu*, 3 vols, 2nd edn, 1837.

Whateley, *Bride-Bush*. Whateley, William, *A Bride-Bush: or, a Direction for Married Persons*, 1619.

—, *Care-Cloth. A Care-Cloth or a Treatise of the Cumbers and Troubles of Marriage*, 1624.

Wheaton, *Family*. Wheaton, R., & Hareven, Tamara K. (eds.), *Family and Sexuality in French History*, Pennsylvania, 1980.

Whitelock, *English Society*. Whitelock, Dorothy, *The Beginnings of English Society*, 1959.

Whitforde, *Householders*. Whitforde, R., *A Werke for Housholders or for them that have the Guiding or Governance of any Company*, 1533.

Wilson, *Shakespeare's England*. Wilson, John Dover, *Life in Shakespeare's England*, 1962.

Winchester, *Tudor Portrait*. Winchester, Barbara, *Tudor Family Portrait*, 1955.

Wolf, *Peasants*. Wolf, Eric, *Peasants*, New Jersey, 1966.

Wotton, *Reliquiae*. Wotton, (Sir) Henry, *Reliquiae Wottonianae*, 1651.

Wright, *Middle-Class Culture*. Wright, Louis B., *Middle-Class Culture in Elizabethan England*, Carolina, 1935.

Wright, *Life of Defoe*. Wright, Thomas, *The Life of Daniel Defoe*, 1894.

—, *Domestic Manners. A History of Domestic Manners and Sentiments in England during the Middle Ages*, 1862.

Wright, *Autobiography*. Wright, Thomas (ed.), *Autobiography of Thomas Wright of Birkenshaw 1736–1797*, 1864.

Wrightson, *English Society*. Wrightson, Keith, *English Society, 1580–1680*, 1982.

Wrightson, *Terling*. Wrightson, Keith, & Levine, David, *Poverty and Piety in an English Village. Terling, 1525–1700*, 1970.

Wrigley, 'Family Limitation'. Wrigley, E.A., 'Family Limitation in Pre-Industrial England', *Econ. Hist. Rev.*, 2nd series, XIX, no. I, April 1966.

—, 'Population'. 'Growth of Population in Eighteenth-Century England: A Conundrum Resolved', *Past and Present*, 98, Feb. 1983.

—, 'Population History'. 'Population History in the 1980's', *Jnl of Interdisciplinary History*, vol. XII, 2, 1981.

—, 'Reflections'. 'Reflections on the History of the Family', in *Daedalus*, Spring 1977.

—, *Demography*. Wrigley, E.A., (ed.), *An Introduction to English Historical Demography*, 1966.

Wrigley & Schofield, 'Population History'. Wrigley, E.A., & Schofield, R.S., 'English Population History from Family Reconstitution: Summary Results 1600–1799', *Population Studies*, vol. 37, 1983.

Wynn, *Family Policy*. Wynn, Margaret, *Family Policy*, 1972.

Zubrow, *Demographic Anthropology*. Zubrow, Ezra (ed.), *Demographic Anthropology*, Albuquerque, 1976.

Index

Index by Sandra Raphael

Printed and bound by CPI Group (UK) Ltd, Croydon, CR0 4YY